Rethinking Jewish History and Memory Through Photography

Rethinking Jewish History and Memory Through Photography

Edited by

OFER ASHKENAZI and
THOMAS PEGELOW KAPLAN

SUNY
PRESS

Published by State University of New York Press, Albany

EU GPSR Authorised Representative:
Logos Europe, 9 rue Nicolas Poussin, 17000, La Rochelle, France
contact@logoseurope.eu

For information, contact State University of New York Press, Albany, NY
www.sunypress.edu

Library of Congress Cataloging-in-Publication Data

Names: Ashkenazi, Ofer, editor. | Pegelow Kaplan, Thomas, editor.
Title: Rethinking Jewish history and memory through photography / edited by
    Ofer Ashkenazi and Thomas Pegelow Kaplan.
Description: Albany, New York : State University of New York Press, [2025] |
    Series: SUNY series in contemporary Jewish literature and culture | Includes
    bibliographical references and index.
Identifiers: LCCN 2024057651 | ISBN 9798855803464 (hardcover : alk. paper) |
    ISBN 9798855803471 (ebook) | ISBN 9798855803457 (pbk. : alk. paper)
Subjects: LCSH: Documentary photography. | Historiography and photography. |
    Jews—Historiography. | Collective memory. | Holocaust, Jewish (1939–1945) |
    Photography—Social aspects. | Photography—Philosophy.
Classification: LCC TR820.5 .R48 2025 | DDC 070.4/9—dc23/eng/20250226
LC record available at https://lccn.loc.gov/2024057651

In memory of Uta Larkey (1953–2024),
an insightful scholar and a wonderful friend

Contents

Part II.
Probing the Boundaries of Documentation:
Jewish Photographic Memory

Part III.
The Photographed Jewish Body:
Agency, Race, Nation

Part IV.
Jewish Photography as a Commentary on Crisis and Violence

Part V.
The Jewish Gaze on the Other "Others":
Migration, Colonialism, Minorities

Acknowledgments

Every academic project and publication benefits and, at times, depends on the assistance and collaboration of fellow researchers and a broad range of institutions. This is particularly true for this volume, which assembles the works of a series of scholars, with a variety of interests and expertise, who frequented a variety of archives and were supported by several grants. It is, therefore, a pleasure to express our gratitude to the many colleagues who contributed in various ways to bringing this project to its successful conclusion.

The project emerged from post-panel discussions at the 2018 Lessons and Legacies conference in St. Louis, for which we co-organized a panel entitled "Holocaust Studies Past the Visual Turn: From National to Global Perspectives and Challenges." We detected the absence of a volume that took stock of the recent and immensely innovative approaches in the intersecting fields of photography, visual studies, and Jewish memory and history. We wanted to go beyond a narrow focus on the Shoah and instead combine attention to photo analysis and a range of related methodologies with explorations of the *longue durée* of Jewish memory, history, and photography. We composed a specific call for papers and also reached out to colleagues, including some of the foremost experts in these fields. We were grateful for the many positive responses. The chosen contributors from various disciplines—many university-based, some independent scholars—agreed to grapple with a list of questions we sent out. In two virtual workshops in the summer of 2021, we discussed preliminary findings and encouraged everyone to engage with each other's work. We held more meetings at Hebrew University in late 2022. We were as pleased with the process as we are with the outcome.

Our greatest expression of gratitude, therefore, is reserved for the volume's contributors, for their diligent work and cooperation, for composing fine chapters or agreeing, as in Marianne Hirsch's and Leo Spitzer's case, to engage in a conversation about the state of the field and their contributions to it. We are thankful for the institutional support we have received from the Richard Koebner Minerva Center for German History and from the Mandel-Scholion Research Center, both at the Hebrew University of Jerusalem; the Center for Judaic, Holocaust, and Peace Studies at Appalachian State University, North Carolina; and—after Thomas's move to a new position—the Program in Jewish Studies and Department of History at the University of Colorado Boulder. We are grateful for the financial support from the Israel Science Fund (ISF 2648/20), the German Israeli Foundation (111.5-2017), and the research funds for the Leon Levine Distinguished Professorship at Appalachian State.

Among the many colleagues who have supported us, discussed pertinent questions, and participated in related conference panels, workshops, and other programs with us, we would particularly like to mention Leora Auslander, Dorota Glowacka, Atina Grossmann, Simone Lässig, Andrea Löw, Jürgen Matthäus, Guy Miron, Dan Michman, Robert Müller-Stahl, Ulrike Pilarczyk, Matthias Schmidt, Swen Steinberg, Anat Vogman, Annette Vowinckel, and Daniel Wildmann—a special thanks, finally, to Ann Pegelow Kaplan for discussing her award-winning photography and photography in general with one of the coeditors for so many years. Since this is a volume about photography, we are immensely grateful to the many archives, research centers, and individual copyright holders for granting the contributors and us permission to reprint images from their collections. In particular, we would like to thank AKG-images, the Art Gallery of Ontario, the Arts and Humanities Research Council (AHRC), Yael Bartana, the Bayerisches Hauptstaatsarchiv, Beit Lohamei Hagetaot kibbutz museum, the Blond family archive, the bpk Bildagentur, the Century Foundation, especially Jason Renker and Lia Tabackman, the Cumberland County Historical Society, the Emanuel Ringelblum Jewish Historical Institute in Warsaw, the Folkwang Museum, especially Petra Steinhardt, the Hirsch-Spitzer Archive, the Iowa Women's Archives at the University of Iowa Libraries, the Israeli Government Media Agency, the Jewish Museum Berlin, the Jewish Museum Stockholm, Mirta Kupferminc, the Magnes Collection of Jewish Art and Life, the Tefen-Haifa Archive of German-Speaking Jewry, the National Museum of African Art—Smithsonian Institution, Nerris Markogiannis, the Photo Archives of the United States Holocaust Memorial Museum, the Photo Archives of Yad Vashem, the Walter Rosenblum Archive, the Smithsonian's National Museum of African American History and Culture, the University of New Hampshire, the University of Washington Libraries, and Greg Wittkopp.

Finally, we are grateful to SUNY Press for embarking on this project with us. James Peltz, SUNY Press's editor-in-chief, has been superb to work with. Likewise, we are thankful to the external readers for their careful review and constructive suggestions.

Ultimately, of course, all mistakes in the present volumes are ours. We are hopeful, however, that readers will regard the following contributions as enriching and insightful as we do and that many will, in turn, engage in the issues raised in this volume in the years to come.

Introduction

OFER ASHKENAZI AND THOMAS PEGELOW KAPLAN

Figure I.1. Andreas Meyer, Jewish illegal immigrants arrive in Nahariya, Mandate Palestine, January 1948. *Source:* Courtesy the Meyer Family Collection, Archive for History and Heritage of German Speaking Jewry in Israel, Haifa University. Used with permission.

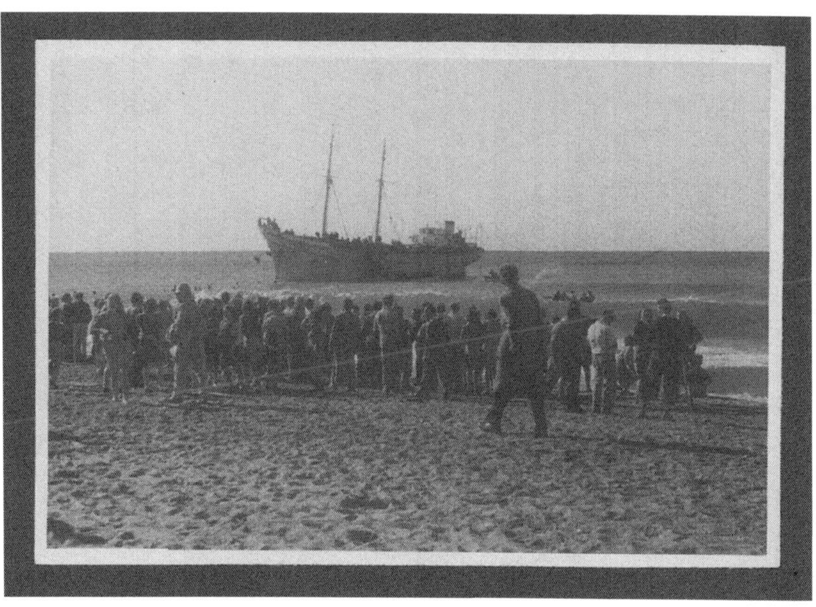

Around noon on January 1, 1948, a wooden boat ran aground a few dozen meters off the Mediterranean coast of Nahariya, a small Jewish town on the northern borders of Mandate Palestine. Setting sail from Genoa, Italy, a few weeks after the historic vote in favor of the partition of the land and the foundation of Jewish and Arab states, the boat was christened the *United Nations*. It carried some 700 Jewish refugees, survivors of World War II and the Holocaust, who sought to immigrate to Palestine illegally, namely, by defying the British authorities' restrictive quota on immigration to the country. The Jews of Nahariya, many of whom had escaped Nazi Germany and only arrived in Palestine a decade earlier, were quick to react. They hurried to the beach, assisted the evacuation of the boat, and helped direct the refugees to hiding places (Hirschfeld, Prism, and Yatom-Tomer, n.d.). And they took photographs to document the event that excited so many in their community. Some of the photographs of that afternoon in Nahariya have since been recurrently reproduced in history books and on postal stamps, propaganda posters, and educational websites. Many of these photographs resemble figure I.1 above, which was taken by Andreas Meyer, a local amateur photographer.

The reproduction of such photographs is hardly surprising, considering the pivotal role played by the illegal *Aliyah* (Ascension) in the foundation myth of the Jewish national movement and of the State of Israel (Halamish 1988; Ofer 1991). The struggle to bring refugees from displaced persons camps in Europe to Palestine provided a potent impression of the agency of Jews in Palestine (who formed effective paramilitary organizations and intelligence agencies that enabled this enterprise). It highlighted Jewish solidarity and a sense of tightened national community (as local Jews participated in the efforts to hide the immigrants from the police and, later, helped the immigrants to assimilate in the new land). It facilitated the portrayal of the post-Holocaust immigrants as primarily uprooted, detached from foreign influences, and ready to assume the local culture and ideology (Shamir 1951; Zerubavel 2002, 121). And it allowed Zionist activists to portray their struggle as waged by the victims who fight (colonial) injustice, rather than of a national movement engaged in an ethnic-based conflict over the land.

Andreas Meyer's photograph is a remarkably powerful visualization of these elements. It features the boat at the center, visibly overcrowded and slightly tilted to its side, alluding to its frailty and to the danger of its possible sinking. The angle of the camera situates the refugees as isolated, surrounded by water, but also shows the proximity of the boat to the heads of the people on the beach, who came to rescue them. The Nahariyans on the beach stand tightly together. This sense of a tightly knit community is emphasized further by the gap on the right-hand side—suggesting that they could spread, but chose not to—as well as by the people on the left-hand side, who direct their gaze to the right, toward their comrades. The narrow strip of water between the heads of the locals and the refugees on the *United Nations* is filled with small rescue boats, sent by the people on the beach. An emblem of agency and overcoming obstacles (symbolically, the waves that are coming toward them), the young Jews of Palestine are depicted here as the power that connects the exhausted crowd on the sea with the vital Jewish community in the land. While the boat is at the center of the photograph, most of it depicts the clear sky above and the vast sea on the sides and in the background. The refugees are faceless; we can see neither their features nor their belongings. They are, evidently, from nowhere, or, more accurately, "from the sea" that stretches in all directions. As such, they appear to be ready, arguably eager, to be molded into the new Jewish community that waits to embrace them once they hit the ground. Furthermore, the long shadows of the people on the sand appear as an allusion to the approaching darkness at the nearing end of the day, and, hence, as an indication of urgency and of the need to take immediate action.

Simply put, Andreas Meyer seems to have caught the fundamentals of the Zionist psyche (and propaganda) in the final months of the British Mandate in Palestine. Yet the photograph is not merely an assembly of Zionist tropes; it also documents a specific event, at a specific time, from the viewpoint of a specific witness. The shadows cast on the sand, consequently, also invoke a real, rather than symbolic, crisis: the lengthy shade suggests that the photograph was taken just before the British forces arrived at the beach (at 3:00 p.m.) and arrested the refugees who had not been evacuated earlier. Within this framework, the photograph exhibits a tense moment for all the people it depicts, oscillating between hope and despair. Already at first glance, therefore, it is clear that this photograph both documents (Jewish) experience and communicates a particular approach—ideological as well as emotional—toward this experience.

But Meyer's approach was still more complicated than the analysis above suggests. In his personal archive, the photograph is displayed within a particular visual narrative, an album, which contextualizes and assigns further meaning to its initial inference. The album presents different scenes from Meyer's time in Nahariya, from his late teenage years to his late twenties. It is not organized chronologically—from the late 1930s to the early 1950s—but rather thematically: one page portrays a few photographs of Meyer and his girlfriend; another is dedicated to the building of a new coffee house; a double page depicts a bicycle trip of the town's children, and so forth. The thematic arrangement leaps back and forth between years. Some pages, including the one of the *United Nations* boat, feature side-by-side images from different years. In this case, the page included the 1948 boat's arrival alongside an image from a cabaret-style play that the local Nahariyans performed in 1939 (this photograph is missing, only the descriptive caption remains); an undated photograph from a costume party (assumingly a Purim celebration); and a 1940 performance of the local choir. This strange assortment of images on this page, in an album that is arranged according to common themes, seems to suggest that the scene on the beach was just another stage performance rather than a fundamental historic event, where the Nahariyans put on costumes and acted out their role (Meyer n.d.).

Thus, when we zoom out from the photograph to its place in the album, namely, to Andreas Meyer's recollections from that eventful period, the Zionist pathos that seems to dominate the *United Nations* image receives an ironic touch. Parallel irony can be detected in other references to illegal immigration in this album. Meyer, for instance, situated an image of the half-sunk refugee boat *Hannah Szenes*, broken and tilted on its side, next to a photograph of a naked toddler lying playfully in the water, on a page that portrays family leisure on the beach. In a retrospective interview, looking back at the series of photographs he took on the day the *United Nations* arrived, Meyer asserted that some of them were taken under entirely different circumstances, on the set of the 1966 film *Judith*, where he helped to design the illegal immigration scene. He could not tell between the different settings: between a photograph of historical reality and a photograph of staged fiction (Anat Vogman, interview with Ofer Ashkenazi).

As Andreas Meyer's visual documentation of Jewish refugees' arrival in Palestine indicates, photographs are vital for the study of the past, of the way it was experienced, remembered, and commemorated. Yet Meyer's album also underscores the multifaceted nature of photographs and their inferences. Maiken Umbach and Jonathan Stafford emphasize in their contribution to this volume that historians must "read" photographs within the various contexts of their production, preservation, display, and viewing. As a growing cohort of theorists and scholars of visual history have demonstrated (Azoulay 2010; Burke 2001; Hirsch 1997; Pilarczyk and Mietzner 2003; Harvey and Umbach 2015), a photograph does not document reality as it "was there," in front of the camera, but rather captures a fragment of reality from a particular perspective and communicates its significance from that perspective. In other words, photography is the practice of paying attention, in which certain experiences are ripped off the ephemeral sequence of mostly disregarded events, to become a meaningful image. Photographs, therefore, comprise and exhibit the process of assigning meaning to experiences—by both its producer and its viewer—and the effort to influence the ways they will be remembered in the future.

Photography is neither history nor memory. The convoluted relationship between photographs and memory has fascinated and bothered generations of critics. Already in the 1920s, facing the rapid popularization of private photography, Siegfried Kracauer distinguished between the photographic image and the "memory image," stressing the former's inability to maintain the abundance of arbitrary details preserved by memories (Kracauer 1995). Roland Barthes argued similarly, "not only is the photograph never, in essence, a memory . . . but it actually blocks memory, quickly becomes a counter-memory" that "fills the sight by force" (Barthes 1981, 91). Contemporary scholars problematize the memory-photograph relationship further by complicating the photograph's role as mediators between personal and public memory. According to Marianne Hirsch, rather than publicly displaying the past experiences of individuals, photography undermines and reshapes memories: "In its relation to loss and death, photography . . . brings the past back in the form of a ghostly revenant. . . . The encounter with the photograph is the encounter between two presents, one of which, already past, can be reanimated in the act of looking" (Hirsch 2001, 231). In other words, as an object, a photograph does not merely represent the past. Instead, it is an ongoing endeavor to turn experiences into historical sources and sites of memory, which, by necessity, are embedded in the present.

In his pathbreaking book *Zakhor*, Yosef Hayim Yerushalmi reminded his readers that "memory of the past was always a central component of the Jewish experience," even if historians were hardly its "primary custodian[s]" (Yerushalmi [1982] 1996, xxxiii). More than four decades after the publication of the first edition, Yerushalmi's words are still poignant. Yet, with an eye on the period since the mid-nineteenth century, they need to be modified and expanded by integrating the integral role and significance of photography and "photographic events" (Azoulay 2010). This volume explores this endeavor in a variety of social and cultural contexts of modern Jewish history. It demonstrates prominent approaches to the reading of photographs—taken by and of Jews—as a means to explore hitherto overlooked aspects of Jewish experiences and of their ever-developing memories. As the ensuing chapters demonstrate, professional photographers of Jewish ancestry often produced images that contemplated the intricacies of Jewishness in the modern world, within the contexts of migration, urbanization, persecution, and other rapid changes in the daily lives and the spaces in which they occurred. The intrinsic multivalence of the photograph allowed them to communicate complex affinities and, at times, the coexistence of seemingly incompatible desires, hopes, and fears (Silverman 2009; Shneer 2011; Benton 2015). As Meyer's depiction of the Zionist enterprise shows, the capability to communicate complex views and emotions is not restricted to professional photography. Private photographs, namely, images that were taken by amateur photographers to document private experiences, often disclose a nuanced mixture of emotions, identifications, and expectations that are crucial for modern historians and can hardly be found in other types of sources (Auslander 2015; Batchen 2000; Campt et al. 2020; Ashkenazi 2022).

Consequently, this book highlights the role played by both professional and private photography in the negotiation of modern Jewish experiences. The technology of photography, and Jews' interest in taking photographs, developed at the same time with major changes in the social environment and daily routines that characterized Jewish lives in Europe, North America, the Yishuv, and elsewhere. Jewish photographers documented and participated in assigning meanings to these changes. While their participation was not always conscious or intended, it left historians with images that encoded their approach to events and the ways they were supposed to be remembered.

Photography is an intricate, multilayered communication of particular positions toward the documented occurrences, which often plays an essential role in the comprehension and remembering of historical experiences. Consequently, this volume raises a series of intersecting questions about the use of photographs in the study of Jewish history and memory. While all the ensuing chapters explore the ways photography can enrich and complicate our understanding of modern Jewish experiences, they evince a variety of different approaches to the concept of "Jewish photography," namely, the extent to which photographs or photographic events could be seen as distinctly "Jewish." Some contributors to this collection examine if (and how) the Jewish background of the photographers or the "Jewish" subject matter gave way to particular aesthetics or style. We believe that these questions are productive inasmuch as they lead to novel and intriguing analysis of photographs and their relations to history and memory. We, therefore, chose to present several perceptions of "Jewish photography," rather than to provide a definitive notion. We hope that this approach will situate this volume at a starting point of a discussion, rather than as its conclusion.

The inclusive framework also allows us to include non-Jewish photographers, and highlight the significant roles they played in documenting and interpreting Jews' routines and encounters with others in changing worlds. The book's chapters show, for instance, that the images of these photographers often raised similar questions about modern Jewish identity, albeit with different premises and different answers to these questions. The chapters of this volume consider the ways photographers, both Jews and non-Jews, sought to influence the memory of the documented event through certain thematic and aesthetic choices. They suggest how scholars can analyze these choices to reconstruct the aspirations and the emotions these images sought to evoke, negotiate or refute.

"Jewish Photography" in Modern History and Memory

There is no such thing as Jewish photography.

—Nahum (Tim) Gidal, "Jews in Photography"

In a sense, the above-quoted comment by Nahum (Tim) Gidal underlines the obvious absurdity of attributing "Jewish" characteristics to a photograph: as Gidal notes, just like "there is no Jewish picture framing," there is no inherently "Jewish" way of taking photos, preserving them, or compiling them within narratives (Gidal 1987). Our perception of "Jewish" in this context, however, has little to do with the inherent qualities of Jews, or with the distinctions of Jewish cultural heritage; instead, we highlight the connections between specific historical experiences of Jews *as Jews*—which are, of course, diverse and varying—and the imagery found in the analyzed photographs. As Lisa Silverman writes in this volume, the particular experiences, the position vis-à-vis the social majority, and the cultural background of the photographers fundamentally influence the significance of the image. Owing to the choices made by the photographer and by the people who preserved, displayed, and viewed the photographs—whether consciously or not—the images contemplate Jewishness and the meaning of Jews' experiences in the particular historical context of its production and viewing. Yet, as Marianne Hirsch and Leo Spitzer note, some fundamental elements of the modern "Jewish" experience—and the photographic documentations of these elements—were not unique to Jews. In a conversation with this volume's coeditors, they argue that "a consciously deliberate self-presentation" by assimilating outsiders, in photos and portraits, was common among other social groups as well. They, therefore, suggest that instead of searching for distinctively "Jewish" characteristics, scholars should focus on the particular depictions of and by Jews in generic photography: replacing the emphasis from "Jews' photography" to "photography's Jews." While the influence of this approach is evident in some of the ensuing chapters, other contributors to this volume still contemplate the notion of Jewish photography as analytical category that enhances our understanding of the particularities of Jewish experiences in their particular historical contexts.

When we speak of photography in this book, we refer to all aspects of the "photographic event" (Azoulay 2010), namely, the act of taking a photograph (the photographer's aesthetic and thematic choices); the appearance of the photographed people (such as dress, direction of gaze, and posture); the development, preservation, and display of the photograph (including choices made by the album compiler and journal editor); and the retrospective interpretation of the photograph by its viewers (and, later, by historians), often aided by a written or oral explanation, and its complex relations to memory (Langford 2006; Edwards 2009). We argue that, in all of these aspects, "Jewish" photographs enabled Jewish photographers, curators, editors, and viewers to communicate a particular position vis-à-vis the photographed reality, namely, an interpretation of the historical events they displayed (Thomas 2009). In other words, photographs exhibited, complicated, and facilitated Jews' agency by determining (or, at least, influencing) the significance of the photographed moment. This volume discusses various ways in which historians can face the challenge of "Jewish photography" and unravel the beliefs, emotions, and notions of agency encoded in the photograph.

The production and consumption of photography had expanded rapidly in the latter half of the nineteenth century, together with the expansion of European and North American middle classes (Zervigón 2017, 24–29). The mass migration, wars, urbanization, and scientific breakthroughs during the decades that followed the first experiments with visual documentation generated both the demand for photography and the supply of cameras, professionals, and raw materials to answer the new demand. By the turn of the century, illustrated magazines around the world regularly printed photographs that exhibited the latest advances in camera technology, promoted commercial goods, and advocated various political causes (Knoch 2006,

218–22; Davenport 1999, 91–94). Across the globe, photo studios spread to answer the public's thirst for photographic images (Berkowitz 2009). While these studios enabled their patrons to record and perpetuate their identity, it also often situated them against "exotic" backgrounds, which linked (bourgeois) reality with fantastic scenes (Gauthier and Staszak 2012; Klein 2023). At the same time, middle-class Westerners were introduced to exotic lands and their inhabitants through travelogue photobooks and illustrated magazines that contributed also to the development of the colonial imagination (Zeller 2010; Hight and Sampson 2013). Ethnographers were likewise excited to direct the camera toward their subject of inquiry, and thereby underscore the genuine differences between members of ethnic groups. Yet the colonized were never merely passive objects of the camera's gaze. They often found ways to display, and reflect on, their identity through photographs (Grandin 2004).

While cameras, films, and related accessories remained relatively expensive until the mid-1920s, the popularity of amateur photography already increased considerably during and in the aftermath of World War I (Starl 1985, 93–95). Numerous soldiers had begun to use photographs to report on their experiences and commemorate their comrades. By sending home commercial postcards or photographs that they took at the frontline, they contributed to the omnipresence of photographs in both the public and private spheres of the 1910s. The war was a catalyst of several significant changes in the technology, aesthetics, and politics of photography. As governments and military leaders sought to employ visual imagery to propagate mobilization for the war, display battlefield successes, and expose the enemy's cruelty, photography became ever more present in the news media (Weise 1998, 21–23; Knoch 2006, 222–26).

Wartime photography accentuated the interrelations between the aesthetics and contents of photographs, both private and commercial, and the ones of other popular elements of visual culture, such as printed reproductions of paintings, illustrated newspapers, films, and, most importantly, illustrated postcards, which increasingly featured generic photographs (Jewish Theological Seminary of America 1998; Silvain, Minczeles, and Wharry 1999). To a great extent, the constant confluence of photographic imagery and other visual representations of modern reality shaped the history of photography and its participation in the discourse about the past. The broader context of modern visual culture is indicated or insinuated throughout this volume. Yet, focusing on photography, this collection does not aim to provide a comprehensive analysis of the ways particular photographs functioned within, influenced, and were influenced by this broad context. Again, we hope the readers will approach the ensuing chapters as a starting point for further inquiries, also in this direction.

These abovementioned developments in photography coincided with the modernization of Jewish experiences, ideologies, and tastes (Lässig 2004). Thus, major aspects of Jewish modernization, and particularly the consequences of mass migration and the embourgeoisement of European Jews, were abundantly documented on camera. Photography offered Jewish entrepreneurs and artists a comparatively easy path up the socioeconomic ladder similar to the cinema or cabaret (Prawer 2005; Otte 2006). Observing this development, Michael Berkowitz has asserted that during the late nineteenth and early twentieth century, in Central and Western Europe, photography had developed to be a "Jewish space," associated with Jewish integration with bourgeois society (Berkowitz 2017).

The depiction of photography as a "Jewish space" notwithstanding, it is crucial not to overstate the separation between Jewish and non-Jewish photography. The Jewish studio photographers of the nineteenth century took photographs of a variety of customers, both Jewish and non-Jewish. The pioneering Hans Biow of Hamburg, for instance, produced celebrated portraits of up-and-coming middle-class Jews alongside non-Jewish aristocrats (Gidal 1987, 440). The aesthetic principles exhibited in photographs of Jews were seldom distinguishable from those of non-Jewish customers; similarly, the imagery produced by Jewish photographers was rarely distinguishable from their non-Jewish contemporaries. Like many of their peers, Jewish photographers represented mostly the place where they learned their profession and the cultural context in which they lived (with its visual tropes and generic imagery), alongside their national, gender, or class identity.

Likewise, Jews rarely posed in photographs distinctively *as Jews* or organized their photographs in a distinctively "Jewish" manner. As Noam Gal demonstrates in his contribution to this volume, the personal, cultural, and political contexts in which the imagery was conceived and displayed shape its meanings no less, and arguably more, than its themes and styles. Simply put, Jewish photographers (and compilers of photography) have not developed distinctive styles. Instead, they normally appropriated familiar imagery and expectations to express particular sensitivities and perspectives. As Michele Klein argues in her chapter, through such appropriation photography played an important role in contemplating and assigning meanings to private Jewish experiences already in the latter half of the nineteenth century. Klein demonstrates how Jewish bourgeois families in the nineteenth century skillfully compiled generic studio photographs in albums to negotiate various perceptions of identity. Individual experiences of Jews have been thus commemorated through the particular arrangements of standard studio images to form distinctive private narratives.

This approach to the documentation and display of Jewish experiences had become even more apparent in the early decades of the twentieth century, with the popularization of private photography, when Jewish amateurs avidly documented their private experiences at home and during travels, emigration, and interactions with others (Umbach and Sulzener 2018; Ashkenazi 2019). The enthusiastic engagement of Jews with photography coincided with, and often responded to, the increasing instrumentalization of photography by advocates of racism and antisemites who sought to expose and exhibit Jews' difference and inferiority (Morris-Reich 2016). Jewish photographers, both professionals and amateurs, often reacted to major trends in racial and antisemitic photography, either by emulating its aesthetic out of context or by suggesting alternative depictions of similar situations. As a result, late nineteenth and early twentieth century photographs introduce scholars of Jewish history with an immense, unparalleled reservoir of sources that directly relate to distinctively "Jewish" experiences from various perspectives.

The positioning of the photographed Jew as the "other" had been a recurring theme of modern antisemitic imagery. As Amos Morris-Reich reminds us in this volume, the emphasis on (certain) Jews' "otherness" was also a significant subject of Jewish photographers. Morris-Reich's analysis of Helmar Lerski's "Orientalist" imagery, however, suggests that photographs can also undermine the alleged natural differences between ethnic groups. He reads Lerski's project as a (failed) attempt to negate racial biases through photographic representations of the "Oriental" Jew.

The depictions of "Oriental" or "Mizrahi" Jews through the lens of European-Jewish photographers, as Ktzia Alon's chapter in this book notes, did not only serve the various objectives of these photographers. They also prompted a broad array of responses and new ways of seeing, displaying, and taking photographs. Jewish photographers in Israel portrayed the Jews of Muslim countries as "exotic" or even "primitive" in comparison with the European Jews. As Alon demonstrates, these "Mizrahi" Jews reacted to such depictions in a number of distinct ways, including by developing an alternative gaze on their social environment, which worked to secure and assert agency.

Time and again, photographic events were profoundly shaped by conflict and war. Similar to many non-Jewish soldiers, European and North American

Jews photographed their frontline experiences during World War I, interacting with generic national imagery in ways that displayed or complicated their adherence to the nationalities they served. Jewish communities by the frontlines were in turn photographed—by Jews and others—to comment on the inherent qualities of the occupiers and of the Jews themselves. The most consequential development in the history of photography, however, occurred during the early 1920s, with the introduction of cheap, small and easy-to-use cameras, such as the box cameras (e.g., of Zeiss and Agfa) and the pocket cameras, first and foremost the 1925 Leica (Koch 2012; Griffin 1995). As increasingly popular journals and handbooks provided knowledge on the practice and aesthetics of photography, a growing public had developed unprecedented photo-literacy (Heiting and Jaeger 2012). Already by the early 1930s, tens of millions of families in the West owned a camera (Campt et al. 2020; Conze, Prehn, and Wildt 2013). Photographs of everyday life and ordinary places—of the home, the street, or a vacation resort—became ubiquitous (Lugon 2008). Art photographers and photojournalists have also participated in this new discovery of the ordinary (Hambourg and Phillips 1989). Paying attention to the fleeting moment, turning it into an image—with a metaphorical and aesthetic significance—these photographers phrased new ways of looking at reality.

Once again, the changes in the technology and practice of photography coincided with radical changes in the lives of Jews: from mass migration, exile, and persecution to unparalleled integration within Western societies and to the rise of Jewish nationalism and its success. Thus, on the one hand, Jews eagerly participated in, and, in some cases, spearheaded the increasing presence of photography; and, on the other hand, the changes of Jewish experiences had been documented on camera in an unprecedented abundance. During the interwar years, Jewish professional photographers helped shape new visual and social sensibilities while documenting life in the modern world. As Joachim Schlör indicates in his contribution to this volume, Jewish photographers contemplated their own belonging in interwar Europe through reflections on alienation and empathy in the urban environment. During the devastating decades between World War I and the early Cold War years, many private photographers had documented the momentous events they witnessed from Jews' perspective.

In their chapter, Christoph Kreutzmüller and Theresia Ziehe highlight the principal interests of Jewish photographers during a time of rapidly increasing violence under the National Socialist regime, as well as the growing restrictions on what could be photographed. This analysis highlights the benefits historians can draw from looking at photographs alongside other sources. As the authors emphasize, understanding the changing political circumstances that allow and restrict photography is crucial for the evaluation of these sources. The political contexts in which a photograph is taken—and the biographical circumstances of its producers and publishers, which still need to be theorized and analyzed, even if, after the "linguistic turn," with much greater sophistication (Pegelow Kaplan 2017)—become particularly significant in the case of migrant, refugee, and exiled Jewish photographers. Documenting the colonial rule in India, for example, German-speaking Jewish photographers demonstrated different forms of agency, going beyond documenting the suffering of fellow Jews. As Rebekka Grossmann argues in this volume, Jewish exiles, migrants, and travelers played a vital role in propagating humanitarian approaches through photographs of the social reality in the European colonies. Similar tendencies can also be seen in the latter half of the twentieth century in the Global North, where certain Jewish photographers seem to assume the position of an "outsider-within" Western societies, who seeks to underline injustice or incongruities within Western ideologies. In their contributions to this volume, Michael Berkowitz and Deborah Dash Moore analyze two different ways in which Jewish photographers negotiated race and class in the United States during the Cold War years. These two chapters show how Jews' positions vis-à-vis racial and class-based identities facilitated new perceptions of Jewishness and of the role Jews should play in the political struggle for equality—even if not without conflict also with leading voices of the African American communities.

The essential intersections between the history of photography and the history of modern Jewish experiences were not limited to the works of Jewish photographers. Non-Jewish photographers, both amateur and professional, had also gazed at Jews through camera viewfinders in (resentful and even violent or rather empathetic) attempts to communicate their understanding of Jews' experiences. While the literature on photography, the Holocaust, and memory is by now substantial and still rapidly growing (e.g., Fresco 2021; Knoch 2001; Struk 2005; Zelizer 2001), Yechiel Weitzman's chapter offers a fascinating rereading of the much-displayed photographs of Moshe Hagerman, the "barefoot Rabbi," who was documented by the German occupiers of his small town, Olkusz. The perpetrators who tortured Hagerman left images that nonetheless, in intricate and insinuated manner, communicate his experience of National Socialist atrocities. Moreover, Weitzman emphasizes that, while these images were taken to satisfy the needs of the perpetrators, they have been incorporated into the memory of the Holocaust in complex and often problematic ways, by Jews and non-Jews alike. As Maiken Umbach and Jonathan Stafford note in their chapter, the omnipresence of perpetrators' images of the kind Weitzman describes had a vital, arguably destructive, impact on the teaching and learning of the Holocaust and its history. The task of contemporary historians and educators, they maintain, would be to overcome this bias of sources and offer new methods for learning history from photographs.

As the examples cited above clearly indicate, while photography had been there right on time to document Jewish renewal, Jewish modernization often ensued or was complemented by the disappearance and destruction of former communities, traditions, and practices through migration or violence. As a close companion of such changes, photography was also an apparatus of commemoration. In some cases, photographs were taken purposefully to document and preserve a soon-to-be-lost Jewish world (Morris-Reich 2022, 149–84). In many other cases, photographic depictions of ordinary moments transformed later into a monument to the loss of entire communities (Hirsch and Spitzer 2020). As Daniel Magilow shows in this book, photographs taken and compiled by Jews and gentiles can also commemorate lost communities by refraining from depicting the reality that preceded their destruction. His analysis of photobooks that portray German-Jewish cemeteries indicates the limits of photographic representation and reveals unique endeavors to overcome such limits.

In her much-discussed work, Marianne Hirsch (2012) has continued to develop and analyze the manifestation of mediated memory, in which photographs often functioned as agents of "postmemory." In her depiction of this concept, it functions as a device employed to communicate memories to viewers who are utterly foreign to the long-gone reality the photographs portray. The selection of photographs from the past, the way they are organized—and, sometimes, described by a knowledgeable narrator—construct an image of the past, a memory narrative encapsulated in the still image. As Hirsch and Spitzer further explicate in this volume, photography thus intertwines and influences modern Jewish memory in dynamic manners, which works to simultaneously preserve awareness of the past and change its meanings. Dora Apel's essay in this book consequently shows how photographs can fill in memory gaps among viewers, and at the same time highlight the complexities and shortcomings of personal memories. Notably, Apel uses photographs as a tool for an inquiry about the past, not as the resolution of her inquiry.

No single volume can encompass all the interactions between photography and modern Jewish history and memory. The selection of the chapters included here reflects our twofold initial intention: to represent a wide variety of themes we deemed crucial for the intersections between photography, Jewish historical experiences, and the commemoration of such experiences; and to explore a wide variety of methodological approaches to the analysis of photographs in the study of Jewish history and memory. Consequently, some topics are underrepresented. Thus, for instance, Jewish nationalism, the Zionist movement's achievements and controversies, and the State of Israel are discussed at length in two chapters—Alon and Morris-Reich—which arguably understate their impact on Jewish experience in the twentieth century. One might argue that the emphasis on the Holocaust and its memory also inadequately stirs the focus of the study of photography away from various other aspects of modern Jewish life. We believe that, besides the obvious, unparalleled importance of the Holocaust in Jewish history and memory, its multifaceted discussion in this volume highlights the various approaches to photo analysis by historians, and the ability of different approaches to shed new light on a well-researched field.

The arrangement of the chapters in this volume seeks to underline some of the most essential questions and areas of research that, we believe, can be considerably advanced through systematic examination of photographs. The order is therefore thematic, rather than chronological, in the hope that the reader will find new connections between subject matters and methodologies, across historical contexts. The first section considers the key concepts that recur throughout the volume. It comprises a discussion that examines the notion of "Jewish photography," and its use in previous scholarship, as well as two chapters that highlight the different agents involved in the photographic event and influence its significance. The second section brings into the spotlight the intricate relations between photographs and "Jewish" memory. While every consideration of photographs takes into account their evolving roles in memory culture, this section focuses on the aspiration to utilize photographs as a commemoration device, or as a means to undermine commonly held perceptions of the past. The third section contemplates photography's participation in the discourse about the "Jewish body," and how this participation intersects with questions about Jewish racial and national identities. The fourth section brings to the fore photographs of Jewish suffering, during or in anticipation of catastrophes. The discussions in this section explore the limits of photographic representation of anxiety and pain, as well as the capability of scholars to probe and overcome these limits. The final section rethinks the concepts of race and "otherness," this time through Jewish photographers' depictions of other minorities or colonized subjects. These chapters suggest that the complexities of such portrayals reveal overlooked aspects of both Jewish history and the history of human rights movements in the twentieth century.

As the chapters below suggest, photographs are indispensable from any discourse about the Jewish recent past, and how it should be remembered. In other words, the photographs discussed in this book participated in an ongoing discussion of Jewish experiences and their changing significance in different historical, geographical, and cultural contexts. Yet the chapters of this volume recurrently emphasize that the relations between photographs, the reality they depict, and the roles they played in the commemoration of the photographed event are anything but plain or direct (Tucker and Camp 2009). Understanding the inferences of photographs requires the development of novel analytical approaches and methodologies, which would focus on the images' affect and on their interactions with other images and texts (Pilarczyk and Mietzner 2003; Edwards 2012; Roth 2009; Buerkle 2009). Owing to the complexity and the seemingly obscure nature of visual sources, studies of Jewish history and memory had traditionally tended to overlook photographs or to incorporate them as mere "illustrations," rather than sources that require methodical analysis (Hirsch and Spitzer 2009; Tucker and Campt 2009). This tendency is slowly disappearing, making way for novel discoveries that enrich our comprehension of Jews' historical experiences, evolving memories, and varying agency throughout late modern history (e.g., Löw 2015; Magilow 2019; Wobick-Segev 2024). The chapters of this book introduce and contemplate a plethora of such discoveries, and demonstrate the advantages of new methodologies to the study of historical photography. They deliberately do not adhere to a single analytical method or a theoretical framework. Instead, they introduce the readers to a variety of approaches in a hope that they will be utilized in and adapted to future inquiries in various realms of Jewish history.

Works Cited

Ashkenazi, Ofer. 2019. "Exile at Home: Jewish Amateur Photography under National Socialism, 1933–1939." *Leo Baeck Institute Year Book* 64 (1): 115–40.
———. 2022. "Reading Private Photography: Pathos, Irony and Jewish Experience in the Face of Nazism." *American Historical Review* 127 (4): 1606–34.

Auslander, Leora. 2015. "Reading German Jewry through Vernacular Photography: From the Kaiserreich to the Third Reich." *Central European History* 48 (3): 300–34.

Azoulay, Ariella. 2010. "What Is a Photograph? What Is Photography?" *Philosophy of Photography* 1 (1): 9–13.

Barthes, Roland. 1981. *Camera Lucida: Reflections on Photography*. Hill and Wang.

Batchen, Geoffrey. 2000. "Vernacular Photographies." *History of Photography* 24 (3): 262–71.

Benton, Maya, ed. 2015. *Roman Vishniac Rediscovered*. International Center of Photography.

Berkowitz, Michael. 2009. "Photography as a Jewish Business: From High Theory to Studio to Snapshot." *East European Jewish Affairs* 39 (3): 389–400.

———. 2017. "Photography as a Jewish Space." In *Space and Spatiality in Modern German-Jewish History*, edited by Simone Lässig and Miriam Rürup. Berghahn.

Buerkle, Darcy. 2009. "Caught in the Act: Norbert Elias, Emotion and *The Ancient Law*." *Journal of Modern Jewish Studies* 8 (1): 83–102.

Burke, Peter. 2001. *Eyewitnessing: The Uses of Images as Historical Evidence*. University of Chicago Press.

Campt, Tina, Marianne Hirsch, Gil Z. Hochberg, and Brian Wallis, eds. 2020. *Imagining Everyday Life: Engagements with Vernacular Photography*. Steidl Verlag.

Conze, Linda, Ulrich Prehn, and Michael Wildt. 2013. "Sitzen, baden, durch die Strasse laufen. Überlegungen zu fotografischen Repräsentationen von 'Alltäglichen' und 'Unalltäglichen' im Nationalsozialismus." In *Fotografien im 20. Jahrhundert: Verbreitung und Vermittlung*, edited by Annelie Ramsbrock, Annette Vowinckel, and Malte Zirenberg. Wallstein.

Davenport, Alma. 1999. *The History of Photography: An Overview*. Focal Press.

Edwards, Elizabeth. 2009. "Photography and the Material Performance of the Past." *History and Theory* 48 (4): 130–50.

———. 2012. *The Camera as Historian: Amateur Photographers and Historical Imagination, 1885–1918*. Duke University Press.

Fresco, Nadine. 2021. *On the Death of Jews: Photographs and History*. Berghahn.

Gauthier, Lionel, and Jean-François Staszak. 2012. "Framing Coloniality: Exotic Photographs in Swiss Albums, Museums, and Public Spaces (1870s–2010s)." *Photography and Culture* 5 (3): 311–26.

Gidal, Nachum T. 1987. "Jews in Photography." *Leo Baeck Institute Year Book* 32 (1): 437–53.

Grandin, Greg. 2004. "Can the Subaltern Be Seen? Photography and the Affects of Nationalism." *Hispanic American Historical Review* 84 (1): 83–111.

Griffin, Michael. 1995. "Between Art and Industry: Amateur Photography and Middlebrow Culture." In *On the Margins of the Art Worlds*, edited by Larry Gross. Routledge.

Halamish, Aviva. 1988. "Illegal Immigration: Values, Myth and Reality." *Studies in Zionism* 9 (1): 47–62.

Hambourg, Maria Morris, and Christopher Phillips. 1989. *The New Vision: Photography between the World Wars: Ford Motor Company Collection at the Metropolitan Museum of Art*. Metropolitan Museum of Art.

Harvey, Elizabeth, and Maiken Umbach. 2015. "Introduction: Photography and Twentieth-Century German History." *Central European History* 48 (3): 287–99.

Heiting, Manfred, and Roland Jaeger, eds. 2012. *Autopsie: Deutschsprachige Fotobücher*. Seidl Verlag.

Hight, Eleanor M., and Gary D. Sampson, eds. 2013. *Colonialist Photography: Imag(in)ing Race and Place*. Routledge.

Hirsch, Marianne. 1997. *Family Frames: Photography, Narrative, and Postmemory*. Harvard University Press.

———. 2001. "Surviving Images: Holocaust Photographs and the Work of Postmemory." In *Visual Culture and the Holocaust*, edited by Barbie Zelizer. Athlone Press.

———. 2012. *The Generation of Postmemory: Writing and Visual Culture after the Holocaust*. Columbia University Press.

Hirsch, Marianne, and Leo Spitzer. 2009. "Incongruous Images: Before, during and after the Holocaust." *History and Theory* 48 (4): 9–25.

———. 2020. *School Photos in Liquid Time: Reframing Difference*. University of Washington Press.

Hirschfeld, Esti, Yossi Prism, and Yoram Yatom-Tomer. n.d. "Ha'apala, Eduyot Toshavei Nahariya" [Testimonies of Nahariya Residents]. Accessed December 15, 2022. https://sites.google.com/site/toldotnahariya1/war/haapala?pli=1.

Jewish Theological Seminary of America. 1998. *Past Perfect: The Jewish Experience in Early 20th Century Postcards*. Library, Jewish Theological Seminary of America.

Klein, Michele. 2023. "Dressing Up: 'Reading' Costume in the Photograph Albums of Nineteenth-Century Bourgeois Jews." *Textile: The Journal of Cloth and Culture* 21 (3): 571–98.

Knoch, Habbo. 2001. *Die Tat als Bild: Fotografien des Holocaust in der deutschen Erinnerungskultur*. Hamburger Edition.

———. 2006. "Living Pictures: Photojournalism in Germany, 1900 to the 1930s." In *Mass Media, Culture and Society in Twentieth-Century Germany*, edited by Karl Christian Führer and Corey Ross. Palgrave Macmillan.

Koch, Hanna. 2012. "Erfahrungen mit der Leica." In Heiting and Jaeger (2012).

Kracauer, Siegfried. 1995. "Photography." In *The Mass Ornament: Weimar Essays*. Harvard University Press.

Langford, Martha. 2006. "Speaking the Album." In *Locating Memory: Photographic Acts*, edited by Annette Kuhn and Kirsten Emiko McAllister. Berghahn.

Lässig, Simone. 2004. *Jüdische Wege ins Bürgertum: Kulturelles Kapital und sozialer Aufstieg im 19. Jahrhundert*. Vol. 1. Vandenhoeck & Ruprecht.

Löw, Andrea. 2015. "Documenting as a 'Passion and Obsession': Photographs from the Lodz (Litzmannstadt) Ghetto." *Central European History* 48 (3): 387–404.

Lugon, Olivier. 2008. "'Photo-Inflation': Image Profusion in German Photography, 1925–1945." *History of Photography* 32 (3): 219–34.

Magilow, Daniel H. 2019. "Cute Jews: Modernist Photographic Forms and Minor Aesthetic Categories in 'Jüdische Kinder in Erez Israel: Ein Fotobuch.'" *Leo Baeck Institute Year Book* 64 (1): 47–71.

Meyer, Andreas. n.d. Nahariya album. G.F.0030-4. Meyer Collection. Archive for the History and Heritage of German Speaking Jewry in Israel, Haifa University.

Morris-Reich, Amos. 2016. *Race and Photography: Racial Photography as Scientific Evidence, 1876–1980*. University of Chicago Press.

———. 2022. *Photography and Jewish History: Five Twentieth-Century Cases*. University of Pennsylvania Press.

Ofer, Dalia. 1991. *Escaping the Holocaust: Illegal Immigration to the Land of Israel, 1939–1944*. Oxford University Press.

Otte, Marlene. 2006. *Jewish Identities in German Popular Entertainment, 1890–1933*. Cambridge University Press.

Pegelow Kaplan, Thomas. 2017. "History and Theory: Writing Central European Histories after the Linguistic Turn." In *Modern Germany in Transatlantic Perspective*, edited by Michael Meng and Adam R. Seipp. Berghahn.

Pilarczyk, Ulrike, and Ulrike Mietzner. 2003. "Methoden der Fotografieanalyse." In *Film- und Fotoanalyse in der Erziehungswissenschaft: Ein Handbuch*. VS Verlag für Sozialwissenschaften.

Prawer, S. S. 2005. *Between Two Worlds: The Jewish Presence in German and Austrian Film, 1910–1933*. Berghahn.

Roth, Michael S. 2009. "Photographic Ambivalence and Historical Consciousness." *History and Theory* 48 (4): 82–94.

Shamir, Moshe. 1951. *With His Own Hands*. Hakibbutz Ha'Artzi.

Shneer, David. 2011. *Through Soviet Jewish Eyes: Photography, War, and the Holocaust*. Rutgers University Press.

Silvain, Gérard, Henri Minczeles, and David Wharry. 1999. *Yiddishland*. Gingko.

Silverman, Lisa. 2009. "Reconsidering the Margins: Jewishness as an Analytical Framework." *Journal of Modern Jewish Studies* 8 (1): 103–20.

Starl, Timm. 1985. *Die Bildgeschichte der privaten Fotografie in Deutschland und Österreich von 1880 bis 1980*. Koehler & Amelang.

Struk, Janine. 2005. *Photographing the Holocaust: Interpretations of the Evidence*. Routledge.

Thomas, Julia Adeney. 2009. "The Evidence of Sight." *History and Theory* 48 (4): 151–68.

Tucker, Jennifer, and Tina Campt. 2009. "Entwined Practices: Engagements with Photography in Historical Inquiry." *History and Theory* 48 (4): 1–8.

Umbach, Maiken, and Scott Sulzener. 2018. *Photography, Migration and Identity: A German-Jewish-American Story*. Palgrave.

Weise, Bernd. 1998. "Das Geschäft mit dem Foto in der Geschichte der Presse- und Illustrationsfotografie in Deutschland." In *Der Bildermarkt—Handbuch der Bildagenturen*, edited by Bundesverband der Pressebild-Agenturen und Bildarchive. BVPA.

Wobick-Segev, Sarah. 2024. "Photography and the Art of Memory Creation: Portraits of a Provincial Jewish Community in the Late 1930s." *Contemporary European History* 33 (3): 942–61.

Yerushalmi, Yosef Hayim. (1982) 1996. *Zakhor: Jewish History and Jewish Memory*. University of Washington Press.

Zelizer, Barbie, ed. 2001. *Visual Culture and the Holocaust*. Athlone Press.

Zeller, Joachim. 2010. "Harmless 'Kolonialbiedermeier'? Colonial and Exotic Trading Cards." In *German Colonialism, Visual Culture, and Modern Memory*, edited by Volker M. Langbehn. Routledge.

Zerubavel, Yael. 2002. "The 'Mythological Sabra' and Jewish Past: Trauma, Memory, and Contested Identities." *Israel Studies* 7 (2): 115–44.

Zervigón, Andrés Mario. 2017. *Photography and Germany*. Reaktion.

Part I

Reading, Curating, and Teaching "Jewish" Photography

Theory and Practice

Chapter 1

What Is Jewish Photography and What Can We Learn from It?

A Discussion with Marianne Hirsch and Leo Spitzer

Ofer Ashkenazi and Thomas Pegelow Kaplan

The pioneering scholarship of Marianne Hirsch and Leo Spitzer has inspired and functioned as a starting point for many current studies on the intersections of photography and Jewish history and memory. The following conversation between these two scholars and the present volume's coeditors delves into key questions about the use of photography in Jewish historiography and memory studies. In drawing on Hirsch's and Spitzer's rich oeuvres, this conversation aims to further set the stage for this volume's main themes and questions.

～

Ofer Ashkenazi and Thomas Pegelow Kaplan: In an often-quoted essay, the German Jewish photographer Nahum (Tim) Gidal asserted that "there is no such thing as Jewish photography, just as there is no specific . . . Jewish picture framing" (Gidal 1987, 437). Yet in the same article, Gidal suggests that, ever since the 1830s, Jewish photographers have demonstrated the propensity to be "explorers and revolutionaries," namely, adversaries of "conservative" documentation. As your studies have often shown, this romantic depiction disregards most Jewish photographers, both professional and nonprofessional. Do you think that a distinct notion of "Jewish photography" can nonetheless be a productive paradigm in the study of modern history and memory? How would you define such paradigm and its boundaries?

MARIANNE HIRSCH AND LEO SPITZER: There is no question that European and new-world Jews embraced photography very quickly and enthusiastically after the mid-nineteenth-century breakthroughs that permitted inexpensive replication and commercialization of photographic images. These decades also marked the era in which Jews increasingly gained admission into the bourgeoisie in many locations in Europe and the Americas—a period in which entrance into the dominant mainstream through assimilation was presented to minority populations as the transformative means toward belonging and eventual citizenship.

In our work, it has been one of our arguments that photography, as a technology of modernity, became an instrument of assimilationism that Jews used to their benefit both as image makers and as the subjects who defined their identity photographically. But in doing so, Jews were not unique. They acted like many other literate minority populations who aspired to bourgeois lifeways and had the means to take photographs or to have their photos taken. It is thus difficult to maintain that "Jewish" photography—photographic images made by Jews as well as photos of Jewish subjects—differs fundamentally from photography taken in this era by Armenians, African Americans, indigenous Africans, or by members of other socially, economically, and culturally ascendant groups.

Let us illustrate this briefly through an example of Leo's: In my book, *Lives in Between*, which examines assimilation and marginality through generational life histories of members of the West African Creole May family, the Afro-Brazilian Rebouças family, and the Central European Jewish Zweig/Brettauer family, photos (especially portraits) display and, thus, confirm manifestations of successful assimilation and rise into the bourgeoisie (Spitzer 1989). Invariably photographs of members of these families—taken in the late nineteenth and early twentieth century by photographers who would certainly have included persons of African descent (in Brazil and West Africa) and Jews (in Central Europe)—show persons that in dress and outward appearance conformed to middle-class standards set by dominant groups in their respective societies.

But the steady rise of exclusionary racism in the second half of the nineteenth century, and the steadfastness of anti-Jewish prejudices also made it imperative for persons in these families to present themselves in the world

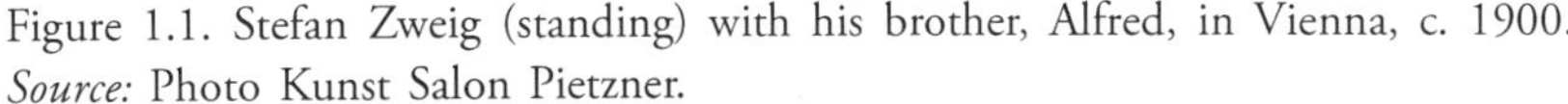

Figure 1.1. Stefan Zweig (standing) with his brother, Alfred, in Vienna, c. 1900. *Source:* Photo Kunst Salon Pietzner.

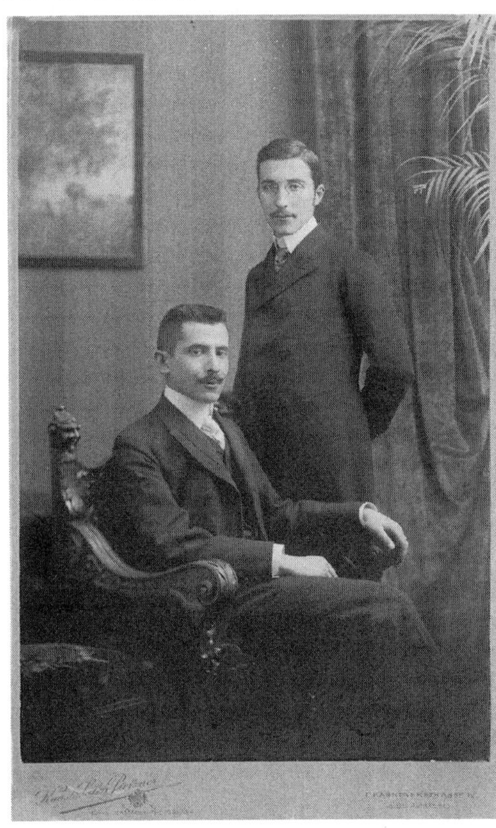

of the white, Gentile ruling groups with caution and circumspection. According to Stefan Zweig, for example, his parents, Moritz and Ida Zweig, who had become very wealthy textile industrialists in Vienna and able to afford the very best of everything, consciously sought to disarm potential hostility to their economic success by belying the stereotype of the money-grubbing Jew—the avaricious Shylock who provoked envy and hatred on the part of the Gentile majority. In their everyday lives, they diverted attention from their "difference"—from their Jewishness and their wealth—by presenting themselves as largely unostentatious in their personal appearance and style of life. Yet in their portraits, which were taken professionally in a studio, they are always elegantly dressed, appearing to conform to a middle-class—perhaps

Figure 1.2 André Rebouças, an Afro-Brazilian engineer in Rio de Janeiro, probably in the early 1880s. *Source:* André Rebouças, *Diario e notas autobiográficas* (Rio de Janeiro, 1938).

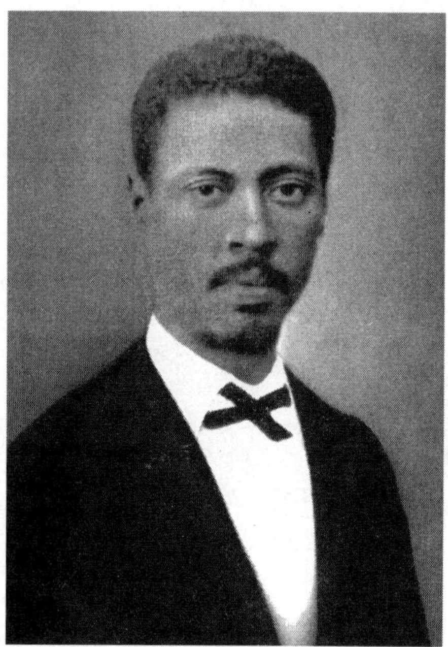

even *haut bourgeois*—style. Was that "look" in their portraits their choice, or were their outfits (suits worn by Moritz, dresses and jewels worn by Ida) costumes provided by the studio for the occasion? The studio portraits thus gave these subjects the opportunity to show off in ways that they avoided doing in everyday appearance—if we are to believe Stefan Zweig.

However, does such a consciously deliberate self-presentation by assimilating Jews in photos and portraits argue that this exemplifies a characteristic of Jewish photography? We would say no. Other assimilating individuals and groups also responded and presented themselves in these complicated and sometimes contradictory ways. In conjunction with other contemporary sources, photographs can thus allow us to understand assimilation and modernization as journeys with pushes and pulls, with ambivalences, false starts, and uneven outcomes.

The photography theorist Ariella Aïsha Azoulay urges us to see photography not through the images themselves, but through events that occasioned them. A photographic event might or might not result in an image, but it organizes our field of vision into what is to be made visible, clear, and recognizable, on the one hand, and what is not considered worth framing and extracting as an image, on the other. The photographic shutter, in Azoulay's view, extracts the image from the surrounding timespace, and it operates according to the mechanisms of power that organize our social and political lives. Its click is controlled by the one who has the power to frame the image and to fix the photographed person or scene into the domain of the visible. As such, for Azoulay, the shutter is a "synecdoche for the operation of the imperial enterprise altogether" (Azoulay 2019, 2). It separates time punctually into a sequence of events—events that are captured to organize a view of history and the makeup of historical archives. By extension, we can argue that Jews' embrace of modernity in response to possibilities of emancipation coincided with a new conception of time and identity shaped by the work of the photographic shutter. And that conception also inflected historiography and the construction of archives. But as often ambivalent aspirants to social integration and inclusion, rather than part of a hegemonic mainstream, their positionality no doubt informs their perspective and gaze, their forms of self-fashioning, and their participation in the practice of photography, professional or amateur.

Looking at photography as an event that organizes time and history, however, also provokes us to be conscious of what is not photographed and what thus remains invisible. If we see photography as a necessarily modern practice dependent on the embrace of modern technologies, we also have to be aware that more traditional Jewish worlds were not and will not be represented in photographic images. It is not just that they remain outside the frame, but that they do not participate in photography as a practice and a way of organizing their world.

Rather than arguing that there is such a thing as "Jewish" photography then, we might argue that modern "Jews" are actually created by photography. And that this applies to other assimilated populations in the era of photography as well. In other words, can we speak not of Jews' photography, but of photography's Jews?

Ashkenazi and Pegelow Kaplan: This nuanced assessment is certainly more than called for. Any proposition that a notion of "Jewish photography" could serve as a productive paradigm also needs to avoid any form of essentializing Jewishness. Yet in your answer you seem to focus on the side of

Figure 1.3. Lotte and Friederike Gottfried strolling the Str. Iancu Flondor (Herrengasse), Cernăuți, Romania, early 1930s. *Source:* Courtesy Hirsch-Spitzer Archive.

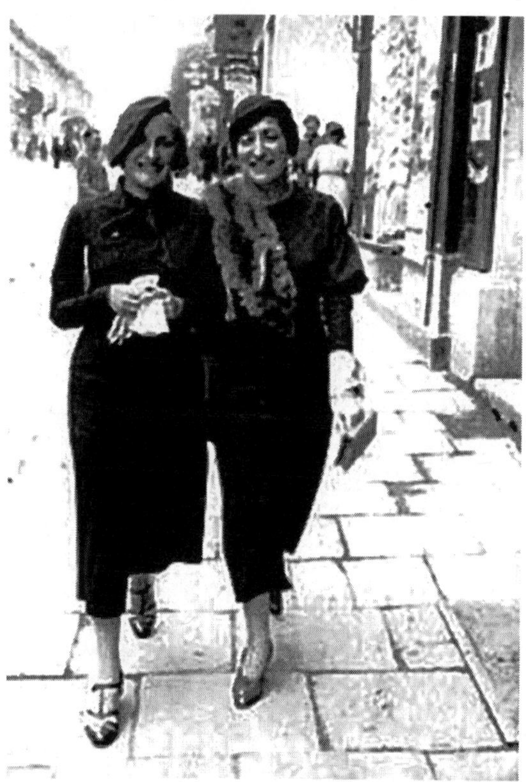

production, rather than the viewing of the photographs. Can aspects of the of reception, interpretations, or "affect" be considered within the—however defined—"Jewish paradigm?" In what ways can reception be integrated into the analysis of "Jewish" photography?

Hirsch and Spitzer: To consider Azoulay, and her argument about photographic practice as an encounter between subjects and as an event that organizes the experience of time and the writing of history, is not only to think about production. In fact, we would say, such a take on photography eschews the distinction between production and reception. In our view, the event, or the events, of photography include its viewing over time, by the makers and the subjects of photographic images, contemporaries as well as subsequent generations. The meanings of images change with different viewings by different subjects and over time.

We appreciate the fact that you share our resistance to any essentialist notion of "Jewish" photography. But here you are asking not only if Jewish photographers mobilize something like a "Jewish" gaze, but also if there is a "Jewish" look through which we engage with photos of Jews, or photos taken by Jewish photographers. We would resist any such general notion, though, in specific historical circumstances, our ways of looking might well be marked by a *Jewish history* of looking.

We are thinking here of the incisive essay by Elizabeth Alexander, "Can You Be Black and Look at This?" in which she argues that Black viewers experienced the televised images of the police beating of Rodney King differently than white viewers (Alexander 1994). That difference is not due to identity, but to an inherited memory of African Americans watching Black bodies being injured and brutalized by white perpetrators, often sanctioned by state power. Jews, also, have inherited scenes of injury that frame our encounter with photographs of persecution, expulsion, ghettoization, and murder.

Our question would be whether this legacy also applies to looking at images of the persecution of others, non-Jews in this case? In *School Photos in Liquid Time*, we placed images of Jewish schoolchildren in European ghettos next to image of Japanese American children deported to US concentration camps, and of African American children violently excluded from equal education. In the book (Hirsch and Spitzer 2020), and its accompanying exhibition *School Photos and Their Afterlives*, which was on display at the Hood Museum of Art at Dartmouth College from January until April 2020, we were thus venturing that the injustice that brought each of these groups to that moment would be visible and palpable to viewers beyond personal or group history and memory. These histories of looking are not the same, but we believe that they can generate ways of seeing that cross identity lines. Such ways of seeing, we would hope, would be particularly attuned to recognizing the workings of injustice and exclusion. In Azoulay's terms, we are all part of the citizenry of photography.

Ashkenazi and pegelow kaplan: This volume demonstrates various ways in which photo analysis enriches our understanding of modern Jewish experience and its memory. In more general terms, how would you characterize the significance of photography in the field of Jewish studies? What new paths have been opened through more sophisticated methodological approaches and readings of photography in the past decades?

Figure 1.4. Graduating students holding their diplomas in the Lodz ghetto with the Nazi-appointed Ghetto Elder and head of the Jewish Council, Chaim Rumkowski, 1941. *Source:* Photo Archive, United States Holocaust Memorial Museum, courtesy of Izak and Rosa Rosenwasser.

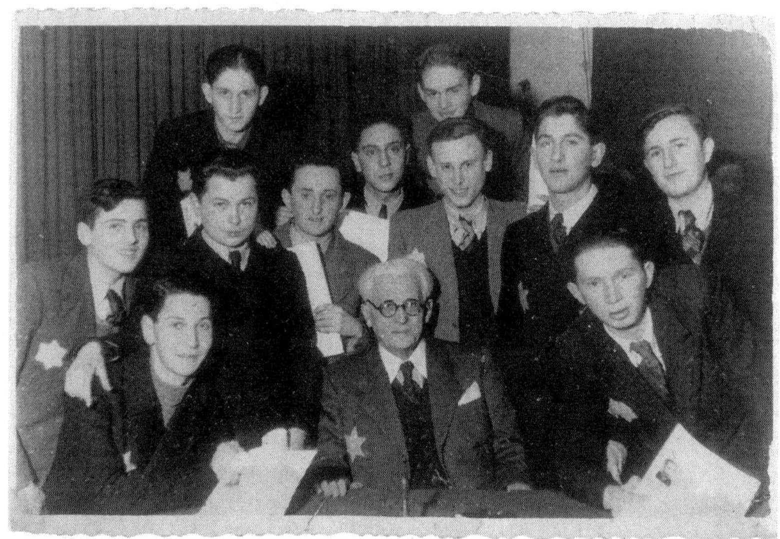

Figure 1.5. Archival caption reads: "Mrs. Ziegler oversees her 9th grade class at the internment camp in Jerome Arkansas," 1942. Classes were typically set up in military style barracks. Photograph by Tom Parker. *Source:* Courtesy Central Photographic File of the US War Relocation Authority. National Archives, College Park.

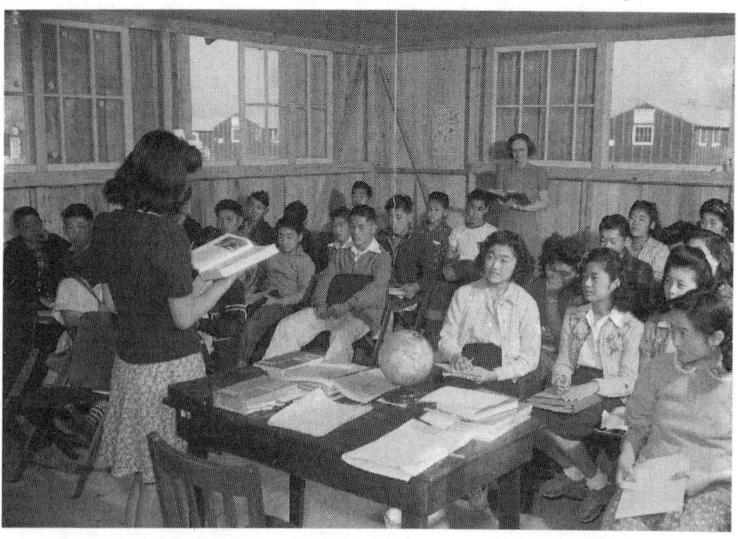

Hirsch and Spitzer: Much recent scholarly work in Jewish studies, at least in the part of Jewish studies that we have both practiced, involves reflections on diaspora and dispersion, as well as on loss and trauma. Documents are often lost or missing or destroyed. Many materials are held in family or community archives, and many are reconstructed on the basis of fragments and traces. Or archival materials sit in state archives that opened them to researchers belatedly or continue to restrict access. Thus, existing archival materials often need to be read and interpreted in creative and sometimes counterintuitive ways.

And yet, because of Jews' embrace of photography from the medium's earliest days, photo archives are multiple and give a rich sense of modern middle-class Jewish life in the late nineteenth, the twentieth, and twenty-first centuries. Photographic documents can at times support, and, at other times, challenge, written and oral accounts, as well as common assumptions about the past. Photographs shape historical analyses, but they also shape individual, communal, and cultural memory and postmemory.

Photographs have played a dominant role in the development of memory studies as a field in the last thirty years or so. Why photos, one might ask? First, one can say that photos offer a window into a lost past, but certainly not a transparent one. Encountering a photograph, we need to ask who took it, when, and how? How is it framed, and what does that reveal about the gaze of the image maker and the work of the shutter? Why and how did it survive? What was the event that occasioned it, and what photos surrounding it were either not taken or did not survive? How do photographs inflect individual, collective, and cultural memory, and what additional documentation is needed to contextualize images that have survived different historical moments? How and why do images become iconic and how do iconic images shape particular visions of the past in favor of others?

These are questions that might be posed of any document, but photography, we believe, sharpens and focuses them because the meanings that photographs carry are so heterogeneous. To decode these meanings, however, we need a great deal of paratextual information—information that is sometimes either unavailable or, in itself, ambiguous.

As images become ever more readily available on the internet, they are also often separated from this necessary contextual information. And, just as often, they are curated by way of labels and captions that frame them in specific ways, ways that delimit our viewing and that we have learned to challenge.

In our work, we have drawn on a number of theoretical approaches to photography, from the ideology critique of the 1980s, to the affective turn connecting photography to feeling in the late 1990s, and the multisensory—haptic and auditory—dimensions of the medium highlighted more recently. Photographs for us are not only historical documents, but they are also, and maybe primarily, historical actors in their own right, and they act in all of these multiple ways. We believe that this analysis of photographs inflects the work of history more generally.

Ashkenazi and pegelow kaplan: Since the 1990s, both of you have contributed numerous complex and insightful works that analyzed a broad range of photographs and photography from the vernacular to the artistic. In particular, you developed a new understanding of (initially family-based) mediated memory, or postmemory, which situated the album at the center of the modern identity-formation process. At first glance, this perception of the album as a vehicle of retrospective narrations of "memories" removes the photographs from the realm of history (namely, from their function as documentations of contemporaneous experiences and approaches to these experiences). Moreover, in *The Generation of Postmemory*, you seem to advocate this division further by highlighting the subjective and "autobiographical" reading of the albums as items of postmemory (Hirsch 2012, 4). How, if at all, do you resolve this tension between memory and history in private photography?

Hirsch and Spitzer: The discussion of photographs as memorial objects should in no way diminish their historical role both at the time of their production and in their later reading and interpretation. It is true that domestic photographs held in family albums or collections have specific meanings for the individuals and families depicted in them, and more generic meanings for others of us who are not in the pictures. But the two of us try not to have either the memorial role of photographs or their historical functions exclude or purge one another. Indeed, as we have argued in our work, individual and collective memories of events and places can shift and be open to different meanings over time. Memories are thus not only a *part* of history but also *have a history*. As such, individual and familial archives—and how they are seen and interpreted over time—are crucial to historical work.

Photographs, like other archival materials, require careful interpretive readings: the evidence they provide is in no way transparent or straightforward. As we suggested above, photographs are indexical and iconic signs, connected materially to the time and place where they were taken, but they quickly assume the role of symbols as well and that symbolic role can seem to disconnect them from history. The portrait of Anne Frank, for example, so ubiquitous in the memory and the history of the Holocaust, is both the portrait of an individual girl, whose diary becomes an important document of the period, and a symbol of the vulnerable Jewish victim. The way that she has assumed this symbolic function is, for us, part of Jewish history, an indication of how the Holocaust is seen and remembered through generations by way of certain images, images that have become iconic representations.

The Tower of Faces in the United States Holocaust Memorial Museum is another case in point. Many of these images emerge from one photographic studio, and all of them are private vernacular or studio images. Installed as they are in the museum, in a tower that resembles a chimney, they tell the story of a town that was destroyed. Their meanings might be personal and memorial for the individuals and families whom they concern, but they are historical and symbolic for visitors to the museum.

HIRSCH: In my article and chapter on "Surviving Images," however, I showed how the repetition of iconic images has the capacity of reducing this history to certain well-known tropes: the gate of Auschwitz, the little boy in the Warsaw ghetto with his hands up, Anne Frank's penetrating gaze—we see these over and over again, at the expense of myriad others (Hirsch 2001). But isn't this also the case with how the history of the Holocaust has been reduced in general? Auschwitz and the gas chamber tend to stand in for so much of it, occluding the experiences of ghettos, of the killing fields in the east, of thousands of varied camps in Nazi-occupied Europe, of hiding, and refugeehood.

ASHKENAZI AND PEGELOW KAPLAN: In your work, you have repeatedly and powerfully identified similarities in specific genres of photos from different historical contexts. In *School Photos in Liquid Time*, for instance, you demonstrate this dynamic in photographs of Jewish school children in Nazi-established ghettos and interned Japanese-American students in American concentration camps of the same period (Hirsch and Spitzer 2020, 137, 7). In "Objects of Return," you examine the role of photographs and clothing in return stories of Holocaust survivors and Palestinians driven from their homes in 1948 and propose "connective readings," "shared tropes," and "concerns for justice and . . . repair" (Hirsch 2012, 206). You have already alluded to this, but can you elaborate on the significance of these resemblances for our historical understanding (or awareness)? In underscoring these resemblances, how can we avoid marginalizing the particularities of historical experiences? In other words, do photographs—because of their generic and iconographic similarities—obscure, rather than enhance, our understanding of particular historical experiences?

HIRSCH AND SPITZER: Both of us are trained as comparatists—Leo is a comparative historian and Marianne's primary field is comparative literature. Even as we have both practiced comparative approaches throughout our careers, we have also been particularly attuned to the limits of comparison and to the uniqueness and untranslatability of particular histories. This is why we have more recently shied away from the term "comparative" and have preferred to speak of "connective histories" (Hirsch 2012; Hirsch and Spitzer 2020). Working on the history and memory of the Holocaust brings the limits of comparison to the fore, on the one hand, but, on the other, it has also sharpened for us the need to reveal connections and resonances with other histories of prejudice, persecution, exclusion, murder, and genocide. Each of these histories is unique but each is also related or connected to others in myriad ways that range from structures of oppression to media of representation. We spoke of this earlier in relation to photos of children in Jewish and Japanese concentration camps.

But to better illustrate how we approach these connections, let us focus specifically on the work school photos do to "certify" grade level and grade ascendancy and participation in a trajectory of socialization defining national belonging and citizenship. We came to that (and what now seems) obvious conclusion methodologically: on the basis of historical and cultural field and archival research we did in the Americas, Europe, and Africa. Certainly, each of the places we examined in some detail (Bolivia, Brazil, the US, Austria and the eastern Habsburg Empire, Romania and the Ukraine, Sierra Leone, South Africa) had unique national and imperial histories that could be studied and detailed on their own. But our consideration of the uses of photography in these different places—and, within photography, of school photos especially—led us to pursue connections between them and to come to conclusions that could not be achieved without a broader, comparative, and multicultural and multinational examination. In each of these places, schools, and the state accredited education they imparted, were central institutions in what Louis Althusser had termed as the "ideological state apparatus" (Althusser 1971). They not only taught students to read and write, but also instructed them in appropriate behavior and civic responsibility, and instilled respect for authority, the established economic order, and capitalist notions of work and time. Photography, which developed technologically and spread throughout much of the world during roughly the same period when nation-states and imperial systems took control over the certification of education, was employed to visually illustrate the "deindividualization" of children in a class and—through set-up common postures, looks, poses—to demonstrate their acquiescence to an imposed group identity. However, school photographs in all of these different national/imperial systems were also made to show what came to be called "before" and "after" change. They were used to attest (often by means of contrasting images taken months apart) to the students' visible transformation (and, by implication, "improvement") over time after the school's "conversionist" education and practices had a chance to take effect. These similar uses and conventions can sharpen the difference between specific cultural and historical circumstances.

ASHKENAZI AND PEGELOW KAPLAN: Within this context, would different genres of photography have different values for scholars of Jewish history? For instance, in various studies you have explored the genre of "vernacular"

Figure 1.6. A class photo in an unidentified municipal elementary school in Czernowitz, Bukowina, Austro-Habsburg Empire, c. 1900. Photos of integrated classes in Habsburg Europe could conceal ethnic and religious differences. *Source:* Blond family archive, courtesy of Arthur Rindner and ehpes website (https://czernowitz.ehpes.com/).

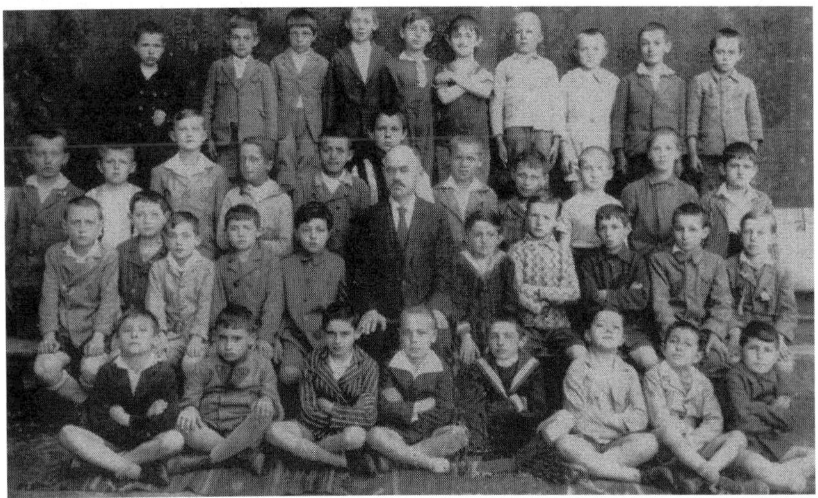

Figure 1.7. Students at the Carlisle Indian School, Carlisle Pennsylvania., c. 1890. Photograph by John N. Choate. *Source:* Courtesy Cumberland County Historical Society.

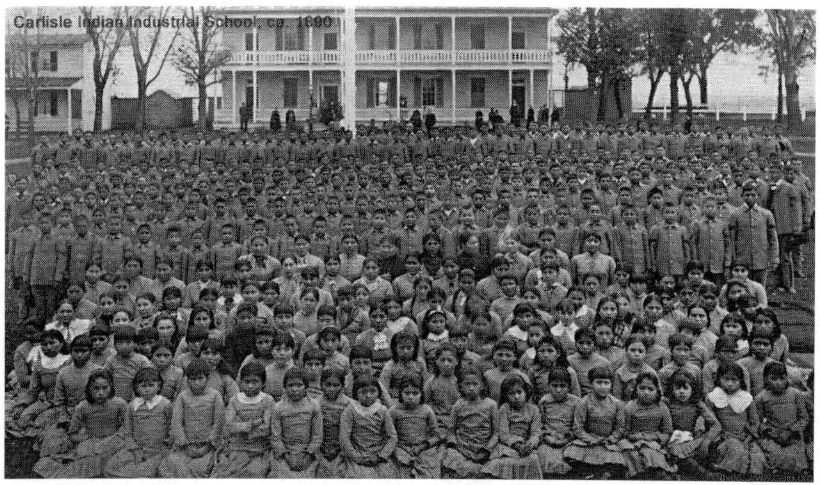

photography, which is characterized by its depiction of "banal" scenes utilizing repetitive, conventional style and iconography. Seemingly, the banality and repetitive nature of "vernacular" photography emphasizes further the tensions between the photograph's alleged ability to "record" what was "really there," and its tendency to reproduce generic imagery (Barthes 1981). As you noted in your article "Incongruous Images," conventional photography can conceal the particular circumstances—such as prevalent antisemitism and the World War—as much as it can reveal them (Hirsch and Spitzer 2012, 147–74; Hirsch and Spitzer 2020, 128–29). While you make a strong case for the use of such photographs in the study of Jewish memory (and memory culture), do you think that historians could also analyze these photographs as "testimonies" of Jewish experience in times of crisis?

HIRSCH AND SPITZER: As you suggest in the previous question and, also, in this one, photographic conventions might seem to risk obscuring particularity and depth in favor of generalized representations that fit into the frames of the medium. "Pictures do lie!" writes the historian Peter Gay in his memoir when he reproduces a 1935 class photo from his high school in Frankfurt in which a classmate puts his arm on his shoulder with easy familiarity. That gesture disguises the fact that that boy, Hans Schmidt, was "already an intolerable Hitler Youth." What kind of historical document is that picture, then, if it "lies?" A really telling one, we would argue. Like other school photos of Jews in integrated school classes in Western Europe in the beginning of the twentieth century, it shows us how Jewish children were educated alongside their non-Jewish neighbors and co-citizens. It shows us how fully Jews participated in state and state-accredited institutions through-out those years, making their exclusion all the more unexpected and brutal.

At the same time, conventional "vernacular" photos, such as family, tourist, street, or school photos, all of which we have worked with, also can show the particularity of Jewish experience especially well, not so much despite, but because of, their repetitive conventional features. In our study of class pictures, we were able to see, at the same time, how state institutions used schooling and photography to assimilate and integrate diverse populations into the mainstream, and how Jewish integration worked differently from that of colonial or African-American subjects whose education remained segregated. The similarity of the photos reveals the difference between these strategies of assimilation, and the responses of those affected, even more strongly.

In more general terms, we would also suggest that many documents used by historians to gain insights into a time or life are strictly conventional and they shape the history that is told as much as photographs shape the scene they record. Letters, newspaper articles, civil documents, memoirs—all these are no less conventional than photographs and require no less inter-pretation and careful contextual reading.

In our work, we have often turned to artists to open up photos and documents to their own interpretations, to show us what these conventional images do and can do. For example, in her beautiful book *Everyone Is Present*, Terry Kurgan relies on her grandfather's journals and photographs to trace the family's circuitous escape journey from Europe to South Africa in the late 1930s and early 1940s (Kurgan 2019). By blowing up the pic-tures, by focusing on details that are marginal or almost outside the frame, she can enter the images, evoke the affect of the time, and thus expand the information recorded in the diaries. The photographs and diaries work together and enhance each other. Kurgan insists that the diaries also require sophisticated interpretation. What does the diarist note, what does he leave out? How does she present herself and others? Photos are archival objects like so many others.

Ashkenazi and pegelow kaplan: The practice of photo analysis (mostly, but not exclusively in the realm of art history) is heavily dependent on intentionality—that is, the conscious intentions and objectives that guided the photographer's choice of subject, depth of field, light, and so on. In your writing, it seems that the conscious intentions of both the photographers and the compilers of the albums are marginal, sometimes irrelevant. With the lack of intentionality, you refer to generic conventions and to particular revisions of them, can you explain your methodology—also in regard to gender analysis that has been a core part of your approaches from the beginning?

Hirsch and Spitzer: It is interesting that you see it that way. We do not privilege the photographer's intentions, you are right, though we see the positionality of the photographer as crucially important. We see the image as the product of an encounter between the photographer, the photographed person, and the viewer—an interaction contingent on the social and political workings of power. It is here that gender, race, and other markers of social difference become important, and we always ask which of these factors shape the photographic gaze and how.

We are interested in the photographic medium and what it makes visible, as well as what it obscures. Thus, we are also interested in the work of the shutter and the frame—in photography as a social practice that organizes social life. And we are especially interested in time and how it works to bring all these concerns together.

In *School Photos in Liquid Time*, we develop the idea, precisely, of liquid time. The artist Jeff Wall's essay "Photography and Liquid Intelligence" has been a helpful inspiration to us in this endeavor (Wall 2007). Rather than on the shutter, or on the event of photographing or being photographed, or on the act of looking, Wall bases his reflections about the "liquid intelligence" of the photograph on the process involved in the developing of analog images. In the darkroom, both the photographic film and the photosensitive paper onto which an image has been projected and recorded is immersed in a liquid developing solution where it changes, often in subtle and unexpected ways, before it is chemically "fixed"—again through liquid immersion—into perpetuity. When he wrote his essay in the late 1980s, Jeff Wall wanted to mark the beginnings of the digital turn that introduces a different technological and temporal regime from the analog. But Wall also sought to complicate the pervasive view of photography as an inexorable apparatus and tool of ideological power and domination—a medium of representation which, when "fixed into permanence," embodies a "dry," and thus unalterable optical and technological "intelligence." In highlighting the "liquid intelligence" of the photograph instead, he revealed its contingencies, possibilities, potentials, and affective registers inherent in the process of image-making. In what we, therefore, want to think of as "liquid time," photographs continue "developing" when they are viewed and reviewed by different people in different presents. "Unfixed," they remain open, active, dynamic, acquiring new meanings in new circumstances.

Such a "liquid" and multitemporal reading displaces the primacy of the photographer and his or her intentions.

As our discussion of Terry Kurgan's work indicates, the workings of this extended and fluid temporality are best illustrated by some of the photo-based artists we regularly turn to in our work to learn more about what photos *do*. Postmemorial artists, especially, use archival images in their

Figure 1.8. Mirta Kupferminc, Mendel Grossman, *The Witness*, 2019. Inkjet print and drawing on cotton paper. *Source:* Courtesy of the artist.

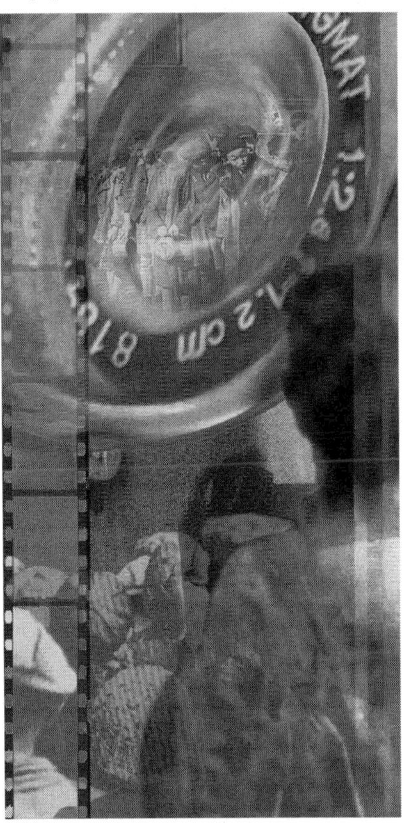

work, reframing, recontextualizing and resignifying them. It is part of their effort to bear witness to and to repair some of the wounds of the past, or to show how the past lives on in the present.

ASHKENAZI AND PEGELOW KAPLAN: Regardless of the status of "Jewish photography" as a distinct analytical paradigm, your studies have intriguingly linked photographs of and by Jews to "activist and interventionist cultural and political engagement." In *School Photos in Liquid Time*, you draw on Gabrielle Moser's notion of the "disobedient gaze" and reflect on "visual action" that turns the violence of conventional school photography on its head. In *The Generation of Postmemory*, you present the work on postmemory as a "form of repair and redress" and explicitly tie it to movements for social change, especially feminism (Hirsch 2012, 225, 6). To what extent do you understand photography as a vehicle of (Jewish) defiance? Is photography, as Ariella Aïsha Azoulay has maintained, a necessarily political act?

HIRSCH AND SPITZER: What you observe in our work is surely linked to the historical moments and situations we engage in our work—moments of political crisis or social change.

HIRSCH: My work on photographs began with family pictures. It was a topic I approached from a feminist perspective critical of the unequal power dynamics of the family and the dominance of the family, and the inequality it perpetuated, in political and social thought and practice. If the conventions of family photography actually undergird these oppressive dynamics, could the same medium also be used to contest and overturn them? Here, as in subsequent work, I looked for examples of such "opposition," to cite bell hooks, or "disobedience," though this term only came to us later.

In order to find examples of how the genre could be reframed and power redistributed, I turned to the work of photo-based artists who could both show us how the medium works and how it can be enlarged and undermined. Photo-based artists who contest the traditional workings of the familial gaze are doing political work. It is this work on family photography that led to my work on memory.

SPITZER: I came to memory first through my work in West Africa involving oral history, and subsequently through my research and writing on refugee migration.

When we both began to work on the Holocaust, we came upon photos that were astounding and astonishing for their very existence. How did images taken in the ghettos come to be, and how could they survive? This was a time when non-Nazi recorded photography was largely clandestine, and yet people risked their lives to record what was happening to them. They took pictures, they developed and hid or buried them along with other records. These were acts of witness that record not only life in the ghettos but also the courage and determination to make this history known in the future. Thus, they were surely acts of defiance as well as precious objects of memory and history. In fact, these images show us how photography is really about the future, and not the past nor the present.

ASHKENAZI AND PEGELOW KAPLAN: We would like to circle back to the "openness" of the photograph. According to the approach you laid out, "disobedience," or even defiance is embedded, therefore, in the openness of photographs to multiple interpretations, including ones that defy oppression. Is it true only for photography, or also for other types of private

Figure 1.9. Children studying in a clandestine school, Kovno ghetto, Lithuania, 1941–1942. Photo possibly by David Chaim Ratner. *Source:* Photo Archive, United States Holocaust Memorial Museum, courtesy of Eliezer Zilberis.

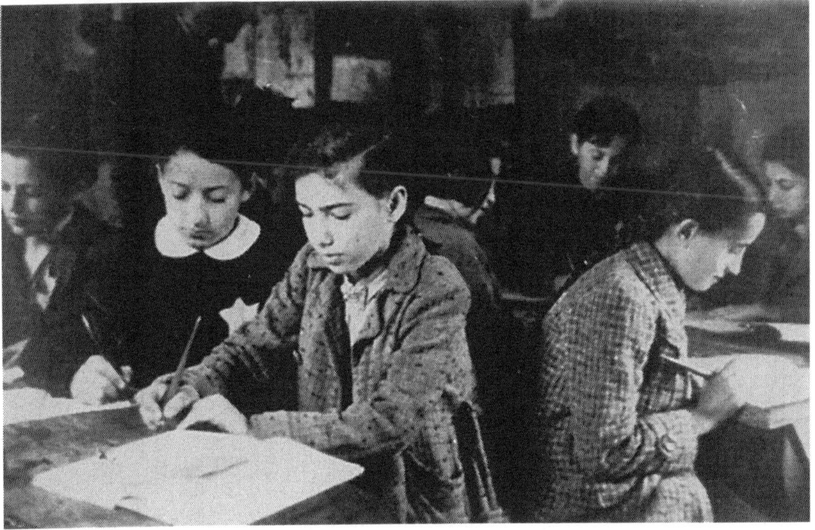

documentations? Or perhaps even official texts? In other words, is there anything special about photography in the hand of the historian? Are photographs taken by Jews in interwar Europe different from other sources they produced?

HIRSCH AND SPITZER: Many of the photographs we have worked with are more than objects and artifacts: they are acts of witness and thus historical actors in their own right. As we have seen in recent years, the existence of still and moving images of police and state violence can have monumental social, political, and juridical consequences. Their evidentiary value is paramount. But are clandestine images from the Jewish ghettos in Europe different from the meticulously produced and salvaged letters, diaries, and related records? All these are not only evidentiary documents, but also haptic traces of lives lived and often destroyed and thus they provide a powerful form of access to the lived reality of the past.

In our own work on the history of Transnistria, we relied on a very tenuous document to find the site of the former concentration camp of Vapniarka (Hirsch and Spitzer 2010). It was a xeroxed image of a photograph of a model made by a camp survivor living in Israel and collected by the Ghetto Fighters' House. Without that image we would not have been able to find the site, which was not only unmarked, but unknown by the local population. The model made from memory, supplemented by prisoners' drawings and memoirs, and by postwar trial records, helped us locate and write about the camp's history. Although several drawings and sketches exist, we have found no photographic images of the site. Would these have even greater evidentiary value?

You are asking about openness to interpretation: Are photographs more open to interpretation than other documents? We believe that as acts of witness, they are as subjective as diaries or letters, or models produced from memory. In addition, we would say that this is also a question about archives, perhaps more than about qualities inherent in these different kinds of documents. Each of these sources demands the same contextual questions about who produced them, when, and for whom. But also: How and by whom were they saved? How are they labeled and classified in institutional archives? And how do they support or complicate other forms of documentation? Vapniarka, for example, was a Romanian-run camp, but is now located in Ukraine. Neither state is taking responsibility for this Holocaust history, and thus private records become even more important in historical research. Romanian, American, German, and Israeli institutions have become the repository for some of these records. Each of these states have

Figure 1.10. Cardboard model of the Vapniarka concentration camp in Transnistria built according to survivors' testimonies by Avi Solomovici-Sela, himself a camp survivor. *Source:* Courtesy Ghetto Fighters' House Archive. Used with permission.

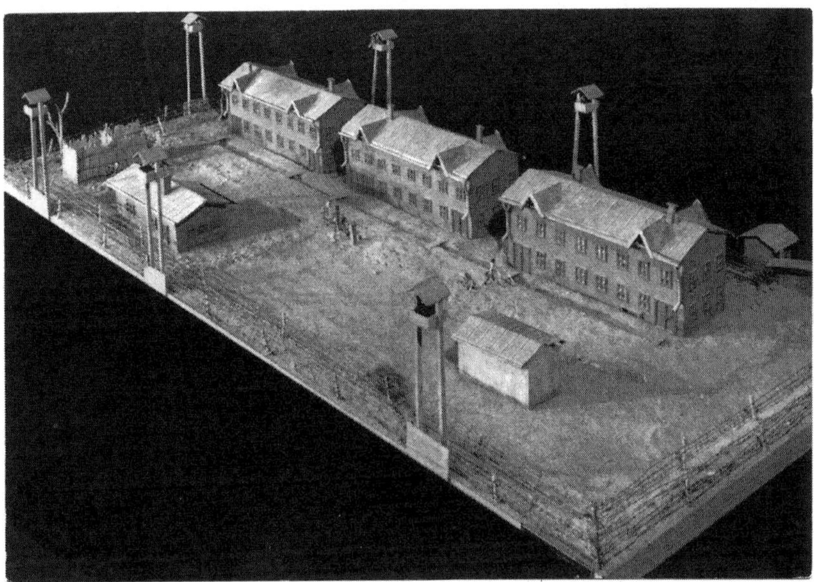

their own political stakes in these histories and these stakes are important to sort out in our work.

ASHKENAZI AND PEGELOW KAPLAN: One of your key contributions to the study of photography explores the aforementioned concepts and approaches of postmemory. In your analysis of postmemory, photographs play a central, if not privileged role as readings of postmemory move from the narrower realm of "familial inheritance" to a broader understanding—also prevalent in your most recent work—of "intersubjective transnational space of remembrance" (Hirsch 2001, 10; Hirsch and Spitzer 2020, 14). How do you see the future of postmemory in the age of digital photography? Would the expansive reservoirs of digitally preserved photographs change (or invalidate) the role of photographs in the construction of identity-narratives?

HIRSCH AND SPITZER: Image archives have certainly expanded and multiplied in the digital age, and they have also become more broadly and instantly available with a click of the mouse. Photographs are no longer material objects stored in albums and transported from place to place. They accompany us on our phone or hard drive wherever we go. This easy availability greatly enhances the role of photographs in identity formation and self-fashioning. Take a look at your phones—how many of the last twenty images you took are selfies? Where did you post them? To whom did you send them? How did they circulate? These are questions for today, but as the technology evolves, so will our means of seeing ourselves reflected in photographs, and our use of them to transmit our histories.

Your question is a great one. We are in an extended moment of transition from the analog image that carries and contains the material traces of the past to the digital image that carries very different kinds of information—information that is in many ways more extensive and precise. Digital images, for example, contain data about the exact time and place when they were taken, as well as about the camera and settings employed in the taking. Extractable by anyone familiar with an editing program like Photoshop, such exact chronological and geographical information in a digital image (which is hardly ever available for an analog image) is of immense evidentiary use to historians and cultural analysts. Digital images (despite their huge quantity) are also more easily sorted and categorized according to the data information they contain than analog ones. But, as we already know, they are also more easily alterable both by humans and by artificial intelligence (albeit, not without leaving traces of their iteration).

How will digital photography impact the future of postmemory? Will the surfeit of images, emails, social media posts, and computer files offer our descendants greater access to the fabric of our everyday lives than we have to the lives of our analog ancestors? No doubt. But they will require no less—and perhaps even greater—interpretive will and critical skill to decode and assemble, and even more suspicion about accuracy, authenticity, and truth. And, certainly, they will require forms of openness and vulnerability on the part of future scholar-descendants that are similar to the ones we have learned in relation to the analog objects we have largely used in our postmemorial work.

Ashkenazi and pegelow kaplan: At least since the mid-1920s, cameras, film-developments, and albums have become relatively cheap and photography a household commodity—even if still to a lesser extent than in the current age of digital photography. As a result, historians of the twentieth century are faced with an unprecedented amount and variety of photographic documents. One of the obvious challenges related to this abundance is the question of the "representativeness" of photographs. For instance, your analysis in *School*

Photos in Liquid Time differentiates between class photos that aim to reinforce individual identities (albeit in a group) and photos that aim to undermine the individuality of group members. Pointing to "links between perpetrator photography and the Nazi killing machine," you present National Socialist photographers' work in the Lodz ghetto that blurs or hides students' faces as an example of the latter (Hirsch and Spitzer 2020, 147–48). Yet, one can find many counterexamples from the 1930s. A considerable number of Jewish photographers, for instance, captured Jewish students in Germany in ways that resemble the "Nazi gaze." Their photographs seemingly deliberately hide faces behind classmates' shoulders or classroom objects. Isn't there a need to differentiate further? What are the premises that would facilitate the analysis of a photograph as "representative" of a broader trend (as opposed to an "incidental" result of the particular circumstances, photographer, and generic conventions)?

Hirsch and Spitzer: It is true in general, of course, that "representativeness" is difficult to establish. There are always individual examples that depart from a larger, more general trend. In this case, however, our observation rests on two specific factors that, again, could illustrate our approach.

The first is the focus on a specific medium and genre—as we have done with school photos. Initially, these were intended for the institution itself, the school and its archives. But as photos became more replicable and easily distributed, these school pictures also became available to the student and the student's family, and to the world at large. Indeed, their visibility and accessibility became a key attribute and function of these images. The images, after all, helped to create a cohort and a generation. They built loyalty and inclusion and helped in the creation of a group identity to which the individual consents to belong, however enthusiastically or reluctantly. If an image neglects this kind of individual visibility and deviates from convention, we need to ask why. It could be incidental, of course, or it could be significant and illustrative of a specific kind of gaze or historical circumstance.

The second factor that helped us read the Nazi images of Jewish children in this way is precisely our comparative/connective methodology. Some colonial images look similar to the Nazi ones. We are thinking of an early 1865 image of Native Tulalip children photographed with their missionary teachers.

Here the teachers stand in front of the children and cover some of them with their bodies. Their aim was to show their power and the domination of

Figure 1.11. Group of young boys in uniform standing behind Catholic missionary Eugene Casimir Chirouse, OMI, and another missionary priest, Tulalip Indian Reservation, Washington Territory, 1865. Photo by William Francis Robertson. *Source:* Courtesy University of Washington Libraries, Special Collections.

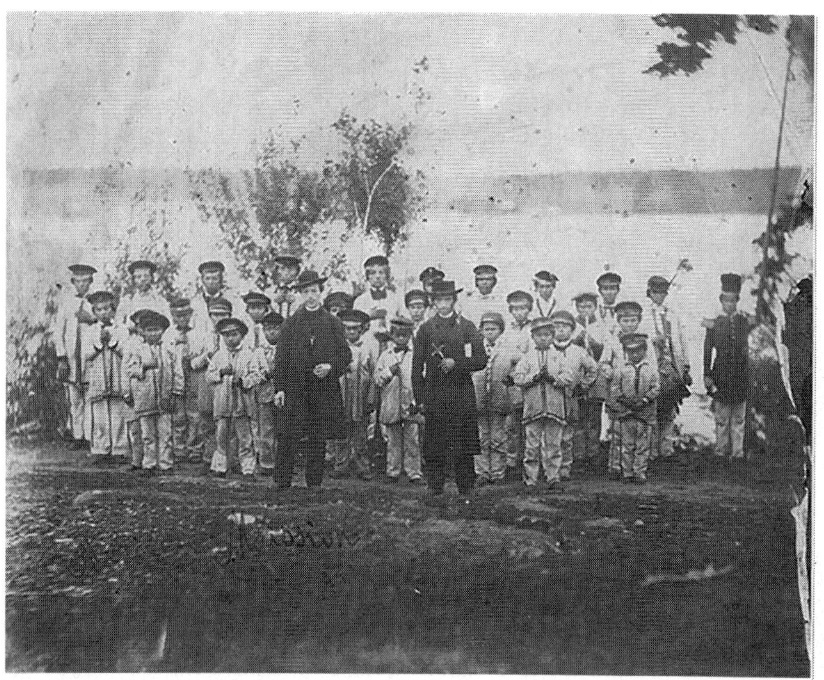

the crosses they were holding up. Putting together images taken by and for Christian missionaries in North America and for the Nazi killing machine in Poland, we concluded that the children and their families were not the intended viewers, but that the photographs, taken nearly 80 years apart, served the purpose of demonstrating the power of conquest and cultural genocide.

Of course, these conclusions are matters of interpretation. In our case, we rely on a visual literacy we have been developing in dialogue with our objects. Each image can teach us how to read it, but it also tells us that it can be read in multiple ways.

Ashkenazi and pegelow kaplan: It seems fair to say that Jewish studies scholars today display much more interest in photography and willingness to incorporate photo analysis in their research than when you first published in this field. Several recent studies—including yours—applied a variety of approaches to understand Jews' experiences and memory through photography: from its social and political functions to its ability to communicate intricate positions and sentiments. By way of summarizing, what are—in your opinion—the most significant insights that the study of photography has provided to the field Jewish studies?

Hirsch and Spitzer: Indeed, photography has been playing a much more prominent role in Jewish history in recent years. Let us answer your excellent question by way of some recent books in the field.

First, we would name the late David Shneer's book *Grief: The Biography of a Holocaust Photograph*. On the basis of one photograph by the Russian Jewish photojournalist Dmitri Baltermants, Shneer not only tells the human lived history of a 1942 massacre in Kerch, Crimea, perpetrated by Nazi forces, but also the history of Russian photojournalism, the contemporary afterlives of these wartime images, their display, and, more generally, the memory of the Holocaust in contemporary Russia (Shneer 2020). This enlarged meditation on history, archives and memorialization is made possible by starting with a single photograph.

Second, we would want to discuss some of the insights of Sara Blair's *How the Other Half Looks: The Lower East Side and the Afterlives of Images*. Blair responds to and contests the images of poverty and abjection that shaped the image of immigrant Jews on New York's Lower East Side through, among others, Jacob Riis's influential *How the Other Half Lives*. Taking Jewish subjects out of Riis's static tableaux, she highlights the dynamic, energetic, and experimental ways of looking, and looking back, developed in this neighborhood in the early parts of the twentieth century. She does this by examining photographs and writing emerging from this rapidly evolving space, and by forging an analytic method that promotes socially conscious and oppositional ways of looking. In this book, photo analysis enables a reframing of the history of Jewish immigrant lives in New York and the United States (Blair 2018).

Third, we want to say a bit more about a work we have already invoked several times in this conversation, Ariella Aïsha Azoulay's *Potential History: Unlearning Imperialism*, a sustained and provocative meditation on the discipline of history, the institution of archives, and the practices of imperialism. Photographs relating to the history of Jewish settler colonialism in Palestine form an important part of Azoulay's corpus, and here she develops an analytic practice that is particularly relevant to our conversation about "Jewish" photography. She enjoins us to look for what the shutter excludes and thus what remains out of view, as well as what eschews understanding even when it is included in the image. Images taken by Jewish Israeli photographers can be read in different ways, depending on whose point of view viewers inhabit or ally with. When Azoulay visits Israeli state archives and their photography collections, she does so accompanied by an imaginary Palestinian "companion" who demands to have his or her view acknowledged and represented (Azoulay 2019). In this way, a different story can emerge, details within the image can be noticed and become significant, captions may need to be rewritten.

In the photos Azoulay herself has collected and exhibited, taken between 1948 and 1953, she finds instances of coexistence and cohabitation that constitute a "potential history" of what could have been. She thus undoes the inevitability of what she calls "regime-made disaster," a way of looking and of doing history that we ourselves have developed through the idea of "liquid time." This is a focus not on trauma and impending or ongoing catastrophe, but on what might have been, and what thus could still be. This reading of photographs as documents not of a past that cannot be changed, but of one that could have led to a different present offers enormous opportunities for Jewish history practiced on the basis of photography.

In trying to write history in this way, we have gone back to an older text, Michael André Bernstein's *Foregone Conclusions: Against Apocalyptic History*. Bernstein warns against a "backshadowing" view of history in which we read the past through the outcome we already know when approaching the material (Bernstein 1994). In looking at photographs of people who were to be subject to catastrophic histories, we try to grant them their own present, that moment before. We try make space for the future they were themselves envisioning when the photo was taken. That envisioned future, we want to suggest, is also very much part of the history we wish to tell.

Works Cited

Alexander, Elizabeth. 1994. "'Can You Be Black and Look at This?' Reading the Rodney King Video(s)." *Public Culture* 7 (1): 77–94.
Althusser, Louis. 1971. "Ideology and Ideological State Apparatus." In *Lenin and Philosophy and other Essays*. Monthly Review Press.
Azoulay, Ariella Aïsha. 2019. *Potential History: Unlearning Imperialism*. Verso.
Barthes, Roland. 1981. *Camera Lucida: Reflections on Photography*. Hill and Wang.

Bernstein, Michael André. 1994. *Foregone Conclusions: Against Apocalyptic History*. University of California Press.

Blair, Sara. 2018. *How the Other Half Looks: The Lower East Side and the Afterlives of Images*. Princeton University Press.

Gidal, Nachum T. 1987. "Jews in Photography." *Leo Baeck Institute Year Book* 32 (1): 437–53.

Hirsch, Marianne. 2001. "Surviving Images: Holocaust Photographs and the Work of Postmemory." *Yale Journal of Criticism* 14 (1): 5–37.

———. 2012. *The Generation of Postmemory: Writing and Visual Culture after the Holocaust*. Columbia University Press.

Hirsch, Marianne, and Leo Spitzer. 2010. *Ghosts of Home: The Afterlife of Czernowitz in Jewish Memory*. University of California Press.

———. 2012. "Incongruous Images: Before, during, and after the Holocaust." In *Performing the Past: Memory, History, and Identity in Modern Europe*, edited by Karin Tilmans, Frank van Vree, and Jay M. Winter. Amsterdam University Press.

———. 2020. *School Photos in Liquid Time: Reframing Difference*. University of Washington Press.

Kurgan, Terry. 2019. *Everyone is Present: Essays on Photography, Memory and Family*. Fourth Wall.

Shneer, David. 2020. *Grief: The Biography of a Holocaust Photograph*. Oxford University Press.

Spitzer, Leo. 1989. *Lives in Between: Assimilation and Marginality in Austria, Brazil, West Africa, 1780–1945*. Cambridge University Press.

Wall, Jeff. 2007. "Photography and Liquid Intelligence." In *Jeff Wall: Selected Essays and Interviews*. Museum of Modern Art.

Chapter 2

Invisibly Jewish

Lotte Jacobi, Photography, and the Boundaries of Jewish Cultural Studies

Lisa Silverman

Figure 2.1. Lotte Jacobi's portrait of her father, photographer Sigismund Jacobi, projects the image of a captured moment of bourgeois gentility, a coveted status for many German Jews. *Portrait of Sigismund Jacobi*, 1920. *Source:* © 2022 the University of New Hampshire. Used with permission.

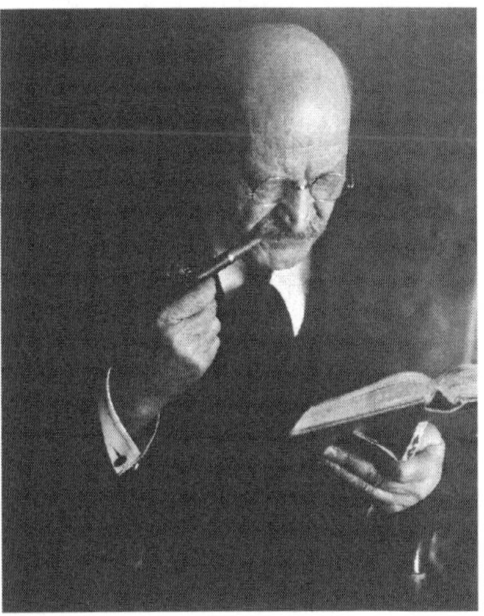

In 1920, photographer Lotte Jacobi took a notable portrait of her father, Sigismund Jacobi. The elegantly dressed figure emerges from an almost black background, into which his dark suit blends. Only his white cuffs and shirt are visible, the latter sporting a cufflink. We do not know where his figure ends and the background begins, save for his hands, one of which clasps an open, apparently weathered and much-thumbed, though not dog-eared, book. In his other hand, he holds a distinguished wood and metal pipe firmly fixed to his mouth, which is also not visible to the viewer. His downcast head conceals his eyes and most of his face. Jacobi's large forehead and the top of his head dominate the photograph along with his round wire glasses and trimmed moustache. Faintly visible in the background is a chair that appears to be made of leather. Jacobi's left hand rests upon its polished black arm. Since he is looking down and his eyes are not visible, the viewer has the impression that Jacobi was unaware his photograph was being taken at all. The image thus emphasizes the illusion that the viewer has stolen a glance of a distinguished figure during a private moment in his fine home. The portrait projects the image of a serious, learned man of the bourgeois or upper-middle class, deliberate in its intent to signify his respected social standing.

To the naked eye, nothing indicates that this is a portrait of a Jew taken by another Jew. There is no Star of David, menorah, Hebrew lettering, or any other religious or cultural item that signifies Jewishness. However, I argue that knowledge of the context in which this and other photographs by Jews were taken illuminates what the naked eye cannot otherwise discern: this photograph signifies the Jewishness of both photographer and subject just as much as those items would. From the point of view of a newly arrived but well-off Jewish family from Eastern Europe, it is unsurprising that both photographer and subject are concerned with his portrayal as an ideal bourgeois German, surrounded by the trappings of a bourgeois or upper-middle class home. The book references the ideals of acculturating middle-class German Jews who, more than others, fixated on ideals of character development and education, or *Bildung*. Historian George L. Mosse, who left Nazi Germany in 1933, highlighted culture as a crucial agent of historical change and the importance of symbols. His seminal *German Jews beyond Judaism*, first published in 1985, focused on Jews' desire to be both German and Jewish. According to Mosse and others, *Bildung*—the formation of character by way of education—replaced religion for the German Jewish bourgeoisie. Since then, Sander Gilman in particular has helped us view *Bildung* as part of a broader narrative of Jewish self-fashioning, building the foundation for studies that take seriously the symbolic substance and representation of everyday occurrences, popular activities, and informal practices. He and other scholars have identified *Bildung* as only one of many Jewish and non-Jewish symbols, themes, and ideas that Jews used to weave their experiences into Central European culture—thus rendering them "Jewish" (Gilman 1991; Lässig 2004; Sieg 2020).

Notably, however, the photograph's Jewishness emerges from what it does *not* reveal: the fact that Sigismund himself is a successful portrait photographer, the third in a generation of photographers who had made their careers in Prussia. According to family legend, Lotte Jacobi's great-grandfather, Samuel, took a trip to Paris around 1840, where he met Louis-Jacques Mandé Daguerre, who popularized photography in Europe. When he returned to Prussia, Jacobi made and sold daguerreotypes—and the family became so closely associated with photography that later, people referred to going to Posen to have a "Jacobi" taken (Trum Hunter 2000). Lotte Jacobi was raised with a very strong association between the family, the profession, and photographs. Samuel's son Alexander and grandson Sigismund—Lotte Jacobi's father—also became photographers; Sigismund took over the family business in Thorn (today Polish Toruń) in 1894. In 1898 he moved the family to Posen (Poznań), where he opened his own atelier in the city center. The name "S. Jacobi" was prominently displayed in large letters above the entrance. However, Sigismund continued to use the insignia of his father Alexander's studio on the back of his photographs, "A. Jacobi," indicating both his pride in the family business and a desire to maintain the generational link in the new studio. Indeed, even its flourishing elegant script—advertising all five branches of the family atelier, with medals displaying the honors bestowed on their photographic achievements since 1894—indicates that the Jacobis worked actively to assure their clients that their studio would capture the refined, sophisticated air they wished to have come across in their portraits. When writing about her life in 1933, Lotte Jacobi herself claimed to have come from one of the oldest families of photographers in eastern Germany, a fact of which she was apparently quite proud.

Though it avoids any reference to his distinguished career, Jacobi's contemplative portrait of her father makes sense as a marker of Jewishness when considered from the standpoint of the position of both photographer and subject as members of a German Jewish family with a long tradition of photographing themselves and others. Lotte Jacobi had moved to Berlin only in 1920, together with her husband Fritz Honig, whom she had married in

1916 and divorced a few years later, and her son Jochen; her father, mother, and sister followed in 1921. They arrived as thousands of other Jews from the East were making their way to the city. However, most of these were Orthodox Jews, whose visible and audible differences in dress, custom, and language made them particularly vulnerable to antisemitic attacks. As many scholars have pointed out, this was often a vexing problem for Jews in Central European cities who were already more acculturated (Gluck 2016; Shapira 2016; Wallach 2017). This includes Lotte and her family who, according to her daughter-in-law, often expressed anxieties and prejudices about these Jewish immigrants from the East and placed a premium on appearing German rather than Jewish (Beatrice Trum Hunter, telephone interview with author, June 17, 2004).

Visualizing Jewish Absence

Jewishness—the quality that makes us describe a person, place, or thing as Jewish—is not a natural state, but rather a social construction fully detachable from people called Jews. This essay argues that photography, as a field in which Jews have long played a major role both in front of and behind the camera, can help us recognize Jewishness as a social construction that is *always* distinct from the Jew, or the thing made by Jews. As I have argued elsewhere, it is only by examining the experiences of Jews *without* making Jewish self-identification the ontological foundation of Jewish experience and history that we can more fully recognize how Jewishness is created, used, covered, reversed, or discarded (Silverman 2011; Berman 2018). To do so is not to deny a work's religious or cultural Jewish content, nor is it to ignore the degree to which its creator self-identified as Jewish. But it is a refusal to make what is visibly, recognizably Jewish about a photographer or their subjects an a priori rule for identifying people, places, and things, worthy of inclusion as part of Jewish cultural studies. It is understanding that a person, place, or thing does not have to be Jewish by anyone's definition in order to engage with the cultural construction of Jewishness.

I emphasize this point because it is often the *absence* of anything that can be identified as explicitly Jewish—and often along with the careful cultivation of what is *not* Jewish—that not only marks, but actually drives so much of the modern Jewish experience (Silverman 2012a). And yet, so many of us continue to overlook the important, invisible, markers of Jewishness that characterize Jews' experiences. Unless there is a direct link between what someone created and their sense of Jewish self-identification, or unless evidence exists that someone was directly affected by an antisemitic act or deed, the assumption continues to be that Jewishness didn't matter. At best, some might reference Jews' general disadvantaged position as outsiders, and explain their efforts toward inclusion as attempts to become insiders. According to this logic, Jews aimed either to become wholly invisible as Jews in their efforts to acculturate to mainstream culture or to fully dissimilate by proudly bearing Jewish symbols or engaging publicly in debates and traditions.

As these examples from Lotte Jacobi's life and career show, photographs can be a rich source of evidence to illuminate the absence of visibly Jewish content and mark the invisible circumscribed codes of behavior that shaped Jews' actions in public and private. They also show how these codes of Jewish difference intersected with other analytic categories such as gender and class. Furthermore, they reveal how it was not only those active, performative gestures that explicitly celebrate or deny traditions, beliefs, and practices of Jews, but also those harder to quantify gaps, absences, and silences, that inform so much of Jewish history. Photographs became popular not only because of their growing accessibility, but also because they were thought to reproduce nature and thus preserve a historical record. Yet it is precisely this belief in the seemingly objective power of photography, along with the subjective, ideological distortions it actually reveals, that compels us to investigate the implications of the socially constructed notion of the Jewish and not-Jewish for both photographers and their subjects. Gisèle Freund (1908–2000), a Jewish photographer born in Berlin, claimed that photography's illusive objectivity allowed it to become a crucial medium for expressing the views of what was seen as the dominant society:

> More than any other medium, photography is able to express the values of the dominant social class and to interpret events from that class's point of view, for photography, although strictly linked with nature, has only an illusory objectivity. The lens, the so-called impartial eye, actually permits every possible distortion of reality: the character of the image is determined by the photographer's point of view and the demands of his patrons. The importance of photography does not rest primarily in its potential as an art form, but rather in its ability to shape our ideas, to influence our behavior, and to define our society. (Freund 1980, 4–5)

Freund's analysis goes to the heart of what was at stake for Jews and photography: knowing when to appear visibly Jewish, or when to hide, evoke, or completely cover that Jewishness, as an important part of Jews' modern experiences. In highlighting the implicit codes that were central to Jews' experiences in the modern era, photographs put to rest the unwritten rule that evidence of Jews' contributions to the creation of culture must be both explicit and visible, or must advance a collective, Jewish agenda.

Photographs are also an especially rich source for showing how constructed ideals of gender inflected the representation of Jews. Jewish men had long displaced their own anxieties by mocking or ignoring Jewish women and idealizing Christian women for their looks. Jacobi's portraits engage with—and often subtly subvert—the difficulties women and Jews faced as they attempted to meet society's expectations about their bodies, appearance, and comportment. As antisemitism became more palpable in the early twentieth century, women, in particular, were expected to clothe, groom, and comport themselves in ways that eliminated any associations with Jewish attributes, an expectation that became a source of extra anxiety. Photography as a career choice thus represented a powerful way for Jews to gain a measure of control over how they were depicted as both part of and separate from mainstream society. Examining portraits Jacobi took of her father and herself, first in Germany, and later in exile in New York, invites us to consider to what extent they explicitly reflect an engagement with contemporary discourses of power, class, and gender, and thus reveal their invisible engagement with Jewish difference.

Consideration of Jewish difference alongside other analytic categories, such as gender and class, adds depth and complexity to our reading of these photographs. Just as reading for gender illustrates how socially constructed gender norms form the basis for the power and control men have over women in everyday life, reading for Jewish difference can help us see how socially constructed notions of the Jew and non-Jew shape the power and control non-Jews wield over Jews, even when the terms of that control are not readily apparent. In this context, rather than trying to identify what visibly Jewish qualities emerge from a photograph, I suggest that it is more fruitful to focus first on why what is socially constructed as Jewish at that time and place might matter to the depiction of that image and how it is interpreted. However, even scholars committed to an examination of the symbolic meanings behind Jewish practices, rituals, and objects find it difficult to let go of the notion that some kernel of authentic Jewishness defines the essence of the Jew (Silverman 2004, 2009).

To that I would argue the following: Think about gender studies and the work feminist scholars have done to show how central its analytic framework remains to historical studies. Due to their efforts, no historian can deny that "femininity" and "masculinity" are cultural constructions that are distinct from actual men and women, but which have had a great impact on the lives of women and men and the culture they created, even if they are not writing about the effects of patriarchy or misogyny per se. But trying to show how Jewish difference is a useful category of critical analysis for Jewish history remains more challenging. Given how integral Jews have been to the creation of culture in modern Germany and Austria, Jewish studies scholars need to rise to that challenge and similarly insist on taking the cultural constructions of Jewishness and non-Jewishness into account, even in scholarship that is not focused on antisemitism and its effects.

But beyond photography, using Jewish difference as an analytical tool in this way can help us unravel some of modern Jewish history's more vexing issues by revisiting past experiences, events, and texts that lend significant insight into Jewish history but have previously been left at its margins because they have not met expected definitions of Jewish content. It also allows for a deeper consideration of individuals whose lives and works reveal an engagement with the categories of the Jewish and the non-Jewish, regardless of their own degree of Jewish self-identification. It moves us beyond a search for visible Jewish content to ask whether the photograph reveals engagement with the relationship between what was perceived as Jewish and what was not Jewish in that time and place—an important point to consider, especially if such an engagement might actually be represented by the explicit *lack* of Jewish content. In other words, the very content that designates these photographs as Jewish is ultimately a matter—to call up Hayden White's sense of historiography of form (White 1987)—of those formal qualities that suggest a profound interrogation of the subtler complexities of Jewish experience.

Bourgeois Origins

Lotte Jacobi was born Johanna Alexandra Jacobi to Siegesmund Jacobi and Maria Lublintzki in 1896 in Thorn, in West Prussia. She was the oldest of three children. Her sister Ruth, who also became a photographer, was born in 1899 (Beckers and Moortgat 2012). A brother, Alexander, arrived in 1902 (Pomerance 2008). Within two years of her birth, her family had moved to the larger city of Posen, and in 1921 to Berlin. From her early years as a photographer in Weimar Berlin to her travels in the Soviet Union in 1932 and eventual exile in England and the United States after 1935 until her death in New Hampshire in 1990, Lotte Jacobi continued to take original portraits of well-known intellectuals, politicians, and entertainers, including actress and singer Lotte Lenya, dancer Claire Bauroff, actor Peter Lorre, painter Marc Chagall, writer Karl Kraus and journalist Egon Erwin Kisch, and Communist leader Ernst Thälmann, as well as Martin Buber and Albert Einstein. Her portraits of these iconic figures reveal her immersion in the cultural, artistic, and intellectual milieux of salon life in 1920s Berlin and beyond. However, Jacobi did not only remain behind the camera. She also actively took part in the worlds of her illustrious clients through social engagement with them at her studio, attendance at Communist Party meetings, trips to the Soviet Union, and even collaboration on photographs and techniques—some of which, as this chapter will show, she used to challenge social and gender norms (Gough 2020).

Photographs that Sigismund Jacobi took of his children even before the move to Berlin indicate that the family was already well embarked on the process of acculturation while living in Posen. A photograph taken by Sigismund in 1899, depicting three-year-old Lotte with the family nanny, is thus not only a family portrait, but also a "calling card" that advertised the type of portraits the studio produced. It shows both woman and child smiling pleasantly; the well-behaved Lotte is carried on the back of her slightly hunched nanny, who is well-dressed in a vest with a ruffled appliqué, ribbed white dress shirt, and long skirt. Lotte is equally well-dressed in a striped dress with puffed sleeves, and fashionable striped socks are clearly visible above her shoes. The well-groomed child and nanny show the styles of comportment, grooming, and child rearing intended to appeal to a middle-class clientele.

The function of Sigismund's portrait was consciously to display what the client desired to show the outside world about class, social standing, and family. And, as Jews became more visible in this new profession, they may have felt the need to conceal their Jewishness in order to conform to what they perceived to be the "idea" of proper bourgeois society. This effacement was felt all the more acutely by Jews both as photographers *and* photographed subjects—like Jacobi and her father—during this period of acculturation. In many ways, this photograph represents one stage in the dynamic of visibility/invisibility that recent scholarship in Jewish cultural history has shown to form a crucial source of social power for Central European

Jews living among populations that never completely accepted them. These scholars note how Jews' supposed desire for an unrequited acceptance from non-Jews actually ebbed and flowed according to circumstance and led to a wide range of active and passive strategies to both signal and cover their Jewishness, depending on their audiences. In other words, Jews' knowledge of these social codes was a crucial strategy of coexistence. It allowed them to flirt with the possibility of appearing Jewish or not Jewish depending on the situation. But how can historians invoke such silences, absences, and gaps as evidence of experience? How can scholars come to terms with qualities of modern Jewish culture that, as Michael Steinberg suggests, are material and palpable, but still "reside below the threshold of articulation" (Steinberg 2007, 18)? I argue that Jewish cultural studies, with its emphasis on the constructed nature of what subjects considered to be Jewish and non-Jewish, can illuminate how Jews and others engaged, reinforced, or subverted the constructed categories of gender and Jewish difference in their lives and works, even when their efforts to do so were not explicitly distinguishable from the efforts of non-Jews.

Jews and Photography in Weimar Germany

Jews in Weimar Germany, for example, as Kerry Wallach has observed, not only had the ability to pass as not Jewish but their reasons for doing so depended on their gender and the specific time, place, and audience. She reminds us that those items created by Jews and that pictured Jews in this period in Germany must always be considered according to the different social considerations Jews faced that influenced their creation. Body shape, facial features, dark hair and eye color, clothing, and other adornments supplied codes of Jewish visibility, an "embodied racialized Jewish coding" that was often a cause of anxiety, particularly for Jewish women. As Wallach notes, Jews relished flirting with stereotypes in order to pass or not pass, suggesting that doing so was a powerful strategy for maintaining a measure of control in public environments (Wallach 2017, 13).

Wallach further argues that in Weimar Germany, new modes of self-identification and intensified antisemitism spread more quickly to broader audiences via advances in technology for mass media. It is in this context that she explores the dialectic of visibility/invisibility as a reflection of Jews' seemingly contradictory impulses to be both visibly Jewish in some cases and invisible in others through literature, newspaper articles, advertisements, performances, contests, and films. For Jews, the idea that you could appear as Jewish or non-Jewish at any given moment, or more Jewish or less Jewish, was widespread. Choosing to remain hidden or to be seen were not mutually exclusive—they were actively chosen by Jews in Weimar Germany to pass for non-Jewish in some contexts and yet still be perceivably Jewish in others. It was less a question of completely passing as non-Jews or overtly displaying oneself as a Jew at all times, but rather a state of ambiguity that could subtly play both sides of this coin—"to be recognizably Jewish without standing out from the crowd" (Wallach 2017, 2–3).

Applying this approach to photography is helpful for understanding the anxieties about appearance that concerned so many Jews in the modern era. Long before the mass popularization of photography in the nineteenth century, European Jews had for centuries been stereotyped and represented in drawings, paintings, and elsewhere as uncivilized, unclean, and ill-behaved. Even after emancipation in Europe, Jews acculturating to the values of the mainstream middle class was not enough for full acceptance. Regardless of their political circumstances or their class, many Jews in interwar Central Europe felt pressured to downplay or even eliminate anything that marked them visually or culturally as Jews. Sander L. Gilman was among the first to note that the general assumption that Jews looked different was also accompanied by a general fear that this difference was elusive—and, therefore, dangerous—since it allowed Jews to "pass" as Germans. Ironically, those Jews who were considered most assimilated were also the ones most concerned about appearing different (Gilman 1996, 70).

By the nineteenth century, stereotypes of deformed Jewish bodies—including bowed legs, fat, hooked noses, and misshapen feet—crystallized in the service of nationalism and eugenics (Gilman 1991). Illustrations and essays increasingly referenced Jews' bodies as deformed, ugly, and thus reflections of a damaged spirit. Such depictions heightened Jews' anxiety about their appearance and behavior and stoked fears that they could never fully assimilate. When Jews attempted to resist these negative associations, antisemites preyed upon their efforts. These tensions are clearly outlined in Oskar Panizza's essay "Der operierte Jud" (1893), a satirical story about a Jew who, at the behest of a non-Jewish "friend," attempts to improve his speech, color and straighten his dark, curly hair, and straighten his bowed legs through painful surgeries. The efforts fail, suggesting that Panizza's essay critiques both Jewish and non-Jewish efforts to "perfect" the Jews' body into an unattainable ideal (Zipes 1991). Thus, Lotte Jacobi's efforts to portray her father not only as any bourgeois German gentleman, but as an exemplary one without any traces of Jewishness whatsoever, reveal an engagement with social codes and a reinforcement of ideals of both gender and Jewish difference.

A Room of Their Own

It is worth considering how the space of the photography studio resembled another close space of social interaction with historical implications for Jewish women, regardless of their level of Jewish self-identification: the salon. Informal social gatherings of Jews and non-Jews, often hosted in the homes of upper-class Jewish women, played a significant role in the development of European literature, art, and politics from the late eighteenth century on. Women were responsible for choosing appropriate guests, constructing programs, and ensuring that discussions, musical and theater performances, and literary readings flowed cohesively. Though they left few permanent traces of their work, they did much more than merely provide backdrops for others' creative endeavors. By the nineteenth and twentieth centuries, salons fostered the introduction of art movements like modernism, the Secession, and the avant-garde, and enabled women to become engaged with political movements, social reform, and organized dissent. According to Emily Bilski and Emily Braun, women who organized salons used them to their own advantage by "speaking and writing, creating erudite identities, holding their own." By fostering salons, otherwise socially disadvantaged women barred from professional spheres could actively engage in cultural exchange (Bilski and Braun 2005, 5–7). At a time when shifting gender norms allowed women more access to public and semipublic spaces such as cafés, restaurants, and dance halls, photography studios mirrored the active participation required of salon hosts and also offered Jewish women new possibilities for self-identification (Wobick-Segev 2018, 23–32).

As sites of creativity, photography studios went a step further: they were not only sites of discussion, engagement, and participation, but also allowed Jewish women to make documented interventions into cultural discourses, producing photographs as evidence of the important social relationships and cultural exchanges that took place there (Berkowitz 2017; Lässig and Rürup 2017; Sachsse 2000). According to Jacobi's daughter in law, her studio provided the opportunity not only to photograph clients, but also to interact with them as writers, artists, musicians, and scientists (Beatrice Trum Hunter, telephone interview with author, June 17, 2004).

However, women were not only disadvantaged due to assumed gender roles. The widespread belief that women photographers had a more intuitive ability to put their sitters at ease, to decorate their studios, and to use a less mechanical approach undoubtedly contributed to the support they received (Rosenblum 1994, 74; Wexler 2000). And, although restrictions on women's career opportunities remained strong in many areas in the early twentieth century, photography—with its relatively low start-up costs and its status as a profession without a long tradition—was an open and attractive career option in both Vienna and Berlin.

How very different, then, is Lotte Jacobi's self-portrait from the portrait of her father. Jacobi appears slightly out of focus, a blurriness that at once calls attention to her profession and the actual moment being photographed. She depicts herself holding the end of the device connected to the camera with which she is taking her picture, thus dispelling any illusion that this could be a private moment captured at home. Instead, viewers encounter a

Figure 2.2. Self-portrait of Lotte Jacobi, 1920. Jacobi's self-portrait actively confronts viewers by challenging gender norms and disrupting stereotypical portrayals of Jewish women. *Source:* © 2022 the University of New Hampshire. Used with permission.

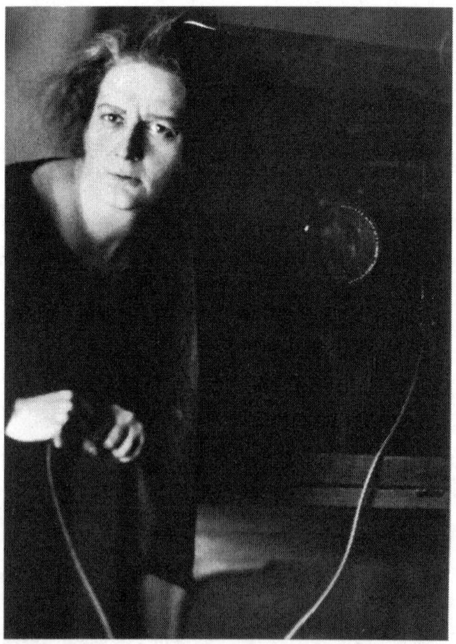

photographer at work—in this case, on herself—a self-conscious and serious act that still highlights that a portrait really only captures a moment in time. Only her hands and her head are recognizable; she is dressed in a formless black dress that is not visible to the eye; her hair is disheveled, grey, and hastily brushed back from her face. Her eyes peer intently and seriously off to the side, as if into a mirror.

As gender studies scholars have long argued, reading texts and images with the symbolic construction of gender norms in mind can help us understand how institutions and texts used the politics of sexuality in addressing female audiences, particularly in the decades before World War II, when women were starting to challenge these boundaries (Petro 1989). That Jacobi bends the boundaries of gender is obvious. She appears as a non-gender-specific, Expressionist figure, whose camera plays as important a role in the photograph as herself. As opposed to her portrait of her father, nothing of the careful styling and self-conscious attention to detail is visible. Instead of a stolen look at a distinguished bourgeois gentleman in a private moment at home, Jacobi's self-portrait actively confronts and challenges the viewer by exposing everything in its portrayal of her face, her gender, and her profession. It seeks to disrupt what was expected in her father's portrait photograph. Just as her father's image conformed to ideals of masculinity and *Bildung* and, therefore, engaged Jewish difference, so does Jacobi's engage Jewish difference by rejecting that very paradigm at a time when Jews—and especially Jewish women—were expected to maintain it.

Like Jewish men, Jewish women were also at times depicted as deformed and ugly, but they also had to contend with yet another visual stereotype: the *belle juive*. Unlike the older stereotype of the ugly Jew, the idea of the darkly beautiful, seductive Jewish woman emerged through nineteenth-century drama and literature, largely out of the imagination of men (Krobb 1993). In Central Europe, some Jewish women took advantage of their newly emancipated status by utilizing this eroticized image to evoke the *femme fatale*, flirting with its power (Silverman 2012b). Yet, even as Jewish women could deploy this stereotype for empowerment, it also pressured them to conform to men's ideals of women as objects of sexual desire. Jacobi's portrait rejects any associations with such ideals by refusing to articulate the contours of her body or to address the viewer directly with a welcoming smile or gaze.

However, the large, cumbersome camera shown in this self-portrait reveals not only her wish to have it in the frame for its dramatic effect, with the long cable and black cloth, but underscores her need to forefront the very act of her own taking of the picture, of the seriousness of being the one to hold the release and of performing the work of a photographer. Jacobi decided to train to become a photographer in 1925, after she had worked in her father's studio for four years. She enrolled at the *Fachschule* in Munich until she was compelled to return to Berlin, where she and Ruth took over her ailing father's studio in 1927 (Beckers and Moortgat 2012, 20, 90). In her next self-portrait, from 1937, when she had already arrived in New York after fleeing Nazi Germany, two years after the death of her father and the "Aryanization" of her studio in Berlin, one sees both continuities and differences with the 1929 self-portrait that engage with the earlier portrait of her father—and, therefore, with both gender and Jewish difference. After the death of Sigismund in 1935, the family emigrated to New York via England and Canada (Pfanner and Samson 2010, 111).

By 1937, she had already opened her first solo studio in New York at 24 Central Park South. But this portrait appears to have been taken in a bedroom, in front of a mirror reflecting an open closet crammed with clothes.

This pose illuminates even further how far she has come from the Jewish family from Posen that sought to acculturate into bourgeois German norms. It is no longer pushing back on gender boundaries—it is

Figure 2.3. Self-portrait of Lotte Jacobi, 1937. In this self-portrait, a year after she opened her photography studio in New York, Jacobi holds a cigarette in a nod to her father's pipe, but with a wink to its role as a signifier of the New Woman. *Source:* © 2022 the University of New Hampshire. Used with permission.

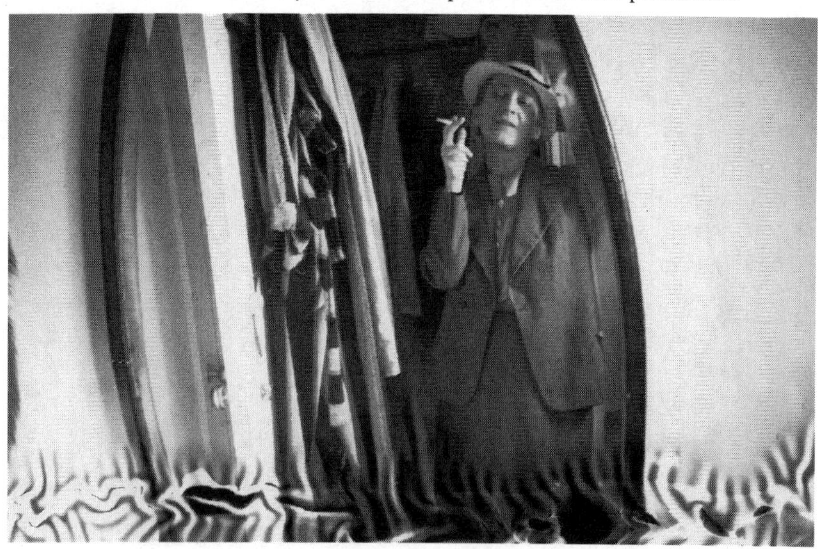

fully reversing them, as she is dressed in a suit as was her father, and her androgyny has now moved toward a portrayal of confrontational masculinity. In this portrait, the figure of Jacobi herself is still marginalized—and not only smaller, but she "looks back" twice at the viewer through the framed mirror that detaches her image from the outside world. This time, one sees the background—not a location staged for a portrait, but the emergence of Jacobi from a closet of clothes, exposing the "behind the scenes" efforts that formed part of fashioning one's image as both a woman and a Jew, as well as Jacobi's efforts to separate herself from them.

Here and in other ways, Jacobi explicitly plays with constructed gender norms by representing how women both reflect and resist the societal expectations that shape their experiences. She wears women's clothing but appears manly. In one hand she holds a cigarette in a nod to her father's pipe, but with a wink to its role as a signifier of the New Woman. But let us not forget its connotations as a phallic symbol; in addition, smoking at this time had connotations as a real "danger" for women, as it had long been associated in art and image with drink, drinking establishments, and sex. Since the late nineteenth century, a number of women photographers had begun to use smoking to signal independence and strength—a way to defy social conventions (Gilman and Xun 2004).

But no less apparent in this photograph, too, is not only how it subverts gender boundaries, but also how it plays with Jewish difference by subverting expectations for how Jewish women were supposed to look. Starting in the 1920s, claims that the New Woman in Central Europe was a danger to society linked her to Jewishness via her sexuality, consumerism, and financial greed (Grossmann 1983, 167). Jewish women in particular subtly hid their Jewishness just below the surface rather than eliminating it entirely. Some remained discernibly Jewish to other Jews, even if their outer appearance and modes of self-presentation resembled those of non-Jewish women (Wallach 2017). Weimar-era periodicals often feature independent New Women coded as just "Jewish enough" to evoke the desired effect on potential consumers. Cover art and advertisements showed figures with dark or curly hair, for example, which was enough to generate consumer desire. Such images, ironically predicated on negatively casting Jewish women as the "ultimate" consumers, would either please Jewish women who saw themselves in them, or attract non-Jewish women who would make consumer choices on the basis of the Jewish woman's mark of approval, even if they felt negatively about Jews in other situations. As Buerkle notes, advertising in Central Europe between the wars initially evoked Jewish women as ideal consumers, but then gradually effaced them as the image of the "Aryan" woman became the ideal and Jews were forced out of the fashion industry (Buerkle 2006, 631).

In Jacobi's portrait of her father, his pipe indicates a captured moment of bourgeois gentility, conforming visibly to gender roles and invisibly to Jewish difference via the erasure of markers of Jewishness and their replacement with those of class. In this self-portrait from 1937, Jacobi's juxtaposition of the camera with her cigarette foregrounded almost defiantly bends the visible markers of gender. However, she retains the invisibility of Jewishness by marking herself as not conforming to any acculturated or assimilation clothes vision of what a Jewish woman in America should be. This portrait shows how far she had come in making this family business her own—as a photographer, a woman, and self-assured Jew, unencumbered by bourgeois social and gender norms. Although they do not contain explicit "evidence" of Jewishness, the photographs here reveal the complexities of Jewish women's self-fashioning in interwar Vienna, illustrating how the symbolic construction of Jewish difference often *implicitly* affected both depictions of women and the terms of address to female audiences, even in the absence of clearly identifiable representations of Jewish (or non-Jewish) elements.

Passing and Photography

The ability to pass or not pass, to cover one's Jewishness or to allow oneself to be outed as a Jew, were powerful tools Jews used to navigate their environments, and as such are often incorporated into photographs and other cultural products. By illuminating and contextualizing these acts, we can show the existence of the invisible contours of Jewishness that proved to be central to the shaping of culture in modern Central Europe. As recent scholarship in Jewish studies has highlighted, Jews' experiences were often shaped by the fact that they lived amid majority cultures that would never fully accept them, no matter how assimilated, patriotic, or wealthy they were, or how non-Jewish they looked or behaved (Silverman 2018). Their strategies for coping depended on time, place, and audience, requiring Jews to maintain a constant vigilance about where they were and who was watching them. But this didn't keep them from participating deeply, significantly, and often playfully in the creation of modern European culture. By focusing on how Jews constructed their own narratives of the past in order to make meaning in the present and to point toward the future, these cultural histories help us see what was previously unseen. Recognizing how Jewish women photographers like Jacobi engaged, reinforced, or subverted the constructed categories of gender and Jewish difference in their lives and works helps us better understand how Jews negotiated society's expectations—and better appreciate the culture they created.

Works Cited

Beckers, Marion, and Elisabeth Moortgat. 2012. *Lotte Jacobi: Photographien*. Wienand.

Berkowitz, Michael. 2017. "Photography as a Jewish Space." In *Space and Spatiality in Modern Jewish History*, edited by Simone Lässig and Miriam Rürup. Berghahn.

Berman, Lila Corwin. 2018. "Jewish History beyond the Jewish People." *AJS Review* 42 (2): 269–92.

Bilski, Emily D., and Emily Braun. 2005. *Jewish Women and Their Salons: The Power of Conversation*. Jewish Museum.

Buerkle, Darcy. 2006. "Gendered Spectatorship, Jewish Women, and Psychological Advertising in Weimar Germany." *Women's History Review* 15 (4): 625–36.

Freund, Gisèle. 1980. *Photography and Society*. Gordon Fraser.

Gilman, Sander L. 1991. *Inscribing the Other*. University of Nebraska Press.

———. 1996. "The Jew's Body: Thoughts on Jewish Physical Difference." In *Too Jewish? Challenging Traditional Identities*, edited by Norman L. Kleeblatt. Rutgers University Press.

Gilman, Sander L., and Zhou Xun, eds. 2004. *Smoke: A Global History of Smoking*. Reaktion.

Gluck, Mary. 2016. *The Invisible Jewish Budapest: Metropolitan Culture at the Fin de Siècle*. University of Wisconsin Press.

Gough, Maria. 2020. "Portrait under Construction: Lotte Jacobi in Soviet Russie and Central Asia." *October*, no. 173, 65–117.

Grossmann, Atina. 1983. "The New Woman and the Rationalization of Sexuality in Weimar Germany." In *Powers of Desire: The Politics of Sexuality*, edited by Ann Barr Snitow, Christine Stansell, and Sharon Thompson. Monthly Review Press.

Krobb, Florian. 1993. *Die schöne Jüdin: Jüdische Frauengestalten in der deutschsprachigen Erzählliteratur vom 17. Jahrhundert bis zum Ersten Weltkrieg*. Niemeyer.

Lässig, Simone. 2004. *Jüdische Wege ins Bürgertum*. Vandenhoeck & Ruprecht.

Lässig, Simone, and Miriam Rürup, eds. 2017. *Space and Spatiality in Modern Jewish History*. Berghahn.

Petro, Patrice. 1989. *Joyless Streets: Women and Melodramatic Representation in Weimar Germany*. Princeton University Press.

Pfanner, Helmut, and Gary Samson. 2010. "Lotte Jacobi: German Photographer and Portraitist in Exile." *Germanic Review* 62 (3): 109–17.

Pomerance, Aubrey. 2008. *Ruth Jacobi: Fotografien*. Nicolai.

Rosenblum, Naomi. 1994. *A History of Women Photographers*. Abbeville Press.

Sachsse, Rolf. 2000. "'Dieses Atelier ist sofort zu vermieten': Von der 'Entjudung' eines Berufsstands." In *"Arisierung" im Nationalsozialismus: Volksgemeinschaft, Raub, und Gedächtnis*, edited by Irmtrud Wojak and Peter Hayes. Campus.

Shapira, Elana. 2016. *Style and Seduction: Jewish Patrons, Architecture, and Design in Fin de Siècle Vienna*. Brandeis University Press.

Sieg, Ulrich. 2020. "The Importance of Bildung: The Jewish Middle Classes at the Eve of World War I." *Aschkenas* 30 (2): 303–12.

Silverman, Lisa. 2004. "Family Business." *Jewish Quarterly* 51 (3): 35–40.

———. 2009. "Reconsidering the Margins: Jewishness as an Analytical Framework," *Journal of Modern Jewish Studies* 8 (1): 103–20.

———. 2011. "Beyond Antisemitism: A Critical Approach to German Jewish Cultural History." In *Nexus: Essays in German Jewish Studies*, edited by William Collins Donahue and Martha B. Helfer. Boydell & Brewer.

———. 2012a. "A Room of Her Own: The Photographer's Salon." In *Vienna's Shooting Girls: Jüdische Fotografinnen aus Wien*, edited by Iris Meder and Andrea Winklbauer. Metroverlag.

———. 2012b. *Becoming Austrians: Jews and Culture between the World Wars*. Oxford University Press.

———. 2018. "Revealing Jews: Culture and Visibility in Modern Central Europe." *Shofar: An Interdisciplinary Journal of Jewish Studies* 36 (1): 134–60.

Steinberg, Michael P. 2007. *Judaism Musical and Unmusical*. University of Chicago Press.

Trum Hunter, Beatrice. 2000. "Some Vignettes of Lotte Jacobi." Unpublished manuscript. Lotte Jacobi Papers, 1898–2000, MC-58, Box 44 f.9. Milne Special Collections and Archives, University of New Hampshire Library, Durham, NH.

Wallach, Kerry. 2017. *Passing Illusions: Jewish Visibility in Weimar Germany*. University of Michigan Press.

Wexler, Laura. 2000. *Tender Violence: Domestic Visions in an Age of U.S. Imperialism*. University of North Carolina Press.

White, Hayden. 1987. *The Content of the Form*. Johns Hopkins University Press.

Wobick-Segev, Sarah. 2018. *Homes away from Home: Jewish Belonging in Twentieth-Century Paris, Berlin, and St. Petersburg*. Stanford University Press.

Zipes, Jack. 1991. *The Operated Jew: Two Tales of Anti-Semitism*. Routledge.

Chapter 3

Photographs, Jews, and Nazis

The Politics of a Visual Archive, Historically and Today*

Maiken Umbach and Jonathan Stafford

Introduction: The Strange Presence of Photography

In a photo, the past becomes present. Historical photos transport the past into the present of the viewer with a powerful sense of immediacy. They are popular tools for historical engagement and education. Photos of the Holocaust, which are widely used in teaching and commemoration, transform us all into witnesses of this darkest history. But most of the Holocaust photos that appear in textbooks, museums, and television documentaries come from a relatively small stock of "iconic" images (Mills and Umbach 2024, 50; Holtschneider 2011). There are exceptions: some museums, such as Yad Vashem and the United States Holocaust Memorial Museum (USHMM), also show a variety of private photos of Jewish life before the Nazis (Liss

---

*We wish to thank the Arts and Humanities Research Council (AHRC) for funding the research underpinning this chapter as part of the project grant "Photography as Political Practice in National Socialism" (principal investigator: Maiken Umbach). Special thanks also go to the members of the Salzmann family, Eva Vichules (née Salzmann), Judith Bryant, and Craig Becker, who were kind enough to contact us and provide valuable information about the after-lives of their family photos, which we used as sources in our research.

1998; Crownshaw 2007; Levitt 2009). But the Holocaust itself is usually depicted through photos taken by others. Many were taken by professionals from the Nazi *Propagandakompanien* (PK) (Uziel 2008; Sachsse 2003; Krol 2008; Arani 2010), or by implicated "hobbyist" photographers (e.g., Wehrmacht soldiers engaging in ghetto tourism). The second genre comprises photos taken by Allied troops, and occasionally accompanying journalists or humanitarian organizations, immediately after the liberation of Nazi camps. Both types show Jewish people and other persecuted groups enduring immense suffering and death. By comparison, photos of the Holocaust taken by Jewish victims, albeit fewer in number, are hardly ever displayed.

Some scholars argue that, irrespective of who took them and why, the shock effect of graphic Holocaust images promotes empathy and solidarity (Hébert 2020; Azoulay 2008; Linfield 2010). Others have raised ethical concerns about the photographers' intentions, the dignity of those photographed, the voyeurism of the modern viewer, and the longevity of the photos' ethical impact (Sontag 1990; Barthes 1981; Struk 2004; Crane 2008). Susie Linfield provides a useful if polemical critique of such views (Linfield 2010, 3–32; Zylinska 2017). These concerns are particularly acute when we consider the perpetrator bias in the PK photos, designed to denigrate Holocaust victims (Raskin 2004). As we shall argue, there is evidence to suggest that such photos are ill suited to creating empathy today. But more benign intent does not always translate into "better" photos. Liberator photos, too, paid scant regard to the agency or dignity of victims. And although the Allies believed that exposing the German population to such images was part of reeducation, it is far from clear that these photos have an automatic ethical effect today. In this chapter, we shall describe our research findings on the impact of such photos on contemporary audiences.

Before we do so, we need to tackle two methodological challenges. The first relates to the evidentiary or lexical nature of photography. Much of the debate about Holocaust photos is predicated on the photos' status as documents and evidence of the "real." This elides differences of perspective, aesthetics, or style, and in the subsequent social uses of photos from the vast archive that depicts Jewish experiences in this period. Curatorial practices in Holocaust museums and memorial sites often reproduce this homogenizing tendency, ignoring the "different perspectives the photographers took towards their subjects, as well as the various purposes for taking photos [and for] the co-operation (or lack thereof) of the subjects" (Holtschneider 2012, 102). This flattens the distinction between, for example, a photo taken by a PK photographer, depicting the downtrodden victims of Nazi violence during the clearing of a ghetto, and the subtle and poetic photos of daily life in ghettos made covertly, and at great personal risk, by Jewish photographers such as Mendel Grossman or Henryk Ross. The question then is not just *what* objective events or sites photos show, but *how* they do so, what perspective they adopt, what visual style and metaphors they deploy, and, of course, how they were subsequently viewed. We shall explore such distinctions in this chapter.

The second challenge relates to the question of how we might define a "Jewish photo." Scholars working with written sources have long pointed out that in studying the Holocaust, it is imperative that we base our analysis not just on official records created by the perpetrators but give due weight to the voices of those who were persecuted and murdered by the regime (Friedländer 1997, 2007; Betts and Wiese 2010). This is relatively straightforward if the alternative archive in question consists of Jewish ego-documents or subsequent survivor testimony. But if photos both reflect and create a particular point of view, then the same principle should apply here. A visual history that relies predominantly on Nazi photography remains irredeemably compromised unless we make efforts to consider the role of Jewish photography as a source in its own right. But the notion of authorship in a photo is complicated. All photos, even private photos, are produced by multiple actors. The photographer's identity and his or her intentions certainly play a role; but so does the agency of those acting in front of the camera, the aesthetic conventions that shape how a scene is framed, and the constraints of a particular photographic situation. Moreover, the meaning of a photo is not fixed in the moment of its production: it is also, and crucially, constituted in the photo's history of consumption (Edwards 1992, 2012). And this social life, too, involves multiple actors. Who decides which photos are preserved and which are discarded may not be the photographer; the same applies to how and where photos are shared and enter public or personal archives; how they are captioned, or combined with other materials, either in print or in personal albums and scrapbooks. This "social" production of photographic meaning typically involves many people and can stretch over long periods of time—in the case of Holocaust images, often over multiple generations (Hirsch 1997, 2012). In analyzing Jewish photos, we need to understand "agency" as distributed between the photographer, the photographed, the assumed and actual viewers at the time, and the contemporary viewer, including ourselves.

The patchiness of the archival records should not absolve us from grappling with these questions. In a research project called "Photography as Political Practice in National Socialism," we explored the private photographic production of ordinary Germans implicated in the regime and the private photography of Jewish people persecuted by this regime (Umbach, n.d., for details of this project).

Our findings draw attention to the role of photography in asserting and defending contested identities and senses of belonging. In many instances, aesthetic conventions to depict a German *Heimat*, and place oneself within it, were not necessarily an expression of alignment with Nazi ideology: it could also, on the part of Jewish families, be a move to reassert and defend their sense of belonging to a culture from which racial legislation was attempting to exclude them. "Jewish photos," we suggest, are photos that tell stories of Jewish people when they are taken, preserved, and shared. While perpetrator photos define the moment of victimization as the singular signifier of identity, Jewish photos told stories: each moment depicted formed part of a story, drew on earlier stories, and was informed by an expectation of a future. What makes a photo "Jewish" is thus not just about the ethnic identity of a photographer, but about the discursive, social quality of photos, the ways in which they form part of a visual conversation over a *longue durée*.

This also relates back to our first challenge: the evidentiary status of photography. Irrespective of who held the camera, we have to be careful not to assume that a photo's "Jewishness" derives from the "realism" with which it depicts the suffering and trauma of the Holocaust (Batchen 2009). Such an assumption would superimpose a thematic focus on the study of Jewish photography from the Nazi years that has deeply problematic, political consequences. This is not to relativize the immense suffering experienced by European Jews between 1933 and 1945. But to view photos from this period as "Jewish" only if and when they depict and display evidence of this suffering is to dismisses as irrelevant, or at least to relegate to secondary importance, photos that focus instead on Jewish agency, individuality, resilience, resistance, and even irony (Ashkenazi 2022). Such photos are rarely used as historical evidence. But they are vital historical sources: they tell stories about Jewish histories and identities that remain hidden in the images that dominate museum displays and textbooks today. They were products of a shared pictorial culture, which encompassed multiple cultural identities and traditions: Jewish and German, Jewish and Polish, Jewish and middle class, and so forth. The very fact that photography was often used to assert one's place within a broader social, cultural, or national story draws attention to these photos' political role: as objects that intervened in, and challenged, the unitary "Jewish identity" conjured up by the Nazi race laws and by the racist photographic production that visualized only Manichean distinctions between "Jewish" and "non-Jewish."

To tackle these questions, this chapter will proceed in three sections. Section 1 will focus on an example of the performance of hybrid Jewish identities. It explores the role of photography in reimagining and reasserting the fundamental entanglements of German and Jewish identities. Section 2 will turn to Jewish photography in ghettos. These photos, taken secretly and in violation of official bans, tell stories during a time when normal agency in shaping one's own life was greatly reduced. The stark contrast between the perpetrator photographs and the narrative and often lyrical quality of Jewish photos created in such settings throws into even sharper relief the fact that the discursive function, rather than its formal content, is what makes some photos "Jewish." At the same time, we have to acknowledge that there is a grey area between these two perspectives; a problem that, as we shall see, has been raised about the official photos created by and for the Jewish ghetto administration. Section 3 will then explore ways of looking at these images today. If histories of reception shape photographic meaning, it is not enough simply to display "Jewish photos" alongside perpetrator images. In the absence of a shared experience between those who created these photos and those who view them today, historians need to develop ways in which the "before" and "after" dimensions of such images can be brought to light: if not literally and completely, then metaphorically and suggestively. This is what we tried to achieve when we created our exhibition "The Eye as Witness: Recording the Holocaust." In section 3, we offer some insights about modern viewing behaviors derived from visitor observations in that exhibition. On this basis, we offer some general conclusions about the politics of Jewish photos in the context of the histories of Nazism and the Holocaust, then as today.

Private Jewish Photos

Jewish photos from the 1930s and 1940s survived in surprisingly large numbers. Some are still in private hands; others have been donated to archives and museums. Some show individuals about whom we know little; others are part of vast archives that span several decades. One such archive is that of the Salzmann family. We have written about this archive elsewhere (Umbach and Sulzener 2018). Therefore, we mainly confine ourselves here to some considerations of what makes such photos Jewish. Like many German Jewish families, the Salzmanns were avid photographers. While clearly the work of amateurs, the photos were taken with considerable aesthetic ambition: many play knowingly with optical devices, such as mirrors, and make dramatic use of light and shadow to create striking visual effects. This aesthetic ambition is matched by the social ambition of their content. Many photos seem to show a bourgeois lifestyle: extensive international travel, elegant attire, car ownership, and the conspicuous consumption of "high culture," especially art and architectures from classical antiquity and the European Middle Ages. By contrast, domestic scenes and quotidian moments are largely absent. The Salzmanns' actual home lives in a working-class district of Berlin were much more modest. The photos show moments in which a perfect life could be "tried out," performed, and transformed into photographic memories, not everyday realities. This was not atypical. Many Germans during this period used their cameras to create images of the life they wished to live rather than quotidian realities (Umbach and Harvey 2015). That does not mean such photos were inauthentic. They recorded aspirations, not realities. These aspirations were coproduced by many actors. Family members posed for the camera, performing the importance of familial relationships, and, albeit less often, friendship networks. They also posed with objects, especially distinctly "modern" objects such as a car. Or they showed people's sense of place: gazing at landscapes or at historical architectures of special significance. They showcased cultural competence; this was reinforced by the practice of arranging such photos in beautifully designed and captioned albums.

Private Jewish photos from the Nazi period have to be read in this context. Rather than documenting a history of persecution, they show, on the surface, the opposite: a life of leisure, enjoyment, and, most bafflingly, of significant ideological alignment with dominant cultural paradigms. The Salzmanns' 1937 holiday album is a case in point. Compared to earlier albums, it especially took an emphatically nationalistic turn—featuring sites, poses, and iconographies closely associated with the official visual culture of the day. Documenting a round trip through Germany, the album shows the Salzmanns appearing in a number of ideologically charged settings, such as the city of Nuremberg, the Olympic Stadium in Berlin, and gothic cathedrals.

Captions in the album are also telling. While just a year earlier, the family were using a loose cursive script, the 1937 captions are written in a pseudo-gothic font. They also adapted their personal appearance in the same way: the dress code becomes more rustic, even folkloristic.

As Leora Auslander notes, the same tendency could be observed in German-Jewish domestic tastes. Analyzing inventories of Jewish property

Figure 3.1. The Salzmann family on holiday, 1937. *Source:* Ruth Salzmann Becker Papers, courtesy Iowa Women's Archives, University of Iowa Libraries, Iowa City. Used with permission.

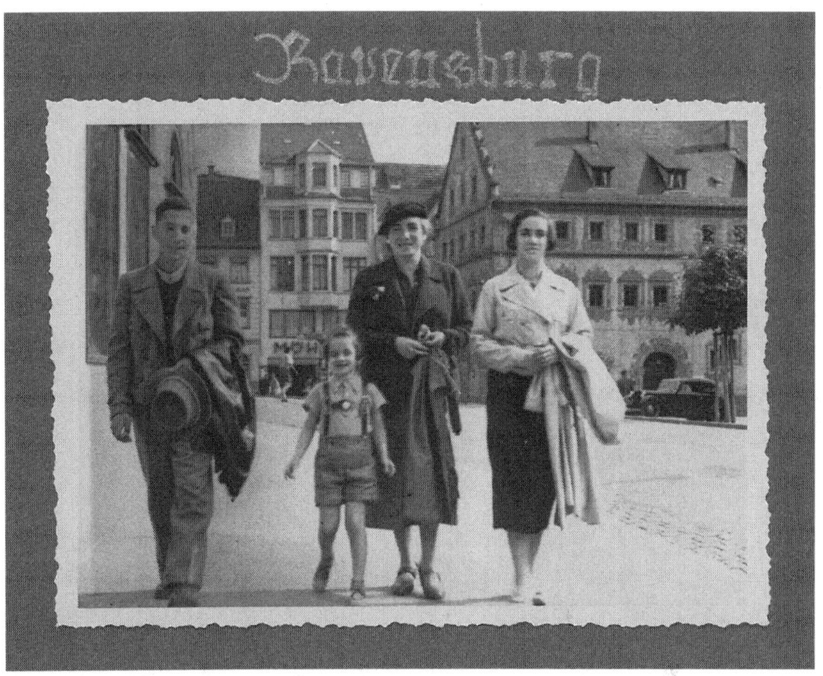

confiscated by the Nazi regime in Berlin, she finds that "a surprisingly large number" of Jews inhabited "homes decorated with Christian religious icons" (Auslander 2002, 314). But such photos do not just document immersion in German culture: they also perform it for a political purpose. "German" culture became the primary topic in the Salzmanns' photos precisely when the Nazi regime excluded Germany's Jewish citizens from this culture, recasting it as supposedly "Aryan." At this moment, the camera could be used to defend and reinforce a Jewish place within German culture. Thus understood, such photos are part of a countertactic, in a de Certeauian sense, to the racial strategies of the Nazi state (de Certeau 1984).

This perspective also explains why many Jewish families photographed their emigration not as a desperate flight, but as a new beginning and adventure—and also an eminently German undertaking. The Salzmanns created an album that documents their emigration: first Ruth packing her bags, then the family emptying and cleaning the old apartment, and loading their possessions onto a truck and into a container with the lines "Berlin–New York" emblazoned on the side (fig. 3.2), and, finally, a series of images on board the *Iberia* during the Atlantic crossing. Similar photos exist from other German-Jewish journeys. A famous collection survives at the USHMM, which shows the journey like one might photograph a cruise: full of excitement, an occasion to be staged, and celebrated, in front of and for the camera (fig. 3.3).

These photos may, on the surface, appear as inadequate representations of the trauma of persecution and flight (Spitzer 1998; Hirsch and Spitzer 2009). And yet, for the families who created them, such photos were celebrations of agency, and also a celebration of Germanness. Not only Jewish identity had long been diasporic: so was German identity. During the nineteenth century, German emigrants settled all over the world, above all, in the Americas (Manz 2014; Penny and Rinke 2015). The Salzmanns saw

Figure 3.2. The Salzmann family's emigration, 1939. *Source:* Ruth Salzmann Becker Papers, courtesy Iowa Women's Archives, University of Iowa Libraries, Iowa City. Used with permission.

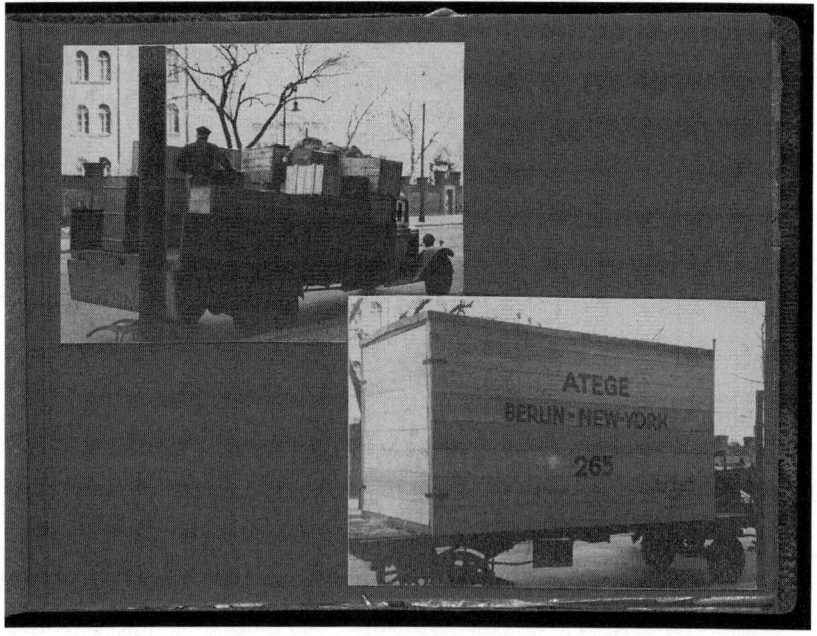

Figure 3.3. Members of the Dublon family pose on the deck of the MS *St. Louis*, 1939. *Source:* Courtesy Photo Archive, United States Holocaust Memorial Museum.

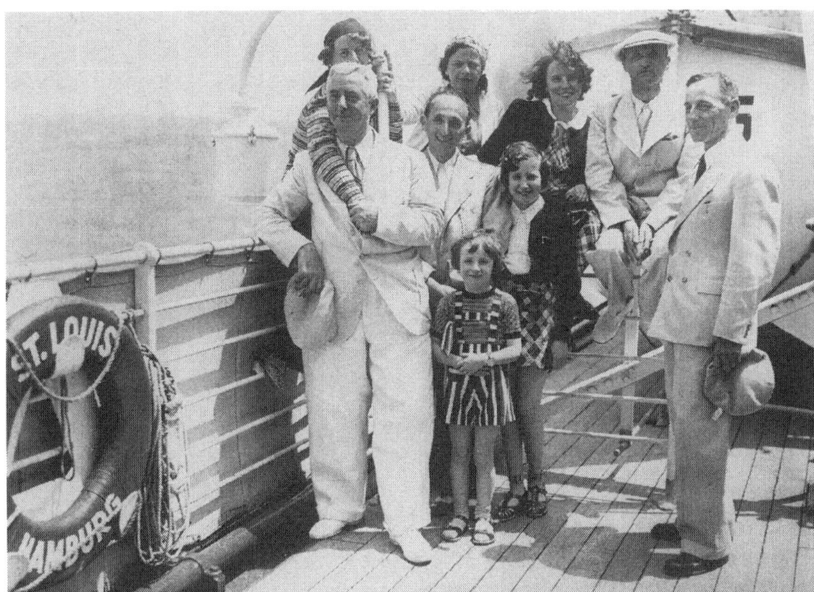

themselves as an eminently German family in that sense, too; they spoke of a "connecting thread, which reaches from East Prussia's Amber Coast across the world's oceans to all parts of the globe" (Umbach and Sulzener 2018, 77–92). This thread enabled many German-Jewish families to leave their homeland behind *without* abandoning their sense of national identity. Such photos are documents of resistance to an identity politics that defined the "national" in both geographically bounded and exclusionary racist terms.

Given this history, it is perhaps not surprising that Ruth Salzmann decided to donate these records to the historical archive of the University of Iowa, and not to a specialist Holocaust museum or testimony collection. As her daughter Judy Bryant later testified, the family did not see themselves first and foremost as Holocaust survivors (Judy Bryant, email to Maiken Umbach, November 26, 2020). These photos were an integral part of family life over many generations. The act of making a private photo archive public was driven by a desire to commemorate and celebrate a family history that was part of a wider German-American history. Because a lot of historical research on Jewish emigration up to 1939 has been shaped by readily available source collections in specialist Holocaust archives, this history has been narrated primarily as one of "victimhood." Private Jewish photos such as the ones discussed here offer us a different perspective onto this history: not one that negates victimhood, but certainly one that reclaims agency, and that does not accept the hegemonic identity politics of the perpetrators, who turned Jews into Others, and victims, as "fact." Only a more expansive definition of Jewish photos, that takes their private meanings into account, can convey a full picture of this experience.

Holocaust Photos:
Jewish Agency and the Viewer of the Future

The Nazi regime employed photography as a means of "Othering" the Jewish population. Photos taken by the official PK photographers, in ghettos, during deportations, and in camps, were designed to denigrate and dehumanize, to tear the "mask of civilization" off the Jewish face. They are important evidence. But relying exclusively on them in Holocaust commemoration today elides Jewish agency, and can inadvertently perpetuate stereotypes (Holtschneider 2012, 101). Hirsch, commenting on the "Warsaw Ghetto Boy" photo in the Stroop Report, sees this iconic image as "deeply implicated in Nazi photographic practices" (Hirsch 2012, 139). And Eva Fogelman suggested that the ubiquity of this image has contributed to the widespread perception of the passivity of European Jews in the face of their persecution (Fogelman 2007). In reproducing the Nazi subjugation—and subsequent murder—of Polish Jewry, the photo does not bear witness to the abundant narratives of Jewish struggle and resistance; it only shows the agency of the perpetrator. The same applies to "hobbyist" snapshots taken, for example, by Wehrmacht soldiers visiting ghettos off duty. The case of Heinrich (Heinz) Jöst, a sergeant who photographed in the Warsaw ghetto, is a case in point. Although the veracity of his account was later called into question, in 1982, Jöst claimed that he had wondered whether it was acceptable to photograph the few more affluent, well-dressed Jews in the ghetto (Schwarberg 2001, 41). By reducing the Jews to poverty and starvation, the Nazis had stripped them of their humanity, specifically of their right to choose whether they should be photographed, the agency to assert the right to photographic self-representation.

Nevertheless, occasionally, glimpses of Jewish agency are visible even in such photos. PK photographer Hugo Jaeger took images of young Jewish women in the Kutno ghetto in 1940, just before they were deported to extermination camps. When Jaeger sold them to Life Magazine in 1965, these images caused a public stir, because they defied simple categorization. But they have been all but ignored in Holocaust scholarship (Arani 2011, 30, 48). These photos are disconcerting because the young women pose and smile for the camera. They were shaped not just by the photographer's ideological brief, but also by the subject's agency. In posing this way, it appears that the young women being photographed embraced the opportunity to create a record of themselves irrespective of the photographer's intentions. Conventions were also at play. Jaeger's subjects would have remembered how to pose for a photograph in "civilian" life, to commemorate family occasions, celebration, or simply to capture the likeness of a person. It is well documented that people who have learnt to smile when a camera is pointed at them do so even on occasions that are anything but happy: the presence of the camera prompts them to recall, and momentarily restore, a "normal" photographic situation (West 2000). But there is also another dimension to this convention: one that, in this case, counteracted the explicit brief of the photographer. Jaeger had been trained in photojournalism: the conventions of that profession conditioned him to select as "good shots" those motifs that conformed to this aesthetic. The resulting photos certainly objectified the young women in it, but this process was more akin to the casting of a young model as an object of the male gaze and desire in a fashion shoot, than to a photographic practice with overtly racist intent. Jaeger's photos, then, were shaped by forces that lay, at least in part, beyond the photographer's control, and that involved *some* Jewish agency. But clearly, this is not enough to make such photos "Jewish," if by that definition we mean photos that primarily express Jewish agency and perspectives, rather than the perpetrator gaze.

Holocaust photos by Jewish photographers are rarer, but they do exist. A poignant example is the famous *Sonderkommando* photos from Auschwitz-Birkenau. As Didi-Huberman argued, they bear witness to the photographer's struggle to render atrocity visible: each subtle mark, each compositional element, even the sequence in which they were taken, can be read as performative gestures, traces of a Jewish agency set against the monolithic power of a seemingly unstoppable genocide (Didi-Huberman 2008). Such resistance took many forms: not all of them are about revealing the crimes of the perpetrators. Many Jewish photos from ghettos show the extent to which Jewish victims of Nazi oppression not only insisted on taking photos of themselves as they wished to be remembered—as autonomous individuals and in loving family scenes. The Jewish photographers who documented lives in ghettos—often at great risk—have been the subject of specialist studies (Klugman 1967; Sened and Szner 1970; Grossman and Smith 2000; Arani 2013). But they are rarely used in mainstream Holocaust galleries or in Holocaust educational materials.

The photography of Henryk Ross is a case in point. Ross and Mendel Grossman were employed by the Jewish Council's Department of Statistics in the Lodz ghetto to document productive labor. Both of them also produced thousands of unofficial images, secretly documenting scenes from daily life. Although Ross's photos were used as evidence in the Eichmann trial in 1961, where Ross also gave testimony, his photos met with little public interest in the postwar era (Struk 2004, 95); others claimed that Ross purposefully withheld most photos (Weber 2004; Bourla 2015). Only much more recently have some images featured in specialist exhibitions, such as *Das Ghetto in Lodz, 1940–1944*, Jewish Museum, Frankfurt am Main, 1990; *Memory Unearthed: The Lodz Ghetto Photographs of Henryk Ross*, touring exhibition (US), 2017; and *Flashes of Memory: Photography during the Holocaust*, Yad Vashem, 2018. Ross's photos rarely conform to preconceptions about the horrors of ghetto life. Some seem ethically ambiguous: they show Jewish children reenacting troubling scenes, or the relative privileges enjoyed by some ghetto occupants, including the Jewish ghetto police. Scholars have debated whether Ross's own complicity with the collaborationist ghetto administration lessens the photos' evidentiary value (Weber 2004; Bourla 2015). Shifting the focus to our concern with distributed photographic agency offers a different perspective. Ross's subjects pose for the camera: they want to be recorded and are determined not to grant the perpetrators a monopoly of documenting ghetto life. Ross's photos thus document Jewish agency, a determination to record, bear witness, and preserve traces of Jewish lives at the very moment when these were existentially threatened. The results were images of an aesthetic and lyrical quality that stand in sharp contrast to the better-known Nazi images. Our example here (fig. 3.4) depicts a Jewish occupant of the Lodz ghetto trudging through the snow, amid the ruins of a synagogue destroyed by the Nazis. The building is destroyed: but its remains, crowned by the Star of David tower majestically over the snow. The photo not only conveys melancholia in the face of loss. It is also an image of defiance: even in the face of annihilation, the spirit of Jewish civilization lived on. Traces of the spiritual life of Europe's Jews persist in the ruins—traces that a future generation can bear witness to. The man in the foreground walks on, his pose is not one of resignation, but determination.

As the Lodz ghetto was being liquidated in 1944, Ross buried his photos and negatives in the hope that they would survive, even as his own survival was less than certain. He would later write: "Just before the closure of the ghetto, I buried my negatives in the ground in order that there should be some record of our tragedy, namely the total elimination of the Jews from Lodz by the Nazi executioners. I was anticipating the total destruction of Polish Jewry. I wanted to leave a historical record of our martyrdom" (quoted in Weber 2004, 27). Ross survived the Holocaust and was able to dig up the box in January 1945. Although much of the material had sustained water damage while underground, around half of his images were rescued (Löw 2015). These photos should be seen as both documents—in depicting the everyday, heroic attempts at survival and maintaining humanity in the ghetto—and as expressions of Jewish agency in their defiant documentation. Burying thousands of negatives was an essential part of this photographic practice, just as much as the process of composing the shot, releasing the

Figure 3.4. Henryk Ross, remains of the synagogue in Wolborska Street, Lodz, 1940. Man walking in winter in the remains of the synagogue on Wolborska Street, destroyed by the Germans in 1939, 1940. Gelatin silver print, 12.7 × 18 cm. *Source:* Art Gallery of Ontario. Gift from Archive of Modern Conflict, 2007. 2007/2365. © Art Gallery of Ontario. Used with permission.

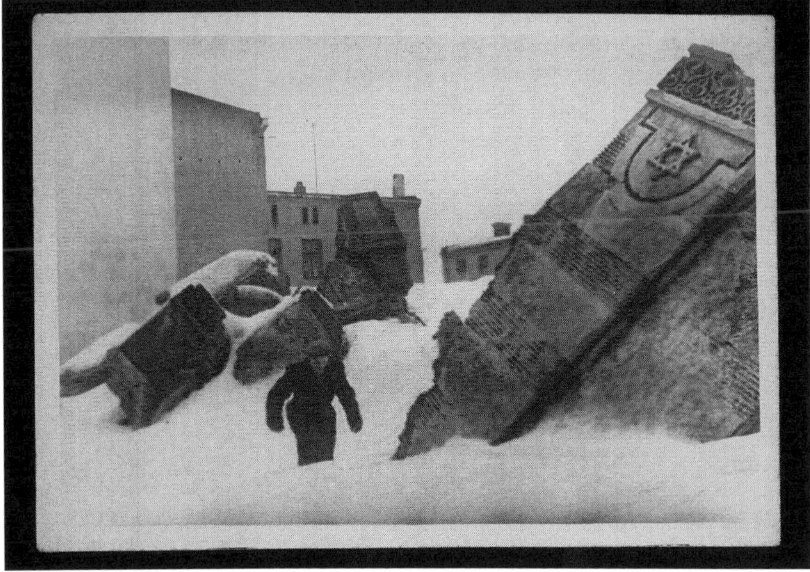

shutter, or developing the film. This, too, involved multiple agencies: Ross enlisted a group of trusted friends to assist in the burial. In bearing the marks of water damage, the surviving photos present an indexical trace, a visible record of the accretions of historical Jewish agency. The lack of attention paid to these photographs is thus troubling. If we understand bearing witness in a broader sense than merely providing evidence, as an active mode of resistance, as an assertion of agency, humanity, and identity, we need to be attentive to *whose* photos we use and *how* they are used, displayed, and encountered in modern commemorative settings.

Transforming the Gaze

We have suggested that "Jewish" photography is not just about the moment of a photo's creation, but also about the memory culture that evolves around images. But is "Jewish photography" still a meaningful term today, if most modern viewers of Holocaust photos are not able to read them as such? And are there ways for us to enable and encourage more knowing ways of seeing than those into which most modern viewers have been socialized? This chapter's final section explores such questions.

Scholars have assumed viewers respond to Holocaust photos emotionally: "There is no doubt that we approach photographs, first and foremost, through emotions" (Linfield 2010, 22). This entails a danger. "Pity," Linfield writes, "creates a top-down relation in which one person's power is predicated on another's weakness; this unequal relationship then presents itself in the maddening guise of generous virtue" (Linfield 2010, 128; Struk 2004, 213). In the tradition of Sontag, others have spoken about emotional overload leading to an affective numbness in response to Holocaust photos (Zelizer 1998, 141). Azoulay concludes that we should "shed terms such as 'empathy,' 'shame,' 'pity,' or 'compassion'" altogether when examining engagement with photographic representations of suffering (Azoulay 2008, 17). Such arguments assume that Holocaust photos, or even photos of suffering more generally, constitute a singular genre. We suggest that to change ways of seeing we need to be more attentive to the heterogeneity and specificity of individual photos, and especially to the question of what "Jewish photos" may convey to viewers today.

To this end, we need to consider an important intermediate stage between the photo's historical creation and its modern reception. This is the role of the imagined future viewer, to whom those who initially created photos of the Holocaust addressed themselves. In Jewish photos, these imagined future viewers range from future generations within a particular Jewish family or community, who use photos to remember loved ones, to a more general sympathetic audience equipped with the different political sensitivities of a post-Nazi future. The Salzmann photos, initially, were family mementoes: but the family also felt that, as political circumstances changed, they needed to be deposited in a public archive. Henryk Ross hoped that future viewers would excavate his buried treasures and view them with new eyes, freed from the constraints of Nazi ideology. For the Nazis, too, however, photos were a record for the future. Many so-called Nazi propaganda photos were not publicized at the time. Perpetrators created archives for "the historians of the future" (Raskin 2004). Confronting the modern-day viewer with the figure of the imagined future viewer of the past, we hypothesized, has the potential to dislodge overfamiliar and purely emotive ways of seeing.

To explore this challenge, a multidisciplinary team of academics from the University of Nottingham and curators from the UK's National Holocaust Centre and Museum cocreated the exhibition *The Eye as Witness: Recording the Holocaust*, which toured the UK from 2020 to 2022. Its aim was to bring Jewish photographic perspectives to the attention of a wider public, and to measure the results. "The Eye as Witness" combined an immersive Mixed Reality experience, display boards of photos accompanied by text and artefacts, photos on interactive digital screens, and an art installation. In the Mixed Reality, visitors step "into" a classical perpetrator image of the Holocaust from the Stroop series of the Warsaw Ghetto, to explore the space and the circumstances of the photo's production and observe the official photographer at work. Thus, sensitized to the issue of perpetrator perspective and bias, visitors then encounter Jewish photos. The aim was not to document a complete history of the Holocaust through Jewish photos: a small number of images were displayed alongside texts that explored why each photo was taken, who its intended viewers were, and how the photo was subsequently used. In this way, the exhibition sought to encourage reflection on the role of photographic perspective. In a digital installation, entitled "The Ethics of Seeing," we then invited the viewer to respond to photos on a touch screen, comparing Nazi images, Jewish images, and more contemporary images. This installation prompted visitors to reflect on issues raised by the exhibition; at the same time, it served as an evaluation tool.

The "Ethics of Seeing," placed near the end of the exhibition, comprised three consecutive screens with six images each, to which exhibition visitors respond through a series of on-screen activities. We presented these images without contextual information such as dates and location, to focus on their immediate visual impact. Results we share here are drawn from the exhibition's first venue, South Hampstead Synagogue in London, recorded in January 2020, and come from 102 individuals. The exhibition tour ended at the time of writing: a fuller comparative analysis of visitor responses in different venue responses will be published in due course. But preliminary findings suggest that responses collected in other venues were very similar.

"The Ethics of Seeing" begins with six classical images of the Holocaust, featuring victims in pitiful conditions, or already dead, taken by perpetrators and liberators. Visitors were asked to choose from a list of textual responses that best capture their reactions to each image, ranging from the emotive (e.g., pity, sadness) to more cerebral responses (e.g., perpetrator/liberator gaze). The results bear out our initial presuppositions: graphic images, especially images of naked bodies, generate less pity than is often assumed, and even less empathy. An American liberator image that depicts corpses at Buchenwald concentration camp (fig. 3.5) failed to evince pity *or* empathy in viewers, with only 3 percent of participants recording either of these responses (the lowest of the six images on this screen). Viewers were much

Figure 3.5. Patron responses, "The Ethics of Seeing," 2020. *Source:* Courtesy of the authors.

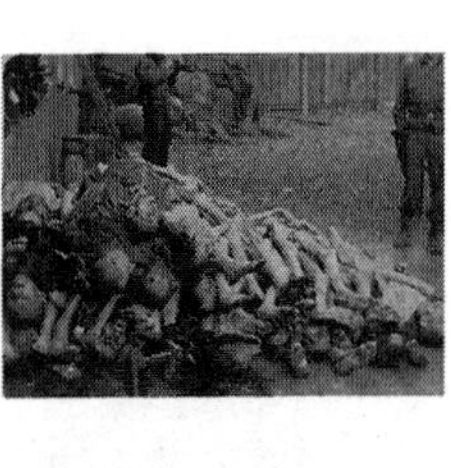

American soldiers view a pile of corpses found behind the crematorium in the newly liberated Buchenwald concentration camp. April 1945.

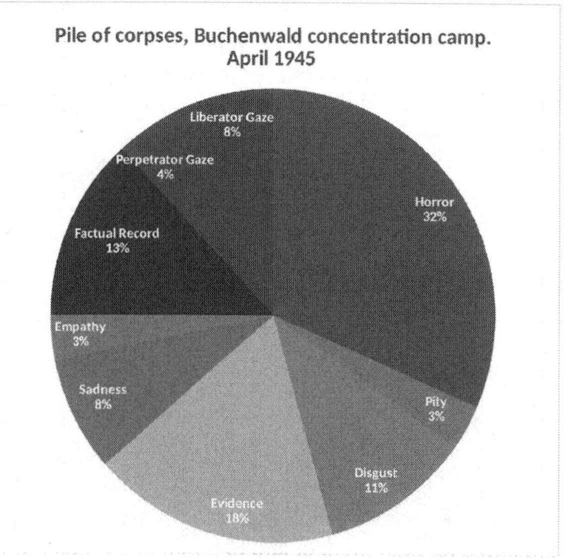

more likely to respond with horror (32 percent) or disgust (11 percent), or to view the image as a source of evidence (18 percent) or factual record (13 percent). For the remainder of the images on this screen, empathy was not a significantly common choice either, noted in only around 10 percent of responses. Although the results suggest that, intellectually, viewers were able to distinguish, to some extent, between perpetrator and liberator photos, there was no notable distinction between these categories in terms of emotional responses.

The second screen features a very different set of photos: with one exception, these were taken by Jewish photographers (two each from the Salzmann and Ross collections). All portray victims as individuals, without resorting to graphic depictions of suffering. We invited audiences to choose from a list of questions these images triggered in their minds, which focus on the kinds of contextual information we regard as important to provide when these photos are exhibited: the identity of the photographer and photographed; the historical narrative that underpins the picture, both at a macro and micro level, before and after; the agency of those depicted. The only photo on screen 2 not taken by a Jewish photographer is one of the Hugo Jaeger portrait photos from the Kutno ghetto, which we discussed above. This image was included to test the ideas regarding agency and "Jewish" photography put forward in this essay—that, without context, the Jaeger photograph bears none of the classic hallmarks of the "perpetrator" image, and even appears to present its subject in a sympathetic light. We measured little curiosity regarding the identity of the photographer for this image: the proportion of respondents who queried "Who was the photographer?" was only 5 percent, the second lowest of the six pictures on the screen. Furthermore, the image provoked little concern regarding the agency of the photographed, with the question "Did this person choose to be photographed in this way?" only being asked by 5 percent of respondents, the joint-lowest of the images. By contrast, respondents were curious regarding the identity of the young woman, with 39 percent asking, "Who was this person?" the highest of any of the images, perhaps provoked by the apparent incongruity of the woman's smile in a series of photos depicting the Holocaust.

Screen 2 also features a photo by Henryk Ross of a Jewish infant, prepared by her parents for deportation (fig. 3.6). This provoked similar responses to the Jaeger image. It was the second highest (32 percent) for respondents asking, "Who was this person?" It was also joint-lowest (5 percent) with Jaeger's image for the question "Did this person choose to be photographed in this way?" Another notable result from screen 2 concerns a photographic

Figure 3.6. Patron responses, "The Ethics of Seeing," 2020. *Source:* Courtesy of the authors.

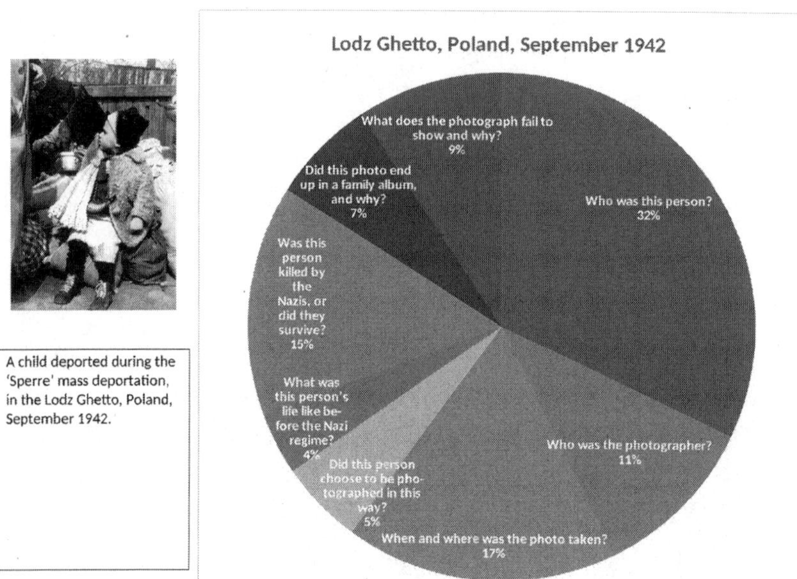

A child deported during the 'Sperre' mass deportation, in the Lodz Ghetto, Poland, September 1942.

self-portrait, taken in a Woolworth self-service photo booth, by the Nortons, a Jewish family who escaped from Nazi-occupied Czechoslovakia. Taken in June 1940 in London, this was the first photo they took after arriving in England. This photo had the highest number (31 percent) of respondents asking, "Was this person killed by the Nazis, or did they survive?" Unlike graphic representations of suffering, this seemingly normal, happy image clearly has the capacity to engage the viewer in a story of Jewish survival against the odds and enables identification. The palpable sense of relief in the image, and the happy embrace of the family members, promotes in the modern viewer a personal investment in the fate of the Jewish people who created the photo, without the aid of any "external" photographer.

On the final screen of "The Ethics of Seeing," visitors encounter photos from three more recent sites of trauma: the civil war in Sudan; migrants at the US-Mexican border; and Melilla, the Spanish enclave in Morocco, which attracts many citizens of African nations who are trying to enter the EU. The images were chosen for the different representational approaches they employed. Participants were invited to rank the photos according to how much dignity they afforded the people they depict. The results confirm our

Figure 3.7. Patron responses, "The Ethics of Seeing," 2020. *Source:* Courtesy of the authors.

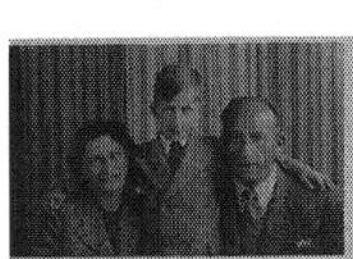

Bob Norton with his parents Karl and Marianne. June 1940, London. Taken in a Woolworth self-service photo booth by a Jewish family who had managed to escape to England from Czechoslovakia.

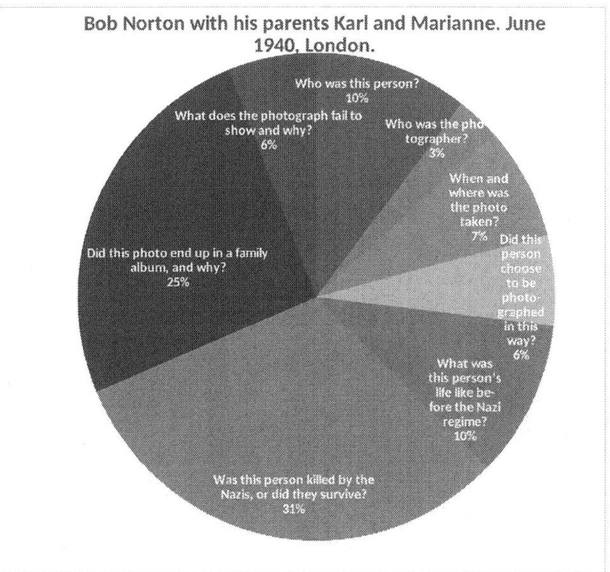

hypothesis: viewers found more dignity in photos whose subjects have been given agency, identity, the opportunity for self-presentation: these provoke reflection on the wider narrative of the people depicted. All of these photos were taken by photographers who had lived for sustained periods among and with the people whom they photographed. Conversely, the photos ranked lowest were those taken by photojournalists, who present their subjects as anonymous victims in sensational shots. Screen 3 gave us an opportunity to assess the relationship between responses to historical images of the Holocaust and to representations of human suffering in the contemporary world, and to invite audiences to apply visual sensitivities developed in the exhibition to new situations. This grows out of our hypothesis that the iconography of historical Holocaust photography continues to inform and provide a framing reference for how we look at contemporary images of suffering—one that appears to be borne out by this data.

Finally, we combined data from the first and third screens to compare ways of viewing different kinds of photos. We divided responders to screen 1 into those who preferred emotional language and those who chose more factual descriptors to record their reactions. We then compared the results with variations in the same viewers' rankings of the contemporary photos on screen 3. One notable result concerned a portrait image by Nerris Markogiannis, who has for many years been stationed with UN Peacekeepers in Sudan (fig. 3.8).

Markogiannis makes a point of not taking graphic images of violence and its aftermath; he chooses instead to create consciously aesthetic, often lyrical, black-and-white photos of survivors and landscapes. "Photojournalists continue to replicate stereotypes in Africa. Malnourished children, either alone and pensive or with their mothers, continue to be favorite subjects. One way to escape from stereotypes, he suggests, is to aestheticize our images" (Umbach 2020). Markogiannis's contemplative, black-and-white portrait shows a young woman and her child inside the UN rescue helicopter, about to be flown to safety. The two were the only survivors of a massacre in Darfur. Those who responded more emotionally to screen 1 tended to rank this image more highly than factual responders (an average ranking of 2.93 vs. 3.12). It seems plausible that those who respond more emotionally to images of suffering felt that the subject of this image was afforded more dignity due to the artistic qualities of the shot, while more factual responders were perhaps concerned by questions about agency: the woman barely seems to register the presence

Figure 3.8. Nerris Markogiannis, a mother with her teenage daughter, refugees from the village of Wadda, on a UN helicopter, 2009. *Source:* UNAMID/Nerris Markogiannis. Used with permission.

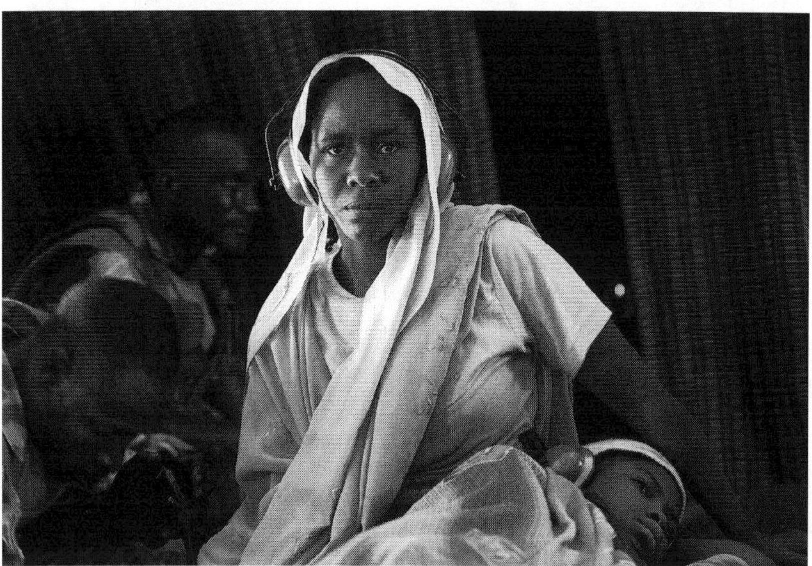

of the camera, she is not "posing." Factual responders tended to rank more highly the photo of an art project with refugee children on the African side of the fence surrounding the Melilla enclave (2.24 against 2.39 for emotional responders). This is certainly an image less concerned with pathos or aesthetic beauty, and more with the positive actions of those depicted.

In this final section, we have explored modern viewer responses. It is clear that there is no singular, uniform response to photos of human suffering. Our viewers of course responded after "The Eye as Witness" exhibition had drawn their attention to questions of identity and agency in Holocaust photography. But the results demonstrate that even a relatively short intervention like this exhibition can be effective in counter-acting a "homogenizing" gaze. It successfully sensitized audiences to the multiple agencies at work in establishing the meaning of a photo and made them attentive to the ethical imperatives of Jewish perspectives.

Conclusion

We see the past through photography. Photos make memories, and they constitute history. This is not just because photos offer a seductively authentic window into the past. Most photos are taken with the future viewer in mind: they are already "historical" at the time of their creation. In assessing the meaning and significance of photos and determining what might be described as a "Jewish" photo, it is important not only to consider the entangled agencies of photographer and photographed. We also need to consider the different temporalities that shape a photo's meanings. Past, present, and the (imagined) future cocreate each image. Each photo is a preemptive act of commemoration, an appeal to the future viewer to engage in a dialogue with the photo and those who act in it. Not only the Nazi regime created photos for the "historians of the future." In their radically different ways, so did Jewish individuals and families. The Salzmanns, who donated their private family albums to a historical archive, saw their personal photography as telling a broader history, and writing their own memories into that history. As Eva Vichules, daughter of Hans and Kate Salzmann, later put it: "All our vacations and important family occurrences were immortalized in photos. Even some of the ones before my birth, and before I knew what they were, were eventually part of my growing up. I 'knew' some of my ancestors that I had never met from their photos" (Eva Vichules, email to Maiken Umbach, September 15, 2019). Photos create lines of communication and bonds of belonging between spaces and generations. In so doing, they also create history. Ruth Salzmann's decision to donate these private photos to a historical archive was motivated by the conviction that they should form part of "history." Jewish photography in Nazi ghettos, too, was motivated by this desire to communicate with future viewers. Henryk Ross, Mendel Grossman, and the other Jewish photographers who, and at great personal risk, chronicled intimate moments of Jewish life in the ghettos in sensitive, quiet, and often lyrical images, also did so with imagined future viewers in mind: those who would later excavate the hidden images and read them differently from the dictates of Nazi ideology. And unlike Nazi photographers, their appeal to the future made no binary distinctions between Jewish and non-Jewish viewers.

It is incumbent on us, as the viewers of that future, to engage sensitively with a photo's language and to appreciate that it is not only the identity of the photographer that makes a photo "Jewish." It is, rather, the photo's ability to narrate stories from a distinctly Jewish perspective: not fixing or classifying identities in a singular moment of persecution, but to convey something that extends beyond that moment, to bring alternative pasts and alternative futures into a dialogue with one another. In this dialogue, the modern viewer exercises a crucial agency, which entails ethical obligations. As we have argued in this chapter, debates about whether or not the emotive impact of shocking Holocaust images are conducive to creating empathy can detract from such obligations. A purely affective reaction to the scene depicted in an image, whatever its nature, is always reductive. While modern viewers are constantly bombarded with graphic and shocking images of human suffering, which seem to invite such an immediate affective response, we can choose to engage differently, and prompt others to do the same. New curatorial approaches, we maintain, can open up new ways of seeing, which are attentive to the "Jewishness," or otherwise, of Holocaust photos. Through Jewish images, we can see and engage with stories that are intimate and unimaginably expansive at the same time: stories of suffering, of resilience and resistance, stories that celebrate Jewish identity and culture at the time when it was most in peril, and stories that continue to resonate in the present.

Works Cited

Arani, Miriam Y. 2010. "Wie Feindbilder gemacht wurden: Zur visuellen Konstruktion von 'Feinden' am Beispiel der Fotografien der Propagandakompanien aus

Bromberg 1939 und Warschau 1941." In *Die Kamera als Waffe: Propagandabilder des Zweiten Weltkrieges*, edited by Rainer Rother. Boorberg.

———. 2011. "Die Fotografien der Propagandakompanien der deutschen Wehrmacht als Quellen zu den Ereignissen im besetzten Polen 1939–1945." *Zeitschrift für Ostmitteleuropa-Forschung* 60 (1): 1–49.

———. 2013. *Mendel Grosman: The Lodz Ghetto (1940–1944) Photograph Collection at the Wiener Library, London*. Deutsch-Polnische Akademische Gesellschaft.

Ashkenazi, Ofer. 2022. "Reading Private Photography: Pathos, Irony and Jewish Experience in the Face of Nazism." *American Historical Review* 127 (4): 1606–34.

Auslander, Leora. 2002. "Jewish Taste? Jews and the Aesthetics of Everyday Life in Paris and Berlin, 1933–1942." In *Histories of Leisure*, edited by Rudy Koshar. Berg Press.

Azoulay, Ariella. 2008. *The Civil Contract of Photography*. Zone.

Barthes, Roland. 1981. *Camera Lucida*. Translated by Richard Howard. Hill and Wang.

Batchen, Geoffrey. 2009. "Seeing and Saying: A Response to 'Incongruous Images.'" *History and Theory* 48 (4): 26–33.

Betts, Paul, and Christian Wiese, eds. 2010. *Years of Persecution, Years of Extermination: Saul Friedlander and the Future of Holocaust Studies*. Continuum.

Bourla, Lisa. 2015. "Shaping and Reshaping Memory: The Lodz Ghetto Photographs." *Word and Image* 31 (1): 54–72.

Crane, Susan A. 2008. "Choosing Not to Look: Representation, Repatriation and Holocaust Atrocity Photography." *History and Theory* 47 (3): 309–30.

Crownshaw, Rick. 2007. "Photography and Memory in Holocaust Museums." *Mortality* 12 (2): 176–92.

de Certeau, Michel. 1984. *The Practice of Everyday Life*. University of California Press.

Didi-Huberman, Georges. 2008. *Images in Spite of All: Four Photographs from Auschwitz*. Translated by Shane B. Lillis. University of Chicago Press.

Edwards, Elizabeth, ed. 1992. *Anthropology and Photography, 1860–1920*. Yale University Press.

———. 2012. *The Camera as Historian: Amateur Photographers and Historical Imagination, 1885–1918*. Duke University Press.

Fogelman, Eva. 2007. "On Blaming the Victim." In *Daring to Resist: Jewish Defiance in the Holocaust*, edited by David Engel, Yitzchak Mais, and Eva Fogelman. Museum of Jewish Heritage.

Friedländer, Saul. 1997. *Nazi Germany and the Jews: The Years of Persecution, 1933–1939*. Weidenfels & Nicholson.

———. 2007. *Nazi Germany and the Jews: The Years of Extermination, 1939–1945*. Harper Collins.

Grossman, Mendel, and Frank Dabba Smith. 2000. *My Secret Camera: Life in the Lodz Ghetto*. Frances Lincoln.

Hébert, Valerie. 2020. "Teaching with Photographs." In *Understanding and Teaching the Holocaust*, edited by Laura Hilton and Avinoam Patt Madison. University of Wisconsin Press.

Hirsch, Marianne. 1997. *Family Frames: Photography, Narrative, and Postmemory.* Harvard University Press.

———. 2012. *The Generation of Postmemory: Writing and Visual Culture after the Holocaust.* Columbia University Press.

Hirsch, Marianne, and Leo Spitzer. 2009. "Incongruous Images: Before, during, and after the Holocaust." *History and Theory* 48 (4): 9–25.

Holtschneider, K. Hannah. 2011. *The Holocaust and Representations of Jews: History and Identity in the Museum.* Routledge.

———. 2012. "Are Holocaust Victims Jewish? Looking at Photographs in the Imperial War Museum Holocaust Exhibition." *Melilah: Manchester Journal of Jewish Studies*, suppl. 1, 91–106.

Klugman, Aleksander, ed. 1967. *The Last Journey of the Jews of Lodz: Photographed by Henryk Ross.* S. Kibel.

Krol, Eugeniusz C. 2008. "Die Propaganda des Dritten Reiches gegenüber Polen und den Polen von 1939–1945." In *Im Objektiv des Feindes: Die deutschen Bildberichterstatter im besetzten Warschau*, edited by Eugeniusz C. Krol. Rytm.

Levitt, Laura. 2009. "Returning to the United States Holocaust Memorial Museum: The Tower of Faces Ten Years Later." In *Photographs, Histories, and Meanings*, edited by Marlene Kadar, Jeanne Perreault, and Linda Warley. Palgrave Macmillan.

Linfield, Susie. 2010. *The Cruel Radiance: Photography and Political Violence.* University of Chicago Press.

Liss, Andrea. 1998. "The Identity Card Project and the Tower of Faces at the United States Holocaust Memorial Museum." In *Trespassing through Shadows: Memory, Photography and the Holocaust.* University of Minnesota Press.

Löw, Andrea. 2015. "Documenting as a 'Passion and Obsession': Photographs from the Lodz (Litzmannstadt) Ghetto." *Central European History* 48 (3): 387–404.

Manz, Stefan. 2014. *Constructing a German Diaspora: The "Greater German Empire," 1871–1914.* Routledge.

Mills, Gary, and Maiken Umbach. 2024. "Teaching with Images: Opportunities and Pitfalls for Holocaust Education." *Holocaust Studies* 30 (1): 47–65.

Penny, H. Glenn, and Stefan Rinke. 2015. "Germans Abroad: Respatializing Historical Narrative." *Geschichte und Gesellschaft* 41 (2): 173–96.

Raskin, Richard. 2004. *A Child at Gunpoint: A Case Study in the Life of a Photo.* Aarhus University Press.

Rollins, William. 1995. "Whose Landscape? Technology, Fascism, and Environmentalism on the National Socialist Autobahn." *Annals of the Association of American Geographers* 85 (3): 494–520.

Sachsse, Rolf. 2003. *Die Erziehung zum Wegsehen: Fotografie im NS-Staat.* Philo Fine Arts.

Schwarberg, Günther. 2001. *In the Ghetto of Warsaw: Heinrich Jöst's Photographs.* Steidl.

Sened, Alexander, and Zvi Szner, eds. 1970. *Mendel Grossman: With a Camera in the Ghetto*. Ghetto Fighters' House and Hakibbutz Hameuchad Publishing House.

Shand, James D. 1984. "The Reichsautobahn: Symbol for the Third Reich." *Journal of Contemporary History* 19 (2): 189–200.

Sontag, Susan. 1990. *On Photography*. Anchor.

Spitzer, Leo. 1998. *Hotel Bolivia: The Culture of Memory in a Refuge from Nazism*. Hill and Wang.

Struk, Janina. 2004. *Photographing the Holocaust: Interpretations of the Evidence*. I. B. Tauris.

Umbach, Maiken. 2020. "Interview with a United Nations Photographer." In *Learning from the Past*, a FutureLearn course. https://www.futurelearn.com/courses/learning-from-the-past/3/steps/923322.

———, principal investigator. n.d. Web page for "Photography as Political Practice in National Socialism." Accessed September 5, 2022. https://www.nottingham.ac.uk/humanities/departments/history/research/research-projects/current-projects/photography-as-political-practice/photography-as-political-practice-in-national-socialism.aspx.

Umbach, Maiken, and Elizabeth Harvey, eds. 2015. "Photography and German History." Special issue of *Central European History* 48, no. 3.

Umbach, Maiken, and Scott Sulzener. 2018. *Photography, Migration and Identity: A German-Jewish-American Story*. Palgrave.

Uziel, Daniel. 2008. *The Propaganda Warriors: The Wehrmacht and the Consolidation of the German Home Front*. Peter Lang.

Weber, Thomas. 2004. Introduction to *Lodz Ghetto Album*, photographs by Henryk Ross, selected by Martin Parr and Timothy Prus. Chris Boot.

West, Nancy Martha. 2000. *Kodak and the Lens of Nostalgia*. University Press of Virginia.

Zelizer, Barbie. 1998. *Remembering to Forget: Holocaust Memory through the Camera's Eye*. University of Chicago Press.

Zylinska, Joanna. 2017. *Nonhuman Photography*. MIT Press.

Part II

Probing the Boundaries of Documentation

Jewish Photographic Memory

Chapter 4

Theodor Herzl *Is* Yael Bartana

Noam Gal

Figure 4.1. Yael Bartana, *Herzl I*, 2015. Photograph series of six images total. Color photograph, fine art print, 60 × 40 cm. *Source:* Courtesy of Yael Bartana. Used with permission.

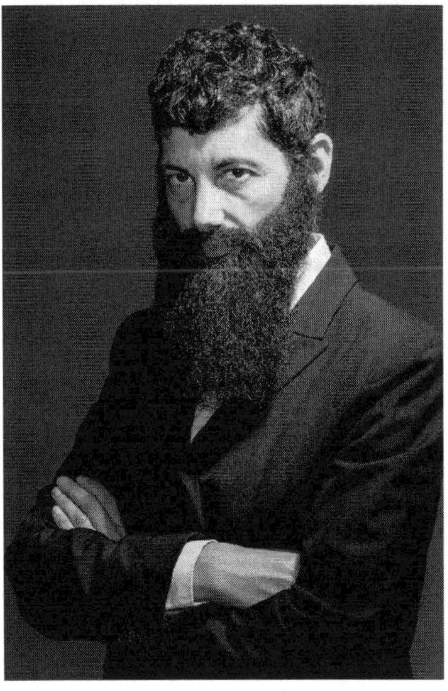

Evidently, most of the readers of this chapter assume they know the person portrayed in figure 4.1. Even when, after a second or so, viewers would probably claim that "this is *not* Theodore Herzl," most would still not identify Yael Bartana, the person who impersonates the forefather of modern Zionism. Within the smaller cultural orbit of contemporary art in Europe, the United States, and Israel, the response would probably be the opposite: "Look, Yael Bartana did Herzl, too." Without diminishing the significance of the Zionist leader in the historical consciousness of that milieu, this response may reflect the status Bartana has gained over the last two decades as an internationally acclaimed and widely exhibited video and installation artist (Germany, for example, selected the artist to represent it at the 56th Venice Biennale, April–November 2024). Whether or not one knows Bartana seems to be crucial for discussing this photographic artwork, so I allow myself to take this rather flat generalization a step further. Both groups—the one that recognizes only the referent of this photographic "stand-in," and the one that recognizes both the historical character and the contemporary artist—would recognize the portrait as a parody because of the same visual elements: the haircut appears to be different than Herzl's, and so do the eyes. Indeed, these clear differences produce what Linda Hutcheon defined as parody, "a repetition with critical distance, which marks difference rather than similarity," strategically employing that difference in resisting heterosexual culture (Hutcheon 1985, 6; 1992, 35). More immediately, both groups simply respond to the fact that it is a recently made color photograph, freshly framed and installed on a museum wall, and not another modest black-and-white authentic document from the archives of Jewish history. Yet the caption that accompanies the photograph describes it plainly as *Herzl 1, 2015*, implying that *he* is back, or at least a version of him (indeed, *version no. 1*) and poses for the camera again. For that reason, Bartana's *Herzl* may strike viewers of both groups as teasing with a simple question: So who am I, really? And why am I doing this? When a work of art imposes such direct questions, we find ourselves on stage, playing with personal identity and collective identity, and how both are shaped and presented by camera-acts.

As in other cases of artistic impersonation in front of the camera, what distinguishes this work from just a common play with costume and make-up (or other forms of traditional masquerade that survive in numerous cultural contexts in the Insta-TikTok-selfie era) is the congruence of the professional perfection of the photographic act with the character chosen for representation and its accumulated public image. Despite its visual simplicity, Bartana's *Herzl* is a more complicated case on the range of what

Philip Auslander called "performed photography," in which "performances [are] staged solely to be photographed or filmed and [have] no meaningful prior existence as autonomous events presented to audiences. The space of the document, i.e., the photograph, thus becomes the only space in which the performance occurs" (Auslander 2006, 2). This sort of camera-body-action, where the artist is the performer and the documenting photographer, goes back to the early days of photography, as in Hippolyte Bayard's *Self Portrait as a Drowned Man* from 1840. Then, as now, it entails a certain break from truth-telling: the uses of the medium of photography in circulating evidence that are then assembled into a consensual history feed into the recognition that the photograph at hand is deceiving. Yet, at the same time, the viewer is prompted to realize a more complicated truth, namely, that the photograph documents a show that *did* happen and presents a human subject whose identity is determined by what the image-surface hides and distorts. Characterized primarily by its "openness to otherness," this genre of performative self-portrait challenges the position of the artist as a photographer, especially when it behaves according to the popular conventions of the photographic portrait, in spite of "its contingency on the one who views or engages with it" (Jones 2002, 949). If we think again of Bayard's self-portrait vis-à-vis Bartana's, the staged subject is a hybrid of the performing character (a dead man or Herzl), the professionally and commercially identified maker (Bayard and Bartana), and an artist critically marked as a performer, a conceptual artist by a certain interpretational discourse (which was not available at Bayard's days but could comfortably land in that context).

While the above photograph is obviously not only a self-portrait of Yael Bartana, it does also create a space where her presence and her present identity intermingle with the identity of another, of a (dead) Other, of past-identifications. Bartana's *Herzl* is exemplary of the capacity of photography to unfold the political mechanics of identity construction in modern times, especially from the national and gender perspectives, as well as to push further the postmodernist potential of deconstructing seemingly coherent identities from within. In such "exaggerated" performative relationship with the camera, the artists "explore the capacity of the self-portrait photograph," as Amelia Jones observed, "to foreground the 'I' as other to itself," while pointing "to the paradoxical 'death' and 'life' of the photographic image and thus, by extension, to the simultaneity of absence and presence—the inexorable passage of time rendering all seeming presence as absence—giving shape to the profound paradox of being human" (Jones 2002, 950, 958). In Bartana's case this existential paradox is highly politicized by the interference of an unquestionably successful national icon. "Successful" here refers both to the political triumph of its subject (the fulfilment of his "Jewish state" vision) and to the effective canonization of his image.

Yael Bartana plays Herzl, this is what we know when looking at this portrait and its accompanying caption, on display as part of the permanent collection of the Jewish Museum in Berlin (also in Bartana's comprehensive solo exhibition *Redemption Now* at the Jewish Museum in Berlin, June–October 2021). That bit of information may disarm the disturbing gaze of the person watching us from this picture. If those eyes still do something to us, if they prompt us to contemplate our own position as viewers, even (for some) our own identity, we will later come to ask how it is achieved and for what purpose. For now, I wish to explore four breaches of normative social categories through which Bartana and Herzl drift and leave tracks, four kinds of trespassing taking place in this unusual artwork that invite us to reflect back on the construction of Jewish collective memory in the camera-ridden age. The investigation of these different breaches aims to illuminate the visual register of some of the main symbols of modern Jewish nationalism before and after (and because of) the establishment of the State of Israel.

First Trespassing

We may well begin with the most professed kind of trespassing, that of gender, cross-dressing, and sexual identity. Bartana's *Herzl* is part of a larger photographic series that started from her attention to the reoccurring fashion of bearded men in contemporary Israeli society. "Wanting to be in man's skin" (Yael Bartana, conversation with author, May 2021), Bartana photographed herself in different portraits, mimicking several stereotypes: as a bearded Jewish Orthodox rabbi and dressed as a right-wing settler, a representative of the Jewish religious communities in the Occupied Territories who achieved his greatest power and influence in the governments under Prime Minister Benyamin Netanyahu during the last two decades. She also photographed herself as "a hipster"—a young, liberal, and secular urbanite, often involved in political leftist causes and social activism mainly influenced by American and European ideas. Both the settler-rabbi and the Tel-Avivian hipster wear what is called a "Herzl beard," and win, under Bartana's careful staging, an effective portrait, a convincing image of themselves, betraying a more general picture of masculinity in contemporary Israel across ideological positions.

The current global popularity of that facial trend notwithstanding, when Bartana performs Herzl the beard turns back from a genre to a particular case, it cannot be captured from other angles but the ones that shaped the historical image of the Zionist leader in the first place: the "Herzl beard" comes back to identify the real Herzl, since Bartana's photograph replicates the iconic image that defines Herzl and represents his project. Neighboring other bearded men, photographed in a similar fashion (indeed, close to fashion-studio practices), our contemporary Herzl is met with the questionable gender of Bartana's subjects.

This question of masculinity and the feminine takes a different shape in each of Bartana's staged impersonations. Yet the case of Herzl is doubly troubling. Not only are we reminded of the misogynic efforts of fabricating "the new Jew," where masculinity played a central role in early Zionist utopian texts—although Herzl himself was a pioneer in advocating women's voting rights—we are actually offered to reconsider the sexuality of their historical authors once again. This process also serves as a reminder of the antisemitic questioning of the "Jewish sexual character" at the time (Pinsker 2008, 107). We are offered such "uncomfortable" ideas specifically in times when facial hair has become a common arena in Western societies for promoting new possibilities for self-identification (Dozier 2005). In this context, Bartana couples the current public interest in transmen identity (still new to most Israelis of 2015) with the contemporaneous academic interest in the social constructions of the nation-state, and particularly that of the "Jewish body" in Zionist and modern Jewish histories. For instance, Herzl's Zionism, according to literary historian Michael Gluzman, is primarily a discourse on the longing for masculinity. Gluzman reads Herzl's 1902 utopian novel *Altneuland*—a seminal text that we will soon revisit—as a narrative of sexual evolution, the maturation of young Viennese lawyer Dr. Friedrich Löwenberg from the feminine, melancholic Jew of diaspora (ridiculed by his friends as "Ophelia") up to the reenergized, healthy, strong, and active male in the "new society" of Zion (Gluzman 1997, 149–50; Kornberg 2007, 44). The author of *Altneuland*, according to Gluzman, propagates corrective masculinity based on European antisemitic stereotypes and nationalistic biopolitics. Such a project for "correcting masculinity" rests primarily on the negation of femininity, a suppressed register in Herzl's ideological heritage that is possibly revived by Bartana's bearded persona. Furthermore, in that reenacted pose, Herzl's beard covers over a female-artist's face with a certain rhetoric of power that served the historical leader on his sweeping political and diplomatic trajectory.

"Herzl's charisma manifested itself in his stately carriage, his baritone voice and elegant German, and, most important, his beauty," writes his most recent biographer:

> In a 1937 essay titled "What Did Herzl Look Like?" Samuel Bettelheim describes Herzl's visage as combining aspects of an English lord and east European rabbi "in his Jerusalemite glory." The First Zionist Congress, writes Bettelheim, would have had little import had there not sat in the Congress president's chair a man who was no less than "a miracle as if King Solomon had arisen from his grave, because he could no longer bear the suffering of his people and its humiliation." Many an observer was fascinated by Herzl's "Assyrian" beard, which bestowed upon him the look of ancient Semitic royalty. The artist Ephraim Lilien depicted Herzl as Moses, that prince of Egypt who rejoined and redeemed his people, and also as the biblical figures Jacob, Aaron, Joshua, David, Solomon, and Hezekiah. (Penslar 2020, 23)

The gender aspect of Zionist identity-construction is recalled from the past to the present, from Herzl to Bartana. This process is complicated by Bartana's self-identification as a Jewish-Israeli living in Berlin, whose emigration from Israel reversed Herzl's life enterprise. Out of her entire oeuvre, this is the first time that Bartana appears in her work (she will do it again in other works since 2015). Notably, in this unprecedented occasion, she chose to show herself as a man, as well as a symbol of Jewish territorial claims—two categories that appear to contradict her identity. The simplicity of this dressing-up shot is of the essence. It stands in stark contrast to Bartana's signature style video megaproductions, attempting for the first time to become a figure herself, a dramatic character, by following a historical figure, who is considered anything but an ordinary person.

Estranging both Herzl and Bartana, this self-portrait was created when Bartana had already secured international recognition as a leading video artist, mostly known for her trailblazing trilogy *And Europe Will Be Stunned* (2007–2011), featured at the Polish Pavilion of the 54th Venice Biennale. The trilogy narrated the imaginary return of three million

Jews from Palestine to Poland and its consequences, through complicated filmic productions in which massive crowds participated in various actions in public spaces, all designed and orchestrated by the artist, who was always behind the camera, never to be seen on screen. Even when in 2012 Bartana materialized some of those "consequences" of the imaginary transfer in the form of a live event at the Berlin Biennale—the *Jewish Renaissance Movement in Poland Congress*—she was not participating as one of the invited speakers. To several extents, it was Herzl who outed her.

The subject of women's representation and the idea of feminine leadership came to hold a central role in Bartana's much later project titled *What If Women Ruled the World* (2017–2020). In between these multifaceted, elaborate video and live productions, *Herzl* seems an interesting stop, a point of intersecting questions of gender and nationalism that have bothered Bartana and shaped her art for a long time. In a 2017 interview with Erica Balsom, she said:

> Women as well as Palestinians were excluded from the Zionist narrative. Women have a different understanding of the state and of the land. I'm so fed up with masculinity being used in the wrong way. My hope is that we realize that achieving equality is not just about having women rule the world, but about transforming our language, structures, and priorities. We live in a very dystopian time. At the moment I don't understand anything about politics. I really don't know how we got here. (Balsom 2017, 140)

In that sense, Herzl's figure seems to serve Bartana as a carrier for what literary historians Jonathan Goldberg and Madhavi Menon termed "queering history," that is, interfering historical narratives with questions on overlooked or outlawed subjectivities, as well as illuminating the faults of normative, teleological, and productivity-oriented conceptions of time and historical progress (Goldberg and Menon 2005). The transhistorical proposition that Bartana stages is itself possible due to queer logic of free passage between social conventions of body and language. Something in Herzl's character and historical positioning brings Bartana out of her artistic "closet," this time facing the camera as a transgender leader.

Figure 4.2. Carl Pietzner, Theodor Herzl, c. 1901. *Source:* Public domain.

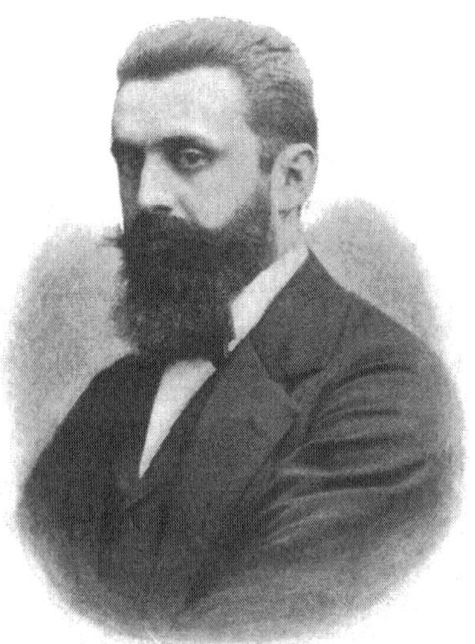

Second Trespassing

The gender-crossing is enabled by another kind of trespassing, well known from photographic manipulations by late twentieth-century artists, namely, the crossing over from one historical moment to another and from one gender to another, such as the works of Cindy Sherman or Gillian Wearing. In Bartana's case we are called to consider the similarity, more than the difference, between Herzl's 1900 moment at Carl Pietzner's commercial photo studio in Vienna, and her self-produced studio shooting in Berlin of 2015. The relation between these two distinct diasporic perspectives on "the Jewish question" and its implied figuration into a calculated visual icon requires some exploration, first of its temporality (the anachronic montage), and then of its fictionality (the "what if" at the basis of political imagination).

Both Herzl and Bartana play, through their photographic portraits, the figure of an opinionated Jewish intellectual in the European diaspora; the seriousness of the former qualifies the genuine demand for his utopian plan, while the irony of the latter qualifies the genuine frustration from that same plan. But Bartana looks just as serious about it. In fact, she superimposes one time-leap on top of another: one is from the century-old promise for national independence (rooted, as it were, in Western colonial imperialism) to its present judgment as based on ethnic and geographic cleansing; the other is the time-leap already proposed by Herzl himself in *Altneuland*. Written around the same time of the official portrait to which

Bartana refers, *Altneuland* imagines a passage in time from 1902 to the year 1923, parallel to a passage in space from Vienna to Palestine. That parallel transition in time and space was mythologized by Nachum Sokolov, who translated Herzl's novel into Hebrew the year of its release. He chose to translate "Alt-neu-land" as "Tel Aviv" after a Mesopotamian town mentioned in the book of Ezekiel. Sokolov explained to Herzl his choice: "This is a Hebrew, Biblical, Israeli name. . . . And it serves as a connection between the new and the old: 'Tel' is an ancient ruin, and 'Aviv' (spring) refers to blossoming and renewal in nature. As a result, you have a ruin that has come back to life, to a new spring: the Old-New Land" (Azaryahu 2007, 36). This translation decision immediately transforms the time difference between 1902 and 1923 narrated in Herzl's novel to a "cosmological" time difference between (biblical) antiquity and modernity. The classification of Europe in the narration and organization of temporalities in *Altneuland* could be confusing, as the European Jew resembles the weak, traditional diasporic body, while the European scientist-entrepreneur resembles the progressive, modern body. In the words of Jeremy Stolow, who unfolds the geopolitical agendas and utopian tropes in *Altneuland*: "The chronotope of 'Palestine 1923' [which the protagonist visits after two decades of isolation in a remote island] is thus the opposite, not only of 'Palestine 1902' but also of the chronotope of 'Europe.' Where the latter appear filthy, unhealthy, and undesirable, the former appears clean and invigorating" (Stolow 1997, 64). Following Stolow's terms, the timelines of Palestine and Europe are now extended again. Fast-forward to 2015, Bartana takes over the stand from where Palestine is seen from afar, thus aligning herself with both the unhealthy character of the shtetl-Jew from the past—which protagonist Friedrich Löwenberg aspires to abandon—and the unhealthy character of a Jewish liberal who cannot bear living in the imperialist colony that has become of that utopian project and withdraws to Europe.

On a different level, Bartana's temporal superimposition introduces fiction and fictional theoretical propositions to our construction of Zionist history: What if Herzl lived today? What if there could be another Herzl? What if Herzl was a woman? What if he was to become an artist as he perceived himself (Penslar 2020, 22, 154–55]? Again, she seems to find the right figure to follow on the tracks of alternative history. *Altneuland* famously carries the motto (now fixed with Herzl's image more than with that novel) "If you will, this is not a legend" (*Wenn ihr wollt, ist es kein Märchen*), completed by the novel's postscript, "But if you do not wish it, all this that I have related to you is and will remain a legend" (Herzl [1941] 2000, 228). This motto places the Zionist national claim as a possibility that rests on foreseeable collective willpower, which seems to belong at the same time to the realm of the imaginary, of the fictional, of folk-tales and dreams. Bartana dedicated her 2013 exhibition at the Wiener Secession to that tension, where she staged an imaginary meeting between Herzl and Freud, residents of the same neighborhood that never met; she titled that exhibition *Wenn Ihr wollt, ist es kein Traum* (Bartana replaces the original *Märchen*, "fairy-tale," with *Traum*, "dream"). Already in *Altneuland*, the time-leap framing the novel is intertwined with a more complicated ontological leap from real to fictional to possibly real again. Stolow concludes:

> [T]he line dividing "dreams" and "fabels" from *Realpolitik* is not always unequivocal in Herzl's writing. . . . In the postscript to *Altneuland*, Herzl hints that "dreaming" implies a certain alloplasticity inherent in all practical engagements with the world: [quoting from *Altneuland*] "I have meant to compose an instructive poem. 'More poetry than instruction' some will say—'more instruction than poetry,' others . . . dreams are also a fulfilment of the time we spend on earth. Dreams are not so different from deeds as some believe. All the deeds of mankind were once dreams, and later become dreams again." (Stolow 1997, 65)

Bartana's confusing historical superimposition brings back, through this genre of staged studio shot, the fictional, occasionally hallucinatory aspect of Herzl's position. This is the Zionist dream that transformed into reality, now made again into a dream, keeping Herzl's promise from the postscript. Moreover, the link suggested here between history and narrative, especially under the poetic combination known as alternate history seems emblematic to both the writings of Herzl and the art of Bartana: "what if" is their shared practice; both are authors of "alternative history" fictions (Hellekson 2001).

A few months before the publication of *Altneuland*, Herzl wrote the short story "The Left Doorbell" ("Die Linke Glocke," eventually published in his 1911 collection *Feuilltons*), where, like in *Altneuland*, we are introduced to a place visited again after many years and revealed as totally transformed. The visitor is the rather mysterious Wendelin who recounts a story before a group of "successful men" about fate and life-changing decisions: he was a disadvantaged young layman when one day, upon his return from the port after figuring out he could not afford boarding a ship to America, he accidently met a wealthy man who gave him a letter to deliver to the near building. Following the address, young Wendelin came to stand in front of two identical doors, not knowing which one is the right destination for his letter. Wendelin pulled the right bell, which led him to permanent employment with the wealthy family that resided there, later marrying their daughter, and becoming a successful businessman. The other door, he came to know years later, led another person who opened it to a life of poverty and a miserable marriage. After older Wendelin finishes his story and leaves the group, one of them reveals that in fact the one who opened the left door was Wendelin himself (Herzl 2002). In Vivian Liska's reading of this story, the idea that success and failure is not a matter of merit but of sheer luck could not be delivered effectively by a loser—"to an assembly of rich and arrogant members of the town's elite, to those who have a stake in considering their own position to be a result of their own merits. The realization that things could be different, that self-confidence based on success is an illusion, must be driven home by one of their equals, by one who made it in the world" (Liska 2007, 168). Yet, beyond the psychological tactics of leading others to reflect critically on their self-deceiving social mobility, the potential of alternate history to convince in its probability seems to rely on staging a confusing duplication: the two adjacent, identical doors in the hallway, and the two mirroring bells. This idea of a confusing similarity between two opposites links Herzl's duality of history-making and fiction-making to Bartana's camera-work—its intertwining of realism and alternatives to reality—and its influence on forming political imagination.

Figure 4.3. Yael Bartana, *Herzl III*, 2015. Photograph series of six images total. Color photograph, fine art print, 60 × 40 cm. *Source:* Courtesy Yael Bartana. Used with permission.

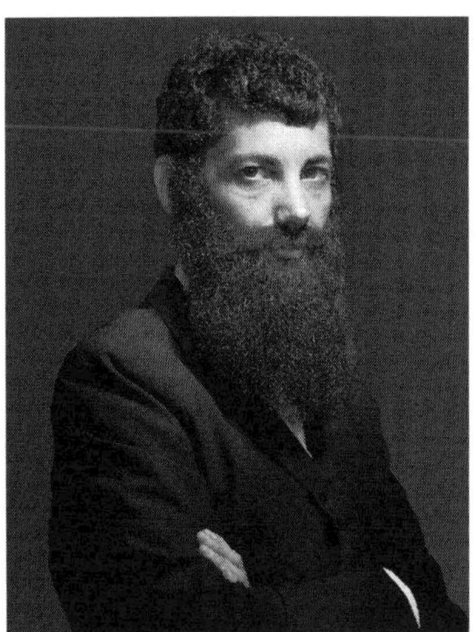

Third Trespassing

In envisaging alternate history as poetically effective, Bartana's camera moves from art making to commercial photography and back, trespassing between two conventionally distinct realms of operation that have tantalized photography since its invention. Photography as a suitable arena for investigating modernity and the myths of modern nationalism, particularly due to its Janus-faced power of bringing certain evidence from reality in a way that would erase other evidence and manipulate collective consciousness and memory. This is also where Bartana feels most at home. When this nature of photography is contextualized between Western colonial powers and colonized spaces and communities of the Levant from the very onset of photography and until today (Behdad 2016), Bartana's art revives critical consequences of camera uses and their representation in certain historiographies. By placing herself in front of the camera, she offers herself as another item in the inventory of modern nationalism—the Zionist project—which, according to Herzl's *Altneuland*, was a primarily technological, scientific enterprise. In other words, Bartana is a late representative of image-making and image-circulation technologies that have accompanied Western imperialism and its territorial and cultural claims from the start. It is a techno-critical history which Ariella Azoulay recently crystalized: "The [camera] shutter is a synecdoche for the operation of the imperial enterprise altogether, on which the invention of photography, as well as other technological media, was molded" (Azoulay 2019, 2). Here it is through Herzl's viewfinder: Upon their travels in the "new" Palestine, *Altneuland*'s protagonists Löwenberg and Kingscourt are invited for a Passover dinner in Tiberias, where a speech by Joe Levy, the founder of a new Jewish national movement, is played on the phonograph. Kingscourt's exclaims enthusiastically:

> "Capital!" shouted Kingscourt. "A brilliant idea, most estimable man of the future. All this while I have been asking myself about the transition period. The finished product is before us. But how did it come about? That's the gist of the matter! We ignorant Europeans knew all about railways, harbors, factories, automobiles, telephone, photo—and Lord knows what other graphs before We ever set foot in Palestine. But how did you transplant them all? I had been intending to ask you." (Herzl 2000, 148)

Bartana seems to invoke this century-old perception that links the construction of national identity and modern capitalist societies with technical progress and investigates its implications for relations between nationalism and the arts. Bartana's *Herzl* is obviously not only an appropriation of a certain technology of image-making, but rather a critical exploitation of its aesthetics and rhetorical power. The commercial portraiture that Bartana appropriates—in this case, directly from the Viennese studio of Carl Pietzner—follows the conventional style of late 1800s portraits. Like magnanimous portraits of the Parisian elite by Félix Nadar of the 1850s to the 1870s, for instance, Pietzner's Herzl exhibited three-quarter posture and a nearly frontal, penetrating gaze of a well-dressed man, which aimed to reflect candor and earnestness. This conventional aesthetics effectively utilized symbols of economic status, ethnicity, and gender to produce an image of superior psychological traits and a justification (or a visual fabrication) of social hierarchy (Kozloff 1976).

Following John Tagg's historical investigation of the cultural precedents of the photographic portrait in the nineteenth century, we may suggest that through such aesthetic conventions Pietzner's work aspired to inscribe social identity more than to describe an individual (Tagg 1993, 36–39). Pietzner thus created one of Herzl's most circulated images, a lasting power that Bartana wishes to exploit and find the means to recreate. These conventions of commercial portraiture serve Herzl's own visual conception of individualism and leadership. As an experienced journalist, he was well aware of the visual impact of an effective photograph, which later served his public reception as a nearly messianic figure in Jewish political and cultural lives. In an often-cited essay, historian Robert Wistrich writes excitedly about Herzl's carefully calculated performance:

> In his physiognomy the core of the Zionist programme already seemed to be contained. The manly figure, the handsome face, the gravity, the impressive beard (recalling the prophets of Israel) and the penetrating, melancholy eyes, embodied for many of his followers the Zionist promise of regeneration. . . . His picture adorned virtually every Zionist meeting hall, office or reading room just as it would gaze out over his followers at future Congresses of the movement. It could be found on trademarks of Jewish ceremonial objects, household articles, canned milk or cigarette boxes. (Wistrich 1995, 2–3)

It is difficult, obviously, to distinguish the impact of a portrait that is the result of a certain photographic practice from the impact carried out by the identity and public performance of the photographed subject, prior to any particularly visual presence (Alexander 2010). But it is this indistinguishability that Bartana challenges with a simple experiment: To what extent would that visual impact of the leader's icon remain once the leader is replaced by an artist? To what extent would that impact survive the transition of the observed object from a mass-produced commodity to an "authentic" artwork, despite their common dependence on current technological and economic systems?

Once taken as an artwork, we should consider these questions about the visual impact of portraiture not only in the context of its historical background, but also in the context of its current (local) visual culture and (international) artistic production—both contexts may inform our iconological investigation of how this photographic portrait "works on us," to follow W. J. T. Mitchell's methodological program (Mitchell 1986, 1996). To produce her *Herzl*, Bartana invites a professional crew of commercial studio photography with the appropriate equipment, but this is done nearly half a century after regular studio portraiture of the kind Pietzner operated in Vienna has globally shifted from its original participation in the maintenance of social hierarchies to the realm of commercial and political campaigns. The latter is especially present within the Israeli social spheres of the last decade, where recurring elections for parliament constantly fuelling political instability with an unprecedented volume of visually and verbally forged content on both printed and virtual platforms. But even for these purposes, the single iconic portrait seems to have lost relevance for contemporary political-celebrity construction. When Bartana created that photographic series, celebrity power could rest no more on a single image or on the singularity of visual evidence but rather the opposite, on the abundance of visual reference, on the constant availability of portraiture, of an endless number of angles by which one can be photographed and seen around the clock by various societies of "followers" (i.e., voters, clients, fans [Thompson, 2005]). There are several photographic portraits of Herzl well circulating through the century that have passed until Bartana's appropriation-art gesture; accordingly, she creates three different *Herzl* portraits, three different poignant shots, but the power of *her* photographic pose (its iconicity, its idol-ness) seems to rely on that of a coherently imagined figure of the past rather than that of a constantly seen figure of a person whose visuality is his/her main product, which must constantly be produced anew. The commercial practices for idol-making are thus appropriated and highlighted by the artist in times when "celebrities are, in fact, the most powerful icons" (Alexander 2010, 324). In this case, the appropriation takes place within a national-ethnic context known for its roots in the prohibition of idolatry. Our opening question strikes again: Who is the photographed celebrity here? Who is the important figure whose status as a visionary of alternate historical narratives is inscribed by this carefully displayed and circulated art-object? Who is this spokesmodel for a newly imagined community in search of a home?

Figure 4.4. Yael Bartana, *Mary Koszmary (Nightmares)*, 2007. Video still. *Source:* Courtesy Yael Bartana. Used with permission.

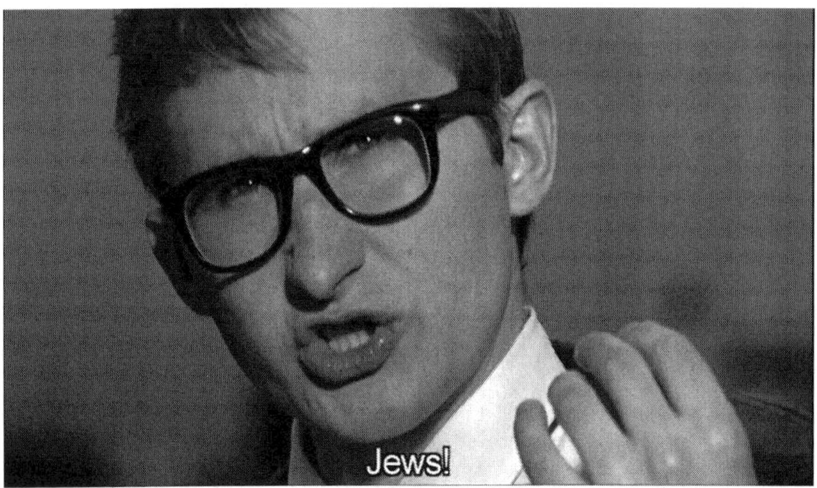

Fourth Trespassing

I would like to conclude my analysis with the most radical possibility of trespassing, in which the artist dares to replace the leader, not on the surface of a simple conceptual photographic action but truly as the generator of a collective change on a national scale. What if Bartana was, indeed, Herzl? Or, more concerning, what if Herzl is not different from Bartana? Under certain circumstances and through imagining alternate histories, the artist *shows* that she *could* be a Herzl, implying that he *actually was* an avant-garde artist working mainly with the medium of transhistorical fantasy. Were the visions-cum-actions of Herzl essentially different from Bartana's art? To dismiss these questions as unworthy of any theoretical consideration would mean that we still approve of art according to a defined distance it maintains from reality. Yet if we are open to considering Bartana's proposition seriously, the answer seems to bring us back to her massive film productions, through which she has achieved her international fame, representing several contradictory fronts on the current discourse on Zionism and the Israel/Palestine conflict.

Her video trilogy mentioned above, *And Europe Will Be Stunned*, opens with an image of a leader, the Polish leftist activist and editor Sławomir Sierakowski, standing in a vacant, deserted stadium and delivering a powerful speech that starts with a loud exclamation, "Jews, countrymen, people!" Sierakowski's appearance, wearing thick glasses and untidy jacket and tie, may fit the stereotype of a journalist more than that of a political leader, thus suggesting already that the "Herzlian" visual image of a journalist-intellectual-leader has changed, however believable or trustworthy we find this sort of leadership-image, which immediately suspends our belief in the presented event. Yet, Sierakowski's speech unfolds as a coherent plea for the long-awaited return of three million Jews to "Mother-Poland" to redeem her from the "nightmares and demons that chase her since they left" (Bartana 2007). The call for a collective act that resonates within an abandoned stadium—a structure made for collective actions—links the two peoples, the Jews and the Poles, by a reciprocal promise: "Heal our wounds," Sierakowski asks the absent Jews, "and you'll heal yours. We will be together again" (Bartana 2007). Meanwhile, a group of kids, dressed in youth movement uniforms, jointly use lime powder to stencil a large slogan on the stadium grass with the words "3,300,000 Jews can change the life of 40,000,000 Poles." From this moment and throughout *And Europe Will Be Stunned*, actions would be performed collectively. They would define a collective under a particular symbolic order that unifies a specific community. Both the collective action and the collective's language are the products of imaginary acts, rituals staged for the camera by nonactors, and texts that not only mimic political demagogues from the past and the present but propose a possible, even if not yet realized, turn of events.

That staged, effective speech is followed by a series of public events featured in the trilogy, such as the erecting of a Zionist settlement at the heart of Warsaw (modeled after the architecture and choreography of the historical "Tower and Stockade" settlement project in Mandate Palestine of the 1930s), or the public funeral of the assassinated leader of the *Jewish Renaissance Movement in Poland*, that is, Sierakowski himself. All these events are "documented" according to the conventional representation and circulation of parallel events in today's media. Consequently, Bartana's trilogy often appears more like news items than video art that documents fabricated stage performances. Looking highly familiar, *And Europe Will Be Stunned* stresses its invitation to test the feasibility of reversing Jewish history to its pre-Holocaust era, when large Jewish communities prospered across European and North African host-nations while Arab communities in Palestine lived under Turkish and then British rule. This is not an act of reconstruction for conserving a lost origin, but rather an act of experimenting with an alternative leeway for an otherwise dead-end conflict.

Moreover, all these events are joint actions, composed and instructed by a single artist who is able to mobilize masses of people. In the first part of the trilogy, *Nightmares*, the members of a Polish youth movement arrange together "Return the Jews" slogans on the stadium grass. In the second part, titled *Wall and Tower,* the "neo-pioneers" collaborate to erect the new settlement in the Warsaw Park, thrilled faces upwards, strong hands carrying heavy load happily. Finally, in *Assassination,* crowds of believers jointly protest and mourn the death of their great leader, all marching in absolute silence. The convincing effect of *And Europe Will Be Stunned* seems to derive from Bartana's assumption that moving a public, indeed, as a director of such a complicated production, requires not merely the collective following of a particular synopsis but rather the fictionalizing-together of historical facts, the sort of spiritual structure known from the maintenance of cultural myths. She directs her community of nonactors of different origins and nationalities according to scripts that seem very familiar, thus training her viewers' ability to fabricate alternate historical narratives as confusingly seductive political programs.

When the trilogy *And Europe Will Be Stunned* was premiered at the Venice Biennale, Bartana was already living in Europe for more than a decade. Her frustration with Israel's violations of the Oslo Accords (which envisaged the two-state solution on the basis of a peace agreement between Palestine and Israel) and the weakening of critical voices in Israeli society during the Second Intifada sent the artist abroad. There, in Berlin and Amsterdam, and for some time in Warsaw and New York, Bartana would constantly look into the fatal dead-ends of Israeli nationalism and militant culture on the one hand, and universalist leftist activism on the other hand; once an activist in her own right, Bartana has gradually developed a critical telescopic view of Israel that allowed her the kind of creative distance and flexible focus that enable the poetic passage between reality and allegory. In a 2012 interview, Bartana admitted: "When I left, in 1996, it was out of personal frustration with Israel, an inconvenience to live there. But at the same time, it's my home . . ." (Edelman 2012). Coming from opposite ends on the anti-Zionist-nationalist range, responses to *And Europe Will Be Stunned* exposed the political ambiguity played out by the artist against the common expectations for a clarified stand regarding either the Israeli occupation or the universal moral lesson of the Holocaust. Especially memorable was the initial refusal of the Israeli minister of culture, Limor Livnat, to attend the opening of Bartana's trilogy at the Polish pavilion of the Venice Biennale, despite its adjacency to the Israeli pavilion, an act that made waves in Poland-Israel diplomatic discourse around the lucrative event. At the same time, those debates further placed Bartana as a representative, if not a full-fledged leader, of a generation of Israeli artists and intellectuals who live and work abroad (mostly in Berlin, London, and New York), while their work refers directly to Israeli affairs. Bartana's fusion of powerful messages and counterhistorical appropriations left many viewers suspicious of the artist's "true" opinion, looking for her "right" ethics (especially since, in the Biennale, she represented not "her motherland" but the very country depicted in the trilogy as responsible for the Jewish trauma).

Accused as a "betrayer" or a "trespasser" both at home and abroad, the responses to her trilogy anticipated a risk that Bartana would dare to further cultivate. The evolution of *And Europe Will Be Stunned* from an imaginary artistic experiment into an actual political movement peaked in the form of the first conference of the *Jewish Renaissance Movement in Poland* (*JRMiP*), which took place in 2012, as part of the 7th Berlin Biennale. During this event, acclaimed intellectuals, journalists, and artists debated "How should the EU change in order to welcome the Other?" or "How should Israel change to become part of the Middle East?" (Lingwood and Nairne 2012). One review summed up this transformation from vision to action rather ominously: "I suspect that for Bartana, this shift from phantasm to reality must have created a difficult situation and generated some pressure. Step by step, and maybe inadvertently, the artist took the place of the assassinated leader. Having created a movement, how should the artist define its aims and agenda?" (Pantenburg 2012, 56). Curator Avi Feldman saw in Bartana's 2012 staged conference a more direct allusion to Herzl's Zionist Congress:

> As baffling as the JRMiP Congress might seem to be in its inter-section of truth and fiction, of legal matters and imagination, Bartana's artistic maneuver is based on creating and facilitating a frame in which differing or even negating powers and ideologies can form an encounter. In the most immediate way, one can say that Bartana appropriates Herzl's first Zionist Congress in order to implement into it diverting views. One example for this is the turning of the Congress to an all-inclusive event dealing with universal and global issues to which not only Jews were invited. (Feldman 2015, 80)

With the realization of an artwork that narrates alternate histories into an operative political body, Bartana seems to leave behind the discussion of whether art must let free of any ideological enlistments or universal moral codes, or whether under such fatal political realities like the one in which Bartana works this option is simply unavailable. Her stubborn push to actualize her stories—recalling Herzl's adamant struggle to turn a utopian fiction to "ist es kein Märchen"—is not driven by the conditions for imagining impossibility that art enables, but by the opposite understanding, that the very attempts of actualizing such art (through fully embracing the rhetorical toolbox that shape leaders) will have real consequences: not only for the artist who may have lost her critical independence and creative distance (often necessary for the production of allegories), but more importantly on the society that the artist now represents (artists, curators, scholars, the "creative class"). Back to Bartana's *Herzl*, we may agree that both actions of the leader (Herzl) and the artist (Bartana) advocate a political vision, where rhetoric is applied onto creative acts. Yet, it is the woman whose role here remains suspect: neither her political stance will be taken seriously (as she is not a real politician nor does she accept the role of representing the Jewish people) nor her artistic act (she cannot be serious with that beard, through such a "selling" photographic genre that is never taken to be intellectually satisfying for the art milieus).

I remember looking at that image, Bartana's 2015 *Herzl*, for the first time. I thought it is where she actually moved to the front, out from behind the camera, announcing her identification with a historical figure that for many represents a national triumph, while for many others represents the birth of a catastrophe. Her gaze to the camera was moving, still. After a few minutes, a slight smile that comes up in many experiences of viewing and comprehending conceptual art left my face, and I let an uncomfortable proposition sink in: this *was* Herzl. His infinitely praised artistic imagination is now carried further by a different kind of European Jewish leader. The artist has come to replace the leader, and the artistic action replaces the political one. I cannot tell where one stops and the other begins, but I feel it demands that I search for the remains of the original from among its present duplications, traces, replacers, and transgressors. Something in the premodern belief in the power of a face of an ambiguous identity, simultaneously abhorred and admired, blasphemous and virtuous, deceiving and promising, shaped my experience of facing it (Mitchell 1996, 75). It wasn't that Herzl and Bartana are one, but rather that they now resided in a (con)temporary equation where the task of indicating clear-cut differences is not so easy and requires much creative investment. When I finished writing this essay, it was somewhere in June 2021, I phoned Yael again, we talked about differences and similarities, the meanings and problems in comparisons. She was in Berlin, witnessing the multiple demonstrations against the last round of Israeli military actions in Gaza. Meanwhile, outside my office in Tel Aviv, Israeli society was violently divided under the endless efforts to replace an increasingly authoritarian and militaristic leadership in Israel. We shared the feeling that the need to imagine alternative leadership and different frames of living and belonging has never been so urgent.

Works Cited

Alexander, Jeff. 2010. "The Celebrity-Icon." *Cultural Sociology* 4 (3): 323–36.

Auslander, Philip. 2006. "The Performativity of Performance Documentation." *PAJ: A Journal of Performance and Art* 28 (3): 1–10.

Azaryahu, Maoz. 2007. *Tel Aviv: Mythography of a City*. Syracuse University Press.

Azoulay, Ariella. 2019. *Potential History: Unlearning Imperialism*. Verso.

Balsom, Erika. 2017. "Embrace Weakness! A Conversation with Yael Bartana." In *Yael Bartana: Trembling Times*, edited by Nicole Schweizer. Musée cantonal des beaux-arts de Lausanne/JRP Ringier. Exhibition Catalogue.

Bartana, Yael. 2007. *Mary Koszmary (Nightmares)*. One channel video and sound installation, 11:00.

Behdad, Ali, 2016, *Camera Orientalis: Reflections on Photography of the Middle East*. University of Chicago Press.

Dozier, Raine. 2005. "Bears, Breasts, and Bodies: Doing Sex in a Gendered World." *Gender and Society* 15 (3): 297–316.

Edelman, Udi. 2012. "Till Imagination Takes Us Back: A Conversation with Yael Bartana." *Ma'arav*, suppl. 12. http://maarav.org.il/english/2012/04/29/till-imagination-takes-us-back-a-conversation-with-yael-bartana/.

Feldman, Avi. 2015. "Performing Justice: From Dada's Trial to Yael Bartana's JRMiP Congress." *On Curating*, no. 26, 70–85.

Gluzman, Michael. 1997. "Longing for Heterosexuality: Zionism and Sexuality in 'Altneuland'" [in Hebrew]. *Theory and Criticism* 11: 62–145.

Goldberg, Jonathan, and Madhavi Menon. 2005. "Queering History." *PMLA* 120 (5): 1608–17.

Hellekson, Karen. 2001. *The Alternate History: Refiguring Historical Time*. Kent State University Press.

Herzl, Theodor. (1941) 2000. *Old New Land.* Translated by Lotta Levensohn. Marcus Wiener.

———. 2002. *Journalistic Stories.* Translated and edited Henry Regenstein. Associated University Presses.

Hutcheon, Linda. 1985. *A Theory of Parody: The Teachings of Twentieth-Century Art Forms.* Routledge.

———. 1992. *A Poetics of Postmodernism: History, Theory, Fiction.* Routledge.

Jones, Amelia. 2002. "'Eternal Return': Self-Portrait Photography as a Technology of Embodiment." *Signs* 27 (4): 947–78.

Kornberg, Jacques. 2007. "Theodore Herzl: Zionism as Personal Liberation." In *Theodore Herzl: From Europe to Zion,* edited by Mark H. Gelber and Vivian Liska. Max Niemeyer.

Kozloff, Max. 1976. "Nadar and the Republic Mind." *Artforum,* September.

Lingwood, James, and Eleanor Nairne, eds. 2012. *And Europe Will Be Stunned—The Polish Trilogy.* Artangel.

Liska, Vivian. 2007. "A Vision out of Sight: Theodor Herzl's Late Philosophical Tales." In *Theodore Herzl: From Europe to Zion,* edited by Mark H. Gelber and Vivian Liska. Max Niemeyer.

Mitchell, W. J. T. 1986. *Iconology: Image, Text, Ideology.* University of Chicago Press.

———. 1996. "What Do Pictures *Really* Want?" *October* 77:71–82.

Pantenburg, Volker. 2012. "Loudspeaker and Flag: Yael Bartana, from Documentation to Conjuration." *Afterall* 30:48–61.

Penslar, Derek. 2020. *Theodor Herzl: The Charismatic Leader.* Yale University Press.

Pinsker, Shachar. 2008. "Imagining the Beloved: Gender and Nation Building in Early Twentieth-Century Hebrew Literature." *Gender and History* 20 (1): 105–27.

Stolow, Jeremy. 1997. "Utopia and Geopolitics in Herzl's Altneuland." *Utopian Studies* 8 (1): 55–76.

Tagg, John. 1993. *The Burden of Representation: Essays on Photographies and Histories.* University of Minnesota Press.

Thompson, John B. 2005. "The New Visibility." *Theory, Culture and Society* 22 (6): 31–51.

Wistrich, Robert S. 1995. "Theodor Herzl: Zionist Icon, Myth Maker and Social Utopian." In *The Shaping of Israeli Identity: Myth, Memory and Trauma,* edited by Robert Wistrich and David Ohana. Frank Cass.

Chapter 5

Paper Tombstones

Photographic Inventory and German Jewish Cemetery Books

Daniel H. Magilow

Introduction: A Scene in a Graveyard

"Eier" (Eggs), an anecdote by the Czech-German-Jewish satirist Maxim Biller, is a short literary sketch that until its crucial final sentences, has little relevance to photography and its roles in modern Jewish history (Biller 2005, 17). "Eggs" recounts the story of Kohn, a Jewish man engaged to Andrea, a German gentile, and his first meeting with her parents at an awkward Easter brunch. As in many of his stories, Biller satirizes contemporary Jewish life in Germany through cringe-inducing details that leave readers laughing while wondering about their laughter's appropriateness. By creating a sense that something is just not quite right in the post-Holocaust interactions of Jewish Germans and non-Jewish Germans, Biller has earned a reputation as an author who is not interested, in one reviewer's words, "in making his work palatable for a non-Jewish German audience" (Wolff 2015). "Eggs" bespeaks Biller's interest in depicting, in scholar Jefferson Chase's words, "the commodification of German-Jewish issues by a mass culture that continually exploits the public's fascination with the Holocaust." And it is this interest that manifests itself at the story's conclusion when Biller specifically references a unique form of contemporary photographic book in Germany (Chase 2001, 112).

119

The moment that gives "Eggs" its title and that points to photography's roles in shaping contemporary discourse about German Jewish history occurs when Andrea's parents gift their future son-in-law an Easter basket. It contains "five ghetto-yellow Nestlé chocolate eggs as well as a photobook about Jewish cemeteries in Lower Saxony" (*fünf gettogelbe Schoko-Eier von Nestlé sowie ein Fotoband* über *jüdische Friedhöfe in Niedersachsen*). The basket is a present from well-meaning future in-laws, but as part of a celebration of a Christian holiday, its contents are inappropriate gifts for a Jew, especially because the eggs' "ghetto yellow" color evokes the branding and ghettoizing of Jews throughout German history. The basket's other item, the photobook about Jewish cemeteries, is one that Biller could reference and expect his readers to recognize because since the mid- to-late-1980s, this genre of photographically illustrated text has flourished in Germany and to a lesser extent in Austria, Poland, and the Czech Republic as well. Photographs are central to Jewish cemetery books (*jüdische Friedhofsbücher*). Each volume consists mainly of pages upon pages of formally redundant, documentary-style, straight photographs of the headstones (*matseyves* in Yiddish or *matzevot* in Hebrew) from old and frequently neglected Jewish graveyards. For page after page, the images systematically record hundreds of Hebrew inscriptions and iconography, which are translated, annotated, and contextualized within Jewish religious traditions and local German-Jewish history. Alongside the photographs, consistent organizational and formal traits include:

- a tendency to focus on cemeteries in smaller rural towns and regions rather than cities in a manner that conspicuously evokes discourses of *Heimat* and rootedness;

- the active involvement of Germans and Jews, frequently academics, as coauthors and translators, the latter of whom are typically Israelis rather than German-born Jews;

- multiple layers of dedications, introductions, and prefaces by civic and religious leaders that legitimate and consecrate cemetery books as institutionally sanctioned forms of public memory and as gestures of German repentance;

- cemetery maps, often on inside covers;

- summaries of Jewish history and traditions for German audiences likely unfamiliar with Jewish nomenclature, calendars, numerology (*gematria*), and tombstone iconography;

- indices, registers, and appendices that exhaustively describe and list the names, professions, and origins of the interred.

As physical objects, *Friedhofsbücher* are generally large format, clothbound, deluxe editions on glossy paper, often with color photographs. Their high production values and granular documentation of Jewish graveyards bespeak significant expenditures of intellectual labor and financial resources. Often commissioned by towns or local religious and memorial authorities, new cemetery photobooks appear regularly, and while an exact census is difficult to establish, dozens of these photographic compendia of Jewish gravestones have been published since the late-1980s (Wiesemann 2005). But for their subject matter, one might even be tempted to call them "coffee table books."

The following chapter adopts a telescoping structure to analyze and understand both the historical context for the emergence of cemetery books and the specific texts and photographs within them. It begins by briefly considering some of antecedents of contemporary *jüdische Friedhofsbücher* and how they used photographs. Then, I argue that as examples of what scholars such as Jeffrey Shandler, Michal Kravel-Tovi, and Deborah Dash Moore have theorized as "Jewish inventory," cemetery photobooks should be approached critically as serving functions beyond just documenting old gravestones (Shandler 2010; Kravel-Tovi 2016, 12). The scholarship on *Friedhofsbücher* is practically nonexistent, but in her analysis of a similar kind of memorial inventorying, the Yad Vashem census of Holocaust victims, Carol A. Kidron identifies an "inherent tension" in the project that inhabits cemetery books as well. This tension consists, on the one hand, of what Kidron terms the "positivist precepts at the heart of enumeration," and on the other, "moral agendas that frame efforts to sustain the symbolic potency of numbers that represent those who count" (Kidron 2016, 65). Attending to these cemetery books as representational forms that have been invested with the power to dispassionately document facts while concurrently advancing moral agendas offers a new approach, one rooted in visual culture, to understanding the tension Kidron identifies in memorial inventorying projects, most of which are purely text-based. To demonstrate this point, the analysis proceeds to a case study of a cemetery photobook from the Swabian village of Freudental to illustrate how cemetery books do not—and, indeed, cannot—just scientifically document and itemize the German Jewish past. They also symbolically reanimate long deceased Jewish communities and recode German-Jewish history. These books are a complex gesture that must be understood as part of broader national projects to atone for the Shoah, work through traumatic local histories, rehabilitate neglected

Jewish spaces, and renegotiate Jews' connections to German *Heimat*. But in trying to accomplish these tasks concurrently, this form of photobook becomes stranded uneasily between scientific documentation and atonement. The reason is that *jüdische Friedhofsbücher* rely heavily on page after page of formally standardized, closely cropped, sharply focused, but profoundly redundant documentary photographs to ground themselves historically and certify a self-assigned forensic project whose audience is unclear. Cemetery books become a text and an artifact that Maxim Biller could use to depict a German Jewish relationship in which, as critic Fabian Wolff describes it, "something is off" (Wolff 2015).

Toward a Genealogy of Cemetery Photobooks

Although deluxe, photographically illustrated *jüdische Friedhofsbücher* are a recent phenomenon, the interest in documenting German-Jewish cemeteries to which they attest is not. Indeed, studying cemeteries has long fulfilled a significant symbolic role in Jewish historiography, although it was not until the late nineteenth and early twentieth century, when the technologies for photomechanically reproducing images in books and magazines became economically viable, that photographs became a common feature. Photographically illustrated or not, these projects were, at least initially, undertaken almost exclusively by Jewish scholars and communities concerned with documenting their own histories. For instance, Europe's oldest Jewish cemetery figures centrally in one key chapter of one of the first histories of a German Jewish community, Moses Mannheimer's 1842 *Die Juden in Worms, ein Beitrag zur Geschichte der Juden in den Rheingegenden* (The Jews in Worms, a Contribution to the History of the Jews in the Rhine Areas) (Mannheimer 1842, 56–64). As Nils Roemer has argued, "Central to Mannheimer's narrative was his retelling of the community's past through the existing physical structures, such as the synagogue, the Rashi chapel, and the cemetery" (Roemer 2006, 63). Roemer convincingly demonstrates that as an institution, cemeteries were important for establishing ethnic and communal Jewish identities as Germany modernized and Jewish populations increasingly concentrated in cities. Jews beyond Berlin used the study of local communities, traditions, and spaces—including cemeteries—to establish their own identities vis-à-vis the metropolitan hub.

Throughout much of the twentieth century, this historical interest in Jewish cemeteries manifested itself in scholarship that frequently although certainly not exclusively focused on the larger, storied graveyards in Berlin, Frankfurt/Main, Munich, and Prague. To be sure, it was only with the late nineteenth century introduction of technologies like autotyping and rotogravure that photographs could begin playing a significant role in this research, and even then, these studies took the form of photographically illustrated books only in rare cases.

Figure 5.1. Plate from *Der alte Prager Judenfriedhof*, 1903, showing a section on the west side of the Klausen synagogue, around the grave of Mardachai Meisel. *Source:* Lubomír Jeřábek, *Der alte Prager Judenfriedhof* (1903).

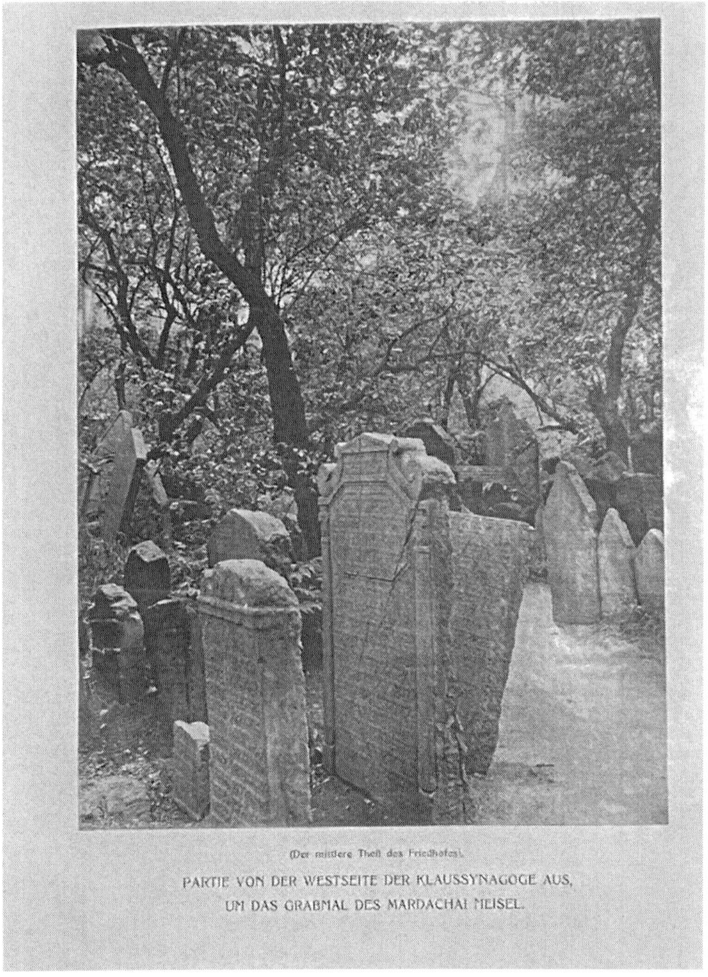

One notable exception was Lubomír Jeřábek's *Der alte Prager Judenfriedhof* (The Old Prague Jewish Cemetery) of 1903, which offered twenty-four full-page rotogravure photographs of the famous cemetery (Jeřábek [1903] 2009). One representative full-page photograph from Jeřábek's book embodies the tensions between documentation, commemoration, and aesthetics inherent to the cemetery book genre. The image shows the tombstone of Mordechai Maisel, the sixteenth-century community leader and the namesake of Prague's Maisel Synagogue. Emanating from the image's upper right corner, soft sunlight suffuses the tree canopy and covers the image's top half, creating the sense that the viewer has stumbled upon the cracked, aging tombstone in a forest clearing. Evocative of Romantic paintings of ruins, the photograph is offered as a sentimental reflection on death and transience. It is a testimony to the long-standing character of Jewish life in Prague. The self-consciously arty, ethereal character accords with early twentieth-century pictorialist photographic practices that aimed to elevate photography to the status of fine art by imitating painting (Rosenblum 1984, 297–98). The photograph is thus a forensic document, albeit one with artistic aspirations.

Another illustrated publication was the fifty-two-page booklet *Der jüdische Friedhof: Seine geschichtliche und kulturgeschichtliche Entwicklung* (The Jewish Cemetery: Its Historical and Cultural-Historical Development) (Cohn 1930). Published by Gustav Cohn (1881–1943), the community rabbi of Leipzig, it included several unattributed photographs presumably taken by Cohn himself. But its photographs were offered as illustration and were not integral to the book's argument. Tim Corbett argues that Cohn's work was a crucial milestone in the "appreciation for the complex historical development of the Jewish cemetery as a cultural space, a communal institution, and a physical place in the landscape" yet also notes that the photographs "were not especially relevant to the text." (Corbett 2018, 300). But Cohn and Jeřábek's books were atypical, and for roughly a half century, between 1933 and around 1980, comparatively few volumes were published about Germany's Jewish cemeteries at all, much less deluxe photobooks. For several decades thereafter, the absence of Jews and the absence of interest led to an absence of new publications.

To be sure, the interest in photographing Jewish cemeteries did persist into National Socialist Germany among Jewish and non-Jewish Germans alike. To reaffirm Jewish belonging in the face of the new regime's antisemitism, for instance, the *Central-Verein-Zeitung* sponsored a photography competition in 1934 that encouraged Jews to photograph synagogues, cemeteries, and other heritage sites to bear witness to "our centuries' long connectedness to the German homeland" (*Central-Verein-Zeitung* 1934). But among non-Jewish Germans, such photographing of Jewish cemeteries did not arise from any interest in historical preservation, nor were the images compiled into photobooks. Rather, it was driven by racist genealogical and demographic considerations: tombstone photographs provided a bureaucratic resource for verifying or disproving Aryan ancestry. The research body responsible for creating these photographic records was the Reich Institute for History of the New Germany (*Reichsinstitut* für *Geschichte des Neuen Deutschlands*), established in 1935 to, in historian Alan Steinweis's description, "infuse a National Socialist perspective into German historical scholarship." In the summer of 1942, the Institute's Research Department for the Jewish Question (*Forschungsabteilung Judenfrage*) began to photograph Jewish cemeteries (Steinweis 2006, 12). The project began with the cemetery in Währing, the 18th district of Vienna, and lasted until at least October 1944. In the interim, the institute produced photographs of cemeteries from Baden-Württemberg, Hamburg, Westfalen, and Lower Saxony. However, this work was not comprehensive—nor did it have to be. Photographing gravestones erected after 1876 was less important, because in that year, the newly unified Germany introduced its system of registry offices (*Standesämter*) to maintain records on births, marriages, and deaths. That bureaucracy could provide information about Jewish ancestry much more efficiently than transcribed and translated photographs of Hebrew headstones ("Gesetz über die Beurkundung des Personenstandes und die Eheschließung" 1875).

For decades after the end of World War II, sustained interest in Jewish heritage in Germany, with its miniscule Jewish population, remained minimal. Consequently, there were hardly any systematic efforts to photograph any of the approximately 2,200 remaining cemeteries (1,900 in the West, 300 in the East). Indeed, cemeteries were more often vandalized than commemorated in photobooks. For instance, historians estimate that between 1945 and 1980, vandals desecrated between 431 and 503 Jewish cemeteries in the Federal Republic, with some episodes generating significant media attention and prison sentences. While cemetery desecration was less common in East Germany, the ignorance of local bureaucrats combined with the absence of influential national Jewish organizations contributed significantly to the decay and neglect of graveyards. It was not until 1992, however, that all desecrations of Jewish cemeteries were categorized as antisemitic acts (Neiss 2010, 92).

However, as part of the broader postwar project of *Vergangenheitsbewältung* (working through the past), attitudes toward Germany's Jewish history were changing by the early 1980s in both East and West, although primarily in the latter. In the East, Cold War politics had long conditioned the approach to creating photographic records of Jewish cemeteries. With their anti-fascist clichés and uncritical, pro-Soviet rhetoric, the few photographically illustrated East German books about Jewish cemeteries that did exist embodied the GDR's institutionalized amnesia toward the Nazi past. Writing in the afterword to *Jüdische Friedhöfe in Berlin* (Jewish cemeteries in Berlin) about Berlin's Weißensee cemetery, one of Europe's largest Jewish burial sites, Secretary for Church Matters (*Staatssekretär* für *Kirchenfragen*) Klaus Gysi wrote that the "The Soviet soldiers' act of liberation is also for our Jewish fellow citizens a liberation in a very personal sense" (Etzold 1980, 62). This tone typifies the sporadic East German photobooks about Jewish cemeteries, especially in the way it obscures continuities between the GDR and the Third Reich and subsumes Holocaust victims under the broader rubric of all victims of fascism.

Figure 5.2. GDR-era book cover depicting the memorial at the entrance to Berlin's Weißensee Cemetery. *Source:* Alfred Etzold, ed., *Jüdische Friedhöfe in Berlin* (Institut für Denkmalpflege, 1980).

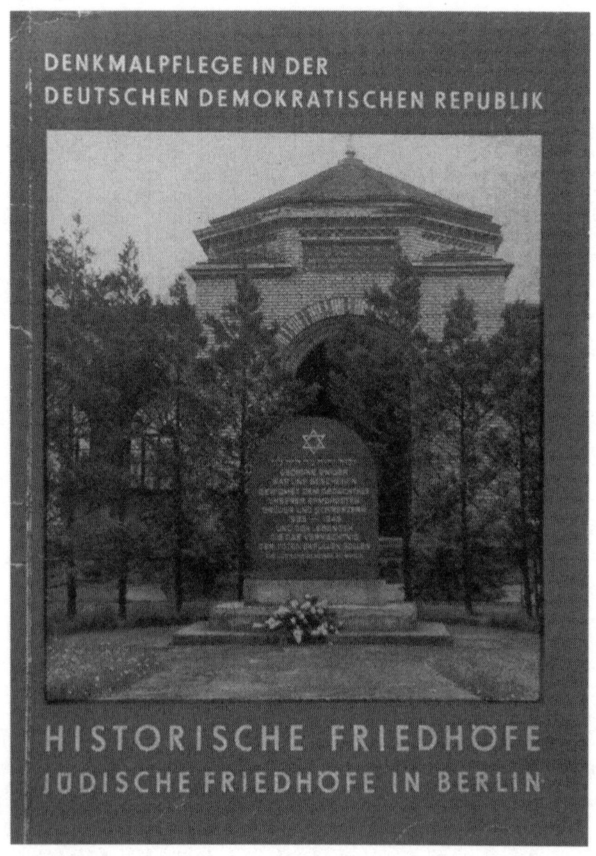

A generalized deployment of photographs contributes to this elision as well. On the cover of one edition, beneath the prominent words "historic preservation in the German Democratic Republic" (*Denkmalpflege in der Deutschen Demokratischen Republik*), one sees a large, tombstone-shaped memorial plaque in front of the similarly shaped entrance building at Berlin's Weißensee cemetery. While the plaque's prominent Star of David and Hebrew explicitly mark this text as Jewish, the monument's inscription describes it as dedicated to the memory of "our murdered brothers and sisters" (*unserer emordeten Brüder und Schwestern*), a vague locution that echoes the universalizing rhetoric of socialist brotherhood. Here, a documentary photograph on a book cover subtly typifies the tendency in the GDR to downplay the Holocaust's ethnic specificity, even as it nominally does just the opposite.

The reorientation toward Jewish history that took place in West Germany in the 1980s, which was usually spearheaded at the local level by civic-minded individuals, was much more significant for the emergence of the type of cemetery photobooks that exhaustively transcribe gravestone inscriptions. In the Federal Republic, memory politics evolved quite differently than in the East. In the Bonn Republic and into the era of reunified Germany, cemetery photobooks emerged and flourished during the "memory boom" of the twentieth century's final decades, a period when, as Jay Winter has argued, "historians young and old . . . found in the subject of memory, defined in a host of ways, the central organizing concept of historical study" (Winter 2001, 57).

One reason for the surge in interest was the development in academic circles of a new orientation toward local history. Particularly among the 1968 generation, curiosity about local memory found one outlet in the turn toward microhistories and history of everyday life (*Alltagsgeschichte*). Specifically, what one might term a "local memory boom" arose from younger Germans' desire to understand—and sometimes expose and atone for—their ancestors' and neighbors' complicity during the National Socialist regime. For instance, among *Geschichtswerkstätten*, the local activist history workshops that emerged to study the history of everyday life, there was recognition of widespread ignorance about Jewish history in Germany that demanded to be addressed (Friest 1989, 248). Rather than focus on grand historical narratives and life in the metropolis, they focused on the places and details that were often ignored as unimportant and could rely on access to local sources, including family photographs, to granularly reconstruct local history. However, the use of photographs in their publications reflected the broader tendency to use photographs primarily as illustration, a state of affairs that lasted at least until the so-called "visual turn," when Holocaust scholarship began to more self-consciously consider, in Sarah Farmer's words, "the particular qualities that make the photographic image function differently than the written documents on which historians traditionally rely" (Farmer 2010, 115).

As a consequence of these popular and academic shifts that opened space for more Jewish perspectives and more work on local history, the trickle of photographically illustrated *jüdische Friedhofsbücher* that began appearing in the 1980s and 1990s grew into a steady stream. The efforts of the Heidelberg-based Central Archives for Research on the History of the Jews in Germany (*Zentralarchiv zur Erforschung der Geschichte der Juden in Deutschland*), a body established by the Central Council of Jews in Germany (*Zentralrat der Juden in Deutschland*), were decisive for this development in its early years. Founded in 1987, this institution began a project to preserve and index Jewish heritage and, between 1987 and 1992, it worked intensively on a photographic documentation of Jewish grave inscriptions, ultimately photographing 53,515 gravestones in 139 cemeteries in West (and later East) Germany. Working both independently and with the *Zentralarchiv* and often at the behest of small towns, specialists, undertook labor-intensive projects for which the goal was "documenting gravestones with at least the most important information about the persons buried there and determining which gravestones are of special cultural-historical significance such that they should be included in the conservation program" (Antmann and Preuß 1996, 232). To this end, they began their work in Baden-Württemberg and, by the time they concluded it, the *Zentralarchiv* possessed photographs of basically all Jewish gravestones in this German state except for a few hundred discovered after the project ended in 1992. The research for each cemetery was presented in the form of standardized, deluxe photobooks. Similar projects have continued to be published ever since this early wave of *jüdische Friedhofsbücher*.

Jewish Inventory, Memorial Inventory, Photographic Inventory

Beyond just examining cemetery books as physical artifacts and historicizing them, but before examining a specific example, it is necessary to analyze what this form of photobook does. "Jewish inventory," a theoretical concept in contemporary Jewish studies, offers a useful lens for this undertaking. The concept helps illuminate these books' twofold function: to document and to memorialize. Inventory refers to, "the creation of a quantified, itemized representation of amassed goods, materials, and artifacts available 'in stock'"

(Kravel-Tovi 2016, 12). As scholars have noted, the practice of making and using inventories has played a formative role in Jewish history, arguably dating back to the first Jewish inventory, the Ten Commandments. In theorizing Jewish inventory, Jeffrey Shandler has convincingly argued that the mere act of making lists about Jewish people, places, words, and things should be counted among the "defining practices of modern Jewish culture," even if it is not usually recognized as such (Shandler 2010). Such list-making spans a wide range of commercial, demographic, eugenicist, political, religious, scientific, and statistical endeavors. From text-based lists documenting the Jewish literary canon to *Schindler's List* to photographic collections of Jewish racial types or visual taxonomies of Chabad houses around the world, one finds a diverse range inventories in Jewish culture (Wisse 2000; Spielberg 1993; Robbins and Becher 2005). Photography's importance in such inventories is tied to the long-standing—if also problematic—tendency to invest the medium with the power to recuperate and document the past in its entirety. In this historicist fantasy, which Siegfried Kracauer critiqued in his 1927 essay "Photography," the photograph offers a spatial continuum that grasps everything that comes before the camera lens, important or not (Kracauer 1995, 50–51). As a representational tool, the camera offers the (false) promise that the past can be fully inventoried and reproduced in a portable format.

Memorials have proven to be especially prominent sites for Jewish counting. Jewish memorial inventorying has a lengthy provenance across the centuries that includes ancient Talmudic notions of a "book of life" that records each person's fate as well as medieval memorial books used to commemorate victims of antisemitic violence. In the second half of the twentieth century, as part of efforts to comprehend the staggering scale of anti-Jewish violence, a myriad of new forms of Jewish memorial inventory emerged as well. These include, for instance, state-sponsored projects like Yad Vashem's Central Database for Shoah Victims' Names, a massive undertaking that aims to catalog all the genocide's casualties (Yad Vashem n.d.). One finds still another common mode of memorial inventory in projects, many of them spearheaded by schoolchildren, that involve the collecting and organizing of a symbolic number (usually 6,000,000) of some object such as coins, buttons, or paper clips (Magilow 2007). Another example, this one from the realm of conceptual art, is Phil Chernofsky's *And Every Single One Was Someone*, a 1,250-page tome that visualizes the scale of the Holocaust by listing the word "Jew" 6,000,000 times (Chernofsky 2013).

Among the many forms of Jewish memorial counting, the compendia known as yizkor books stand out in particular because of the ways they use photographs to document Jewish life before the Holocaust. Usually the product of *landsmanshaftn*, immigrant support societies in Israel, the United States, South America, South Africa, and elsewhere, these yearbook-like publications commemorate Jewish communities, mostly in Poland, that were destroyed during the Holocaust. Central to the genre if not necessarily present in every book, Jonathan Boyarin writes, "are lists of the names of the dead that indicate the close link between the books and the ritual of *yizker* that shares their name" (Boyarin 2010). These necrologies establish personal links between the living and the dead. While they differ in size and scope from short pamphlets to multivolume tomes, yizkor books also recuperate destroyed Jewish communities using narratives of local history, accounts of a town's civic, political, educational, athletic, and religious organizations, biographical sketches of important community members, and, most relevant in this connection, copious photographs of families and local organizations (Horowitz 2011; Kugelmass and Boyarin 1998).

Figure 5.3. Photographs of Jewish life before the Holocaust in Moses Einhorn, *Wolkovisker Yizkor Book*, 1949. The images show (top left) a May Day demonstration on the city's main street, (bottom left) a Jewish soldiers' march, (top right) a group of high school students in 1930, and (bottom right) a group of young women from the town. *Source:* Moses Einhorn, *Wolkovisker Yizkor Book* (self-published, 1949).

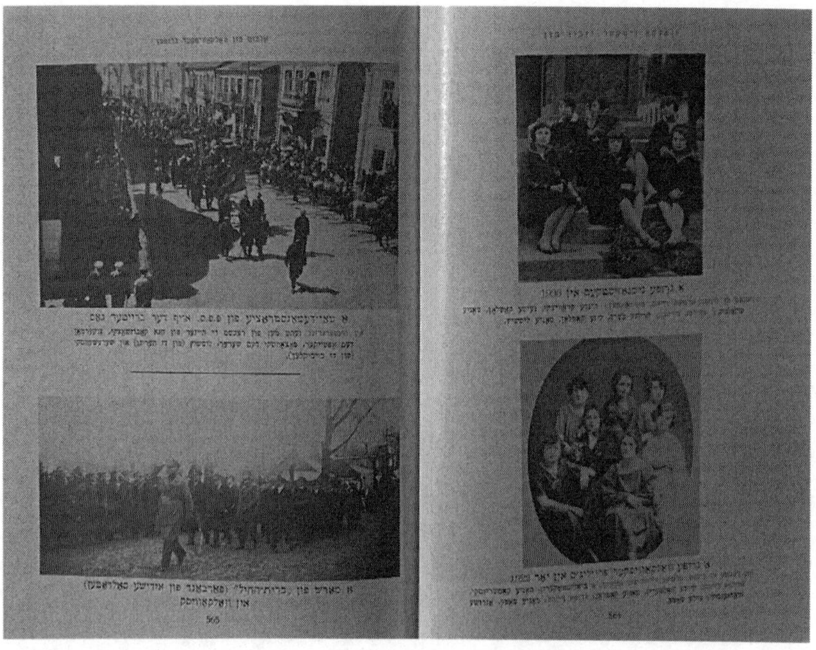

As one can see in a typical illustrated spread from the *Wolkovisker Yizkor Book* of 1949, a representative early postwar example of the genre, the photographs in yizkor books record quotidian Jewish life before the Holocaust (Einhorn 1949). The images depict a May Day demonstration in Volkovysk (today Vawkavysk in Belarus), a march of a Jewish veterans' organization, a group of high school students, and a group of young women. By representing collectives, these photographs stress that Jews had long-standing ties to specific places and institutions. With their candid, vernacular character, they resemble the kinds of images in family albums, and, like family albums, they also enshrine certain values and notions of community (Magilow 2011). Images of harmonious coexistence predominate. These sorts of photographs establish coherence among Jews in the past, create a bridge to that lost age, and represent Jews as people whose history consists of more than just the Holocaust. Commonly offered as gestures of German-Jewish reconciliation, *jüdische Friedhofsbücher* attempt a similar act of temporal bridging. But there is a notable difference: they displace the memory of Jews who were murdered in the Holocaust and deprived funerals onto a memorial inventory of the tombstones for Jews who died before the Holocaust and who did receive proper burials.

Concisely summarizing Shandler's argument about how memorial inventories create collectives, anthropologist Michal Kravel-Tovi distills two key points, both of which aptly describe cemetery photobooks. The first, she writes, is that "inventories are performative, discursive, and conceptual projects [that] constitute the very categories, items, and elements they register. . . . Books, persons, movies, or jokes become 'Jewish' as they are included in 'Jewish' lists; their Jewishness is constructivist rather than essential." And second, inventory is a "technique of cultural salvage, that, by its very undertaking, redeems dispersed items from potential obliviousness or disappearance" (Kravel-Tovi 2016, 13–14). In Shandler's phrasing, the very act of inventorying "betokens something endangered or in need of transformation" (Shandler 2010, 19). Both of these dynamics—positing and thereby constructing Jewish communities and salvaging them—are central to the work cemetery photobooks do in text and photograph, and they are also constitutive of this genre's "Jewishness." Following Kravel-Tovi's argument, the "Jewishness" of Jewish cemetery books is not so much a function of the taking and assembling of standardized photographs of headstones and transcribing and translating their texts. Rather, it inheres the very act of focusing that forensic project toward a subject matter understood historically as Jewish. *Friedhofsbücher* memorialize deceased Jews from across the centuries and reconstitute them as unified wholes.

To affect this keeping of accounts, *jüdische Friedhofsbücher* draw on the lengthy history of using photographs of things and people for inventorying, practices that date back to the medium's early years. William Henry Fox Talbot, the inventor of the positive-negative process known as the calotype (or Talbotype), imagined that inventory would be one of photography's most important uses. For instance, in *The Pencil of Nature* (1844), often considered one of the first photobooks, Fox Talbot included two sharply focused, frontally shot, linearly composed plates of carefully organized sets of expensive objects, *Articles of China* and *Articles of Glass* and emphasized his image's potential value should these objects ever be stolen (Talbot [1844] 1989). To be sure, such nineteenth-century optimism about photographic inventory's benefits finds a counterpart in the camera's use in systems of surveillance and control and in the creation of databases of criminals. John Tagg and Allan Sekula have demonstrated that photography played a critical role in the emergence of the modern industrialized nation-state and was, in Tagg's phrasing, "bound up with the emergence of new institutions and new practices of record keeping" (Tagg 1988, 5; Sekula 1986). Anthropometric and physiognomic projects by Alphonse Bertillon, Cesare Lombroso, Francis Galton, and others were all heavily invested in the notion that massive photographic inventories could predict criminality. Moreover, these sorts of endeavors typified photography's widespread use in creating archives of racial types, a practice that reached an apotheosis in Nazi Germany's racial inventories (Morris-Reich 2016).

The Jewish Graveyard in Freudental

At this point, it is useful to scrutinize the structure, contents, tone, and photographic practices of a single cemetery book to understand the textuality of the genre, that is, to see how, as text-photograph hybrids, this form of Jewish memorial inventory uses photographs to reconstruct and reconstitute German Jewish communities even as they supposedly just document dilapidated cemeteries.

While each *jüdisches Friedhofsbuch* has its idiosyncrasies, the 1996 title *Der jüdische Friedhof in Freudental* for the eponymous Baden-Württemberg village of roughly 2,500 is broadly representative of the genre and thus offers a valuable case study (Bez 1996). The following thick description of its multiple layers of dedications and introductions, didactic texts about Jewish history and culture, maps of cemeteries, and pages upon pages of transcriptions of

Figure 5.4. Cover of the German Jewish cemetery book *Der jüdische Friedhof in Freudental*. *Source:* Ludwig Bez, ed., *Der jüdische Friedhof in Freudental* (Kohlhammer, 1996).

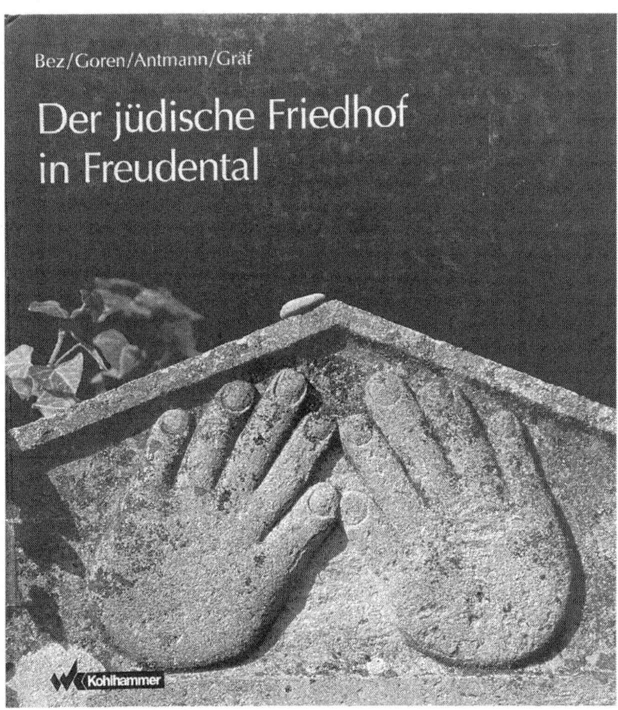

standardized black-and-white tombstone photographs illustrates what these photobooks are and how they mythologize German Jewish communities and retroactively ascribe unto them a historically questionable coherence.

Through text and image, this photobook comprehensively documents one town's long-neglected and long-forgotten Jewish cemetery. As Benigna Schönhagen rightfully stresses in her 1997 review of *Der jüdische Friedhof in Freudental*, "The photographs' quality is notable, as they illuminate the text as much as possible and yet are more than just pure inventory photos, particularly because they are often enlargements that try to convey the look and feel of the tombstones." Schönhagen points to the duality of cemetery books, which, in her words, "fluctuate between sober documentation and an artistically recreated approximation of the quiet cemeteries, remote from settlements, with their mossy, half-eroded tombstones whose peaceful radiance one can hardly elude" (Schönhagen 1997, 412). *Jüdische Friedhofsbücher* like

Der jüdische Friedhof in Freudental are offered as forensic archaeological registers, but through their enlarged, vertically cropped photographs of *matzevot*, they formally resemble tombstones and thus become an affect-eliciting form of memorial inventory.

Der jüdische Friedhof in Freudental was the work of residents of this small village near Stuttgart who, around 1980, began to reexamine their town's long Jewish history. As in many other villages in the region, Jewish life in Freudental dates back centuries (Alemannia Judaica n.d.[a]). In 1731, regulations favorable to Jews led to the establishment of a permanent local Jewish community in Freudental and by 1770, a synagogue had been erected. The first Jewish cemetery, the *alte Friedhof*, had been established in 1723, but Friedrich I of Württemberg ordered it closed in 1811 so that he could have a summer home and royal hunting lodge built there. A report from 1845 describes how headstones were repurposed as building material and how "the Jews watched quietly as the gravestones of their ancestors were used in the construction of a hunting lodge." The second and more recent cemetery, the *neue Friedhof*, served as the main cemetery thereafter for the town's small but proportionately significant Jewish community. By the middle of the nineteenth century, approximately 40 percent of Freudental's inhabitants were Jews. Many worked as farmers and dealers of cattle and textiles. This number declined to approximately 10 percent—50 out of 500—by 1933. On *Kristallnacht* (November 9–10, 1938), SS and SA men armed with axes destroyed the synagogue and set it aflame. Freudental's Jewish community ended on May 4, 1942, when the last remaining Jew, the synagogue *shammes* (sexton) Sigmund Laser, was deported and eventually murdered in the Maly Trostinec concentration camp (Bez 1996, 7). By the end of World War II, all of Freudental's Jews had either emigrated or been murdered (Alemannia Judaica, n.d.[b]).

In 1980, engaged residents established the Registered Society for the Support and Sponsoring of the former Freudental Synagogue (*Förder- und Trägerverein ehemalige Synagoge Freudental e.V.*), which restored the town's old synagogue and transformed it into an educational and cultural center. Ever since, the Pedagogic-Cultural Center of the Former Synagogue (*Pädagogisch-kulturelles Centrum Ehemalige Synagoge Freudental e.V.*) has served as a museum that also publishes books and other materials about Freudental's Jewish heritage (Pädagogisch-Kulturelles Centrum n.d.).

In 1996, the Pedagogic-Cultural Center published *Der jüdische Friedhof in Freudental*. This cemetery photobook begins with several prefaces and didactic texts about Jewish traditions and tombstone iconography that serve multiple and sometimes divergent purposes. It typifies the way that cemetery books combine the functions of memorials and reference books while not committing fully to either genre. The prefatory texts create a highly developed framework intended to guide how readers interpret the formally consistent and thus highly repetitive series of photographs that follows. On the one hand, these texts stress this photobook's documentary importance as a sober, scientific undertaking intended to rehabilitate Freudental's Jewish cemetery and systematically document its eroding gravestones. It is a work of historical preservation. On the other hand, they depart from this scholarly mission by framing the volume with remarks from civic and religious authorities, some affiliated with Jewish organizations. In frequently nostalgic, platitudinous, and ahistorical tones, these officials announce that this compendium is not just an archaeological project, but also a gesture of reconciliation between Germans and Jews, albeit an act of moral accounting that takes place in the latter's absence. These introductory texts confer metaphoric importance to the graves by anthropomorphizing them as a community. They are, in one local official's words, "the oldest, most visible, and most accessible witnesses to German-Jewish culture in Freudental" that open "a door to a world that no longer exists. They tell of the people devoted to Jewish religion, culture, and tradition who lived here for hundreds of years and are a source for understanding history" (Bez 1996, 4). These and subsequent short texts about, for instance, Jewish nomenclature, the differences between the legal names and Hebrew names of the deceased, and name changes born of assimilation (e.g., Krönle became Karoline, Regele became Regina) all indulge in the provincial, nostalgic tone of *Heimat* discourse, which as historian Celia Applegate understands it, "represents the modern imagining and, consequently, remaking of the hometown, not the hometown's own deeply rooted historical reality" (Applegate 1990, 8). By idealizing the histories behind the subsequent formally redundant pages of black-and-white tombstone photographs in this manner, *Der jüdische Friedhof in Freudental* reimagines the village as a multicultural space that some contemporary Freudentalers wish it had been, not as the intolerant place that it regrettably was for much of its history. That intolerance resurfaced in 2007 when the cemetery was vandalized (Alemannia Judaica n.d.[b]).

After the capsule descriptions of the Jewish calendar, numerology, and traditions comes the centerpiece of *Der jüdische Friedhof in Freudental:* pages upon pages of enlarged, annotated photographs of the 435 gravestones in the cemetery. With their standardized, numbered, and information-rich layouts, these images confer rigorous order onto the neglected old graveyard. The entries are grouped two per page, except in the case of several tombstones

Figure 5.5. Representative annotated photographs from *Der jüdische Friedhof in Freudental* showing the tombstones of (top) Rösle Levi and (bottom) Hanna Heumann. *Source:* Ludwig Bez, ed., *Der jüdische Friedhof in Freudental* (Kohlhammer, 1996).

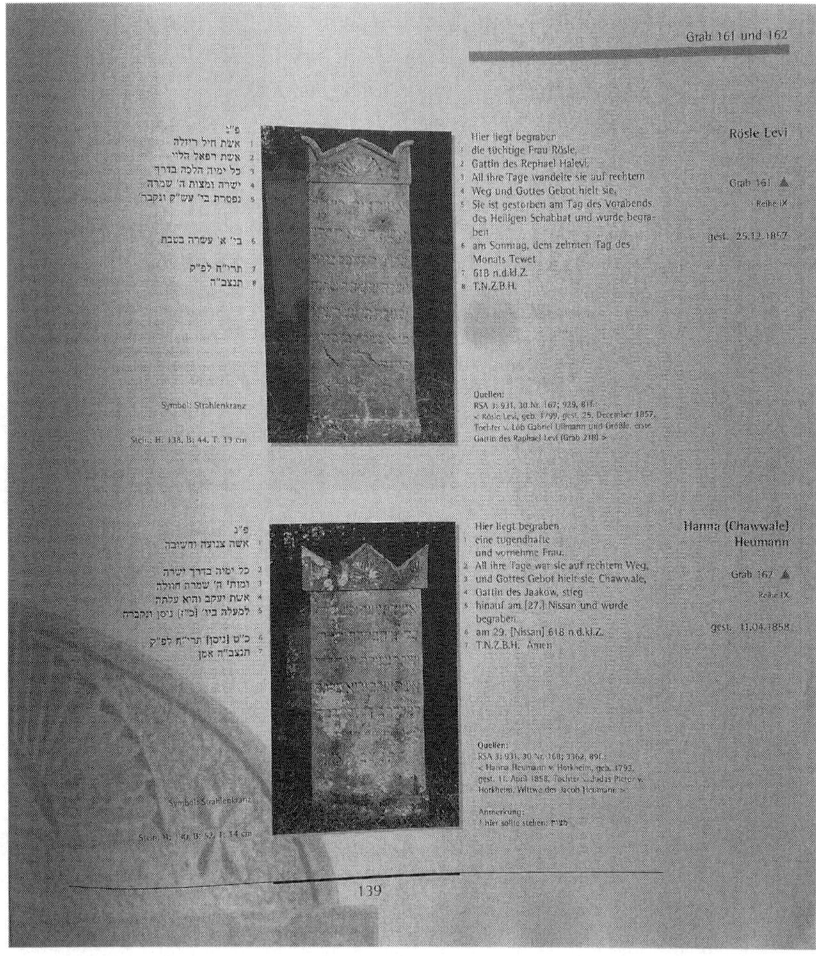

Grab 161 und 162

פ״ט
1 אשת חיל רייזלה
2 אשת רפאל הלוי
3 כל ימיה הלכה בדרך
4 ישרה ומצות ה' שמרה
5 נפטרת בי' עש״ק ונקבר'

6 בי' א' עשרה בטבת

7 תרי״ח לפ״ק
8 תנצב״ה

Symbol: Strahlenkranz

Stein: H: 138, B: 44, T: 13 cm

Hier liegt begraben
1 die tüchtige Frau Rösle,
2 Gattin des Rephael Halevi,
3 All ihre Tage wandelte sie auf rechtem
4 Weg und Gottes Gebot hielt sie,
5 Sie ist gestorben am Tag des Vorabends
  des Heiligen Schabbat und wurde begraben
6 am Sonntag, dem zehnten Tag des
  Monats Tewet
7 618 n.d.Kl.Z.
8 T.N.Z.B.H.

Quellen:
RSA 3: 931, 30 Nr. 167; 929, 81f.:
< Rösle Levi, geb. 1799, gest. 25. December 1857,
Tochter v. Löb Gabriel Ullmann und Größle, erste
Gattin des Raphael Levi (Grab 218) >

Rösle Levi

Grab 161 ▲

Reihe IX

gest. 25.12.1857

פ״נ
1 אשה צנועה והשובה

2 כל ימיה בדרך ישרה
3 ומותי ה' שמרה חוולה
4 אשת יעקב והיא עלתה
5 למעלה ביו' [כ״ז] ניסן ונקברה

6 כ״ט [וניסן] תרי״ח לפ״ק
7 תנצב״ה אמן

Symbol: Strahlenkranz

Stein: H: 140, B: 52, T: 14 cm

Hier liegt begraben
1 eine tugendhafte
  und vornehme Frau,
2 All ihre Tage war sie auf rechtem Weg,
3 und Gottes Gebot hielt sie, Chawwale,
4 Gattin des Jaakow, stieg
5 hinauf am [27.] Nissan und wurde
  begraben
6 am 29. [Nissan] 618 n.d.Kl.Z.
7 T.N.Z.B.H. Amen

Quellen:
RSA 3: 931, 30 Nr. 168; 3362, 89f.:
< Hanna Heumann v. Horkheim, geb. 1793,
gest. 11. April 1858, Tochter v. Judas Pictor v.
Horkheim, Wittwe des Jacob Heumann >

Anmerkung:
1 hier sollte stehen: חוולה

Hanna (Chawwale)
Heumann

Grab 162 ▲

Reihe IX

gest. 11.04.1858

139

whose lengthy text inscriptions justify that they take up their own page. Each grave entry includes a photograph and lists the name of the deceased, the date of death, and the row and number of the tombstone. Hebrew and German transcriptions appear, respectively, to the left and right of each photograph, while other notations record the headstones' dimensions and identify its iconography. Beneath each image is an entry citing additional sources with biographical information, including family relationships with others buried in the cemetery.

For instance, page 139 of *Der jüdische Friedhof in Freudental* presents two photographs against the backdrop of a large, faded detail image of the *Strahlenkranz* (nimbus or halo) of a tombstone. According with the format of all the book's tombstone images, the black-and-white photographs are sharply focused, frontally lit, and cropped closely into rectangles. The tombstones cover almost the entire image space. The close-up shooting angle enlarges the text, which makes the inscriptions and any ornamentation highly legible. The top photograph shows grave 161 and the adjacent text translates its Hebrew: "Here lies buried / the excellent woman Rösle / spouse of Raphael Halevi. / She behaved properly all of her days /and obeyed God's command. / She died on the eve / of the holy Sabbath and was buried / on Saturday, the tenth day of the month of Tewet / 618 n.d.k.Z / T.N.Z.B.H." The three-digit number "618" followed by the acronym לפ״ק, translated as n.d.kl.Z or *Nach der kleinen Zahlung* ("using the short form"), indicates that the year occurred within the current millennium in the Jewish calendar. In this case, 618 thus means 5618, or 1858. T.N.Z.B.H. is the abbreviation for the religious formula תנצב״ה (*Tehi nishmato tzrura btzror hachayim*), "May her soul be bound up in the bond of life." The entry lists the headstone's dimensions as 138 cm tall × 44 cm wide, and 13 cm deep, and identifies the symbol on it as a *Strahlenkranz*. The entry also cross-references Nazi-era records of the Reich Kinship Office (*Reichssippenamt*, RSA), the bureaucratic entity ultimately tasked with deciding who was or was not Jewish (Schulle 2001). It describes the deceased as "Rösle Levi, born 1799, died December 25, 1857, daughter of Löb Gabriel Ullmann and Größle, the first spouse of Raphael Levi (Grave 218)."

The close-up photograph below on the same page is formally identical. It, too, is cropped such that the tombstone covers most of the image, which transforms the photograph into a metonymy for the tombstone. The rectangular composition, frontal lighting, and sharp focus are again intended to make the inscription and the crown-shaped ornament atop the tombstone visible and legible. The tombstone's enlarged text reads: "Here lies buried / a virtuous / and elegant woman. / She was on the right path all of her days / and obeyed God's command. Chawwale, / wife of Jaakow, passed / on the twenty-seventh of Nissan and was / buried / on the twenty-ninth of Nissan 618 n.d.kl.Z. / T.N.Z.B.H. Amen." The annotations again list the measurements (130 × 52 × 14 cm), designate the symbol as a *Strahlenkranz,* and cross-reference another source for biographical data ("Hanna Heumann v. Horkheim, born 1793, died April 11, 1858, daughter of Judas Pictor v. Horkheim, Widow of Jacob Heumann"). Another note corrects an orthographic mistake in the Hebrew inscription. These formally identical photographs render more than 400 gravestones in the cemetery legible. Through their sheer volume and repetitive character, they bespeak the tremendous amount of archaeological and epigraphic work necessary to produce a book like *Der jüdische Friedhof in Freudental*.

Following the dozens of pages of tombstone photographs is a curious photograph depicting a tombstone-like memorial erected in 1988 to Jewish Freudentalers who were war veterans (see fig. 5.6). "To the memory of

Figure 5.6. Photograph of a monument in the Freudental cemetery dedicated to Jewish citizens of Freudental who died in the First World War, from *Der jüdische Friedhof in Freudental. Source:* Ludwig Bez, ed., *Der jüdische Friedhof in Freudental* (Kohlhammer, 1996).

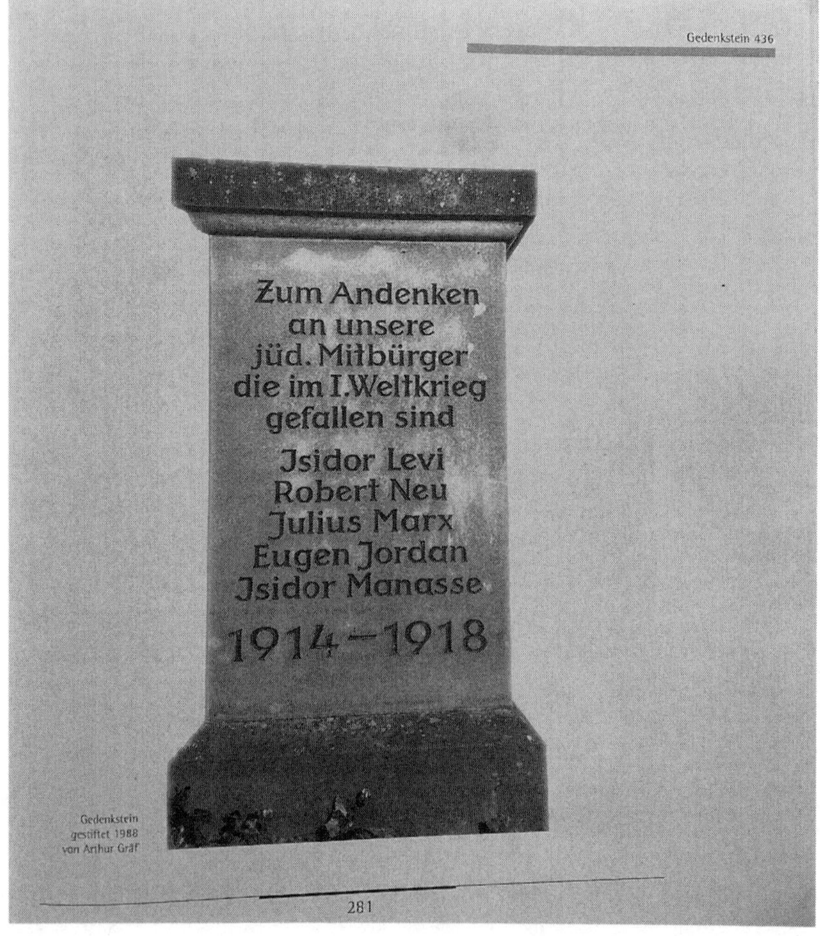

our Jewish fellow citizens who died in the First World War: Isidor Levi, Robert Neu, Julius Marx, Eugen Jordan, Isidor Manasse, 1914–1918." This photograph of the memorial is notable for several reasons. Like the larger tombstones that take up entire pages because of their long inscriptions, this photograph also covers the whole page. It is framed against a completely white background, which makes it appear as though the photograph had been cut out and pasted onto the page, like a photomontage. The absence of background gives it a sense of being detached, even stranded. The memorial's text mentions the last Jew buried in the cemetery: Julius Marx, an émigré who died in 1970 and was repatriated to his native Freudental for burial. However, this photograph of a memorial is not actually an image of a remnant of the old cemetery, but an act of counterfactual historical revisionism. The memorial imagines a more tolerant Freudental in which the town's own residents might have created such memorials to honor Jewish soldiers who died as German patriots, and thus like the photograph of the memorial tombstone itself, suspended against a white background, it is divorced from history. It hypothesizes a village where conservative notions of *Heimat* are not incommensurate with religious and ethnic diversity.

Accessing Jewish Life through Jewish Death

Multiple imperatives animate the ongoing production of German Jewish cemetery books: to recuperate local German Jewish histories, preserve fragile cultural heritage, atone for the Shoah, educate younger generations, and effect reconciliation between the descendants of shattered communities with descendants of the perpetrators. These motives are sincere and well-intended, and hundreds of forensic tombstone photographs are the means to this end. These photographs authenticate, document, validate, and atone for German Jewish history. But as Maxim Biller recognized in his literary sketch "Eggs," this unique form of photobook nevertheless remains the material deposit of an ongoing, continuously renegotiated, and frequently awkward relationship that displaces a past that cannot be reconstructed—the anonymous murder of German Jews—onto one that can.

Formally, this displacement is visible in the Russian doll–like nested layers that render this genre an example of what psychoanalyst Jacques Lacan described as metonymic displacement. That is, from the specific, individual tombstone photographs all the way up to the broader level of the entire genre, cemetery photobooks create a chain of attempts to compensate for absences. For instance, each *gravestone* is a sign of the absent (i.e., no longer alive) body interred underneath it. The *representations of the gravestones*, the photographs, in turn point to another absence: the lack of proper burials for genocide's victims, which has been displaced onto the gravesite of someone who was in fact afforded such a burial decades earlier. Using photographs of the gravestones of their ancestors, a memorial is created for descendants whose only resting spot was, to invoke Paul Celan's iconic poem "Death Fugue" (*Todesfuge*), "a grave in the clouds" (*ein Grab in den Wolken*). The *memorial inventory*, the collection of these photographic representations of gravestones (i.e., the cemetery book), uses a long-neglected and vandalized graveyard to compensate for still another loss, the destroyed small-town Jewish community. And in its entirety, the *genre of the memorial inventories of the representations of gravestones* becomes a kind of collective, symbolic tombstone for all absent victims of the Shoah. If, as Jacques Lacan argued, desire hides within the metonymic displacements of language, then this chain of displacements that inhabits the photographic inventory of *jüdische Friedhofsbücher*, as a form of language, draws attention to the manifest desire to resurrect and properly memorialize destroyed Jewish lives and communities (Lacan 2005, 431). But in the wake of the Holocaust, one wonders if this desire can ever be fulfilled or if it leads only to a void and the sorts of awkward interactions depicted in Maxim Biller's "Eggs."

Using cemeteries and photographs of their gravestones to access and inventory Jewish history is problematic and overdetermined because Jewish lives are framed as something to be accessed through Jewish death. But in this regard, cemetery books are not unique. To the contrary, they participate in a long-standing and sometimes-criticized tendency in Holocaust studies that reduces research into German Jewish history to a kind of mortuary work or body counting. Rejecting this approach and writing with reference to the neglect and desecration of Jewish synagogues, cemeteries, and memory in Galicia (Ukraine), Omer Bartov has argued "that studying the manner in which the Jews were killed told one very little about the manner in which the Jews had lived; in fact, it brought them into history for the sole purpose of depicting their extermination" (Bartov 2007, xi). But the focus in cemetery books on the dead as the way to recuperate the living is only one reason they are conceptually problematic.

Another reason is that for all their noble intentions, *jüdische Friedhofsbücher* embody a discontinuity between the agents of memory (deceased Jews from the nineteenth and early twentieth centuries) and the objects of memory (their descendants and other Jews murdered in the Holocaust). Cemetery books seek to overcome a rupture in tradition using photographic inventory. But the rupture may simply be unbridgeable because the remnants of the tradition are scant. One can reasonably ask if the well-intended gesture of documenting and rehabilitating neglected Jewish graveyards through photography has the unintended side-effect of reifying, exoticizing, and essentializing Jews. Cemetery books do not—cannot—provide a sense of closure to the cataclysm of the Holocaust. They can gesture in this direction, but, in the end, they remain mere paper tombstones.

Works Cited

Alemannia Judaica. n.d.(a). "Freudental (Kreis Ludwigsburg) Texte / Berichte zur jüdischen Geschichte des Ortes." Accessed January 19, 2025. http://www.alemannia-judaica.de/freudental_texte.htm.

———. n.d.(b). "Freudental (Landkreis Ludwigsburg) Jüdische Geschichte / Betsaal/ Synagoge." Accessed January 19, 2025. http://www.alemannia-judaica.de/freudental_synagoge.htm.

Antmann, S. Michal, and Monika Preuß. 1996. "Das Projekt zur Erfassung jüdischer Grabsteine in Baden-Württemberg." *Denkmalpflege in Baden-Württemberg—Nachrichtenblatt der Landesdenkmalpflege* 25 (4): 231–43.

Applegate, Celia. 1990. *A Nation of Provincials: The German Idea of Heimat.* University of California Press.

Bartov, Omer. 2007. *Erased: Vanishing Traces of Jewish Galicia in Present Day Ukraine.* Princeton University Press.

Bez, Ludwig, ed. 1996. *Der jüdische Friedhof in Freudental.* Kohlhammer.

Biller, Maxim. 2005. *Moralische Geschichten.* Kiepenhauer & Witsch.

Boyarin, Jonathan. 2010. "Yizker-bikher." *The YIVO Encyclopedia of Jewish Eastern Europe.* https://yivoencyclopedia.org/article.aspx/Yizker-bikher.

Central-Verein-Zeitung. 1934. "Unser Amateur-Photo-Wettbewerb." June 21.

Chase, Jefferson. 2001. "Shoah Business: Maxim Biller and the Problem of Contemporary German-Jewish Literature." *German Quarterly* 74 (2): 111–31.

Chernofsky, Phil. 2013. *And Every Single One Was Someone.* Gefen.

Cohn, Gustav. 1930. *Der jüdische Friedhof: Seine geschichtliche und kulturgeschichtliche Entwicklung.* Verlag Franzmathes.

Corbett, Tim. 2018. "Gustav Cohn's Jewish Cemetery: A Cultural History." *Leo Baeck Institute Year Book* 63:299–318.

Einhorn, Moses, ed. 1949. *Wolkovisker Yizkor Book.* Self-published.

Etzold, Alfred, ed. 1980. *Jüdische Friedhöfe in Berlin.* Institut für Denkmalpflege.

Farmer, Sarah. 2010. "Going Visual: Holocaust Representation and Historical Method." *American Historical Review* 115 (1): 115–22.

Friest, Dagmar. 1989. "Alltagsgeschichte der Juden: In Search of New Approaches to Jewish History." *German History* 7 (2): 248–52.

"Gesetz über die Beurkundung des Personenstandes und die Eheschließung." 1875. *Deutsches Reichsgesetzblatt* 4:23–40.

Horowitz, Rosemary, ed. 2011. *The Memorial Books of Eastern European Jewry: Essays on the History and Meanings of Yizker Volumes.* McFarland.

Jeřábek, Lubomir. (1903) 2009. *Der alte Prager Judenfriedhof.* Reprint. Karolinum.

Kidron, Carol A. 2016. "Breathing Life into Iconic Numbers: Yad Vashem's Shoah Victims' Names Recovery Project and the Constitution of a Posthumous Census of Six Million Holocaust Dead." In *Taking Stock: Cultures of Enumeration in Contemporary Jewish Life,* edited by Michal Kravel-Tovi and Deborah Dash Moore. Indiana University Press.

Kugelmass, Jack, and Jonathan Boyarin, eds. 1998. *From a Ruined Garden: The Memorial Books of Polish Jewry.* 2nd ed. Indiana University Press.

Kracauer, Siegfried. 1995. "Photography." In *The Mass Ornament: Weimar Essays,* edited by Thomas Y. Levin. Harvard University Press.

Kravel-Tovi, Michal. 2016. Introduction to *Taking Stock,* edited by Michal Kravel-Tovi and Deborah Dash Moore. Indiana University Press.

Lacan, Jacques. 2005. *Écrits.* 1st complete Eng. ed. Translated by Bruce Fink. Norton.

Magilow, Daniel H. 2007. "Counting to Six Million: Collecting Projects and Holocaust Memorialization." *Jewish Social Studies* 14 (1): 23–39.

———. 2011. "Yizker Books and Photographic Form." In *The Memorial Books of Eastern European Jewry: Essays on the History and Meanings of Yizker Volumes,* edited by Rosemary Horowitz. McFarland.

Mannheimer, Moses. 1842. *Die Juden in Worms, ein Beitrag zur Geschichte der Juden in den Rheingegenden.* Frankfurt/Main.

Morris-Reich, Amos. 2016. *Race and Photography: Racial Photography as Scientific Evidence, 1876–1980.* University of Chicago Press.

Neiss, Marion. 2010. "Friedhofsschändungen." In *Handbuch des Antisemitismus: Judenfeindschaft in Geschichte und Gegenwart: Begriffe, Theorien, Ideologien,* edited by Brigitte Mihok and Wolfgang Benz. De Gruyter Saur.

Pädagogisch-Kulturelles Centrum Ehemalige Synagoge Freudental. n.d. "Geschichte der Synagoge." Accessed January 19, 2025. https://web.archive.org/web/20240808134945/https://pkc-freudental.de/archive/197.

Robbins, Andrea, and Max Becher. 2005. "770." In *The Jewish Identity Project: New American Photography,* edited by Susan Chevlove. Yale University Press.

Roemer, Nils. 2006. "Between the Provinces and the City: Mapping German-Jewish Memories." *Leo Baeck Institute Year Book* 51:61–77.

Rosenblum, Naomi. 1984. *A World History of Photography.* Abbeville Press.

Schönhagen, Benigna. 1997. Review of *Der jüdische Friedhof in Freudental,* edited by Ludwig Bez et al. and *Der jüdische Friedhof in Schwäbisch Hall Steinbach,* edited by the Stadtverwaltung Schwäbisch Hall. *Schwäbische Heimat* 48 (4): 411–12.

Schulle, Diana. 2001. *Das Reichssippenamt: Eine Institution nationalsozialistischer Rassenpolitik.* Logos Verlag.

Sekula, Allan. 1986. "The Body and the Archive." *October* 39:3–64.

Shandler, Jeffrey. 2010. *Keepers of Accounts: The Practice of Inventory in Modern Jewish Life.* David W. Belin Lecture in American Jewish Affairs 17. Frankel Center for Judaic Studies, University of Michigan.

Spielberg, Steven, dir. 1993. *Schindler's List.* Universal Pictures Home Entertainment.

Steinweis, Alan. 2006. *Studying the Jew: Scholarly Antisemitism in Nazi Germany.* Harvard University Press.

Talbot, William Henry Fox (1844) 1989. *The Pencil of Nature.* Reprint edited by Larry Schaaf. Hans P. Kraus, Jr.

Tagg, John. 1988. *The Burden of Representation: Essays on Photographies and Histories.* University of Massachusetts Press.

Wiesemann, Falk. 2005. *Sepulcra Judaica: Bibliographie zu jüdischen Friedhöfen und zu Sterben, Begräbnis und Trauer bei den Juden von der Zeit des Hellenismus bis zur Gegenwart.* Klartext Verlag.

Winter, Jay. 2001. "The Generation of Memory: Reflections on the 'Memory Boom' in Contemporary Historical Studies." *Canadian Military History* 10 (3): 57–66.

Wisse, Ruth. 2000. *The Modern Jewish Canon: A Journey through Language and Culture.* Free Press.

Wolff, Fabian. 2015. "Something Off." *Jewish Review of Books,* no. 23 (Fall). https://jewishreviewofbooks.com/articles/1869/something-off/.

Yad Vashem. n.d. "About the Shoah Victims' Names Recovery Project." Accessed January 19, 2025. https://www.yadvashem.org/remembrance/names-recovery-project/about.html.

Chapter 6

Displaced and Dreaming in Postwar Germany

The Lure of the Motorcycle and the Briefcase

DORA APEL

Telling our stories helps reveal who we are. The ongoing construction of memory through the interpretation of family photographs contributes to both a personal and a collective way of knowing that helps us discover new meaning about the past and thereby alters contemporary Jewish memory. Although Jewish identity is inevitably inflected by the Holocaust, those of us born later only know the past through representation—films, texts, testimonies, stories, and photographs. We remember the atrocities suffered but also the resistance and the resilience, which has the potential to evoke memory activism in the form of political struggle against ongoing oppression and persecution (Assmann and Conrad 2010; Apel 2020).

In this chapter, I present a family memoir from 1945 to the early 1950s, using family photographs to tell a story about my parents as Holocaust survivors and how they might have imagined their future lives while living in German displaced persons (DP) camps. As memory studies scholars have demonstrated, seeing through the eyes of others helps us to empathize with those whose experiences may be very different from our own, but who embody and connect us to larger communities and histories (Hirsch 1997, 2012; Grossmann 2012, 2021; Landsberg 2004; Apel 2002, 2020). While some historians tend to use images to illustrate history, my purpose here is to read family photographs in order to place the personal on a continuum with the collective, to connect the private with the cultural. As Patricia Holland observes, "A concern with local and family histories, women's history, the history of everyday life and history from below has given a new significance to personal pictures as historical documents" (Holland 2009, 122).

Since the photograph as an object is not commensurate with the subject pictured, the photograph must be understood as a construction based on choices made by the persons who may be pictured, the photographer, and the viewer. The photo therefore produces meaning in a variety of ways: through composition, location, and lighting; by what is included as well as excluded; by clothing, decor, body language, and facial expression. Vernacular photos reflect the agency of the photographer who frames the image and the agency of the people who help determine their own representation at the instant the camera clicks. But neither can control all the circumstances or how the photo may be interpreted by a future viewer. Strangers, for example, may know little of a subject or the surrounding circumstances, while family members may know a great deal. Photographs thus do not speak for themselves and may produce different meanings at different times and in different arenas. They may raise questions that can never be answered. But as they enter the matrix of personal and cultural remembrance, the way they are interpreted and reinterpreted over time may change our view of the past, of the subjects and events pictured, and even of ourselves.

Although the past at issue here is the subject of surviving Jews immediately following the Holocaust, I would argue that there is nothing distinctively "Jewish" about the photographs themselves as aesthetic objects despite the fact that the subjects are Jewish and, most likely, so are the anonymous photographers. Yet we might see yearnings and desires that are distinctly Jewish, if not only Jewish, at this moment in history, when the joy of survival, mixed with the grief of loss, underlay the pictured personas of a traumatized generation of European Jews forced to contend with suffering, catastrophe, and the need to forge a new life.

Though I have been familiar with these photographs all my life, I never discussed them with my parents and have only recently come to study and understand them in new ways. In some, taken immediately after the war, the traumatic shock of war is still visible; in others, taken a few years later, my mother and father are pictured separately while living as displaced persons in Munich, each with an object or "attribute" that offers a critical clue to their sense of themselves, their hopes and aspirations for their lives to come at a transitional moment open to self-reinvention.

For a Holocaust survivor, the years of living as a displaced person were a kind of interzone, a limbo of time when who you were before no longer mattered and who you were going to become, if you were relatively young, was indeterminate and open-ended. Their past lives as they had expected to live them were gone and the future was unknown. It was a time of grief, anxiety, and suspense, but also a time of renewed living, of trying to prepare yourself for an uncertain future after seeing your former life wrecked. The story of the Jews in the DP camps has unfolded in all its complexity only recently (Dwork and Van Pelt 2009; Patt and Berkowitz 2010; Shephard 2011; Cohen 2012; Nasaw 2020).

At the least, you might be willing to imagine, to pretend. You might perch atop a motorbike with your young son as if you could see yourself taking off down the street like a free spirit unburdened by the ghosts of the dead.

My mother Ethel is about forty-four and my brother Max almost four years old. I wasn't born yet. My brother lightly grips the handlebars while my mother merely reaches with straightened fingers to touch the end of

Figure 6.1. Ethel Apel with her son Max, Gabersee DP camp, Munich, 1950. *Source:* Courtesy Dora Apel.

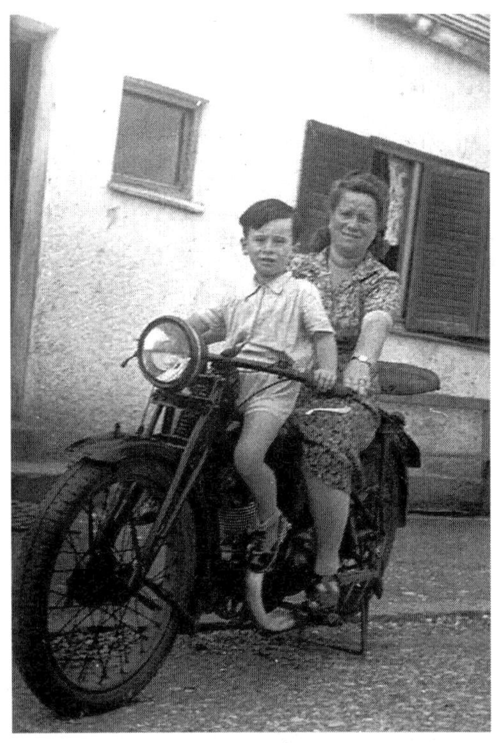

the bar. Max looks a bit discontented; perhaps he is annoyed at having to share this moment on the motorbike with his mother. He smiles in another photo where he is perched on the bike alone. My mother's expression is one of indulgent amusement and ambivalence, a hint of impatience or discomfort etched in her furrowed brow. Taken in the summer of 1950, it seems likely that she gamely mounted the motorcycle in her flowered dress and sandals, her light brown hair arranged in the fashion of the day, only for the purpose of taking this photo with her young son, as if they were going on an adventure.

With my father, Samuel, my mother and brother lived in displaced persons camps in Germany for about five years. My father had escaped the German advance into Poland and crossed the river Bug into the USSR, leaving behind a wife and child when they thought only the men would be in danger. He was deported to a slave labor camp in Siberia. His wife and child soon went into hiding but were denounced and murdered. My mother also fled Poland with her first husband, who died of typhus shortly thereafter; she was evacuated from the border region to Bukhara in the Uzbek Soviet Socialist Republic. There she and my father eventually joined forces and made their way back to Hrubieszów, their hometown in Poland, as the war came to an end.

There were seven million people who lived in DP camps across Europe in the first year after the war ended. These included former forced laborers, prisoners of war, partisans who had fought against the Nazis, concentration camp survivors, and people who had fled or hidden, including the 200,000 Jews who survived the war in the Soviet Union, my parents among them. The DP camps also included Nazi collaborators. The majority of DPs were soon repatriated to their home countries, but almost a million people no longer had a place to go (Nasaw 2020).

In Germany, the Jewish DPs lived in some 200 camps established by the American, British, and Russian powers that occupied Germany after the war. Conditions were harsh and crowded and food was rationed. The camps remained under the control of the Allied military, but the United Nations Relief and Rehabilitation Authority (UNRRA) eventually managed operations, while Jewish voluntary organizations delivered supplementary food and supplies. The sudden growth of a Jewish population in Germany in the immediate postwar period, however, meant this devastated and homeless population now had to live among the perpetrators, who did not welcome them. Having to contend with their own harsh postwar conditions, many Germans viewed the Jews with fear, contempt, resentment, and hatred. But the DPs adapted and developed a vibrant life in the camps, electing central committees and organizing congresses. Some of the larger camps had their own newspapers, theater groups, sports clubs, and competitions.

The DP camps also had their own assigned photographers who photographed everyday life, especially in the American and British occupation zones administered by UNRRA. They depicted diverse aspects of daily life such as school, work, recreation, holidays, celebrations, and activities sponsored by Jewish voluntary organizations (Center for Jewish History n.d.). In many camps, photographs would then be sold to camp residents (West 2014, 179). The Central Jewish Historical Commission, organized immediately after the war, began collecting thousands of documents and photographs of Jewish survivors, including those taken in DP camps, and there are now many photographic archives and collections (Nasaw 2020, 78–82).

In one such DP camp photo in my parents' possession, an apparent celebratory group dinner, a felt sense of community is evident among those gathered, including young couples with children. There was a huge marriage boom followed by a huge baby boom among Jewish survivors, with the Jewish DP birth rate among the highest in the world. The effort to put children into the frame, as seen here, spoke to the determination of surviving Jews to compensate for their losses by creating new families and

Figure 6.2. Ethel and Samuel Apel, back row on the right, Schlachtensee DP camp gathering, 1946. *Source:* Courtesy Dora Apel.

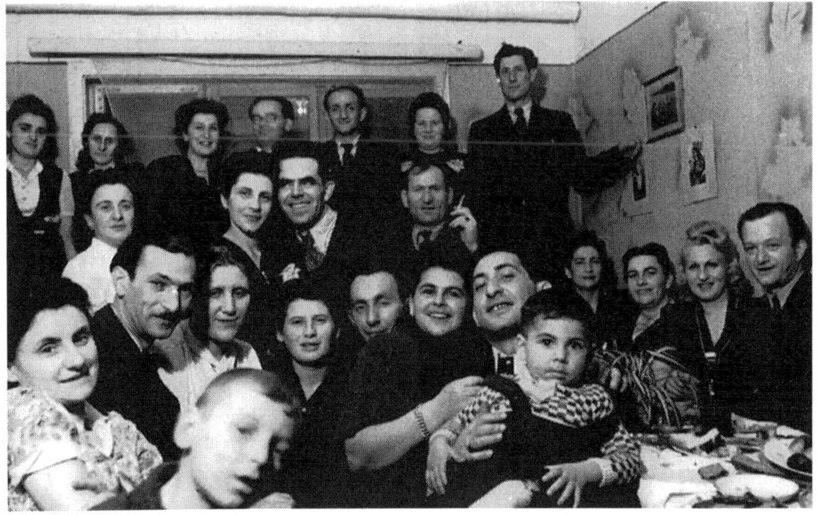

generations (Grossmann 2009, 188–93). As Atina Grossmann notes, precisely because the Nazis had "prioritized the annihilation of women, children, and the 'unfit,' life was reborn and identity remade through the reconstruction of gendered roles and sexed healthy bodies" (Grossmann 2007, 204). The focus here is on healthy, strong bodies and young mothers and fathers with well-fed children. People crowd together, some cheek to cheek, also suggesting their desire for closeness and support.

My mother, too, was pregnant at the time of this photo, though her body is blocked from view as my parents stand at the back in the right corner. They were overjoyed with the extra rations for pregnant women, she later told me, more than with the pregnancy itself, for which she would not have the support of her murdered mother and sisters. Without Jewish doctors or female relatives they could rely on for help, pregnancy necessarily brought Jewish women into contact with German doctors and nurses, which traumatized my mother further when she gave birth to my brother. Just as she was losing consciousness under ether for a C-section, she heard the nurse say to the doctor, "You know she's Jewish" (Apel 2020). In the photo, both of my parents seem a bit aloof from the party, and my father, towering above the group, perhaps not entirely prepared for impending fatherhood, extends his arm along the wall as if searching for something solid and steady to hold onto.

Of the approximately 250,000 Jews in DP camps, less than 57,000 were allowed to immigrate to the United States, my parents among them (Nasaw 2020, 532). The number surely would have been higher if the United States had welcomed refugees for resettlement, but the US immigration law of 1924 severely restricted immigrants by country of origin and imposed other restrictions. Special efforts to allow in Jewish war refugees were opposed by Republicans and southern Democrats who embraced Judeo-Bolshevik conspiracy theories, which suggested that those who had lived in the Soviet Union were likely Communist sympathizers or secret spies. They demanded that such refugees be barred from entering the United States. The Displaced Persons Act finally passed by Congress in 1948 was highly discriminatory, granting visas only to those who were reliably anti-Communist, including those who had collaborated with Nazi occupation forces, served in Waffen-SS units, or committed other war crimes, though this was not publicly revealed for another three decades. The majority of Jews who had survived the war in the Soviet Union ultimately went to Israel (Nasaw 2020, 12–13).

My brother was born in the DP camp in Berlin called the Düppel Center by the Americans but known as Schlachtensee to the DPs, after a nearby S-Bahn station. It was the largest camp in the American zone in Berlin and closed in 1948. My parents and brother were then transferred to Camp Gabersee in the Munich district, which closed in June 1950. They then went to Camp Grohn, a former US military base in Bremen, with a stop along the way at Camp Wildflecken. From Bremerhaven (the city's harbor), they departed for the US in December 1950 on the USS General Harry Taylor, according to the Statue of Liberty-Ellis Island Foundation ship manifest records.

An assigned camp photographer in all likelihood took the photo of my mother and brother on the motorbike. Though my parents are no longer available to answer questions, it nonetheless seems possible to learn something about this seemingly hopeful moment of displaced living for Jews in postwar Germany by examining the visual evidence of those who are pictured and even those who are not.

As far as I know, my parents never owned a motorbike, nor, more importantly, would my mother have ridden one. Indeed, the mother I grew up with would have been terrified to ride a motorcycle, especially with her young son. She was highly cautious, risk-averse, not particularly athletic, and intensely overprotective of her children. She did not even drive a car, finally getting her license at the age of fifty-two, a venture that didn't last long. Though she would creep down the road, never going more than thirty miles per hour, she somehow lost control of the car one day and landed at the top of a steep hill, embarrassed and unable to explain how she had gotten there. The car had to be towed back down to the road. My brother, father, and I agreed she should give up driving and she meekly complied; I suspect she was relieved.

Yet this black and white photo with deteriorating white edges, recalling the first half of the twentieth century, pictures a different woman. Motorcycles were widely deployed in Germany and her pose echoes that of mostly young and adventurous men, including Wehrmacht soldiers, who proudly presented themselves for the camera on their riding machines. In the presence of her child, my mother, a bit hesitant and uncomfortable, tries to present herself as the kind of woman who might defiantly ride a motorcycle, a woman who is daring and independent, not the sheltered young woman who grew up in a strictly Orthodox home. Among many such women, the rupture of their lives and their traumatic war experiences undermined long-held beliefs and conventions, including for my mother. In this moment, despite whatever doubts and misgivings she may have, she seems to claim agency as a free Jewish woman at a time when limited agency could be had. She is a woman who might hop on a motorbike and throw caution to the wind, who might fashion herself to be whatever she wanted to be. "If I had been born in America," she would later say, "I would have been somebody. I would have gone to college and studied math or bookkeeping or accounting."

Displaced persons lived in a kind of interregnum between life as they knew it before and what would come after. We might see it as a form of suspended animation. Though my parents had endured the physical and emotional suffering of war, the shock of losing their families and homes—in this photo on the motorcycle, taken only a few years later, you would not guess any of this. After shrinking to eighty-six pounds during her years of deprivation and starvation in the Soviet Union, the first six weeks of which were spent sleeping on public benches while terrified of being imprisoned by the NKVD (Soviet state security agency), in this photo my mother has doubled her weight to a well-rounded girth and projects a calm and placid demeanor. The pain is now invisible. She is dressed and groomed like a respectable bourgeois woman, a woman who wears a flowered dress with a silver pin on her collar and a watch with a metal band, a woman who is confident enough to pose astride a motorbike as if she owned that too. How did she acquire this finery so shortly after losing everything?

Like many others in postwar Germany, my father began to trade on the black market. As David Nasaw explains, most trading was small-scale for food items, with cigarettes, soap, chewing gum, and items from Red Cross packages constituting the primary form of currency. But every camp also had larger operators who accumulated items such as jewelry and other portable wealth that would help them start a new life elsewhere and easily could be converted to money anywhere (Nasaw 2020, 149). My father was one of those operators. Eventually he acquired a diamond necklace, gold bracelet, and diamond rings for my mother; a gold-trimmed set of Rosenthal China; two sets of crystal wine decanters and glasses, one light and one a deep wine-color; a silver candelabra; a silver menorah with a set of lions whose heads opened for the insertion of oil and cotton wicks; and a set of sterling silver flatware. My parents even covered some of their teeth in gold, as was fashionable then. Along with these treasures, my mother preserved what photos she could of her family and brought those with her to America, too. There are no photos of my father's prewar family. Having grown up poor, they most likely never owned a camera.

Those black-market goods with which my father bejeweled his wife and made enough money to start their new life in America perhaps included items confiscated from Jews during the war. Perhaps this was the case with the pin and the watch. Did the Jews who traded on the black market consider this? Did it matter? Or was it seen as a way of redeeming the historical injustice by transforming such goods into a means of survival and defiant living?

Where is my father when the photo was taken of my mother and brother on the motorcycle? There is a second photo of my brother alone on the bike but none of my father. Why didn't he assume the masculine-defined role of motorcycle rider?

Perhaps he wasn't there that day. But I think there is another reason my father is absent from this photo even if he was present. If my mother aspired to physical courage and fierce independence from religious strictures, my father sought a level of intellectual achievement and cultural refinement that was taken out of his reach when he was still a boy. At the age of ten, his mother died of suspected stomach cancer, leaving behind four children for her husband to raise alone on his wages as a forest laborer. My father was forced by his mother's early death and his family's poverty to quit school at the sixth-grade level and go to work sewing hatbands into hats. In this way he stumbled into a profession as a hatter, although after the war he never went back to making hats. He not only accumulated the accouterments of culture by trading for crystal, silver, and china, but was averse to having his photo taken unless he was dressed in a suit, white shirt, and tie. The father I grew up with did not allow casual snapshots in work clothes and would make the family wait while he went upstairs to change, even for a casual group snapshot.

As social constructs, photos must be understood as performative presentations of the self, in which we strive to project the person we want to be at a given moment and as we wish others to see us; photos may become a way of creating our own narrative about our lives (Apel 2020, 175–84). If my mathematically inclined mother, from an affluent but traditional background, aspired to physical courage and independence, my father, from an impoverished background of physical labor, aspired to educated middle-class respectability and refused to be pictured in any other way.

The earliest photo I have of my father was taken when he was released from the slave labor camp in Siberia. He was not yet in control of his presentation. I assume he had it taken for an identity card. He was a deeply private man who guarded his emotions, but in this photo, wearing a heavy coat, the harrowing effects of trauma and deprivation are plainly written on his face. His hair is crudely chopped, his face slack with exhaustion, his eyes dark and hooded.

Figure 6.3. Samuel Apel after his release from a Siberian slave labor camp, early 1940s. *Source:* Courtesy Dora Apel.

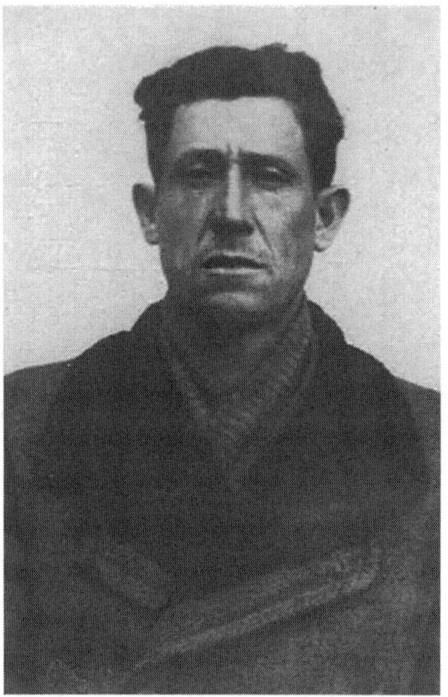

Memoirs about the Soviet forced labor camps describe long hours of labor in forests, mines, and farms; hunger and minimal food rations; climate extremes; serious epidemics, including typhoid and malaria; legions of bedbugs and lice (Goldlust 2017, 47). My father referred to the remote and isolated labor camp only a few times when I was a child. I remember him describing armies of biting red ants crawling up the walls of the wooden barracks in summer; digging tunnels through snow that fell two stories high in winter; being covered in lice; sleeping head to foot like sardines in their barracks. But it became clear that in addition to the torment of his imprisonment—the intense overcrowding, the vermin, the cold, the deprivation, and the forced labor itself—he was also wracked by guilt and shame.

My father's first wife and five-year-old daughter, who went into hiding when it became clear that everyone was in danger, had been betrayed by another Jew who then turned up in the forced labor camp with my father and confessed. During a family Passover seder when I was ten, my father told us this story and when I asked him what he had done on learning this, he said, staring into his matzo ball soup, "I killed him." My mother jumped up and shouted that it wasn't true, and the subject was permanently dropped, but decades later, long after my father's death, my mother admitted to me that she knew nothing about it.

The wretchedness is there in his eyes, the damage that will never be entirely undone. It is impossible to know what ate at him more—his inability to protect his wife and child or his response to the man who had betrayed them.

When Germany attacked its Soviet "ally" in 1941 in Operation Barbarossa, the Soviet Union signed a pact with Poland on July 30 that same year in which Stalin declared previous agreements with Germany null and void and agreed to "amnesty" the Poles and Jews held in prisons and labor camps, who were gradually freed. After his release from the camp, my father, along with other freed Jews, traveled south to Bukhara for the milder climate of the Central Asian republic of Uzbekistan. There he ran into my mother, with whom he had been acquainted before the war.

In Bukhara, barter and rationing were the primary means of survival and my mother was selling cloth. Having both lost their spouses, my father proposed that they become partners. They cut their bread rations in half and sold those too, and in this way saved enough money to buy black-market passports back to their hometown of Hrubieszów in Poland before the war formally ended. They were anxious to see for themselves who might be left after reports that everyone they loved had been killed, and my mother hoped to recover a family photo album. This was not possible when she learned that her parents' former home was now occupied by Poles who sometimes shot and killed returning Jews they feared were trying to reclaim their property. The loss my parents confronted was devastating, especially for my mother: seventy-two members of her extended family, including her parents, her three sisters, and their husbands and children had all perished. She always lamented not having a picture of her parents.

My mother had two offers of marriage: one from my father and the other from a man she told me was a former town mayor, who had returned to Poland from the Soviet Union with my parents and proposed to her on the train. He was the kind of man her father, who was deeply religious, would have chosen for her—a learned man from a religious family—the opposite of my father, who was self-taught and irreligious. "Your father would never have approved of me," my father said to my mother after they were married. She denied it but they both knew it was true.

My mother's first husband had been a man chosen by her father. She was in love with someone else at the time yet had respected her father's wishes, as she told me with a mixture of pride and ruefulness. But she laughed mischievously as she recounted how the man she was actually in love with seized her after the wedding ceremony for the first dance, the one traditionally reserved for the just-married couple, scandalizing the guests, and providing her with a delicious moment of rebellious pleasure.

She had been married for only a year before her first husband died of typhus. While living in Bukhara, she, too, contracted typhus and was hospitalized. My father walked several miles to the hospital each day to visit her and bring her a pillow. Despite the certainty of the hospital nurse that she would die, my mother returned to life from the brink of death.

A formal studio photograph was taken of my parents and the former mayor, my mother's suitor. My mother stands in the center wearing a dark dress with her mouth painted in a rosebud and a small white flower at her bosom. Her face is grave and stoical. On the left is the former mayor, wearing an ornately embroidered yarmulke, signaling not only his piousness and adherence to tradition but also his love of decoration and his affluent upbringing. His pale skin and black-rimmed glasses convey the impression of a scholar. He inclines his head toward my mother as if they are close, but there is a hint of consternation or defeat in his eyes.

Figure 6.4. Ethel and Samuel Apel, on right, with friend, c. 1945. *Source:* Courtesy Dora Apel.

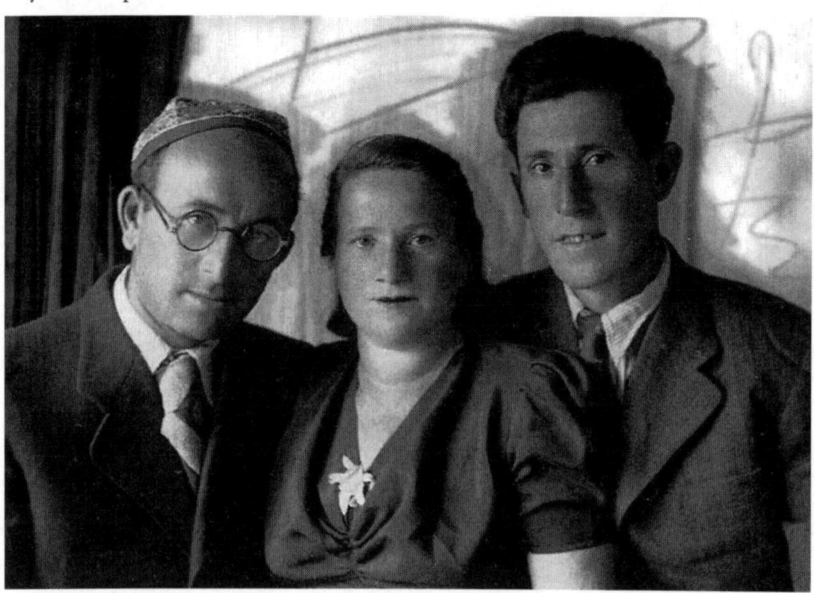

My father stands behind her, leonine, his mane of black hair rising straight back, his teeth showing without quite smiling, a look of triumph or satisfaction in his eyes. A proud and irreverent freethinker, he rejects tradition and wears no yarmulke at all. The apparently hand-colored black-and-white studio portrait makes them all seem slightly waxen, slightly unreal, as if some part of them is still caught up in a traumatic elsewhere.

But what prewar towns in Poland had Jewish mayors? Despite the fact that Jews constituted only about 10 percent of the national population in Poland, and most Jews lived in the larger cities, there were a handful of Jewish mayors in villages in southeastern Poland, where Hrubieszów is located. The Jewish mayors were replaced by Ukrainians from the east following the Soviet invasion of 1939 (Snyder 2015, 117–43). Hrubieszów itself had about 7,500 Jews, about half the town's population of 15,000.

The photo raises other questions: What kind of photography studio has chaotic lines scribbled on the wall as a backdrop? And why was it taken? After looking at this picture for decades, I have come to realize that my parents look younger here than in any other postwar photos, that this photo must have been taken soon after their return. My mother told me that she and my father were married in the home of a surviving Jew in Hrubieszów, that my father found ten people for a *minyon* and located a bottle of vodka with which to celebrate. This must be their wedding photo, taken in the home where they were married, with the former mayor as their witness.

Figure 6.5. Ethel Apel, detail of group portrait, c. 1945. *Source:* Courtesy Dora Apel.

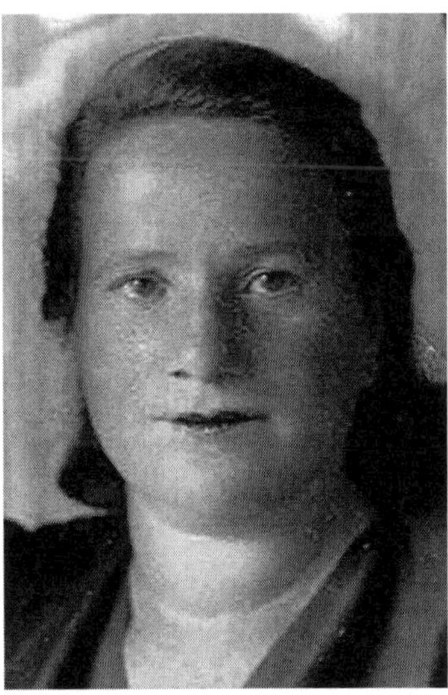

My mother is the most self-contained of the three, even as she sends her sorrowful gaze straight into the camera. It's as if she is appealing to us, her future viewers, to comprehend her grief, her survivor's guilt, and her unlikely choice. This time she doesn't choose the man her father would have preferred, but the one who comforts her, who makes her laugh, who walked miles to bring her a pillow, who is as disillusioned as she is.

They could not stay in Poland, where Jewish homes, shops, farms, land, and factories had been seized by Polish neighbors, and where pogroms, beatings, and shootings of returning Jews found popular support. Crossing the border was illegal but seeing no future for themselves in Poland with its economic wreckage and ongoing antisemitic hostility, my father arranged for them to be smuggled in the back of an ambulance to the American-occupied sector of Berlin. Tens of thousands of returning Polish Jews likewise fled Poland and smuggled themselves, in desperate need of food, clothing, shelter, and medical care, into the American zone of occupation in Germany.

In a photo taken several years later, my father looks proud and self-confident. He is on his way to work after opening a dry goods store with three partners in Munich while living at the Gabersee DP camp. Wearing a secondhand sportscoat and tie and swinging a briefcase, he might be an academic on his way to university or a businessman attending an important meeting, his briefcase filled with vital papers.

Figure 6.6. Samuel Apel on way to work, Munich, late 1940s. *Source:* Courtesy Dora Apel.

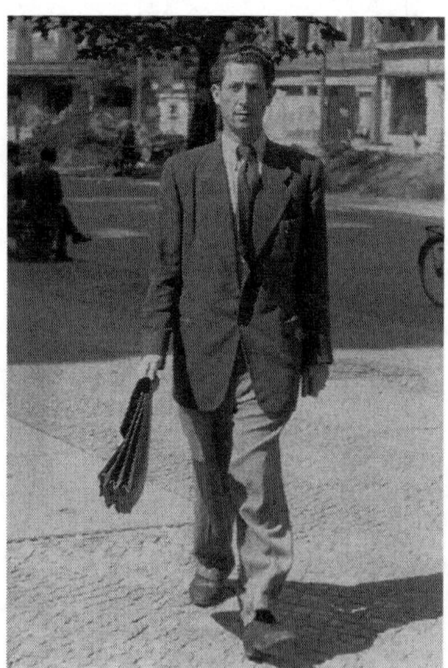

This photo might serve as a counterpart to the one of my mother and brother on the motorbike. The motorcycle and the briefcase become attributes, like objects in Renaissance portraits, which express something important about the subjects represented. If the bike signified mobility and independence for my mother, the briefcase signified mental over manual labor for my father. If my mother betrayed a certain ambivalence, my father was purely delighted.

But just as my mother never actually rode a motorcycle, a briefcase was something my father never carried in his later life. Only in this transitional moment, still full of possibilities, was he the kind of man who might wear a jacket and tie to work and carry a briefcase.

Thus, it makes sense that my father would have declined to pose on the motorcycle, even if he had been there, even if he were wearing his suit and tie—especially then. Besuited men with briefcases didn't ride motorcycles. It seems no accident that it was my mother who assumed the role of masculine bravado astride the bike. Once they left the limbo of unsettled displacement for a new home in New Jersey, it was she who first learned the new language of English and became the buffer between my father and the new world, negotiating life with gentile America for both of them.

Though my parents are gone, the photos remain. The identity card photo of my father and the wedding portrait were shot according to studio conventions and formal protocols that help account for the stiffness of the figures and the rigid poses. Taken soon after the war ended, the relentless frontal gaze of the camera captures something of their ongoing trauma.

The later photos with the motorcycle and the briefcase, however, are both taken outdoors in self-chosen poses. These photos picture them the way they saw themselves at a moment of renewal and reinvention, constructing hope for a future in which they might be the kind of people they imagined themselves to be—a fearless modern woman and an intellectual man. They may not have ridden motorcycles or carried briefcases in their later lives, but they sought to achieve these aspirations in other ways. These photographs now represent for me an essential picture of those aspirations. In this way, they also help define aspects of postwar Jewish history, memory, and identity.

My father saved the money he made on the black market and for $25,000 bought five acres of land with four chicken coops and a ten-room farmhouse in southern New Jersey. With the purchase of 5,000 baby chicks, my parents became newly minted chicken farmers. They worked from dawn until dusk and eked out a living. In four years, there would be a chicken blight, and half the chickens would die; the rest would not lay as many eggs as before. They would not be able to buy a car or a washing machine for another four years. Eventually they started a poultry route, selling whole-sale chickens and eggs door to door, my mother doing most of the talking and selling, my father driving the car. In his spare time, he read a Yiddish literary journal that arrived in the mail every month and debated politics and world events with his friends, especially his closest friend, a journalist.

They were not the only ones who, with no previous experience, turned to poultry farming. By 1952 almost three thousand Holocaust survivors from Eastern Europe had settled on small farms in New Jersey. "The Jewish chicken farmers of New Jersey could once boast that they formed one of the most productive concentrations of egg-growers in the United States," notes the *New York Times*, though by 1986 they had become "a subject for historical research and nostalgia" (Berger 1987). Automation and mechanization on massive industrial factory farms combined with the high cost of grain feed caused the decline of small farms in New Jersey and many Jewish farmers suffered as a result. But the 1950s was the heyday for the Jewish chicken

Figure 6.7. Ethel and Samuel Apel on front steps of their new home in Vineland, New Jersey, early 1950s. *Source:* Courtesy Dora Apel.

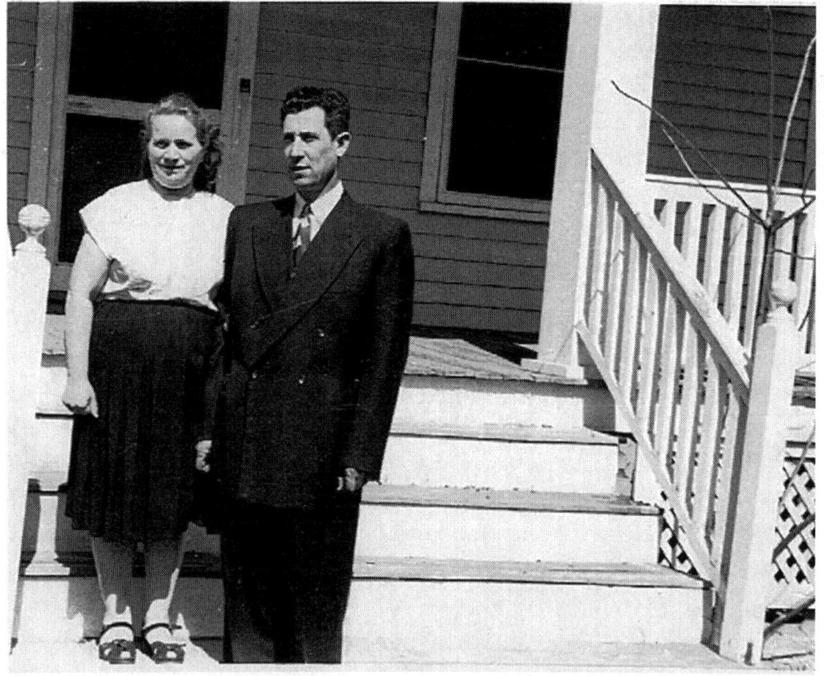

farmer, who broke the stereotype of the urbanized Jew, owned his own land, and worked for himself, often with support from the Jewish Agricultural Society and the Hebrew Immigrant Aid Society, and aided by proximity to markets such as Philadelphia and New York.

Wearing a new skirt and blouse and a crisp new suit, my parents pose proudly in a photo on the front steps of their new home in Vineland. If the motorcycle and the briefcase symbolized escape and freedom, my parents had escaped and were free; they were integrated into a Jewish community of fellow survivors and farmers that allowed them to maintain a connection to their homeland, to Yiddish, to Jewish culture and traditions.

Yet I can't help wondering if they were dislodged from the lives they had dreamed of living. My father, especially, struggled on the farm and on the stock market, too, where he lost most of his remaining money. When my mother sent him hunting for a store or business to buy, he always returned empty-handed until finally my mother established the door-to-door poultry route. The intellectual life he aspired to was always present yet always out of reach.

But my mother's resilience never failed her. She lived to be 101 years old. After my father died at sixty-two, she first got a job cutting apart chickens. Then she rented out bedrooms to boarders and turned the remaining stock market investments into a viable source of income, often ignoring the advice of her investment broker and following her own instincts as to when to buy and sell. She also turned down five proposals of marriage from widowers she knew, valuing her independence and saying, "I can't find a man as witty and intelligent as your father was. They just want me to wash their socks."

And she was one of the few who had survived the Holocaust in the USSR to receive German reparation money for support. Although the largest number of Jews who survived the Nazi genocide did so in the Soviet Union, comprising the majority of Jews in the DP camps, their suffering had gone largely unrecognized, though many thousands died of hunger, exposure, and disease. Until relatively recently, those who returned from the Soviet Union were not considered "survivors" at all, not only by historians but often by concentration camp survivors, and their experience of Soviet exile was not regarded as a legitimate and important part of the story of the Holocaust (Jewish Virtual Library n.d.; Grossmann 2012). In a private email to me in the late 1990s, a well-known historian insisted that my parents were not Holocaust survivors because of their Soviet exile. But as many scholars now argue, the lost and forgotten memories of the Soviet experience must be integrated into our understanding of the Holocaust (Adler 2020; Edele, Fitzpatrick, and Grossmann 2017; Jockush and Lewinsky 2010).

The narrow and historically blind definition of "Holocaust survivor" that most people, including historians and camp survivors, embraced until recently was reinforced by the fact that all representations of "the survivor" in films, documentaries, novels, and museums, as well as in the scholarly literature, focused solely on the concentration camp survivor. As Atina Grossmann observed in her December 2010 presentation to the annual conference of the Association of Jewish Studies " 'Deported to Life': Reconstructing the Lost Story of Polish Jews in the Soviet Union during World War II" (quoted in Goldlust 2017, 74), this contemporary image of the "Holocaust survivor," in its myriad cultural representations, "does not in fact reflect the historical experience of most survivors."

The question of flight to the USSR was especially crucial for residents of Hrubieszów, as Eliyana Adler notes: "In the fall of 1939, Jews across western Poland faced a momentous dilemma: whether to stay in their homes under Nazi occupation or to flee to the area controlled by the Soviets. The question was particularly acute for residents of Hrubieszów, mere kilometers from the new border at the Bug River" (Adler 2014, 1). Most stayed. Few survived. About 2,000 men were killed early on in the death march from Hrubieszów and Chelm in December 1939 (Adler 2014, 4–6). Of the 400,000 Jews from western Poland who entered Soviet territory in 1939, about 250,000 were repatriated in 1946, and of 350,000 or so Polish Jews who survived the war, approximately 70 percent had returned from the Soviet Union (Adler 2014, 17).

German reparations—known as *Wiedergutmachung*—were only awarded to those in concentration camps, labor camps, or in hiding but did not include those in the Soviet Union. My mother nevertheless testified that she was in hiding and received a reparations award, which meant that for the rest of their lives, my parents had to keep their Soviet experience secret. My mother was always afraid she would be found out and lose the monthly compensation on which she depended. As reported in *Haaretz*, it was not until January 2012, five years after my mother's death, that Germany recognized the victimization of and offered compensation to those who had escaped to the Soviet Union (Weiler-Polak 2011).

At the end of her life, my mother felt she had lived a good life and was grateful for what she had. In a photo taken with me at the Jewish assisted living home where she resided, now white-haired and in fragile health but perfectly lucid and still attempting to look her best, she smiles at the camera with a serene and knowing look. She felt fortunate to have settled in the relative safety and stability of America, for her children, her grandchildren, her friends, even as she lived with the lingering alienation of exile, the keenly felt losses, the grief, the thwarted ambitions, the former economic hardships, and the secrets. She was happy to still be alive.

Carefully protected and placed in a family photo album by my mother, who loved pictures and shared them with her children, the photos taken after the war preserve a link to the past and to the transformation of my parents from war refugees to American citizens. They not only represent individual and family identity but also become historically illuminating and constitute a heritage that goes back in time as far as possible since my parents possessed no photos of themselves taken before the war (save one in a Yizkor book of my mother at age twenty-three as part of a Zionist youth group). The postwar photos become a legacy of the past for her children and succeeding generations but also enlarge our cultural understanding. Yet photos are always subject to reinterpretation. By selecting and ordering a series of images from my mother's photo album in this chapter, I have constituted a new family

Figure 6.8. Ethel Apel at 101, with Dora Apel, at Fleischman Residence, 2007. Photo by Greg Wittkopp. *Source:* Courtesy of the photographer.

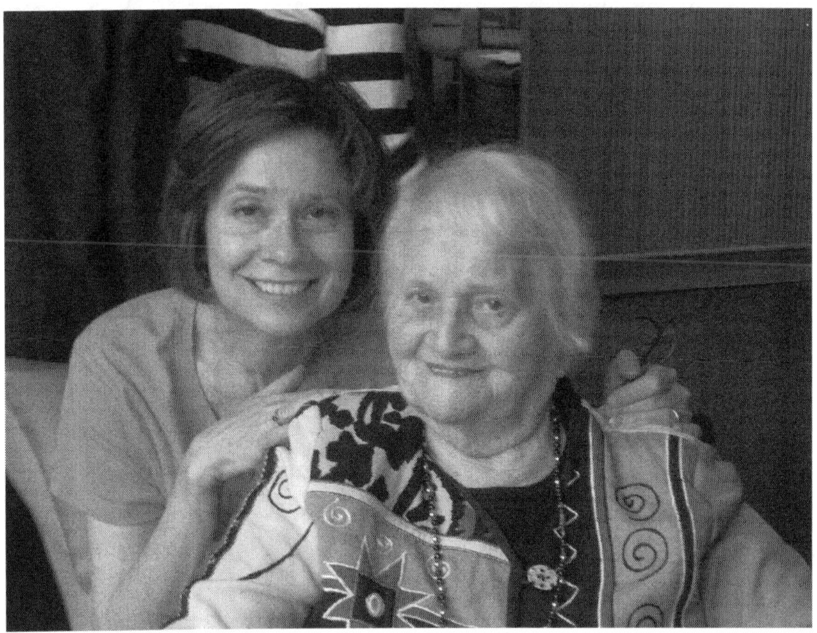

album that helps construct a narrative of struggles and desires from the vantage point of the present. Beyond the meaning these photos have for me and my family, family albums have a historical resonance that surpasses the intentions of the subjects or the photographers. Documenting emotions and events that otherwise would be lost, photographs help place personal hopes, fears, and aspirations on a continuum with social history, shaping and transforming both family remembrance and historical Jewish memory.

Works Cited

Adler, Eliyana R. 2014. "Hrubieszów at the Crossroads: Polish Jews Navigate the German and Soviet Occupations." *Holocaust and Genocide Studies* 28 (1): 1–30.

———. 2020. *Survival on the Margins: Polish Jewish Refugees in the Wartime Soviet Union.* Harvard University Press.

Apel, Dora. 2002. *Memory Effects: The Holocaust and the Art of Secondary Witnessing.* Rutgers University Press.

———. 2020. *Calling Memory into Place.* Rutgers University Press.

Assmann, Aleida, and Sebastian Conrad, eds. 2010. *Memory in a Global Age: Documents, Practices, and Trajectories.* Palgrave Macmillan.

Berger, Joseph. 1987. "Film Set on Jewish Farmers in Jersey." *New York Times*, May 31. https://www.nytimes.com/1987/05/31/nyregion/film-set-on-jewish-farmers-in-jersey.html.

Center for Jewish History, Displaced Persons Camps and Centers Photograph Collection. n.d. "Abstract." YIVO Institute for Jewish Research. Accessed October 1, 2022. https://archives.cjh.org/repositories/7/resources/3244.

Cohen, Gerard Daniel. 2012. *In War's Wake: Europe's Displaced Persons in the Postwar Order.* Oxford University Press.

Dwork, Debórah, and Robert Jan Van Pelt. 2009. *Flight from the Reich: Refugee Jews 1933–1946.* Norton.

Edele, Mark, Sheila Fitzpatrick, and Atina Grossmann, eds. 2017. *Shelter from the Holocaust: Rethinking Jewish Survival in the Soviet Union.* Wayne State University Press.

Goldlust, John. 2017. "A Different Silence: The Survival of More than 200,000 Polish Jews in the Soviet Union during World War II as a Case Study in Cultural Amnesia." In Edele, Fitzpatrick, and Grossmann 2017.

Grossmann, Atina. 2007. *Jews, Germans, and Allies: Close Encounters in Occupied Germany.* Princeton University Press.

———. 2012. "Family Files: Emotions and Stories of (Non-)Restitution." *German Historical Institute London Bulletin* 34 (1): 59–78.

————. 2021. "Trauma and Adventure in Transit: Jewish Refugees of India and Iran." Lecture at the Zekelman Holocaust Center. https://www.youtube.com/watch?v=0Lk64jmSGzE&t=3s.

Hirsch, Marianne. 1997. *Family Frames: Photography, Narrative, and Postmemory.* Harvard University Press.

————. 2012. *The Generation of Postmemory: Writing and Visual Culture after the Holocaust.* Columbia University Press.

Holland, Patricia. 2009. "'Sweet It Is to Scan . . .' Personal Photographs and Popular Photography." In *Photography: A Critical Introduction*, 4th ed., edited by Liz Wells. Routledge.

Jewish Virtual Library. n.d. "Conference on Jewish Material Claims against Germany." Accessed September 18, 2022. https://www.jewishvirtuallibrary.org/conference-on-jewish-material-claims-against-germany.

Jockush, Laura, and Tamar Lewinsky. 2010. "Paradise Lost? Postwar Memory of Polish Jewish Survival in the Soviet Union." *Holocaust and Genocide Studies* 24 (3): 373–99.

Landsberg, Alison. 2004. *Prosthetic Memory: The Transformation of American Remembrance in the Age of Mass Culture.* Columbia University Press.

Nasaw, David. 2020. *The Last Million: Europe's Displaced Persons from World War to Cold War.* Penguin.

Patt, Avinoam, and Michael Berkowitz, eds. 2010. *"We Are Here": New Approaches to Jewish Displaced Persons in Postwar Germany.* Wayne State University Press.

Shephard, Ben. 2011. *The Long Road Home: The Aftermath of the Second World War.* Vintage.

Snyder, Timothy. 2015. *Black Earth: The Holocaust as History and Warning.* Tim Duggan Books.

Weiler-Polak, Dana. 2011. "Germany to Compensate Jews Who Fled the Nazis in the Soviet Union." *Haaretz*, December 25, 2011. https://www.haaretz.com/jewish/2011-12-25/ty-article/germany-to-compensate-jews-who-fled-the-nazis-in-the-soviet-union/0000017f-f0ae-d497-a1ff-f2ae465a0000.

West, Tamara. 2014. "Remembering Displacement: Photography and the Interactives Spaces of Memory." *Memory Studies* 7 (2): 176–90.

Chapter 7

Reactivating Nineteenth-Century Jewish Portrait Albums in Institutions

Cultural Memory and Connected Histories

Michele Klein

Jews who lived in western and central Europe, Scandinavia, and in the British, German, Austro-Hungarian, Russian, and Ottoman Empires in the nineteenth century participated in the worldwide mania for acquiring and collecting reproducible self-portraits printed on photographic cards that were invented in France in the 1850s. In 1936, Augustus De Beer deposited in the Toitū Settlers Museum, Otago, New Zealand, two albums containing his German-Jewish parents' photographic cards (Colonial Family Album n.d.). Between 1943 and 1945, prior to their own deportation, the Nazi-appointed Central Jewish Museum curator and art historian Dr. Josef Polák and his assistant, who were tasked to sift through the movable property of deported Jews from Prague and environs, chose to preserve 121 Jewish albums (Sidenberg 2020, 78–79). These people had a sense of the importance of the vintage albums for the understanding of Jewish and national history, although museums had not collected such books. Twenty-four institutions entrusted with similar nineteenth-century albums became tombs for these visual remnants of past lives, guarded by property or access rights, awaiting an active effort to extract their microhistories and hidden memories.

Only three of the ninety-seven Jewish family portrait-card albums in museums, libraries, and archives have ever been exhibited. The whereabouts and digitization status of these albums is described briefly below, after the case studies that research and discuss two such books. This chapter sets out to recover Jewish collective and cultural memory from these vintage photographic collections, and to extract interconnected narratives of Jewish history whose significance extends, as their donors likely hoped, beyond the families of those who compiled them long ago.

How can these vintage photographic collections, curated by nineteenth-century bourgeois Jews, activate Jewish cultural memory? I adopt Aleida Assmann's definition of "cultural memory" as composed of the "canon," the "actively circulated memory that keeps the past present," and the "archive," the "passively stored memory that preserves the past past" (Assmann 2008, 98). The passive memory in an institution's storerooms—in this case, in a portrait album—remains in the past until someone looks for it and revives it. I contextualize the photographic collections in these albums with the aim of informing historical consciousness in the present. I look for the possibility that an album might serve as a "site of memory," a site with a symbolic aura and a transmittable memorial function that bridges the past, present, and future, as envisaged by Pierre Nora and Jay Winter (Nora 1989, 12; Winter 2008, 62).

How might these photographic collections impact our understanding of Jewish history? I argue that the albums' contents link families, conversations, and activities of the nineteenth-century Jewish bourgeoisie in what Sanjay Subrahmanyam termed "connected histories" (Subrahmanyam 1999). Although each album displays family members of all ages within their social world, in disparate locations and across national borders, their stories link middle-class Jews as well as the Jewish and non-Jewish bourgeoisie, including national or cultural figures. The albums, frequently housing women's portrait collections, may be studied today to connect the past with the present of Jewish women and children, as well as men.

Subrahmanyam formulated the concept of "connected histories," which David B. Ruderman adopted to rethink early modern Jewish history (Ruderman 2010). I propose this concept of connectedness as an interpretative tool to understand the nineteenth-century Jewish bourgeoisie. Ruderman identified forced or voluntary Jewish mobility, the loosening of rabbinic authority, and changing identities as several of the distinctive features that formed the basis for common cultural experiences of early modern Jews that link them around the world. The cultural experiences of nineteenth-century bourgeois Jews were similarly characterized by mobility, changing identities, and the weakening of religious observance. The Jews' struggle to acquire citizenship and civil rights, as well as their exploitation of new business opportunities and international connections to achieve financial power, linked the nineteenth-century Jewish bourgeoisie worldwide (Sorkin 2019; Grange 2015). Wealthy middle-class urban Jews, wherever they lived, engaged in philanthropic activities and internalized the values and behaviors of the leisured class. They strove to look and behave like the non-Jewish bourgeoisie (Klein 2023). While every album is unique, I argue that its hidden narratives of migration, newfound national identity, and aspirations for social inclusion beyond the family and Jewish community linked the nineteenth-century Jewish bourgeoisie, wherever they resided.

Most of the dozens of albums consulted for this study reveal little, if any, visible signs of Jewishness. The albums' staged, studio images reflect instead the gender norms as well as the era's values of respectability, loyalty, femininity, and masculinity. A few undigitized albums display a portrait of a rabbi dressed in the apparel of his profession, and one shows a man wearing a Jewish prayer shawl. However, all the nineteenth-century albums compiled by Jews embody bourgeois Jewish experience as modern citizens of the world, whose daily dress did not distinguish them from non-Jews. Their Jewish experiences, invisible in their self-portraits, only become evident when the photographs are contextualized. Therefore, I follow Lisa Silverman's lead in seeking the unarticulated aspects of Jewish experience in archival visual material—in this case, the albums' photographs—and the contingency of this "Jewishness" within the cultural and historical framework of the era (Silverman 2009, 108–10).

I also embrace the approach of Laura Leibman, who pioneered the study of the material culture of Jewish women who left little in their own words, to bring forgotten Jewish women into our collective consciousness and restore their agency (Leibman 2020). Photograph collections are remnants of a worldwide material culture that democratized the aristocratic penchant for portrait collection, a culture in which middle-class women were active and evident, and in which men also participated. In the nineteenth century, collecting was deemed a male pursuit, but a rapidly growing academic literature has identified a significant number of women collectors (Stammers 2021). Women's collection of portraits, their curation of family history, and their preservation show female agency, even though most of the portraits were taken by male photographers. Women chose the dress in which they and their children posed for their portrait, to reflect their social status. They also selected to whom they presented their self-portraits and their albums (Klein 2023, 573). Several albums in the database described below were compiled by young single women who stopped collecting portraits after their marriage. Portrait collection resembles other collecting activities of nineteenth-century bourgeois women with leisure, such as the collection of sketches or poems in a sentiment album and the collection and pressing of flowers (Kunard 2006; Stammers 2021).

The Jews' albums do not differ physically from the many albums of bourgeois non-Jews preserved in institutions worldwide. While each album is idiosyncratic, they have common features, characteristic of the genre. Each book is a memory object containing photographic portraits, each of which is also a memory object, as described below. The front cover is sometimes personalized with a family crest, the owner's initials, or artwork designed to convey status, as the album was traditionally placed in the parlour for visitors to peruse and discuss. The albums' thick cardboard, gilt-edged pages have precut apertures into which collectors inserted their photographic carte-de-visite (11.4 × 6.3 cm) or cabinet (10.8 × 16.5 cm) portraits, mostly acquired through social exchange. The album enabled portrait collectors to become curators, who arranged their photographs to engage and impress visitors as well as to preserve souvenirs of loved ones, dispersed relatives, and new acquaintances. Some, with missing or added portraits and labels, show signs of twentieth-century editing, when names were added to portraits of people who remained in living memory. Many Jewish albums spanned three or four generations.

This study presents case studies of two albums, compiled by two very different Jewish women, which are publicly accessible online. To use Assmann's terminology mentioned above, I reclaim their passively stored, archival memories to activate their cultural memory, by contextualizing the portraits. I find parallels with portraits in other albums of bourgeois Jews who had similar experiences. I identify the connected histories of the Jewish bourgeoisie that they portray—their cultural experiences of migration, social marginality, philanthropy, and newfound national identity, beyond the Jewish family and community. In addition, I propose their presentation within the institutional setting as sites of cultural memory. Finally, I outline my database and discuss the challenges of reactivating these albums' performative function.

Albums as Memory Objects

Nineteenth-century portrait albums provided the social context for memory that transcends the span of a lifetime. Spectators viewed, touched, and discussed them. Portraits on display generated conversations, storytelling, and shared memories. Thus, albums were intended for social use, serving as performative as well as memory objects. In 1925, Maurice Halbwachs (1992) used the termed "collective memory" to refer to memory triggered by or elicited in a shared "social frame," such as the family, the community, or the nation. The album's photographic portrait collection provides such a social frame and therefore, I argue, may serve as a site of collective memory, or (to use Assmann's term) cultural memory. The "memory boom" (Winter 2001) that evolved from Halbwachs's work in the late twentieth century generated widespread interest in reexamining and discussing vintage albums, yet few nineteenth-century *Jewish* albums have been studied in a scholarly fashion, let alone as memory objects and nonverbal memory texts.

Art curator Elizabeth Siegel (2010, 6–7), who studied hundreds of nineteenth-century American albums, none of which were compiled by Jews, argued that these albums shaped the way Americans imagined memory and history, and continue to do so today, through the stories told when viewing them. Elizabeth Edwards, a visual and historical anthropologist, considered vintage albums and their photographs material forms of memories that elicited patterns of telling, repetitive talking about and around, shaping and reshaping what is remembered. The social performance of album-viewing, accompanied by commentary, anecdotes, and discourse, she noted, activates memory and historical narrative, interwoven with private fantasy and public history (Edwards 1999, 226; 2006, 38). Therefore, blank spaces in an album, where a photograph has clearly been removed, are also important, as they indicate lost memory. Art historian Martha Langford (2008) has shown that such social album-viewing can be revived today.

This chapter uses Langford's method of inquiring what an album's portraits appear to signify and symbolize as well as what they may hide. I follow her example in viewing the portraits as memory texts, imagining the conversations that an album triggered, and translating these into lived experience. In this way, she revived the orality of forty-one nineteenth-century albums preserved in the McCord Museum, Montreal, whose conversations were suspended following their consignment to the institution (Langford 2008).

Trauma is inherent in the biographies of some of the Jewish families whose albums survived the twentieth century, including in one of the case studies below. Marianne Hirsch, whose German-speaking family lived in Rumania before the Holocaust, recovered memory from old family photographs. Using her imagination, she converted family memory embedded in the old prints into living memory relevant to the present (Hirsch 1997). Hirsch's concept of "postmemory" refers to memory reconstructed from photographs, within the living context of a traumatic family narrative, by a deeply connected later generation that has no empirical knowledge of the first-generation subjects portrayed. She used old photographs as transitional objects, missing links that connect generations. "Postmemorial work," defined by Marianne Hirsch, "strives to reactivate and reembody more distant social/national and archival/cultural memorial structures by reinvesting them with resonant individual and familial forms of mediation and aesthetic expression" (Hirsch 2008, 111). Trauma is not, however, a central theme in the reactivation of the informative and performative functions of the two albums discussed below.

Two scholarly studies have each viewed a nineteenth-century Jewish album as memory objects with significance beyond family history. Lavi Shay's study of the mostly unlabelled album of Jerusalemite banker Hayim Aharon Valero (1846–1923) revealed the international culture of Jerusalem's cosmopolitan elites and focused on the early history of portrait photography in the holy city (Shay 2014). Art historian Nebahat Avcıoğlu (2018) examined an album compiled by Hungarian-born Elisabeth Leitner, née Saphir (1842?–1908), mother of British politician Lord Amery. Her collection of multicultural portraits and souvenir cards from a variety of eastern and western countries bears witness to her lifelong experience of displacement, from Budapest to Turkey in childhood, and later to Germany, England, India, and back to Europe. Avcıoğlu highlighted Leitner's cultural entanglements, her continental and intercontinental connections that are not recognized by national historiographies and comparative histories (Avcıoğlu 2018, 200, 220). Leitner's family life was broken up by trauma and migration, as in the case of countless other Jews in and since the nineteenth century.

The case studies below contextualize two albums, revive their orality, extract their hidden memories, compare them to other albums of bourgeois Jews, and transform them into living, connected histories.

Rosa Burchardt's Album

The album that Rosa Burchardt (1821–1893) made for her husband, the wealthy merchant Hermann Burchardt (1820–1904), was exhibited in a showcase in the Jewish Museum of Berlin (JMB) from 2005 until 2015 and reactivated through a media installation that remained on display until 2017.

Digital images of the individual portraits and page views are visible on the Museum's website (Jüdisches Museum Berlin n.d.[a]). The museum's exhibition of this album aimed to inform spectators about nineteenth-century Jewish, German, and European history, as experienced by the Burchardt family; it did not relate to Jewish memory in any form. The Museum "read" the album by lingering over some pages to extrapolate meaning, and ignoring others. I lingered over different pages, as I read the album, and extracted different narratives. My reading of the Burchardt album necessarily involves speculation, imagination of lives lived and family aspirations, in addition to historical contextualization. Other people who study this collection may continue to discuss the album in novel ways.

The album's known biography suggests it as a candidate for the "imaginative investment, projection, and creation" that Hirsch has used in postmemorial work (2008, 107). The album passed from Rosa and Hermann, via their son Edgar and his wife Camilla, who evidently added her own collection of portraits, and then to their only child, Lilly, in whose apartment in Berlin her grandson, Stefan Albert Mautner, discovered it, after her death in 1972. With Hungarian citizenship, Lilly, her Hungarian husband Alexander Poór, her two daughters, and a carriage-load of their valuables escaped Berlin to Budapest in 1943. The Poórs were persecuted and deported to the Budapest ghetto in January 1945. Liberated shortly afterwards by the Soviets, Lilly and her husband returned to Berlin with all her belongings in 1949. Mautner donated the albums to the JMB in 2000.

It is noteworthy that this album was curated by women collectors, women who recognized the importance of memory. The portraits that Rosa Burchardt collected triggered her memories. When arranging and preserving the photographs, she created a historical archive, which was both her story and history. After Rosa died, her daughter-in-law and granddaughter maintained its function as a family memorial by adding new generations to the album.

The Burchardt album's cover, fashioned from a glazed ceramic tile, was decorated with a floral bouquet that represented the ingathering of the Burchardt family displayed within, as Rosa's dedicatory frontispiece made clear. Inside are some 200 photographic portraits dating from 1840 until circa 1920–1930, years after the Burchardt couple had died. The first half of the book shows the couple's nuclear and extended families. Eight pages in the center of the album depict mostly unnamed acquaintances: Dr. Kilian (a famous obstetrician); Austrian consul Paul Lessler wearing a brocaded uniform; a little-known German princess; a young woman whose portrait shows her family crest; and other unnamed children, men, and twice as many women. Did the doctor attend Rosa's births? Did the consul and the princess frequent her salon, or did she meet them at a public venue? I imagine her pondering over these pages, reminiscing on her meetings with these people. The last third of the album displays three mini-collections: some twenty portraits of daughter-in-law Camilla Burchardt's ennobled Hungarian-Jewish family and cousins, as well as five portraits of her daughter, Lilly, as a child and young woman; twenty-two commercial portraits of the era's national celebrities, including royalty, Prussian generals, and the pope, discussed below; and fourteen souvenir cards (the antecedents of postcards) from various European tourist sites.

The museum's installation showed only a sampling of pages from the Burchardt album, alongside textual commentaries, each relating to one highlighted portrait on the page displayed. The pages and texts were chosen to convey the bourgeois Jewish family's strong patriotism, admiration of the German emperor and the House of the Hohenzollern, and the couple's elevated social standing. The texts aligned the family's values with those of the bourgeois society in which they lived, and noted a few of the era's political events, including the introduction of compulsory military service, the Franco-Prussian War, and the kidnapping of Edgardo Mortara. The texts also summarized the technology of the photographic cards. They compensated for the silence of the album regarding the family's Jewishness, by explaining how their Jewishness impacted their lives.

What aspects of Jewish cultural memory are hidden in this visual archive? As mentioned above, there is nothing particularly Jewish in any of the portraits. It is the context in which they are embedded that reveal Jewish experience. First and foremost, Rosa intended this album as a family memorial, a virtual salon uniting the nuclear and extended family with their non-Jewish social and political world. I believe it represents a class of Berlin Jews, wealthy immigrants from Eastern Europe, acculturating to bourgeois life in the capital. It also embodies the class of Jewish financiers in Europe's capitals, who had cross-border dealings. Finally, as the JMB texts pointed out, it leads to the discovery of some limits on Jews' emancipation in Germany.

The first page of portraits in the Burchardt album is dated 1861: we see Rosa, the *salonnière*, who maintained and entertained in the palatial family home in Berlin; Hermann, the successful oil-cloth manufacturer; their eldest son, thirteen-year-old Martin, in a top hat and three-piece suit, looking every bit a businessman in the center of the page; and Martin's six younger siblings. The installation then displayed a page with more portraits of the couple's seven children, dated 1862. The accompanying text explained that the youngest child, Arthur Wilhelm, photographed with his brother Stefan, died that year, aged only five. The JMB did not show the colored, memorial portrait of little Arthur, copied from the earlier photograph, enlarged and mounted in an oval frame, all alone on the following page (fig. 7.1). Standing out among the album's predominantly black-and-white portraits and facing two photographs of each parent, it is significantly the only image in the album to have a whole page to itself. The blue tunic attempts to bring the wistful little boy back to life, evinces pathos, and revives the tragedy of the child's death, a heartbreak that every parent dreads. I imagine Rosa's emotion as she contemplated Arthur's innocent face. I feel her ardent desire to ensure that he will always remain cherished within the Burchardt family, a Jewish family.

The frequent use of repetition in the Burchardt album—the double displays of Rosa and Hermann, the sons in soldier dress, some other family members, and celebrities—is a common feature of nineteenth-century albums. In my view, the Burchardts' repeated acquisition of dignified self-portraits

Figure 7.1. Memorial photograph of Arthur Wilhelm Burchardt (1857–1862). Unnamed photographer, c. 1862. *Source:* Courtesy Jewish Museum Berlin, gift of Albert Stephan Mautner. Used with permission.

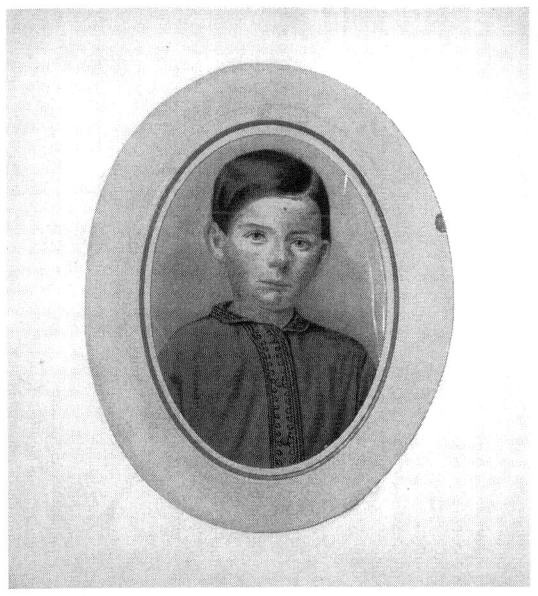

reflects their concern with their social image. Langford considered the repetition "an emulative act of remembrance. . . . A place of memory is thus imaged; but more significantly, the condition of memory, or something that reminds us of memory is figured and absorbed through this repetition" (Langford 2008, 141).

The album's portraits of Hermann's parents, Elias and Henriette Burchardt, and its memorial portraits of Rosa's parents, Meyer and Rebecca "Bertha" Markwald, dated 1840, were not shown in the JMB exhibition. For me, these retrieve the hidden memory of their migration, an experience shared by many nineteenth-century Jews and by Jews throughout history. Rosa was born in Pomerania's largest Jewish community, Märkisch Friedland, East Prussia, now Mirosławiec, Poland. Rosa, her parents and siblings moved to Berlin in the 1830s, where her father was photographed before he died, aged only forty-six. Elias Burchardt started the family's oilcloth business in Sonnenburg an der Warthe, later the site of a concentration camp, now Słońsk, Poland. His children were born there, including Hirsch, who called himself Hermann after gaining citizenship in Berlin in 1847. Translocation and the change of name enabled a fresh beginning, but it also involved the challenges of acculturation that every immigrant faces, still today, of gaining an income, finding a new home, and creating a new social life. Like the JMB, I imagine that Rosa and her family saw no need to recall their migrant history. Yet this history connects today's viewers with the collective memory of Jewish migration, from small town to big city, and all that this entailed. At least thirty Jewish albums in the database, including Leitner's album, incapsulate migration narratives. Migration for economic, marital, or political reasons was a notable characteristic of Eastern and Central European Jewish history, as well as German Jewish history. Wealthy Jews, including the Burchardts, who moved to Europe's financial and cultural centers sought acceptance among the social and economic elite and extended their financial activities across national borders.

In another portrait that was not shown in the JMB installation, Hermann posed proudly, wearing the regalia of a Grand Officer of the Equestrian Order of the Republic of San Marino. Soon after Burchardt received this honor, in 1874, the Berlin magistrate granted him permission to wear the honorific cross-shaped medallion, topped by a crown, on a striped ribbon around his neck, and the star-shaped medallion with a central white cross, affixed to his jacket. San Marino honored foreigners distinguished in politics, sciences, or arts (Ministry of Foreign Affairs n.d.). Hermann evidently made a significant monetary contribution to the microstate. Whereas Berlin newspapers in the nineteenth century referred to him as a merchant, a Hungarian newspaper, *Esti Kurir*, described him as hugely rich private banker with links to the major German and European banks (*Esti Kurir* 1927, 7). I imagine that San Marino's highly visible medallions promoted Burchardt's status when he wore them at public events. They certainly symbolized his international connectivity.

A JMB text noted that the King of Portugal awarded Hermann the title of baron in 1878, yet he was forbidden to use it in Berlin. An archival manuscript reveals that King Luiz honored Burchardt in recognition of his donation to the Portuguese Asylum of Dona Maria Pia (Albert Mautner, personal communication, August 28, 2022). In Judaism, helping the needy is a religious obligation. However, some historians have argued that wealthy nineteenth-century Jewish financiers engaged in non-Jewish philanthropy at home and abroad to enhance their social status and acculturation in their city of residence (Green 2005, 647–48; Schijf 2015). Only one Jew had been ennobled by the German monarch in the 1870s, and only three more prior to 1905 (Cecil 1970, 778). Excluded from the monarch's inner circle, Burchardt did not stand a chance of ennoblement in Berlin.

The effort to overcome marginality is a notable aspect of bourgeois Jewish experience, which is hidden in the portraits of Jewish soldiers in the Burchardt album and in over two dozen other nineteenth-century albums compiled by Jews (Klein 2023, 581–84). Ten portraits of Burchardt men, fully armed and in military dress, announce a new proudly nationalistic concept of Jewish masculinity. A JMB text commented, however, that Jews were barred from becoming military career officers. The installation's attentions to these portraits as well as to the German military celebrities at the end of the album revive the memory of the military culture of the era, in which young bourgeois Jews in France, Italy, and Austro-Hungary engaged enthusiastically, thereby asserting their citizenship and newfound nationalism (Penslar 2013, 36).

JMB's texts, entitled "A Proud Hussar," "Soldier and Jew," "A Consummate Kraut," and "A Man in Uniform," link the Jewish album with local military history. Rosa and Hermann's son Edgar served in 1872–1873 as a private in the Second Regiment of Dragoon Guards, a company without much status, and his brother Georg's service was likely similar. In 1874, another brother, Johann "Hans," wore the tunic and decorative bib that defined him as a lancer. Two years later, color and black-and-white portraits of twenty-one-year-old Stefan Burchardt (1855–1895), the youngest surviving Burchardt son, show him dressed in the uniform, spurred boots, and saber of the Second Rhineland Regiment of the Hussars, no. 9, which he bought himself. The JMB's texts explained the origins of the Hussar uniform and weaponry, the Hussars' reputation as wild, daring men, and the history of Edgar and Georg's characteristically German helmet, the *Pickelhaube*, literally "spiked cap." It also summarized the history of conscription as it related to Jews. Rosa's sons may not have seen action during their minimal, one-year service in their cavalry regiments, in contrast to their uncle Heinrich Burchardt (fig. 7.2), whose medal bears witness to battlefield experience.

Court photographer Hermann Günther photographed Heinrich (1836–1896) and his nephew Gustav (1844–1919) in military dress in 1871 and 1866 respectively. These photographs, and especially the ample facial hair of these two men, which mimics the fashion adopted by the German Emperor and his generals, similarly stress the men's strong identification with and desire to be seen and accepted as Germans, which shapes

Figure 7.2. Hermann Günther, portrait of Heinrich Burchardt as a soldier, Berlin, 1871. *Source:* Courtesy Jewish Museum Berlin, gift of Albert Stephan Mautner. Used with permission.

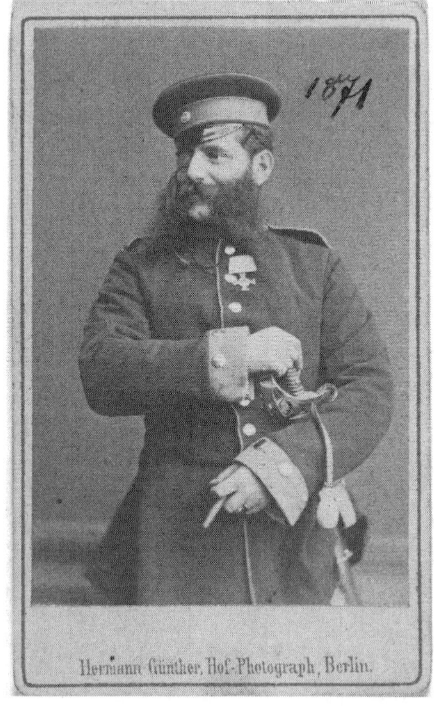

the cultural memory embedded in the album. Photographed during or just after the Franco-Prussian War, already married and a father, Heinrich posed with one hand on his weapon, the other holding a cigar. His sword-knot, the loop on the hilt of his sword by which it was attached to his wrist for combat to prevent its loss, denotes his rank as a sergeant. The JMB interpreted Heinrich's weapon and medal as indicating manliness and bravery, whereas the cigar he holds in his left hand denotes relaxation and leisure, a privilege of the wealthy, His cross-shaped military medal that is also a Christian symbol, similar to that in Moritz Oppenheim's painting *The Return of the Volunteer*, 1833–1834, was affixed with a broad ribbon to his buttonhole. Both the famous historic painting and the portraits of the Burchardt soldiers can be seen as a manifesto for the civil rights of the Jews and, for the Burchardts, an endorsement of the viability of the Jews' German identity (Berman 1993, 59–61).

The Jews' military portraits bely the bourgeois Jews' marginal position in high society. They relay the impression of full and much-desired acculturation. These photographs of visible German identity and invisible Jewish identity contrast markedly with photographs of Jews in the Nazi era, when the Burchardts' descendants and all other Jews were stripped of power and found their Jewishness was made visible by a yellow patch.

Celebrity portraits, of national leaders, including the Prussian and French royal families, Prussian generals, and Pope Pius IX, and the souvenir cards from European travels at the end of the album likely belonged to Rosa and were inserted at some stage in the empty pages at the back of her album, a useful storage place for such cards. The collection of celebrity cards formed part of the global photographic culture of the era (Plunkett 2003), in which Jews fully participated. Collectible celebrity portraits, associated with the era's wars, dominated discussion in the newspapers and the salons of Europe in the late 1860s and the 1870s, when Rosa amassed her collection. I therefore conclude that these portraits connected the Burchardt family to an imagined European community that was not Jewish. The six portraits of Pope Pius IX, including four in color (fig. 7.3), bring to my mind the collective Jewish memory of Church antisemitism. The JMB ignored Rosa's annotation, "8 Debr., 1869, Concil [sic]," on one of the colored portraits of the Pope, which likely dates most, if not all of the papal collection and the views of Rome displayed in the Burchardt album. This note suggests that Rosa, Hermann, or both, visited Rome at the time of the First Vatican Council, which did not change the Catholic Church's mistrust and hostility toward Jews or alter its accusation that Jews murdered Christ (Kertzer 2001).

(Only in 1964–1965, did the Second Vatican Council change its approach, denounce antisemitism and call for mutual respect and dialogue.) I see in the Pontiff's raised hand for benediction a culturally significant and chilling reminder of his support for all efforts to convert Jews as well as his custody of the secretly baptized, kidnapped, Jewish boy, Edgardo Mortara (Kertzer 1997). This papal portrait might have led Rosa and the visitors in her salon to discuss the fact that some Jews chose baptism voluntarily, which her son Edgar strongly condemned. The conversion of Jews to Christianity is an issue embedded in Leitner's and in at least three other Jewish albums.

How could Rosa's album be made to serve as a site of cultural memory of symbolic value to visitors? The new metaphorical "Family Album" in the JMB's core exhibition offers an idea for reframing the Burchardt album,

Figure 7.3. Portraits of Pope Pius IX. Unknown photographers, 1869. *Source:* Courtesy Jewish Museum Berlin, gift of Albert Stephan Mautner. Used with permission.

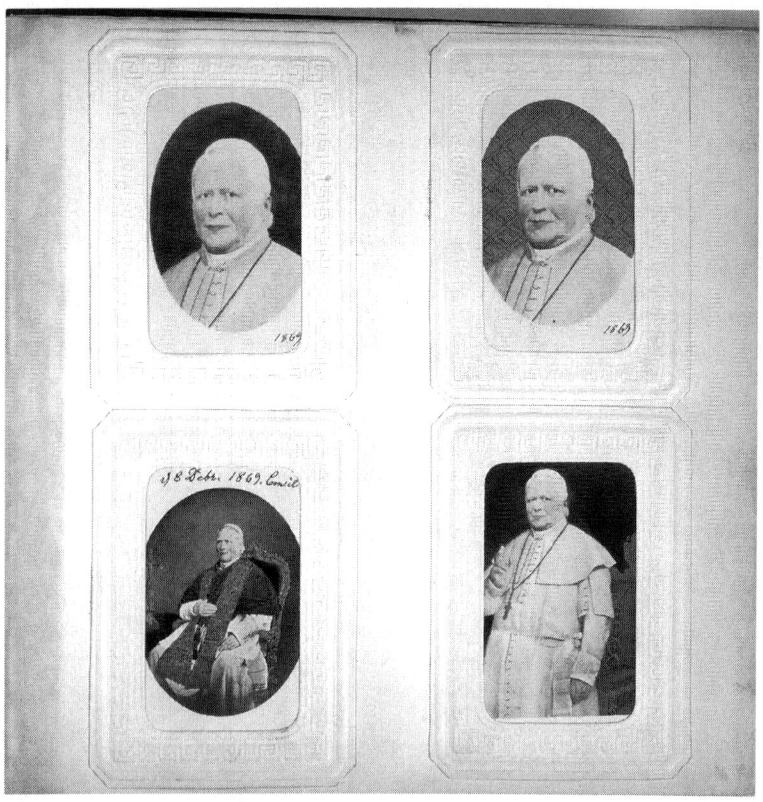

with its portraits of men, women, and children, as a site of memory for retelling personal stories of kinship, bereavement, migration, identity, or social aspirations, and for learning about, imagining, and discussing Jewish bourgeois history that engages all age-groups. Touch-screens on a five-meter-wide wall enable visitors to view and enlarge digitized images of some 500 historical photographs, documents, and other objects, tracing the life paths of several generations of ten families (Jüdisches Museum Berlin n.d.[b]). Explanatory texts in the JMB's new display allow visitors to reconstruct the historical legacies of German Jews. This composite "family album" abandons the family curatorship of the vintage album and changes the definition of an album, as the new "album" is no longer a book containing a collection. Nevertheless, presented in this way, together with other Burchardt archival materials, Rosa's album could enable spectators to "touch" her images, and view the contextualizing documents that reveal the hidden experiences of the four generations represented between its covers. Moreover, just as Rosa's album was added to after her death, so too, the curator could add photographs of later generations, if they agreed, to tie the past to the present. Using the interactive display, visitors could imagine and discover the social networks between Jews and with non-Jews, within and across national borders, migrations, and translocations, as well as the trauma that has characterized and impacted Jewish cultural memory.

The women who collected, arranged, and preserved the photographs in this album enabled us to revive the cultural memories of the German-Jewish and European bourgeoisie. My imagination of long-dead conversations as viewers lingered over the album's pages over a century ago, and this discussion of the Burchardt album revives the album's orality and performative function, converting the photographic archive's passive memory into living cultural memory. The narratives of Jewish migration, Jewish international philanthropy, and nationalism, extrapolated from the portraits, connect to those in other albums of the same era, and to Jewish experience of these phenomena in the twentieth and twenty-first centuries.

The Philipsons' Album

One or two Swedish sisters, a generation younger than Rosa and far less wealthy, compiled a portrait album that is preserved in the Jewish Museum of Sweden (JMS) (Judiska Museet n.d.). It has enabled the retrieval of a different, yet connected history of the female bourgeoisie from the silence of the photographic archive. At least seven of the ten albums in this museum were compiled by women, which exhibit a few ladies who had notable careers.

The JMS digitized both sides of each card within their ten albums, cataloged the name of each subject and photographer as well as the date of photography, when known. The albums' photographic collections are publicly accessible online, without page views, precluding the opportunity for seeing them as a site of memory. Nevertheless, this manner of digitization enables contextual research that can help activate the passive archive, as Aleida Assmann (2008, 99–102) envisaged, to revive hitherto unknown or ignored narratives of Jewish history. Kristina Mittag-Leffler kindly located archival documents that enabled the contextualization of this album and the JMS' Andreas Schein helpfully provided informal page views of the Philipsons' album. These revealed ten undigitized portraits of cultural celebrities, as important to the reading of the album as those of the Burchhardts' generals, emperor, and Pope.

Hélène Philipson (1863–1955) acquired the album, printed with drawings and popular English verses of the period on some of its pages, when she studied in England. She was the third of the five children of Swedish-born Hildegaard Jacobson and Philip Philipson, who was born in the Baltic seaport Åbo, now Turku, Finland. Philip appears to have settled in Stockholm circa 1852, where he made a living as a merchant, like his father. In 1862, his excellent Hebrew and musicality gained him the post of cantor at Stockholm's Great Synagogue. Hélène graduated from the Higher Teachers' Seminary, taught English and German, and championed the teaching of English as a basic foreign language in Swedish schools. She actively promoted temperance among young working-class women and became part of a group of educated women who encouraged women to go out to work. Her eldest sister, Bertha, inherited her father's musicality and became a piano teacher. A young man in military uniform, one of the few men in the album, on a page showing two of the Philipson daughters, suggests that this is Ivan, the couple's only son who died in 1888, aged twenty-eight. Jenny, who worked as an office clerk, was the only sibling who married. She died childless, aged thirty-three, in 1898. The youngest sibling, Sara Adèle (1870–1924), attended university and graduated with a bachelor's degree in 1893. She taught at two of Stockholm's most progressive schools founded by women; a girls' high school that also trained poor women to become teachers, and a coeducational high school favored especially by Jews for its religious freedom. She strove to promote the wages and pension rights of academic women as well as girls' health care. She served as secretary of the

Association for Women Academics, and as a board member of the Swedish Women's National Federation, which drew attention to women's issues and forged international cooperation. The unmarried sisters lived together. In 1952, Hélène, who outlived her siblings, entrusted the album to a friend, Greta Erhardt, née Björkman, wife of military doctor and artist Richard Erhardt. Greta eventually consigned it to the Jewish Museum of Sweden, without any other documents.

The Philipson collection of fifty-two portraits spans from the early 1860s to 1907 and sheds light on the essentially female world of unmarried, bourgeois Jewish women, a topic little explored in academic studies beyond biographies of those who used their wealth to engage in public endeavors (Ashton 1993). I have not found any statistics for the percentage of bourgeois Jewish women who remained single, or regarding their higher education and employment. Ten percent of Jewish women above the normal age of marriage in 1851 Britain and 20 percent of those of German-Jewish origin in 1900 Portland, Oregon, remained unmarried (Toll 1983, 314). Adèle was among the rising number of single women who attended university in the last decade of the nineteenth century.

The album displays sixteen portraits of the Philipson siblings, from early childhood until adulthood, some female relatives and possibly a few male relatives as well. Its unnamed photographs are mostly of women, young and old, and a few children; of the six men exhibited, one is likely Philip. The album's portraits were photographed in Stockholm and other Swedish towns, locations in Norway, Denmark, Germany, as well as in St. Petersburg, London, and Paris. Four commercial portraits of women and girls in traditional Swedish dress, wearing striped aprons, floral bodices, and tight caps that hide their ears, were photographed in Leksand, a northern lake-side resort known for its traditional handicrafts. Are these souvenirs of a visit to the resort, or were they a gift from a friend? I believe that they reflect the sisters' pride in women's handwork, which a childless Jewish woman activist, Emma Zorn, née Lamm, promoted in 1905, by setting up the first Swedish home handicrafts association (Sandström 2021). They may also be seen as expressions of nationalism; the European bourgeoisie, including Jews, as several albums show, sometimes had themselves photographed in national costumes (Klein 2021; 2023, 593).

This photographic collection includes noticeably few men, except for the ten male international celebrities. The album's frontispiece displays a portrait of Esaias Tegnér (1782–1846), a Swedish poet, professor, and bishop, whom the *Encyclopedia Britannica* designates as Sweden's first modern man. The album connects him with Hans Christian Andersen, Shakespeare, Goethe, Longfellow, Tolstoy, Beethoven, Chopin, and others exhibited in this collection. I believe that the celebrities convey the Philipson sisters' adoption of the German ideal of *Bildung*, self-formation through high culture, typical of the Jewish bourgeoisie in Scandinavia as well as elsewhere (Aatsinki, Annola, and Kaarninen 2019; Kaplan 1991, 119). The Swedish album is not unusual in displaying literary and musical celebrities. Five other Jewish women's albums similarly display portraits of European musical celebrities, theatrical stars, poets, and writers linking the private lives of the album-compilers to European high culture. The Philipson celebrities can therefore be seen as another connective thread between young, bourgeois Jewish women throughout Europe, who gained fluency in several languages, read fine literature, and played the piano.

Although predominantly showcasing women, the Philipson's album is hardly the "space of femininity" that Patrizia Di Bello found in the aristocratic (non-Jewish) British women's albums that she studied, which showcased motherhood (Di Bello 2007, 24). In the two images in the Philipson album that show an adult holding a child, the adult is male. These two portraits contrast with the military-virile males of the Burchardt album and challenge the collective consciousness of the non-domestic role of men in bourgeois society. One portrait shows a young man, dressed in the fashion of the 1860s, gently holding the hand of a small assertive-looking girl, standing defiantly on a chair (fig. 7.4). The young man watches his daughter intently. He had no need for concern, as we notice. Behind her chair, the photographer's stand held her in place. This portrait, by an unknown photographer, conveys fatherly love in a manner that is rarely seen in the photography of the era. It contrasts with portraits of mothers holding their children in other Jewish albums, who often have their eyes on the photographer and not on their offspring.

Reviving the Philipsons' album expands the memory of the fin-de-siecle Jewish bourgeoisie to include the marginalized culture of single women, particularly those who looked out for other single women and girls, asserted their intellectual independence, challenged gendered stereotypes, and found purpose in public service. The concern of bourgeois Jewish women to keep up with the latest fashions (Kaplan 1991, 31) connects most of the albums in the database. Femininity was a middle-class status symbol, and bourgeois fashion advertised a lady's virtue (Wilson and Taylor 1989, 25). However, in the latest known portrait of Adèle, aged twenty-nine, taken in Lillehammer, Norway, in 1899, she wears a necktie, held in place with a small pin on

Figure 7.4. A portrait of an unknown young man and girl. Unknown photographer, c. 1869. *Source:* Courtesy Jewish Museum of Sweden. Used with permission.

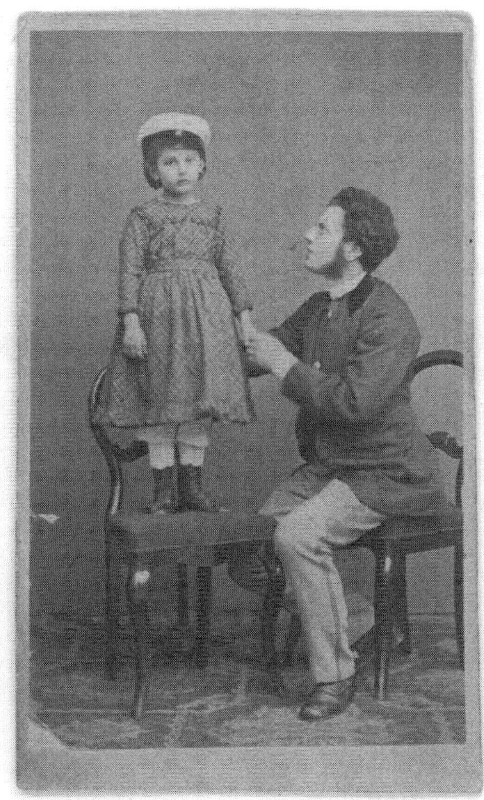

the four-in-hand knot (fig. 7.5). Whereas bourgeois women often sported decorative bows under their chins, Adèle's was knotted in a male fashion. A portrait of Hélène, taken in the German university town of Marburg, a few years earlier, shows her with short hair around her face. Both the necktie and short hair were associated with masculinity and suggest that the two women took a small step toward challenging the accepted feminine ideals of dress and hairstyle. A third young woman wore a bow-tie for her portrait, pinned beneath her chin to her high-necked dress. In the late 1880s and 1890s other "new women" (MacPike 1989, 372) sought to redefine themselves professionally, or sexually through their looks. Two British albums show a Jewish man who redefined himself sexually by cross-dressing (Klein 2021, 78–79).

Figure 7.5. Charlotte Barth, portrait of Adèle Philipson, Lillehammer, August 22, 1899. *Source:* Courtesy Jewish Museum Sweden. Used with permission.

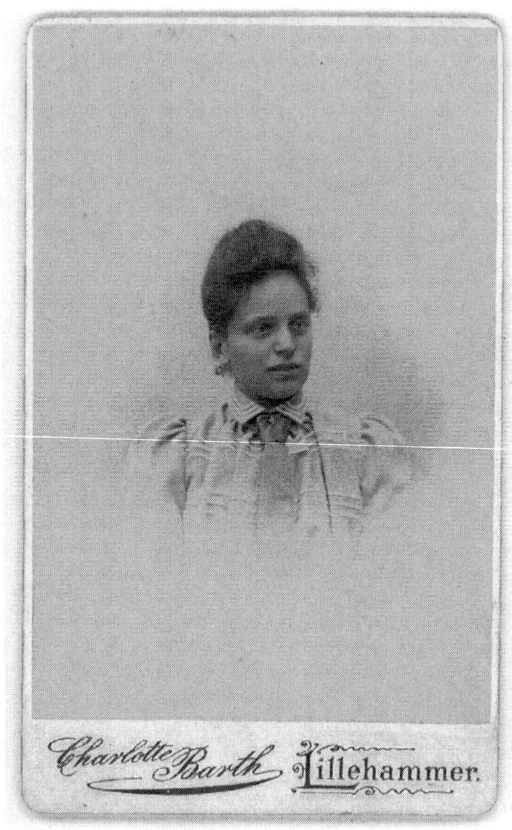

As in the Burchardt album, the Philipsons' Jewishness is not seen in the album. The album connects the sisters to the aspiration for new identities seen in the German-Jewish album above and other Jewish albums (Klein 2023). It associates the sisters with the early feminist culture at home and abroad and with those who challenged gendered stereotypes. The presence of the album in the Jewish Museum of Sweden reflects its significance as a historical artefact, as one of several Jewish women's photographic collections.

The Philipson sisters' will, which dictated the distribution of their estate after death, shows their strong bonds with their relatives and with the Jewish community in which they had been raised. It specified their desire for the preservation of the family's heirlooms—painted portraits, silver, and a few jewels, relics of their parents' and grandparents' bourgeois life-style—by their surviving relatives, or by the Jewish community. The women also bequeathed funds for Jewish education and the education of needy Jewish students.

Adèle and Hélène do not appear in the *Swedish Women's Biographical Dictionary* (*Svenskt kvinnobiografiskt lexicon* n.d.), although Adèle is listed by Uppsala University's digital archive on the topic of the sociology of education and culture (Skog-Östlin 2003). The album is a catalyst for reviving the archival memory of Philipson and the other Swedish-Jewish activists of her generation, who are unknown internationally.

The Jewish Museum of Frankfurt (JMF) offers an example of how the Jewish Museum of Sweden might create a site of memory for the retelling of stories about Swedish Jewish women activists, using some of the Philipson portraits together with portraits of other Jewish women in the JMS's albums and collections, who had an impact outside the family. Women from the Frankfurt collections may include social worker Gerda Meyerson and her sister Agda Meyerson, a nurse who were both active in bringing about social change as well as pianist and music teacher Wilhelmina "Mina" Josephson and actress Olga Raphael, who later became an activist in giving refugee aid. The JMF's interactive media installation, which opened in 2021 in the museum's Frank Center, aims to transform passive cultural memory into living history. It draws on thirty archival family photographs of members of the extensive Frank family, from the nineteenth and first half of the twentieth centuries, as well as other digitized objects, including documents and letters in order to make the Frank family's history accessible to all ages (Familie Frank Zentrum n.d.). The Frankfurt media station takes the form of a large table with digital images of archival objects. The visitors can drag an object into a circle on the table, where a family story pops up, giving the object new life within the canon of memory.

The Philipsons' album could be animated in this way, together with some of the other Jewish women's albums in the JMS collection, to generate a site of Jewish women's history associated with International Women's Day and stimulate discussion of women's agency. Such an installation would necessarily be selective, as was the Burchardt installation, and is not a surrogate for the vintage family albums. However, it would enable the transfer of the memory of Adèle and Hélène Philipson, and their contemporaries, who were changing the roles of women in society, into the canon of cultural memory and the living history of Jewish women.

The Database

As mentioned in the case studies, the two albums discussed above have narratives in common with other nineteenth-century Jewish portrait albums that survived the twentieth century. To date, I have located such albums in the Jewish Museums in Amsterdam, Brussels, Berlin, Copenhagen, Frankfurt, Paris, Prague, Stockholm, and Vienna; the National Libraries of Israel and Sweden, and the University Library of Göteborg; the Anglo-Jewish Archive, Southampton, UK, the French National Archives, the Central Archives for the History of the Jewish People, Jerusalem, the Churchill Archives, Cambridge, UK, and the Rothschild Archive, London; British houses open to the public—Nymans, formerly the home of the Messel family, Broomhill, where the Salomons family lived, and the Freud Museum, London; as well as the Center for Jewish History, New York, the Nordic Museum and Göteborg City Museum, and the Toitū Settlers Museum in New Zealand. Most of these institutions have few nineteenth-century Jewish albums, although the Jewish Museum Prague has twenty, most of them looted by the Nazis (Sidenberg 2020).

Forty of these institutionalized albums are visible digitally, online, page by page or as individual portraits to viewers who know where to look. In addition to the Burchardt album exhibited by JMB, the album of banker and philanthropist Eduard Todesco and his wife was displayed to the public at the Jewish Museum Vienna, in material form, with some portraits reproduced and shown digitally. Another fine album, in private ownership, created by an Italian-Jewish count, Augusto Corinaldi, was exhibited at the MEIS National Museum of Italian Judaism and the Shoah, Ferrara. An exhibition scheduled to open in 2026 at the Jewish Museum Prague will showcase its albums (Michaela Sidenberg, personal communication, March 4, 2024). Seven institutions have not digitized any of their albums. Without public awareness of their existence, albums become repositories for forgetting (Volpe 2009, 16).

The database excludes card albums that house only portraits of celebrities, or those of a particular nineteenth-century photographer. It also excludes vintage albums devoted to indigenous peoples, historical sites or events, or travelogues. Unlike the thousands of odd nineteenth-century portrait cards on web platforms, such as Europeana, and those circulating on Pinterest, Ebay, and Instagram, the portrait albums literally bind together the people that made up the collectors' milieu, providing a social frame for collective memory. These books also attest to the photographs' historical integrity and enhance their value as a primary historical source, especially when their provenance and subjects are known.

When nothing is known about an album's biography and subjects, their texts remain hidden or do not reveal any identifiable names, and relevant archival material is lacking, contextualization and the activation of cultural memory (as Assmann envisaged) are particularly challenging.

Conclusion

Nineteenth-century Jewish portrait albums have been exhibited in three museums to illustrate the past life of the Jewish bourgeoisie in Berlin, Vienna, and Ferara. In each exhibition, a beautifully bound album exemplified the ostentatious material culture of wealthy Jews of the era. This chapter, however, challenges this static approach to Jewish history by attempting to bring the album's photographic collections back to life, through contextualization, questioning, discussion, and imagination, following the examples of Langford, Hirsch, and others. To this end, it considers such albums as social frames of Jewish collective and cultural memory, embedded in which are shared concerns, values, and narratives about family, society, and nation that impact the Jews' self-definition. All the vintage Jewish albums, from disparate locations, spanning the second half of the nineteenth century, some with twentieth-century additions, picture a personal or family perspective of bourgeois social history. Many of them house collections made, curated, and preserved by women who left little in their own words and whose other activities are either unknown or long forgotten.

The two case studies of albums that display women's portrait collections, presented above, examined the semiotics of some of their portraits as well as archival textual documents that provide their backstories. They also identified visual and conceptual parallels with other Jewish albums. One album was compiled by a married woman who was born in Eastern Prussia in 1821, lived in considerable wealth in Berlin, and bore seven children; the other belonged to female teachers in Stockholm, unmarried siblings who were born a generation later. Although the albums' microhistories differ significantly, both have hidden stories of migration and Jewish kinship. Both of them also depict interactions between Jews and non-Jews and explore new identifications, which have characterized bourgeois Jewish experiences worldwide. Rosa Burchardt redefined herself in Berlin through her husband's financial success, through her son's noble relatives, and as a nationalistic German. The Philipson sisters in Stockholm defined themselves through their own agency, as educators and social activists, while retaining their Jewish identity. The Swedish case study points out the dearth of knowledge about the scope, culture, and experiences of middle-class, Jewish single women in nineteenth-century Europe; a direction for future research. The case studies restored hidden memories of bereavement, migration, philanthropy, nationalist sentiment, and marginality, and revalued these as living Jewish history. The cultural memory of many other Jewish albums can be characterized similarly.

The study of the genuinely historic albums is hampered by their fragility and often also their lack of visible textual material that can give them meaning. Although digitization has rendered some albums preserved in institutions publicly accessible, this process dematerializes, dehistoricizes, and decontextualizes the vintage albums, limiting the retrieval of their historical narratives and memory work. Nevertheless, the concept of a family album can be redefined and presented as a site of memory, as proposed above, using modern techniques of digital display and spectator interaction, following the examples set by the metaphorical albums currently on display in the core exhibitions of the Jewish Museums of Berlin and Frankfurt, while the original book is safely conserved in carefully controlled conditions. The study and display of a nineteenth century album reinstates its original performative function, by stimulating questioning, discussion, imagination, and memory work, and transforming its archival contents into living history.

Recognizing that rights, digitizing systems, staff availability, and funding priorities limit public accessibility, I, nevertheless, call for enabling scholars to access the albums' page-views and the photographs' hidden texts, both of which are necessary for reactivating the albums' memory and for reconstructing their historical narratives. One-off digitization of both sides of every photographic card and every two-page spread will enable the album's future usage, for memory work and exploration of local, regional, and transregional nineteenth-century Jewish history, without harming the original object. The albums can then be reproduced and reimagined in new forms and formats, while still maintaining the essence of the original composition. Finally, I wish to credit the foresight of descendants and curators who chose to preserve nineteenth-century Jewish albums. This study validates their premise that nineteenth-century albums are cultural heritage objects worthy of preservation. It argues that they frame the interconnected Jewish bourgeois culture, transcend family history, and embody cultural memory, when their performative and informative functions are recovered through contemplation, contextualization, and discussion.

Work Cited

Aatsinki, Ulla, Johanna Annola, and Mervi Kaarninen. 2019. Introduction to *Families, Values, and the Transfer of Knowledge in Northern Societies, 1500–2000*, edited by Ulla Aatsinki, Johanna Annola, and Mervi Kaarninen. Routledge.

Ashton, Dianne. 1993. "Souls Have No Sex: Philadelphia Jewish Women and the American Challenge." In *When Philadelphia Was the Capital of Jewish America*, edited by Murray Friedman. Balch Institute Press.

Assmann, Aleida. 2008. "Canon and Archive." In *Cultural Memory Studies: An International and Interdisciplinary Handbook*, edited by Astrid Erll, Ansgar Nünning, with Sara B. Young. Walter de Gruyter.

Avcıoğlu, Nebahat. 2018. "Immigrant Narratives: The Ottoman Sultans' Portraits in Elisabeth Leitner's Family Photo Album, circa 1862–72." *Muqarnas Online* 35 (1): 193–228. https://doi.org/10.1163/22118993_03501P009.

Berman, Russell A. 1993. *Cultural Studies of Modern Germany: History, Representation, and Nationhood*. University of Wisconsin Press.

Cecil, Lamar. 1970. "The Creation of Nobles in Prussia, 1871–1918." *American Historical Review* 75 (3): 757–95.

Colonial Family Album. n.d. 1936/118/2 and 1936/118/3. Toitū Otago Settlers Museum, Dunedin, New Zealand.

Di Bello, Patrizia. 2007. *Women's Albums and Photography in Victorian England: Ladies, Mothers and Flirts*. Ashgate.

Edwards, Elizabeth. 1999. "Photographs as Objects of Memory." In *Material Memories*, edited by Marius Kwint, Christopher Breward, and Jeremy Aynsley. Berg.

———. 2006. "Photographs and the Sound of History." *Visual Anthropology Review* 21 (1/2): 27–46.

Familie Frank Zentrum. n.d. "'Früher wohnten wir in Frankfurt . . .': Das Familie Frank Zentrum erinnert an jüdische Familiengeschichte aus Frankfurt." Accessed April 24, 2024. https://www.juedischesmuseum.de/de/sammlung/familie-frank-zentrum/.

Grange, Cyril. 2015. *Une elite parisienne: Les familles de la grande bourgeoisie juive (1870–1910)*. CNRS.

Green, Abigail. 2005. "Rethinking Sir Moses Montefiore: Religion, Nationhood, and International Philanthropy in the Nineteenth Century." *American Historical Review* 110 (3): 631–58.

Halbwachs, Maurice. 1992. *On Collective Memory*. Translated and edited by Lewis A. Coser. University of Chicago Press.

Hirsch, Marianne. 1997. *Family Frames: Photography, Narrative, and Postmemory.* Harvard University Press.

———. 2008. "The Generation of Postmemory." *Poetics Today* 29 (1): 103–28.

Judiska Museet. n.d. "Fotoalbum i skinn med guld- och metalldekor." Accessed January 12, 2023. https://digitaltmuseum.org/0210211126018/album.

Jüdisches Museum Berlin. n.d.(a). "Fotoalbum angelegt von Rosa Burchardt (1821–1893) für ihren Ehemann Hermann (1820–1904)." Accessed January 12, 2023. https://objekte.jmberlin.de/object/jmb-obj-102787.

———. n.d.(b). "The Family Album." Accessed January 12, 2023. https://www.jmberlin.de/en/family-album-panel-discussion-livestream.

Kaplan, Marion A. 1991. *The Making of the Jewish Middle Class: Women, Family, and Identity in Imperial Germany.* Oxford University Press.

Kertzer, David. 1997. *The Kidnapping of Edgardo Mortara.* Knopf.

———. 2001. *The Popes against the Jews: The Vatican's Role in the Rise of Modern Anti-Semitism.* Knopf.

Klein, Michele. 2021. "Louis XIII, Richard I and the Duchess of Devonshire: Nineteenth Century Jews in Fancy Dress Costume." *Images* 14 (1): 54–81.

———. 2023. "Dressing Up: 'Reading' Costume in the Photograph Albums of Nineteenth-Century Bourgeois Jews." *Textile: The Journal of Cloth and Culture* 21 (3): 571–98.

Kunard, Andrea. 2006. "Traditions of Collecting and Remembering." *Early Popular Visual Culture* 4 (3): 227–43.

Langford, Martha. 2008. *Suspended Conversations: The Afterlife of Memory in Photographic Albums.* McGill-Queens University Press.

Leibman, Laura Arnold. 2020. *The Art of the Jewish Family: A History of Women in Early New York in Five Objects.* Bard Graduate Center.

MacPike, Loralee. 1989. "The New Woman, Childbearing, and Reconstruction of Gender, 1880–1900." *NWSA Journal* 1 (3): 368–97.

Ministry of Foreign Affairs, International Economic Cooperation and Telecommunications. n.d. "Honours." Accessed January 12, 2023. https://www.esteri.sm/pub2/EsteriSM/en/Dipartimento/Onorificenze.html.

Nora, Pierre. 1989. "Between Memory and History: *Les Lieux de Mémoire.*" *Representations*, no. 26, 7–24.

Penslar, Derek J. 2013. *Jews and the Military: A History.* Princeton University Press.

Plunkett, John. 2003. "Celebrity and Community: The Poetics of the Carte-de-visite." *Journal of Victorian Culture* 8 (1): 55–79.

Ruderman, David B. 2010. *Early Modern Jewry: A New Cultural History.* Princeton University Press.

Sandström, Birgitta. 2021. "Emma Amalia Zorn." *Svenskt kvinnobiografiskt lexicon.* Accessed January 12, 2023. https://www.skbl.se/sv/artikel/EmmaAmaliaZorn.

Schijf, Huibert. 2015. "Titled Outsiders: Jewish Nobility in the Nineteenth and Early Twentieth Centuries." In *Nobilities in Europe in the Twentieth Century:*

Reconversion Strategies, Memory Culture and Elite Formation, edited by Yme Kuiper, Nikolaj Bijleveld, and Jaap Dronkers. Peeters.

Shay, Lavie. 2014. "Ha-albom ha-mishpakhti ha-rishon be-Yerushayim" [The First Family Album in Jerusalem]. *Kathedra*, no. 152, 110–81.

Sidenberg, Michaela. 2020. "Intimate Galleries: Photographic Albums from the Collection of the Jewish Museum in Prague." *Judaica Bohemiae*, no. 2, 69–80.

Siegel, Elizabeth. 2010. *Galleries of Friendship and Fame: A History of Nineteenth-Century American Photograph Albums*. Yale University Press.

Silverman, Lisa. 2009. "Reconsidering the Margins." *Journal of Modern Jewish Studies* 8 (1): 103–20.

Skog-Östlin, Kerstin. 2003. "Philipson, Sara Adéle." Sociology of Education and Culture, Uppsala University. http://www.skeptron.uu.se/broady/arkiv/a/ffo/kap-philipson-adele.htm.

Sorkin, David J. 2019. *Jewish Emancipation: A History across Five Centuries*. Princeton University Press.

Stammers, Tom. 2021. "Women Collectors and Cultural Philanthropy, c. 1850–1920." *19: Interdisciplinary Studies in the Long Nineteenth Century*, no. 31. https://doi.org/10.16995/ntn.3347.

Subrahmanyam, Sanjay. 1999. "Connected Histories: Notes towards a Reconfiguration of Early Modern Eurasia." In *Beyond Binary Histories: Re-imagining Eurasia to c. 1830*, edited by Victor Lieberman. University of Michigan Press.

Svenskt kvinnobiografiskt lexicon. n.d. Accessed January 12, 2023. https://www.skbl.se/.

Toll, William. 1983. "The Female Life Cycle and the Measure of Jewish Social Change: Portland, Oregon, 1880–1930." *American Jewish History* 72 (3): 309–32.

Volpe, Andrea L. 2009. "Archival Meaning: Materiality, Digitization and the Nineteenth-Century Photograph." *Afterimage* 36 (6): 11–16.

Wilson, Elizabeth, and Lou Taylor. 1989. *Through the Looking Glass: A History of Dress from 1860 to the Present Day*. BBC Books.

Winter, Jay. 2001. "The Generation of Memory: Reflections on the 'Memory Boom' in Contemporary Historical Studies." *Canadian Military History* 10 (3): 57–66.

———. 2008. "Sites of Memory and the Shadow of War." In *Cultural Memory Studies: An International and Interdisciplinary Handbook*, edited by Astrid Erll, Ansgar Nünning, with Sara B. Young. Walter de Gruyter.

Part III

The Photographed Jewish Body

Agency, Race, Nation

Chapter 8

Zionism and the "Jewish Pathos Formula" in Helmar Lerski's Type Photographs

Amos Morris-Reich

Method is nothing else than reflective knowledge, or the idea of an idea; and that as there can be no idea of an idea unless an idea exists previously, there can be no method without a pre-existing idea.

—Benedictus de Spinoza, *The Ethics*, proposition 38

This chapter reflects on the method of one particular photographer, arguably the most prominent photographer working in British Mandate Palestine: the German-born Swiss-American Jewish art photographer Helmar Lerski (Ashkenazi 2016, 91–123; Morris-Reich 2022, 58–86). It explores elements of the "Jewish pathos formula"—the image of Jewish suffering and pain—in one particular project of Lerski's. Given that the pathos formula pertains to forms of gestures and fleeting and ephemeral aspect of the image, what the following addresses is a very restricted feature of the image that is at the same time impossible to "prove." The pathos formula, a concept developed by the renowned art historian Aby Warburg, is intangible, elusive, and never present without the subjective investment of the observer. Not really a formula, "pathos" touches on a certain psychic energy of images and their ability to express pain and suffering as essential human features. Warburg belonged to a generation of German Jews that would have been horrified by the very idea of exploring a specifically "Jewish pathos formula"; if ancient Greek and Renaissance Italian art are understood as standing for all of the Western world, the question of whether one can then speak of a "Jewish pathos formula," how it relates to the "general" pathos formula, and its conditions or constraints, must await future discussion.

Be that as it may, Lerski's photographs of Jewish and Arab types do produce a certain "Jewish pathos formula." I will later discuss the relationship between this form of pathos and Zionism, but a no less significant complication pertains to the status of the image in photography (Olin and Morris-Reich 2019, 193–99). Professional photographers, certainly art photographers of Lerski's caliber, use elements drawn from the world in order to create an image. But they already have an image in their mind. And as the image is not unrelated to the world, the relationship is circular. The analysis of how they make use of reality to create an image is complicated not only because of the practical, silent manipulations photographers employ, and not only because the image they produce is related in complex ways to the image they had in their mind in the first place, but also because the process involves the notion of the image. Unlike a visual object, the image lies at the meeting point of the visible and the imaginary. Conceptually, it is hard and maybe impossible to define and fully stabilize the notion of the image, and, empirically, the image involves irreducible subjective and associative features.

Lerski's project also involves at least two significant political contexts. The first of these is the role played by racial photography in the contemporaneous science, art, and popular culture (Webster 2021). While Lerski was highly preoccupied with compositions of light and shadow, the Jewish and Arab types project on which I expand below is also about the very notion of types and typicality. Types are very difficult to define, but they have to do with the space between the universal and the individual (or, in philosophical terms, a specific difference). For the following, we must remember that Lerski carried out this project at a time when physical anthropologists, geneticists, ethnologists, and members of many more disciplines were looking at similar kinds of phenomena to substantiate the existence of races and distinctive types. Did Lerski actually believe that there were Jewish and Arab types and that he, as a photographer, was documenting them? While he may have wanted to prove that race is an ideological construction rather than a biological category, one of my main arguments in this chapter is that his method caused him to undermine his own undertaking because it emphasized all the dichotomies that photography is capable of expressing so well: between men and women, Jews and Arabs, urban and rural people, rich and poor, young and old, European and Mizrahi.

The second important context is that of Zionism. It is crucial that Lerski first conceived of this project as being about Jewish types and then expanded its scope to include Arab types as well. What did this change in the project intend to indicate? To Lerski's chagrin, the completed project was never exhibited in a museum or published in book form. The questions involved in why it was not shown intersect with another question that cannot be avoided either, even though it completely transcends the case, a question pertaining to the relationships among Zionism, photography, and colonialism (though the word *relationship* is somewhat inapt here, implying as it does that the three are separate or separable in the first place): Was Zionist photography colonialist? And if so, was that because of the nature of Zionism or because of the nature of photography? From a postcolonial historical perspective with which we grapple, photography is often recognized as a colonialist and Orientalist instrument not only because it was part of Western imperial and colonial expansion, an instrument of domination over non-European and non-white subjects, but because it was an expression of the white man's gaze, fixing and stabilizing the image of the Orient. This is a question of "method," that is, of the "idea of an idea" of Zionism and of photography. The image is capable of containing opposites, ambiguities, and self-contradictions. But did Lerski drag reality into the imagination, through the photographic apparatus, or did he, on the contrary, push imaginary types into reality?

In the Western cultural imagination, the *image* of "the Jew" is unquestionably tied to the Christian ethos. This iconography is complex and comprises conflicting, at times contradicting images: for instance, it includes a bearded male Jew, crying and suffering, occasionally with violence being inflicted upon him; and at the same time, other generic images involve antisemitic tropes, such as the Jew as money-lender; as member of a secret, powerful cabal controlling the world; or as a lazy parasite (Lipton 2014; Nirenberg 2015). It is part of the complexity of the image's inference that a photograph can allude to possible interpretations in many ways, involving cues, inversions, and displacements, that are irreducible to its figurative content in the narrow sense. Lerski's pathos formula, I argue, provides viewers with such implicitly instructive cues. It is, evidently, an inherently gendered formula, which is most palpable in photographs of men, with their emphasis on beards and working hands.

The aspect of the pathos formula in Lerski's types project that I am interested in here could be termed "an explosion," by which I mean a dramatic destabilization of the Jewish image. At what moment and under what conditions does such an explosion occur? Lerski's project, focusing on types in Palestine, offers an intriguing site for the exploration of this question. This case, in complex ways, involves politics and culture, Zionism and humanism, the "Old Jew" and the "New Jew," the image and photography. What makes this case particularly interesting is the fact that Lerski himself was engaged in an intriguing form of photographic experiment, which appears to have gone wrong.

At the beginning of this analysis I will consider Lerski's photographic method, then gradually move to exemplifying my claim with photographs. I argue that Lerski had an elaborate method that he extended to this particular project, and that this method was most unsuited to his apparent motivations and goals. I will then turn to the question of the "Jewish pathos formula," suggesting that the destabilization and "explosion" of the Jewish image is tied to the infiltration of *unheimlich* sensation into some of the photographs, which was unintended by Lerski.

Lerski's Method

Lerski's biography is well-known, and I will only repeat here very briefly what is necessary in the current context: Born in Germany to a family of Eastern European Jewish background and brought up in Switzerland, Lerski moved to America, returned to Germany in the midst of World War I, and played a significant role in the development of German cinema during the Weimar Republic years. He moved to Palestine in 1930 and returned to Switzerland a month before the State of Israel was established in 1948. Politically, Lerski's biography is quite idiosyncratic and seems to contradict the familiar contemporaneous trends. He moved to Palestine before the Nazi Party came to power in Germany (though till 1939 he also continued to spend much of his time in Europe), so while he was both a refugee from Germany and a Zionist pioneer, he was also not quite either of those in the full sense of the term; and while the exact motivations for his move are partially obscure, from his scrapbook and the wider context we can situate him socially and politically as partaking of a middle-class, left-wing, liberal, humanist, universalist, German-Jewish outlook.

Artistically, Lerski first became a still photographer under the influence of his first wife, Emilie Bertha Rossbach, in America. His early photography shows elements of pictorialism, expressionism, and pathos. When he moved back to Germany, he developed a unique (as well as complex and expensive) photographic technique based on the enhancement and manipulation of natural light through the use of mirrors. In Weimar Germany, he published an acclaimed photographic album entitled *Everyday Heads* (Lerski 1931). It is important for the types project that the individuals he photographed for this first volume, who he portrayed in a way that resembled the generic portrayals of movie stars and celebrities, were factory workers, homeless people, and beggars, a fact that Lerski disclosed in a numbered but nameless list appended to the end of the book. In the "Jewish and Arab Types" project Lerski was not fully consistent with regard to the naming of the photographed persons. While the Mizrachi and Arab people he photographed were not identified and remained anonymous "types," some of the Ashkenazi ones were identified and named and some were not. I mention this partial inconsistency because, first, it complicates the Orientalist gaze that we intuitively identify in the types project, and, second, because this may be seen as indicating that the first project was also related to types.

The Jewish types project was Lerski's first planned still-photography project in Palestine. His motivation for conceiving and carrying it out was clearly as much political as it was artistic. In a very elementary sense, it was intended to counter, with regard to race, the antisemitic and racist photographic projects that were taking place in Germany, in the same way that his first volume had done with regard to class. At the same time, the project is clearly related to the attempt, integral to Zionism, to transform not only the existence but also the image of the Jew from the "old," passive, weak one to the "new," strong, active, confident one.

There was probably also a political motivation behind Lerski's decision to change the project to encompass Arab types as well, which was quite a unique decision in the context of the period (Avineri 2017). The British Mandate regime in Palestine followed the peace treaties that ended World War I, which emphasized the principle of self-determination. The Mandate also followed the Balfour Declaration, which, while it included Britain's contradictory promises to both Jews and Arabs, stated the British commitment to the creation of a "national home" for Jews in Palestine. Consequently, during the British Mandate years, Jewish and Zionist organizations were busy building the institutions of the future Jewish society and national entity. The

Palestinian leadership (as part of a broader Arab coalition) rejected virtually any plan for a Jewish national presence in the region. This rejection was not coupled with a vision of a Jewish-Arab Palestine, but rather with the ambition to create an exclusively Arab presence in the region. Hence, even though in actuality the Jewish and Palestinian populations were practically mixed—for various purposes and to various degrees—none of the major political players was guided by a vision of a joint Jewish-Arab future (a fact that was acknowledged in the Peel Commission Report of 1936, which called for a territorial partition of the land). What is important, then, is that Lerski's voice is a Jewish voice: the decision to expand the Jewish types project to endorse Arab types as well situates him within the liberal, bourgeois left-wing Jewish camp, in the orbit of the Brit Shalom vision of a shared binational Jewish-Arab territory, space, and society. In terms of the main contemporary political streams of the early 1930s, this position was intellectually significant but politically marginal.

Lerski's decision to expand the project and include Arabs was embedded in and reflected the binational Zionist ideology. Notably, the envisioned project distinguished between the two categories rather than simply studied the multitude of Palestine at the time, which both was wider than these two categories and sometimes confounded them. By including Arabs, Lerski was recognizing their presence in Palestine, a recognition that had both political and ideological ramifications. Yet the more he advanced in the execution of the project, the more he betrayed the essentialist aspects of the types themselves. Edward Said might have concluded that Lerski succumbed to his imagination; I want to suggest that the medium undermined the artist's intentions: photography can be very treacherous.

The single most important thing for the analysis I present here is the fact that he brought an already fully developed method to the new types project. It consisted of his "idea of the idea" of photography, which was essentially about the photographer creating an image through the use of light. He constructed his photographic scenes geometrically, using a large-format camera, plates, and heavy mirrors. The mirrors had to be carried, placed on feet, situated, and adjusted. Then the photographic subjects had to be positioned in the studio space, where they then had to remain perfectly still for a comparatively long time. This method created heavy, theatrical, pathos-filled photographs. Lerski had developed and enhanced this method in the previous years; it immigrated to Palestine with him.

Notably, Lerski's use of the same method despite his migration from Germany to Palestine was an active decision (no less active than a decision to change it). Historians of photography erroneously sometimes view the history of photography as independent of the history of art in general and of painting in particular. Photographers' sensitivity to light is a case in point. It is critically important to situate Lerski with regard to his peers in Palestine, who contended with the question of light. Take, for instance, his contemporary, the painter Joseph Zaritsky (Bar Or 1998). Zaritsky reinvented himself when he arrived in Palestine. He immersed himself in the new place and created a style that was based on his (imaginary and mythical) conception of the land's unique light. Leaving behind the figurative style he had acquired in Russia; he embraced a new style and technique that were meant to address this new light. Another approach to light in Palestine can be traced in the expressionist painting of Naftali Bezem. In depicting workers and sailors in the Port of Haifa, Bezem, a committed socialist, disregarded the specificity of the light and created a universal light instead, suggesting that workers all over the world were the same. In photography, meanwhile, there were Zionist and Israeli photographers (all of them later than Lerski) for whom the question of local light was very important, including Peter Merom, Micha Bar-Am, and Boris Carmi. Of course, the discussion of Mediterranean light cannot be understood without the context of the debate in France and its contrast, northern light, which was related to an "organic" conception of light, much of which was mythical and imaginary. Like the happy impressionists in the south of France, the Zionist painters and photographers displayed differing degrees of self-deception and fantasy, as if they, too, were in the south of France rather than in the hot land of Israel, with its yellow light. Lerski's use of light should be understood against the background of such options and ongoing discussions among artists.

Thus, Lerski could very well have considered altering his method based on the assumption that it would work differently in Palestine, because of its different light conditions, its different scenery, and its different population. Yet, instead, he stuck to his "mechanical" notion of light. In an almost vulgar, violent way, Lerski set aside the question of the organic "local" light and continued to place his rational structure of mirrors at the center of his work. This was not just a theoretical stance, but also a political one. He took the method and technique that he had developed in a studio in Berlin and placed it on his roof in Tel Aviv. Rational rather than capricious, universal rather than local, and mechanical rather than organic, his language of light was, in certain respects, so unique that it was almost a private language. Moreover, Lerski could have replaced his heavy camera with a light Leica, with which he could have toured and photographed on site, forming a direct relationship with Jewish and Arab types in their natural environments. In order to photograph using plates, the photographer has to hold the world still, whereas with the light Leica, already widely available in the 1930s, the world could be photographed in motion, while still retaining sharpness.

In Lerski's estate in the Folkwang Museum in Essen, Germany, we find examples of such "free" photographs, made with a 35mm camera in Palestine. His market photograph (fig. 8.1) demonstrates his use of such cameras. It is much less planned than are his project (studio) photographs. But Lerski apparently went looking for external lighting conditions to match his intended bathing of the scene in Middle Eastern light, and behind the only man looking at the photographer we can see a patch of light on the wall that looks like an abstraction of a window crossed by vertical bars. Lerski probably did not wander into this scene by accident. He lived in Palestine and was familiar with the light conditions at different times of day. With large cameras such as he used, focus is difficult. He seems to have sought the

Figure 8.1. Helmar Lerski, a market scene in Mandate Palestine. *Source:* Courtesy Fotografische Sammlung, Museum Folkwang. Used with permission.

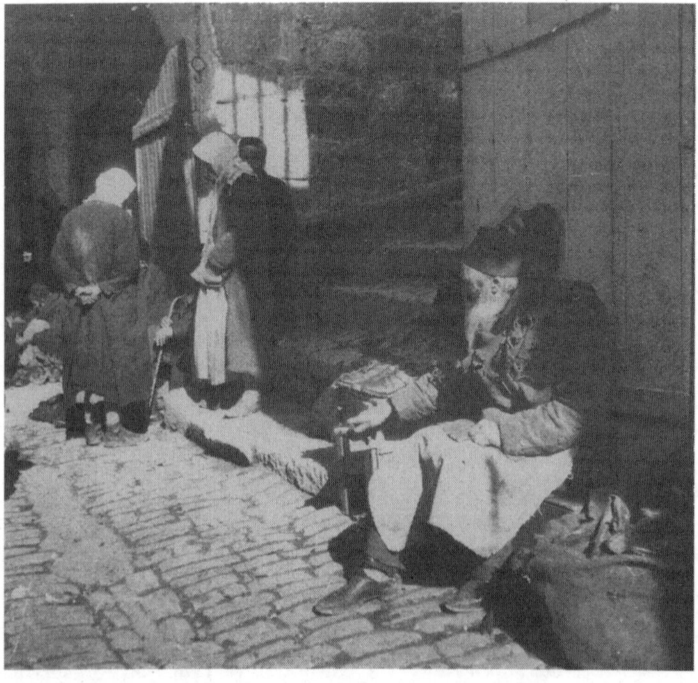

shade; a square, large-format 6×6 Yashica or Rolleiflex allows a lot of light to enter, so the depth of field was such that he was able to capture both the beggar in the foreground on the right and the distant beggar, crouched on the ground at the far left of the picture, keeping them both in focus, whereas in the studio, if the photographic subject makes even the slightest movement of an eyelid, the photograph comes out blurred. With this kind of camera, the photograph is probably taken from the photographer's waist and what he photographs is not identical with what he sees.

Apart from the partially obscured man in black against the wall on the steps, none of the people in the scene is facing the observer. The splash of light against the wall (already mentioned above): even a "standard" street photograph such as this one shows Lerski treating light carefully. We can also note the hands here, how many hands appear in the photograph: the hands of the beggar in the foreground, a hand dug deep into a pocket, hands holding a stick, hands holding each other behind a back, the hands of the distant beggar. Finally, the two beggars—at the far right and the far left—are holding their heads tilted at the same angle, but the photograph frames the one on the right as if he were outside the frame: Lerski is looking at all of them, but he is also looking through the perspective of the beggar on the right, and the photograph produces the impression that the man in black against the wall is looking back at the beggar. Should I comment on the fact that there are no women in the photograph? This is a market in Jerusalem in the 1930s, so maybe we should not be surprised. The market is a male Oriental site, and the photograph expresses this male Orientalism: women are excluded from important segments of the Oriental public sphere, and the photographic frame here also excludes women. The photograph becomes a document of its memory. "Street photographs" are generically quick, sensitive, and filled with humor and affection, qualities altogether absent from Lerski's planned "Jewish and Arab Types" project. By *not* changing his method, therefore, Lerski wanted to show the method's universal applicability, but in actuality, this is not how things worked.

The renowned American photographer Ansel Adams, Lerski's slightly younger contemporary, is a helpful point of comparison here, since both were preoccupied with a method for expressing an image that preceded the photographic act. Both were engaged in attempting to express, through a rigorous, meticulously thought-out, and highly controlled process, the idea that photography is about an image formed in the imagination of the photographer: Lerski with his mirror technique and Adams through the zone system that he formulated. In a certain sense, it does not matter at all to

Lerski what he photographs; what Lerski photographs, in the end, is his own method, his own "idea of the idea" of photography.

Applying the same method that he had earlier employed in the context of class, now in the context of race, Lerski demonstrates his staunch commitment to a universal, humanistic conception of humans, unwilling to succumb to the multiplicity of the world outside. But every student of photography is taught in the very first weeks of study, often with examples that highlight differences—such as an image of an "interracial" wedding—that certain challenges are inherent to photography. The amount of light needed for a balanced photograph differs markedly depending on whether the photograph involves dark-skinned or light-skinned persons; if both of those appear in the same frame, the photograph seems to highlight differences and thus to contradict the essence of the photographed event, namely, the overcoming of differences. Lerski's method works differently when it is applied to different "kinds" of objects. While Lerski wanted to counter the racist and antisemitic uses of photography, even such a trivial thing as skin color had an effect on the photograph. These photographs of two young boys from the "types" project provide a revealing example (figs. 8.2 and 8.3). Even aside from the fact that their hair is differently textured,

Figure 8.2. Helmar Lerski, item from "Jewish and Arab Types." *Source:* Courtesy Fotografische Sammlung, Museum Folkwang. Used with permission.

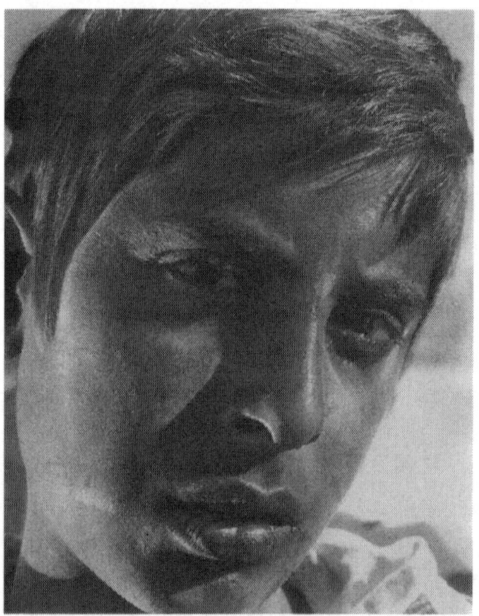

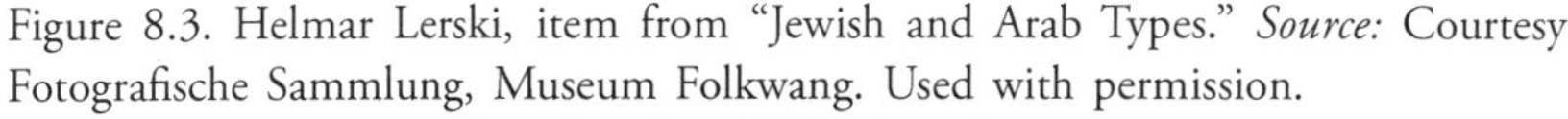

Figure 8.3. Helmar Lerski, item from "Jewish and Arab Types." *Source:* Courtesy Fotografische Sammlung, Museum Folkwang. Used with permission.

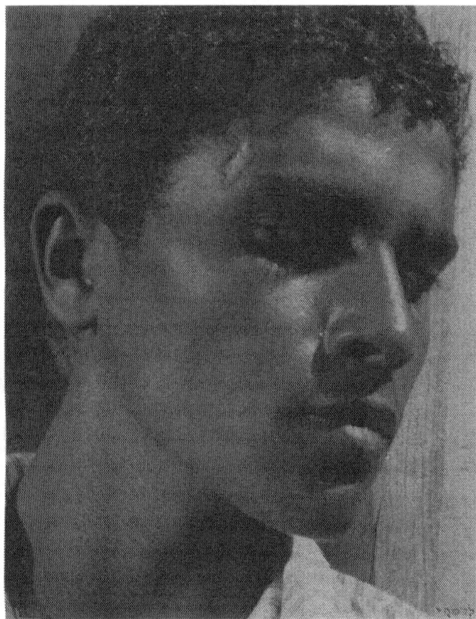

one can easily see that one has light skin and hair, while the other has dark skin and hair, and that his handsome features are stronger, as well as the fact that one is of Ashkenazi and the other of Mizrahi background.

I wish to relate the following examples of the significance of Lerski's method to several general impressions I took away from seeing all of the prints of this series (more than 500 of them). After having observed several photographs from the series, I began to have the feeling that I had already seen the photographs before. In other words, they operated like a powerful cliché. Of course, Lerski did not intend the viewer to see all the photographs at once. Yet it is nonetheless worthwhile noting that looking at the prints in succession had a cumulative and clustering effect. The photographs managed to create the impression that each individual Yemenite (or Jew, or Arab) stood for all Yemenites (or Jews, or Arabs), as if Lerski were really sampling these respective types. Finally, one had the feeling that Lerski had really managed to capture the "Yemenite," the "Jewish," and the "Arab" types (figs. 8.4, 8.5, and 8.6).

Most of the people Lerski photographed for the types project were unnamed and remained anonymous. They really are, in that sense, "types." But some of the people he photographed are named; one of these is a woman named Yehudit Orenstein. Here is an Orientalist moment: European

Figure 8.4. Helmar Lerski, item from "Jewish and Arab Types." *Source:* Courtesy Fotografische Sammlung, Museum Folkwang. Used with permission.

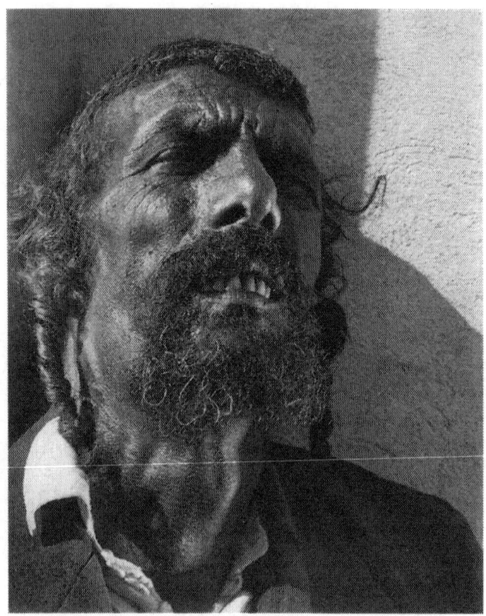

Figure 8.5. Helmar Lerski, item from "Jewish and Arab Types." *Source:* Courtesy Fotografische Sammlung, Museum Folkwang. Used with permission.

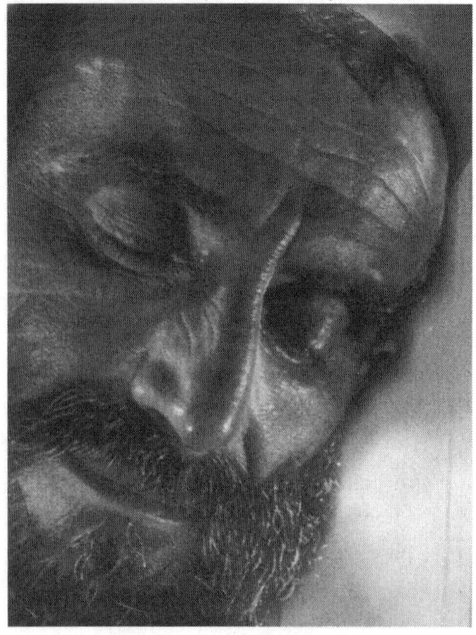

Figure 8.6. Helmar Lerski, item from "Jewish and Arab Types." *Source:* Courtesy Fotografische Sammlung, Museum Folkwang. Used with permission.

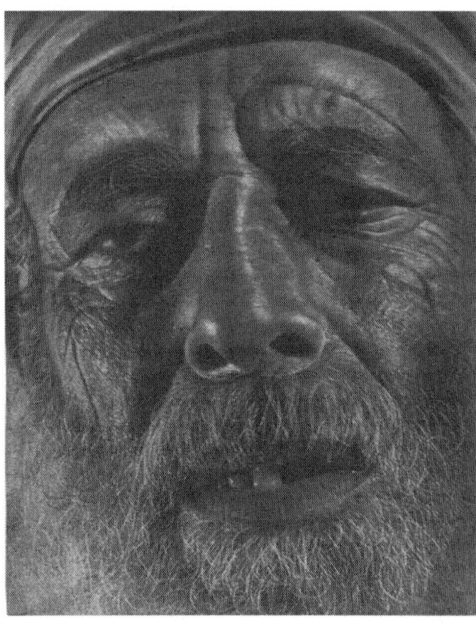

Jews are named, but Arabs, and Jews from Arab countries, are not. But we saw that in the first book, *Faces of the Everyday*, in Germany, people were photographed anonymously, too. Was he Orientalist there, too, or does the Orientalism depend on the place the photographs were taken or the place they were viewed? There is no straight answer to this question. Lerski clearly did employ the same method, the same lighting, and the same mise-en-scène strategies for all of his photographs. He used the same photographic languages for European Jews, for Arabs, and for Jews from Arab countries. In this respect, his method seems to have been devised as a vehicle against racism, which highlights individual idiosyncrasies and thus indicates the faults of ethnic-based categories. At the same time, however, his method did produce different results for the light-skinned Yehudit Orenstein and other European Jews than it did for the dark-skinned Yemenite or Bedouins. In this sense, while Lerski used the same technique, his method predetermined results that underscored differences.

Since the light falls differently on Yehudit Orenstein's skin than it would if she had a darker skin, Lerski's attempt to employ photography to negate race theory undermines itself. He has dressed her in a white cloth and lifted her face so that the smooth areas of her cheeks receive light; he has decreased the contrast between light and shade; and we can tell from the few locks of hair escaping from the head covering that her hair is blond or light brown. Caught in his own method, Lerski *emphasizes* the complexion of the photographic subject. If we compare the light falling on Orenstein's skin with the light falling on the skin of maybe the most famous photograph from this series, the photograph of a Yemenite man, we notice that the shadow in the photograph of the Yemenite man is darker, making a starker contrast, while the shadow in the photograph of Orenstein looks touched by light in comparison, even though, from the slim white line in the middle of the frame of each photograph, we can tell that the condition in which the two photographs were taken was the same. Lerski's *method* works differently with different complexions.

Ansel Adams deployed his zone system on mountains, elevating the landscapes to the sublime. While we could actually compare those photographs with Lerski's, who also elevated his subjects, it is easier to make the comparison between Lerski and Phil Perkis, who was a student and follower of Adams's and applied elements of Adams's method to street photography. The zone system is particularly effective for minimizing differences between people with different skin color. Observe Perkis's 1984 black-and-white photograph made at Jerusalem's Jaffa Gate. Perkis is employing a method of gradation based on underexposure. For this reason, rather than a strong contrast between black and white, there are only shades of black and white; in fact, there is no actual black or white, but only shades of gray. When the photograph was developed, it was again underexposed, and, finally, it was printed on very soft paper. Now, if we try to analyze the person in the crosswalk at Jaffa Gate, we can see that it is pretty clearly a man, we can even infer from his curly hair texture he looks non-European, but we cannot tell from his skin or hair whether he is Jewish or Arab, Ashkenazi or Mizrahi (and maybe even more important, the photograph does not particularly elicit the question). And the reason for this is that Perskis's method does not easily enable us to make these kinds of distinctions in the photograph. In his first book, *Faces of the Everyday*, Lerski's method compelled the viewers to consult the list at the end of the book to realize what he or she was "really" seeing in the photograph. Had he wanted to reach the same outcome in his Palestine type project, his best way to achieve this would have been to use a method that played down physiological differences.

But Lerski's ideological or political motivations did not trump his aesthetic agenda, which was to use the faces of his subjects to create forms. Their faces thus simply became the surfaces of the photographer's projection of light for the purpose of abstraction. True to his artistic vision, Lerski remained committed to his method and aesthetic aims. But this commitment to artistic principles resulted in a contradiction right at the core of his project: by contrast to the evident outcome, Lerski did not want to accentuate natural differences between members of different "races" or "types," but rather to show them as superficial.

The question of the source of the image (whether it originates in the artist's mind or in the world) is basic to nineteenth-century art, which clearly connects Lerski with that artistic tradition. The question is thus not specific to photography, although in this case there is an additional apparatus that comes in between. But this dynamic is relatively new, because early Renaissance paintings of Jesus entering Jerusalem, for instance, were conceived entirely from the artist's imagination: the painter did not see Jerusalem, Jesus, or the donkey. Only following Alberti, who conceived the painting as a window onto reality, could the question arise of whether, despite the fact that I see something, it might actually not be that thing after all (Alberti 1972). Imagination has been inserted into reality, and the more the two mix—when you intersect the real with the imaginary "Jew" or "Yemenite Jew"—the more convoluted the shape, but also the sharper the crisis. You cannot know which of the two (the real or the imaginary) is the one you are seeing, which is exactly the case in many photographs in this series.

Figure 8.7. Helmar Lerski, item from "Jewish and Arab Types." *Source:* Courtesy Fotografische Sammlung, Museum Folkwang. Used with permission.

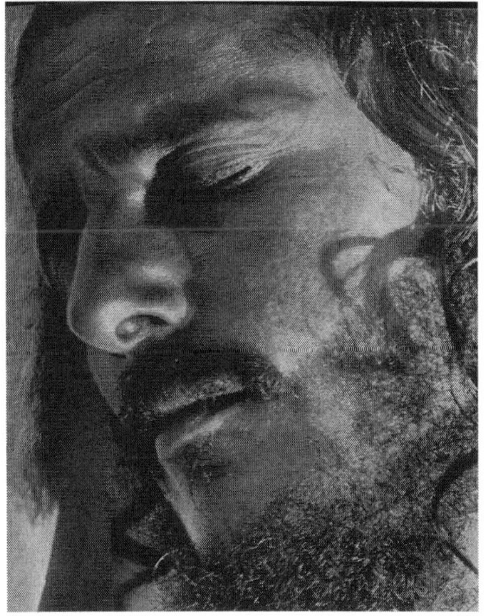

Lerski structures the picture of a Yemenite man to fit the composition, rather than structuring a composition to fit the subject. In other words, Lerski's Yemenite portrait in this series is, eventually, at the service of the composition (and in cutting the head from the shoulders, Lerski is closer to cinematic composition than to nineteenth-century painting). With a simple manipulation of light, Lerski could have situated a Bedouin or Yemenite Jew as an Italian or Dutch noble person, elevating the status of the photograph (to that of a painting) and elevating the status of the photographed subject (to that of a nobleman). From a postcolonial perspective, this is a form of Orientalism. Lerski, however, does not seem to be interested in the authenticity of the portrayed Arab or Jew but rather, like László Moholy-Nagy, in aesthetic abstractions. Abstraction is the idea that form and content merge—a green blotch in a picture can be what the picture is saying, or what it is about, as it causes you to ask whether what comes next will be a completing or contrasting blotch. As Lerski never moved to an abstraction that was free of the figurative, we can situate him between conceptual art (Duchamp) and figurative art (Picasso). And while we do not ask whether Kandinsky "represented" social reality or his own mental reality, the question of "representation" does come up with regard to Lerski, because photography maintains a relationship with representation. But the truth is that the reality that Lerski "represents" is much more his own reality than that of British Mandate Palestine. He does not easily yield to the postcolonial framework: he never denied the presence of the Palestinians, both in the sense that his photographs do not hide the conditions of their production and in the sense that he did specifically include Arabs in the project. If the postcolonial framework does not only suggest that the colonizers does not recognize the existence of the subalterns, but that their colonial methods of representation represent them as "types" rather than individuals, it is not accidental that scholars engaged in postcolonial criticism of Zionism, such as Ariella Azoulay, do not engage with Lerski. While there is ambiguity in Lerski's treatment of his photographed persons, as individuals and as "types," it hard to claim that Lerski did not recognize the existence of the Palestinians without a great degree of violence to his explicit and implicit aims (Azoulay 2008).

The Pathos Formula

The pathos formula is related to subtle gestures and maybe unprovable qualities of images in relation to the expression of human pain and suffering.

Aby Warburg, who developed the notion, helped to redefine the methods of art history, blurring the limits between interpretation and poetic invention (Warburg 1999, 553–58; Didi Huberman 2016). The question of anachronism is central to Warburg's thought, and he developed a nonlinear and highly associative vision of history, in which the identification of pathos is always inseparable from the emotive and energetic investment of the observer. The discussion of pathos in Lerski's photographs cannot be fully separated, then, either from the images that preceded the project under discussion by centuries or from those belonging to the decade that followed.

Since the early centuries of Christianity, solidified through Augustine's doctrine of Jewish witness, the image of the exiled Jew, after the destruction of the Temple, had been associated in Western imagination with the lamentation, humiliation, and suffering. However, it is important to note this nuance: the crying and suffering Jew does *not* elicit human compassion. This, for example, is also the case for the photographs of suffering Jews surrounded by soldiers or uniformed police officers that were taken by the German perpetrators during the Holocaust (like the "barefoot rabbi" Yechiel Weizman discusses in this volume). It is clear that both the surrounding men and the photographer—and the intended viewers of the photograph—neither felt nor expected others to feel empathy with the Jew. Yet, these photos often echoed other images of suffering in Western society.

Compare, for instance, fig. 8.8, the photograph of a bearded Jewish man kneeling and being humiliated by German police officers before being subsequently murdered in a mass shooting in 1942, with the graphic renditions of the *Death of Orpheus* in a fifth-century BCE vase painting (fig. 8.9). The similarities and tensions between the "Jewish pathos formula" and the "general" (Greek/Western) one become apparent.

The most important elements of the pathos formula in the current context are related to primitive levels of human existence, both psychologically and in evolutionary terms, including the haunting power of images, related to what Warburg viewed as their quality of "survival" or the "afterlife" (*Nachleben*), their essentially phantasmal quality, and their being unconscious with respect to time. Discussing the pathos formula in Lerski's case within the framework of these larger questions, then, I ask: Can one speak of a "Jewish pathos formula"? Is there anything specific about it? And has Zionism, intent on transforming the image of "the Jew," changed anything in this regard?

Is it necessary to know that the figure in the photograph is Jewish in order to identify the "Jewish pathos formula," and does this mean that,

Figure 8.8. Humiliation of a Jew in Poland, Luków, fall 1942. *Source:* Courtesy Photo Archives of Yad Vashem. Used with permission.

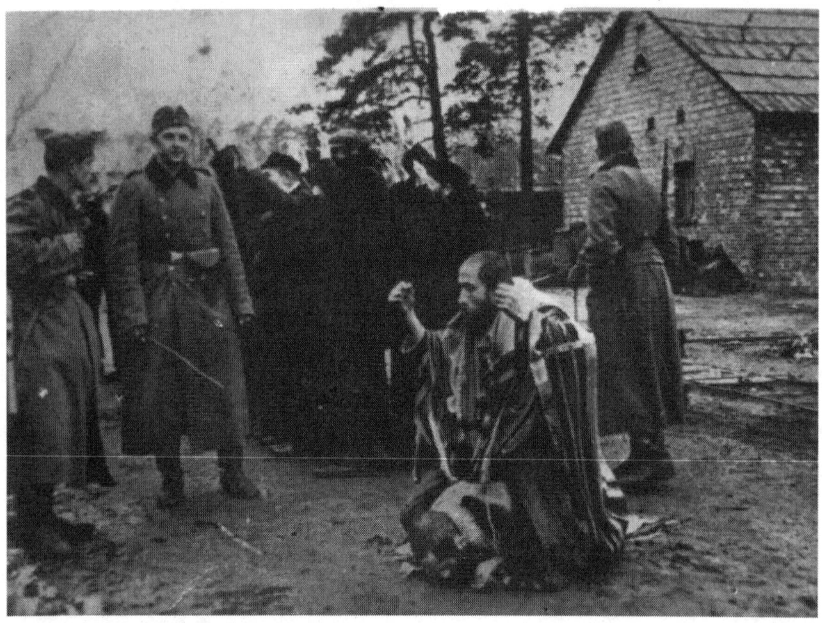

Figure 8.9. *Death of Orpheus*, 1497. Woodcut from Ovid, Metamorphoses. Venice. *Source:* Public domain.

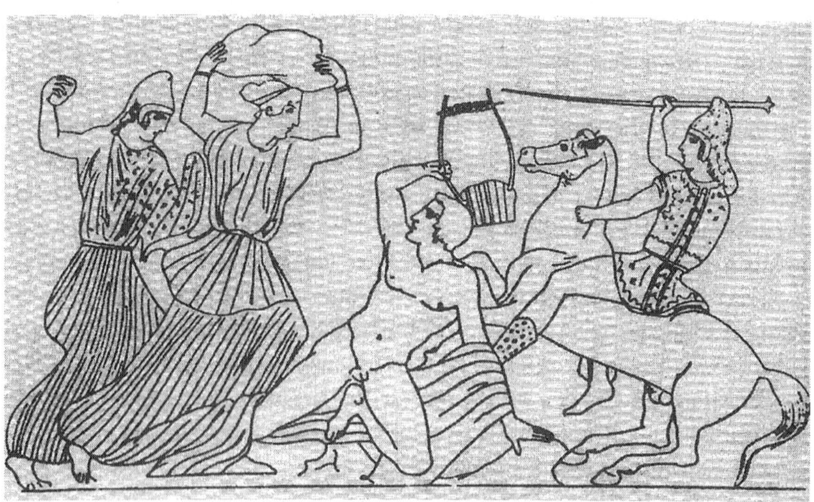

in fact, there is nothing specifically Jewish about it? In contending with these questions, we should not forget that Lerski imposed his photographic language on the world, without much regard for reality or concern with its distortion, much like Shakespeare, who wrote *The Merchant of Venice* when there were practically no Jews in England. Still, the play's Shylock has shaped how generations of actual Jews have been seen and encountered ever since.

With regard to pathos, Lerski's net had only very large holes, so to speak; it did not catch smaller, nuanced reverberations of pathos-ridden imagery, but only the grand, familiar (and often stereotypical) visual tropes. Look, for instance, at this photograph of a Moroccan Jewish porter, from Lerski's types project (fig. 8.10): His eyes are shut and his mouth open, some of his teeth are missing, and his clothes are torn and dirty. Apart from the suffering expression, there is something primitive about the figure, and Lerski gives enormous weight to the man's ear, which is almost double the size of a what a normal ear would be according to the conventions of naturalist

Figure 8.10. Helmar Lerski, item from "Jewish and Arab Types." *Source:* Courtesy Fotografische Sammlung, Museum Folkwang. Used with permission.

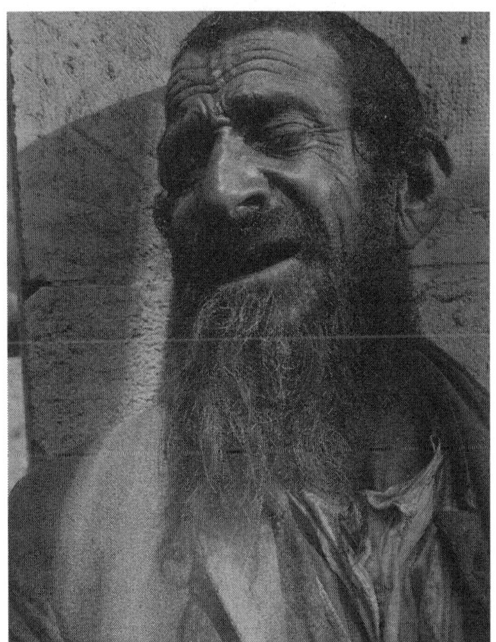

drawing. Here the "Jewish pathos formula" is featured almost explicitly with emphasis on the beard and hands as generic signifiers of will and power. Lerski does not attempt to portray the porter based on the encounter with him, but instead powerfully projects elements of pathos onto his figure. The thing about photography, as Vilem Flusser argued, is that the world submits to photography's projection (Flusser 2000). Lerski looked for a certain photographic form, a site of projection, and chose his subjects—the specific man—to fit the image he wanted to project. Can we deduce anything from this photograph about the social reality of Palestine in the 1930s? Was this man in fact a happy man? The photograph has something horrid about it, echoing a variety of cliché images: The crying Jew praying for redemption at the Wailing Wall; the cursed, wandering Jew; the Jew kneeling before his execution by a Nazi soldier; and Art Spiegelman's *Maus*, who in itself reverberated the Nazi propaganda imagery.

Another variant of the "Jewish pathos formula" in Lerski's types project links the image of the Jew with Jesus on the cross, the ultimate example of pain and suffering. Bringing together primitivism, spiritualism, and expressionism, these photographs by Lerski can be compared with Emil Nolde's 1912 "Prophet." Figure 8.5 serves as good example of this formula, where a bearded Jew, his eyes shut, facing down, his face filling the entire frame like a Christian icon, connect Jewish pain and suffering with the iconography of Christian art. The elements of the "Jewish pathos formula" that can be found in Lerski's expressive photographs of bearded Jewish men, constitute instead an uncanny infiltration into the photographs. The elements are very close to the surface, and "flickering" rather than stable, but the gaze is nonetheless led to them.

Conclusion

Helmar Lerski's photographs of Jews and Arabs in 1930s Palestine intersect core questions in the photography and Jewish history nexus, including imagination or reality in the photographic image; the specifically contentious context of postcolonial theoretical stances, photography's *and* Zionism's Orientalism; and the relationship between diverse photographic methods and (intended and unintended) photographic and political outcomes.

In this chapter, I have suggested that Helmar Lerski's photographs of Jews and Arabs in 1930s Palestine result in the strange resurfacing of elements of the "Jewish pathos formula" in a project carried out within a Zionist culture intent on transforming the image of the Jew. His commitment to a photographic method he used in Germany produced images that conflicted with his ideological convictions—by underscoring differences between "types"—and at the same time turned individuals into both abstract shapes and pathos-ridden references to Jewish and Western clichés. This "explosion" of inferences was, apparently, unintentional. Yet it was the most consequential aspect of Lerski's endeavor to portray the dwellers of Mandate Palestine.

Helmar Lerski's three planned still-photography projects were all carried out using the same method and technique, bringing together his aesthetic commitment to abstraction through the projection of light with a humanistic commitment to a shared human core. But each of his projects did this through a different entry point: the first project, *Everyday Heads*, carried out in Weimar Germany, focused on class (Lerski 1931); the second project (discussed here), "Jewish and Arab Types," carried out in British Mandate Palestine, focused on race and ethnicity; and the third project, called "Metamorphosis through Light" (Lerski 1982) and also carried out in Palestine, focused on individuality. In a certain way, however, all three were based on the same aspirations and vision.

Artistically and aesthetically, all three projects were intended to demonstrate the sovereignty of the photographer: The ability to establish an image and to show that the photographer could trick the observer into recognizing something that was not there (or failing to recognize something that was). For instance, in the context of class, a beggar could be portrayed as a film star, and in the context of individuality, the same individual could be rendered as a knight or a martyr, and this could be done using the projection of light alone. In this new "nation of photography" (as in *The Family of Man*, only a couple of decades later and on a much larger scale), photography was to convey that humans were basically the same and capable of education (Stimson 2006).

But in Lerski's second project, "Jewish and Arab Types," things worked out differently. Photography can be treacherous, and Lerski ended up aggravating all the dichotomies that he opposed. Two political contexts framed this project: "racial photography," which was closely tied, especially in Germany, to antisemitism; and Zionism, which attempted to transform the image of the Jew. It would be a mistake to reduce Lerski's project to either or both of these political contexts. Yet this project also cannot be separated from these two contexts. And both of them trickled into the photographs. But for the explosion that I have described to take place, something additional had to happen.

I have suggested that this explosion may be related to the rattling of the structure in which the Jewish image originated and within which it is fixed. The image of the Jew in Western culture does involve the crying, suffering, bearded Jewish man, who elicits not human compassion but rather indifference, or maybe mockery, if not a touch of contempt. Using some of the qualities of images that Warburg explored, especially the durability of expressions of pain and suffering and their trickery or double-sided nature, some of Lerski's photographs of highly expressive bearded Jewish men, which were intended, maybe more than anything else, as photographic experiments in abstraction, rather than corroborate the image of the "new" Jew, crossed all the way to the other side, recharging the "old" image of Jewish existence as tied to pain, suffering, and violence.

Works Cited

Alberti, Leon Battista. 1972. *On painting; and, On Sculpture, the Latin texts of "De pictura" and "De statua."* Translated by Cecil Grayson. Phaidon.

Ashkenazi, Ofer. 2016. "Zionism as a Cure for Weimar Crisis in Lerski's Avodah." In *Three-Way Street: Jews, Germans, and the Transnational,* edited by Jay Howard Geller and Leslie Morris. University of Michigan Press.

Avineri, Shlomo. 2017. *The Making of Modern Zionism: The Intellectual Origins of the Jewish State.* Basic Books.

Azoulay, Ariella. 2008. *The Civil Contract of Photography.* Zone.

Bar Or, Galia. 1998. *Hebrew Work: Israeli Art from the 1920s to the 1990s.* Mishkan Museum of Art.

Didi Huberman, George. 2016. *The Surviving Image: Phantoms of Time and Time of Phantoms: Aby Warburg's History of Art.* Penn State University Press.

Flusser, Vilem. 2000. *Towards a Philosophy of Photography.* Reaktion.

Lerski, Helmar. 1931. *Köpfe des Alltags: Unbekannte Menschen.* Hermann Reckendorf.

———. 1982. *Verwandlungen durch Licht/Metamorphosis through Light.* Edited by Ute Eskildsen and André Gelpke. Luca Verlag.

Lipton, Sarah. 2014. *Dark Mirror: The Medieval Origins of Anti-Jewish Iconography.* Metropolitan.

Morris-Reich, Amos. 2022. "The Boundaries of Photographic Intention: Helmar Lerski's 'Failed Project.'" *Photography and Jewish History: Five Twentieth-Century Cases.* University of Pennsylvania Press.

Nirenberg, David. 2015. *Aesthetic Theology and Its Enemies: Judaism in Christian Painting, Poetry, and Politics.* Brandeis University Press.

Olin, Margaret, and Amos Morris-Reich. 2019. "Epilogue: Photography and the Question of the Image." In *Photography and Imagination*, edited by Margaret Olin and Amos Morris-Reich. Routledge.

Spinoza, Benedictus de. 1992. *The Ethics; Treatise on the Emulation of the Intellect; Selected Letters.* 2nd ed. Hackett.

Stimson, Blake. 2006. *The Pivot of the World: Photography and Its Nation.* MIT Press.

Warburg, Aby. 1999. *The Renewal of Pagan Antiquity: Contributions to the Cultural History of the European Renaissance.* 1st ed. Translated by David Britt. Getty Research Institute for the History of Art and the Humanities.

Webster, Christopher. 2021. *Photography in the Third Reich: Art, Physiognomy and Propaganda.* London.

Chapter 9

Photography and Racism in Israel
A Telegraphic Sketch of Three Processes

Ktzia Alon

This chapter underlines the significant role photography played in the negotiation of "racial" identities (and the social hierarchy that accompanied it) within the Jewish society of Israel. The long-standing bias against "Eastern," or "Mizrahi," Jews—namely, the ones who immigrated to Israel from North Africa or Middle Eastern countries—has been well documented by scholars, intellectuals, and artists. Photography had played an important role in promoting and displaying this bias. Official photographers of the national institutions and the major Zionist news outlets creatively participated in defining and exhibiting the alleged inherent inferiority of Mizrahi immigrants and their descendants. Yet photography also enabled Mizrahi Jews of different generations to express their identity and communicate their experiences from their perspective. Reclaiming agency through photography, Mizrahi photographers provide an alternative outlook on the social power structure of the Israeli society and its vital tensions, as well as suggest possible resolutions for these tensions.

The first part of this chapter, "Photographing the Mizrahi," briefly touches on the subject of "Oriental Jews" as objects of Zionist photography, which has been produced by the establishment and official institutions over many decades. In the second part, "Photography as an Oriental Medium,"

I discuss the globalization of photography and the utter democratization of the medium, unparalleled by any other art media. The particular focus will be on Israel, with its Ashkenazi (European or Western) hegemony, where photography as a medium is going through the process of "Orientalization"—an inevitable outcome of the above-mentioned democratization. The third part, "Toward a Conceptualization of the Oriental Modus in Photography," presents Mizrahi alternatives to the hegemonic gaze. It concisely discusses works by artists who sought to challenge that gaze and offer new ways of seeing the Mizrahi subject.

I wish to emphasize that the present chapter is not intended to delineate a clear chronological transition; these three movements are simultaneously underway nowadays in the rich Israeli photography-space. Encompassing the abundance of contemporary photographers, willing (or unwilling) subjects of photography, and the presence of photographs in various media and social networks, the photography-space simultaneously gives voice to the hegemony and to its challengers. Also, this chapter will not convey the findings of a completed independent and comprehensive research project but constitute more of an exposition of the field and its significance.

Photographing Mizrahi (Oriental Jews)

As several studies demonstrated, in various historical contexts photography has functioned as a suppressive tool wielded by the powers that be. The privilege of remaining in the shade, invisible behind the camera, while exposing the other to the blinding sunlight, is a characteristic of hegemony. Men took photographs of women as a direct sequel to the oil paintings depicting naked women; various conquering colonial forces, be they military personnel or anthropologists, obsessively documented the conquered natives; the wealthy elite classes photographed the life of the poor.

The beginning of photo-art in Eretz Israel is characterized by a candid manifestation of this balance of power. In her pioneering study of this topic, Rona Sela posed this fundamental question: "Can photography in the above-mentioned period [of the pre-1948 years] be defined as being colonial" (Sela 2000, 17)? Her clear answer is that the photographers' "implicit intention was to bring to the West the exotic and seductive East, while searching for the Biblical reality of the desolate country, which in their eyes has hardly changed" (Sela 2000, 19). Later on, she writes,

The holy places and the natives were photographed in order to glorify their ancient Biblical image, and many times were used as memos to be sold to the West. The photographers looked for the Biblical appearance—the exotic, romantic and the magical—to fit within the accepted stereotype of the Holy Land prevalent in the West. The Westerners were glad to discover that the Biblical world was preserved, and that there's an under-developed, primitive and backward world to be conquered. Many of the images of the Arabs and the Jews in the photographs of the non-Western photographers in the 19th century reflect mostly Orientalism and Primitivism. Research shows that only a small percentage of the local population was genuinely exposed. (Sela 2000, 20)

Indeed, there are photos of Orientals (Jewish and Arabs) by the dozens, cast as extras for the role of "the ancient people of the Bible," which served as decoration for the realistic depiction photographed for the benefit of viewers abroad, for themselves, and for their friends; in some photographs, the emigrating photographers played the role of "the enlightened Westerners returning to their fathers' land" (Alon 2005). In order to achieve the perfect fantasy, highlighting the dichotomous contrast between the photographers and the photographed, the Orientals were required to put on fancy dresses, to assume staged postures and wear the "desired" expression. According to Sela: "[The European-born photographer] Suskin, for example, during the years 1906–1920, out of the attraction for the other, and the enthusiasm and the desire to adopt the local customs, took pictures of Jews wearing Arab clothes. During the first two decades of the 20th century Jewish photographers took the Arab 'other' as a model of the [authentic] man of the land in order to build-up their own self-image" (Sela 2001, 21). Many decades later, after the foundation of the State of Israel, the photographic depiction of the Mizrahi other was institutionalized. The ongoing waves of Jewish immigration from Arab countries (with Orientalist code names such as "The Magic Carpet" and "Ali-Baba") were documented by photographers of the Government Press Office (GPO). These photographers were constantly visiting the *maabarot* (transit camps) where Mizrahi immigrants dwelled and endeavored to produce the "right" image of the newcomers. In the newspapers and newsreels of those days, photos of Mizrahi Jews were abundant.

The Jewish photographers who were active at the beginning of the twentieth century in the Islamic countries, such as Yihya Hayavi, who worked in Yemen, David ben-Rahamim in Aden, and many photographers in Iraq, took pictures of many Jews living there, but were not welcome to do the same in Israel. Today they are all but completely forgotten.

In a 2012 article, Ariella Azoulay referred to the Palestinian space—which has been often invaded by cameras—as "an unbounded [Photography] Studio." "An entire territory taken over by a photography studio," she writes, "is an indication of the defective civil status of its native population. In this context, the defective status manifests in the possibility of photographing Palestinian men and women in the public domain, at all hours of the day, at every kind of activity, even in their private living space, which had become accessible to chance cameras" (Azoulay 2012, 168).

Replacing "Palestinian men and women" by "Mizrahi men and women," we shall get a precise description of the lowly place of Mizrahi Jews and their "defective" civil status. For many decades (and to the present day), Mizrahi Jews have been exposed to the hegemonic gaze: in the environment of their hastily erected housing projects and the "development" towns; their *Moshavim* (cooperative settlements); their *Moshavot* (farming communities of private farms); the dilapidated neighborhoods in the cities; the "empty fridge" in their houses; and their holidays and festivals (such as Yom Hillula, celebrated in memory of a saintly rabbi, next to his tomb, and the *Mimouna*, a traditional North African Jewish feast held the day after Passover)—all are considered a free "unlimited (photography) studio." Voyeurism, exotification, and racial and stereotype labeling have been and still are the main tools in this intensive photo-invasion.

Contemporary Israeli scholars have highlighted the ways mainstream photographers have enthusiastically engaged in the incorporation of the Mizrahi image into the state ideology. Take, for example, this observation on the paradigmatic work of one of Israel's most prominent photographers:

[The photographer] Michah Baraam, one of the most important and fertile creators of the Israeli "visual memory," took in 1958 a shot of a "woman trooper," one of the central icons of the "immigration absorption" pantheon. The picture displays for discussion all pairs of contrasting notions relating to "absorption" of Olim: the teachers versus the pupils, the knowledgeable versus the ignorant, the white versus the black, men versus women, the old versus the young, West versus East. The language of photography reinforces the differences and endows them with a "natural" halo: just as the educational practice of placing the woman trooper opposite the Mizrahi pupil, the camera reinforced the ontological validity of the teacher representing the absorption authorities versus the immigrant pupil. (Abutbool, Greenberg, and Muzafi-Heller 2005)

In another photo taken by Baraam (2011, 56), there's a variation on this theme: a light-haired woman instructor teaches a dark-complexioned boy. The photos, meticulously engineered, were regarded as a perfect imitation of reality, exemplifying a most valuable incontrovertible truth. Couples of photos spread on opposite pages of Baraam's catalog underline the stereotype the Mizrahi woman is locked in (Baraam 2011, 170–71). In the picture on the right, the Mizrahi woman is depicted surprised and amazed at the Picasso drawings, while on the opposite page, on the left, she is seen at home, in her farm (*moshav*), holding a tethered goat, implying she is a shepherdess. Tel Aviv museum (and by symbolic equivalence, Israel itself) is conceived to be a socializing agent, providing the "primitive" women accessibility to progressive Western art.

Institutional and mainstream Israeli culture have seldom depicted Mizrahi women as cultured, broad-minded leaders. This is, by and large, still the case today. In this context, one may mention the many Mizrahi women who were pillars of culture, such as the novelists Shoshana Shababo and Jacqueline Kahanoff, the choreographer and songwriter Sarah Levi-Tannay, the political activist Vicky Shiran, and many others, who were suppressed, have been banished from Israeli "national" culture and were disregarded throughout the last century. Today they are unfamiliar to most Israelis, and I assume the same is true for the readers of the present chapter. Needless to say, Zionist visual imagery had no place for them and completely ignored them and their work.

Mizrahi Jews have been viewed by Zionist and Israeli photographers from an "Ashkenazi" point of view, namely, cast as the exotic "other" to the "norm." Symbolically, the Israeli Government Press Office does not recognize "Ashkenazi" as a distinct category, as opposed to "Moroccans" or "Hindu," the categories that seem to refer to "strange" or "nonnormal" Jews. This taxonomy served to equate "Ashkenazi" with "Israeli," thereby becoming a transparent, all-engulfing, nondiscerning category.

The list of categories in the official photo archive is a living manifestation of the invented transparency of the Ashkenazy in Israel. It allegedly entails the right, solely preserved for it, to be classified and cataloged by participating in an event, but not by appearance or place of origin, a right denied the Mizrahi. As a paradigmatic example, I wish to examine the visual representation of the immigrants coming to Israel from India.

These photos were taken in the settlements Mesillat Zion and Nevatim, where the immigrants from India were sent upon arrival in Israel. The Israeli government archive holds ten photos under the category "Mesillat Zion." Four of them show the process of voting in the years 1955, 1956, and 1959. Three out of these four photos are of women (figs. 9.1 and 9.2).

Is this a coincidence? Undoubtedly, a hidden narrative guided the photographer Fritz Cohen, year after year, to Mesillat Zion. The theme "voting Indian Jews" that is "acquiring a knowledge of Democracy" is a compliment to the life-saving and westernizing fantasy the photos reflect: "We have come to bring you the West" (Hirsch 2014). Photos of the voting days in an Ashkenazi settlement were considered either "not exotic enough" or "not quite interesting."

Transparency, gliding into "the obvious" is the genuine right to not be discriminated. The very photo that is intended to depict the guidance into the symbolic order of democracy actually demonstrates the defective citizenship they are guided toward and manifests their lowly status as citizens. These

Figure 9.1. Fritz Cohen, elections for the Third Knesset, Mesilat Zion, 1955. *Source: Courtesy Israeli Government Media Agency.*

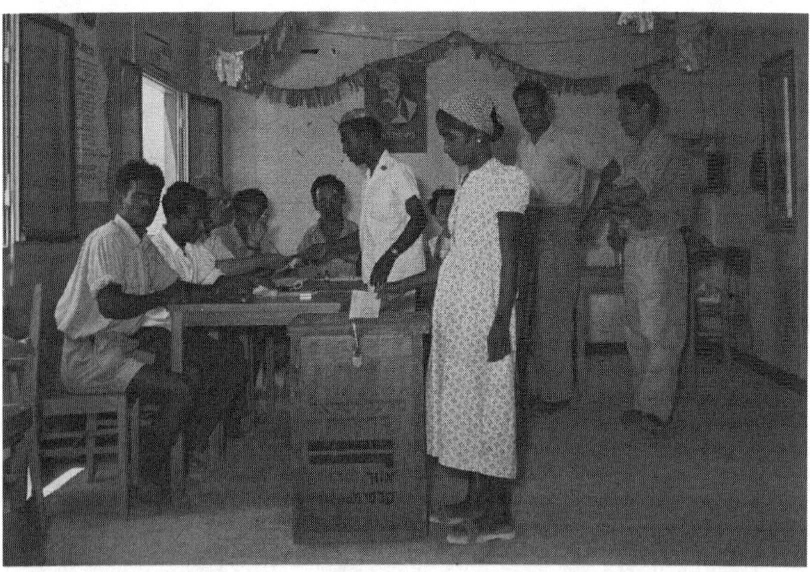

Figure 9.2. Fritz Cohen, elections for the Fourth Knesset, Mesilat Zion, 1959. *Source:* Courtesy Israeli Government Media Agency.

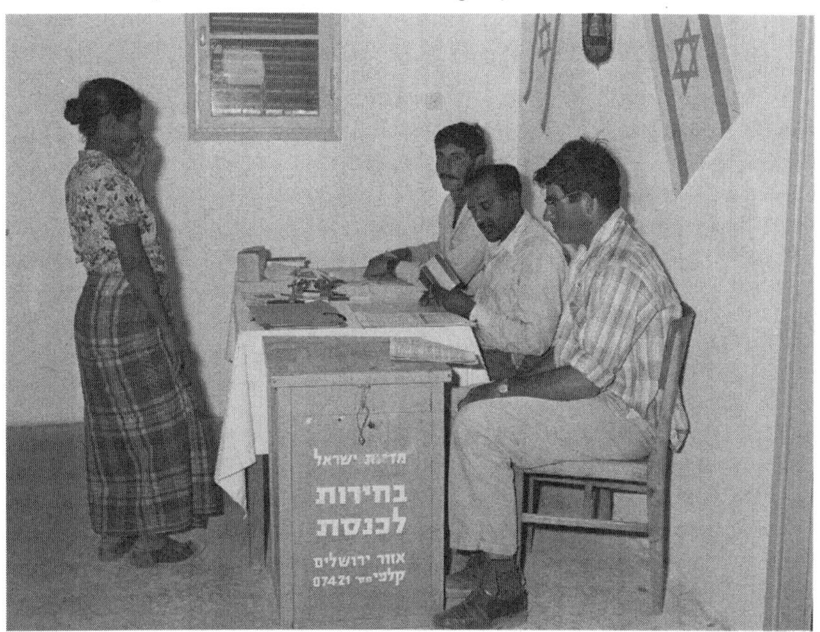

photos are in the capacity of "a transparent camouflage" of the dogmatic image and the dissimilar attitude they are going to suffer from. The racism here is augmented with an effeminizing attitude; that is, deflection toward the pole recognized as feminine, a well-known technique of Otherizing. The Indian body is depicted as a fenced-off body. The Jewish-Indians, like the Mizrahi congregation, went through a process of being subjected to racism and effeminizing, of which these photos are only a visual symptom. This tendency has not changed after the 1950s. In the 1980s, one could still find in the GPO catalog the following photograph titles: *An Ethiopian Woman Studying Hebrew, An Ethiopian in His Modern New Kitchen, An Ethiopian in Front of the Computer.*

I would like to go back to Ariela Azoulay's words quoted above: "An entire territory taken over by a photography studio is an indication of the defective civil status of its population. In this context, the defective status manifests in the possibility of photographing Palestinian men and women at all times, at every kind of activity, even in their private living space, which had become accessible to chance cameras" (Azoulay 2012, 168). Israel being an ethno-national state, where the distinction Jew/non-Jew is immeasurably sharper than the dichotomy citizen/noncitizen (this brings to mind a host of artificial categories that govern the Israeli discourse about—mostly Arab—"others," such as "temporary resident," "resident," or "subject"). There's a direct straight line connecting the invasive eye of the camera and the recurring claims of various politicians that these immigrants—from both India and Ethiopia—were not "real" Jews.

Racism and deliberate positioning are evident when we examine the representation of the fenced-in masculine body. Consider the following. Toward the end of the 1950s, a shot of some unemployed persons in Ashkelon taken by Boris Carmi was published in *Dvar-Hashavua*. A large group of "Mizrahi-appearance" men is pressing toward the camera lens, threatening to flood it, to invade it, to shove it. They are standing side by side, squeezed against each other, severe-faced, their gaze at the camera unflinching. Their faces are solidly opaque, angry, insolent, expectant, ironic, jeering, bitter, or cruel. One and all, they are looking up to the camera with a look of seeming reproof—the camera in this photo is the establishment. The lens, which is too close, tries to record the multitude, expresses anxious fear of this raging mob. The camera is "us" who are afraid of "them." But "they" are anonymous, incapable of engaging in a dialog, defiant, furious, and masculine (Shenhav, Hever, and Motzafi-Haller 2002, 294).

This stereotype is still prevalent in the Israeli subconscious and is a robust obstacle on the road of openly presenting the Mizrahi male to the public eye, especially as a group; I shall discuss the point in the third part of the article. A totally different repertoire of attributes was adopted for the photographed Ashkenazi Jew: against the background of the well-known icon of a large library, indicating a broad education of the subject to be photographed, and a well-chosen painting or an elegant writing-desk, a formal and official position, full of dignity was staged, alongside an appropriate clothing and a flattering environment (Hazan 2009, 11).

Again, Rona Sela phrased it poignantly in the context of the Jewish-Arab dichotomy: "The National Institutes sought to create a heroic stereotype of a new Jew of the land—proud, fair, bigger than life, with European facial features (sans individual identity) and always on-the-go and busy. The image of the pioneer, who fulfilled by his very masculinity the Zionist idea, became an elitist and mythological icon" (Sela 2001, 40). This is the desirable repertoire, in the light of which the others were sorted. The black-haired and the dark-complexioned were unable to enter into the coveted square of the "pioneer." The Mizrahi soma is ever conceived as "Other."

Noa Hazan's extensive examination of photos of Mizrahi women demonstrates how even the subjects and their basic staging constituted an image of the "inferior" Mizrahi woman (Hazan 2013). A representative list of her findings would include a picture of a weaving woman, staged as "a living object" in the exhibition *Home Labor in the Country*; a photo of a "Yemenite bride" doll, displayed in the Israel Museum, where the photographer decided to place it in conjunction with a girl in shorts, as if hinting at the primitivism and patriarchy the Yemenite were extricated from, by bringing them up to the land of Israel. A photo of Yihya Hayavi stands out in this collection. Hayavi, a Jewish photographer who worked in Sana'a, the capitol of Yemen, at the beginning of the twentieth century, presented an alternative depiction of Yemenite Jews, and especially Jewish women. As Hazan emphasizes, Hayavi did not share the sensibilities of the European born Jewish and Zionist photographers of the time, which gave rise to the mainstream narrative of the backward "Eastern" Jews. Of particular interest in this context are the photographs Yosef Tzadok's took in Yemen in the late 1940s (Tzadok 1956). These photos bring the style of Orientalist Zionism to a climax. For instance, his Jewish wedding picture depicts the couple from a close range, with a remarkable excess of ornaments and signifiers that couple "traditional" with "strange" and passive. The young Jewish bride seems to be imprisoned in a cascade of jewelry and her intricate dress. Tzadok's arrangement of the photograph thus highlights the difference between the traditional, backward, and passive Jews in the photo and himself, the photographer, who left Yemen and triumphantly returned as a Zionist activist. Liberated, he appears to have come to free the oriental Jews from their tradition.

The Ashkenazi Zionist gaze was not only dominant at the time, but also plays a major role in the historiography and memory of Israeli photography. A few young curators and researchers of art photography in Israel, among them Guy Raz and Rona Sela, have passionately and skillfully reclaimed forgotten and suppressed photographers. For example, in 2003 two retrospective exhibitions of the photographer Abraham Suskin were held, curated by Guy Raz. The Tel Aviv Museum exhibited *Photos of Tel Aviv*, and, in the museum of Tel Hay, *Photos of the Laboring Settlements*. Undoubtedly these were the two dominant perspectives by which Israel wanted to imagine itself—"the Laboring Settlements" (a name implying the others do not labor) and Tel Aviv (other places ignored). Yet, notably, the photographers whose legacy was researched and their work exhibited were almost exclusively Ashkenazi (Sela 2001). The only notable exception to this trend is the photographer David Seri. Seri had worked in Mandate Palestine since 1928, studied in Bezalel, but was side-tracked, probably owing to his place of origin, to be a goldsmith. Perusing the exhibition catalog titled *David Seri, Photos 1930–1950* (curated by Guy Raz) of the 2004 exhibition in Beit Ha-Omanim in Jerusalem is an eye-opener for those who were accustomed to the official repertoire of "Mizrahi photos." These photos burst with splendor, elegance, joy, and camaraderie. The 2004 exhibition was the first time these photographs were displayed in public.

A comparison of the shots taken by Seri and those by Hayavi reveal some similar aesthetic themes (undoubtedly, there is here a vast field for future research). Hayavi's life story is typical for Mizrahi artists in Israel. Even though he was the only photographer in Sana'a, Yemen, upon arriving to Israel he discontinued his work in the profession and became a laundry handy man. The photography arena in the land was dominated by European, mostly German-Jewish photographers (Sela 2001, 17).

Banishing the Mizrahi point of view is a tangible expression of the fact that Israel was established without "a Mizrahi view-point" at work. According to Ella Shohat, the "oriental" point of view was imagined by the Ashkenazi Jews of Israel through the same process that disinherited Palestinians of their property. Mizrahi Jews were likewise disinherited from their roots, history, and culture (Shohat 1986). It is not a coincidence that the four Israel Prize laureates for photography—Michah Baraam, Alex Levac, Peter Merom, and David Rubinger—are all Ashkenazi males.

A Yemenite Portrait, a 2012 exhibition in the Israel Museum, delivers a none-too-happy salutation from the past. It presented a profusion of Yemenites photographed at the beginning of the twentieth century by Ashkenazi photographers in Eretz Israel. Although the catalog text that was written by the exhibition curator Guy Raz shows some awareness of the problems connected with the historical racism toward the Yemenite community in Israel, he decides to exclude all photos taken by Seri and Hayavi.

The social activist Dr. Rafi Shovali, in a revealing article, points to a group of parameters afflicting the exhibition with neo-Orientalism (Shovali 2012). For example, the persons in the photos are not named, and the catalog has no use for the visual and textual material of the Yemenites themselves. One of the Yemenite community leader's pictures is displayed in the book six times, each with a different caption. Consequently, Shovali, argues that the exhibition is nothing but another demonstration of the Museum's entrenched bias. A central museum for Israeli art, the Eretz Israel Museum in Ramat Aviv is, so to speak, an "Ashkenazi territory," where most curators and presenting artists are from European-Jewish descent. Traditionally in Israel, curatorship is largely an Ashkenazi profession. That might be one of the reasons for the lack of Mizrahi presence. The curator, accordingly, failed when he refrained from inviting Yemenite artists to write about their own culture and its significance.

This shortcoming repeats the characteristics of the Ashkenazi-Yemenite encounter in the mid-twentieth century, which was determined by prejudice, stereotyping, and racism. The photographers of the young State of Israel took pictures for commercial use, creating marketable postcards: lucrative exoticism made for tourists. Another motive was Zionist propaganda. Propaganda photos were meant for fundraising for the Zionist cause. In many instances, the money that was raised by showing the "primitive" Yemenites was directed for purposes other than the Yemenites themselves. Another reason for taking pictures was race-classification. Many photos were taken after a meticulous staging of the subjects by the photographer. The Yemenite subject had to obey the instructions of the photographer as to the posture of his body and even the direction of his gaze. There was no cooperation on an equal basis, just the stage-managing of the photographer. The photographer is described by Raz as representing a (*Halutz*-pioneering) technological front, facing the Yemenite who represented the social lagging rear.

The exhibition catalog received a very warm and welcoming critique in *Haaretz* and in the opinion of Gilad Meltzer, the critic, the exhibition succeeded in presenting the racist situation of the Yemenites and condemning it. Several photographs of the exhibition and the accompanying catalog have become well known icons of the "Yemenite" Aliyah: washerwomen, house cleaners, an exotic beauty, a peddler, a street cleaner, a porter, a teacher cum community sage, newspaper boys (selling *Haaretz* newspapers), goat-milkmen, Gath-chewers, and workers in traditional handicrafts, such as gold crafting and embroidery (Meltzer 2012).

Having to deal with photographs taken in the past is like dealing with dangerous materials. A picture is a place wherein power struggles, social status, routine patterns, and thought models are merged and intertwined, many a time invisibly so. A photograph may be seen as "a surface area," which seems to be mimetic, simple, and clear, but in fact it contains a multitude of elements that, to use Marxist terminology, constitute its genuine, invisible structure. Contemporary curatorship dealing with this material must "peel" the cargo secreted behind each picture, and place it in present-day context, hopefully more conscious of the biases of the past, and more ethical, fair, and decent. In time, one may hope, we will be able to broaden our perspective.

Raz himself has only this to say about the term "racial classification": "In a series of photos, whose context became clear to me only toward the end of this exhibition, it seems that [the photographer] Lilian had in mind not only documentation for the benefit of his artistic work, but also for the benefit of Anthropological research, which is identified with ethnicity research" (Raz 2012, 48). As Dafna Hirsch notes, "In the first decades of the 20th century the eugenic movement was globally spread, and its adherents came from all over the political spectrum. . . . Their classifying Jews as a race was happily adopted by Zionist scientists" (Hirsch 2007, 160). When many of these doctors immigrated, these notions and pseudoscientific researchers came over with them to Palestine. In the words of Hirsch: "Already by the end of the 19th century ethnicity scientists, some of them Jews, defined Jews as a race while at the same time they distinguished various ethnic elements within the Jewish race. . . . Conceiving the East-European Jews within the context of Zionist settlement in the 'East' as 'Caucasians' entailed their segregation from the Mizrahi Jews. These were sometimes deemed 'primitive races' of Jews" (Hirsch 2007, 179). For whom and for what purpose were the photographs in the exhibition taken? What was the motive behind this act? It seems the exhibition evades telling its own story, the story behind the photos themselves.

The ultimate fantasy at the root of the eugenic research in Palestine was "merging the two communities," which later on came to be known as "the melting pot." Even today, when faced with attempts to raise awareness of the imbalance of power in Israel, many argue that the "ethnic economic gap" will gradually diminish as long as we do not talk about it.

Photography as an Oriental Medium

Photography was deemed to be worthy of entrance into the Hall of Fame of the Israeli Arts only in the 1990s (Gueta and Orit 2008, 315). However, the acceptance of this medium to the holy of holies created an immanent difficulty: What is an art photographer, and who is to be conceived of as "an artist," and who should be called merely "a photographer"? Socialization mechanisms were called upon for help. An artist is whoever was trained as an artist in the recognized art schools, in the departments dedicated to the training of "art photographers."

It seems there is no art medium as multilayered as photography, precisely because of its availability and popularity: creating a good picture is not complex, and operating a camera needs no years-long study. The amateur and the professional photographers go almost through the same technical activities. Also, because of its immanent mimesis, everyone feels they have an "understanding of photography," in contrast to other disciplines where education is a prerequisite. Hence the need for habitus-dependent hierarchies, which are independent of skill. "The History of Art," Pierre Bourdieu points out, "is a description of making an art-production discipline, capable of creating an artist (as opposed to a craftsman)" (Bourdieu 2004). Transparent, though high, walls, together with aggressive gatekeepers, blocked reality's efforts to prove the obvious, that "anyone with a camera can produce excellent photos" (Flusser 2014). It should not be forgotten that in Israel the mechanisms for creating the artists' habitus, and his socialization, are often racially biased or even recall racist mechanisms, as demonstrated by Sara Chinski: already since the first days of Bezalel Art School, a distinction by ethnic-based parameters was implemented (Chinski 2015).

In her seminal article about the meagerness of quality-material in art, Sarah Breitberg Semel defined the desirable artist to be one "who belongs to the protected working-class of Eretz Israel, who is a graduate of the youth movements and the Kibbutz, the essence of first-class Israel" (quoted in Chinski 2015). Sara Chinski's vehemently protests that "no wonder this text found many adherents, being a text where the measure of self-flattery, ethnocentricity, historic fakes and indifferent lordship has reached heretofore unknown records within the dialog" have fallen on closed ears, and are still muted (Chinski 2015, 118). Homi Bhabha's words naturally resonate with this sentence: "Two forms of identification are involved with the imaginary, narcissism, and aggression. These are two forms of 'identification,' which establish the ruling strategy of the colonial force" (Bhabha 1994). Local arrogant narcissism, homogeneity of form and ideas, together with aggression toward others—these are the paradigmatic pivots related to the policy of museum management in Israel.

Thus, the ability of press photographers to "cross the line" over to the higher category of art photography is extremely limited. No wonder, the few who managed the crossover are Ashkenazi. A perusal of the list of those photographers who achieved canonic fame as a result of a museum exhibition will reveal an absolute Ashkenazi majority (Nizri 2000).

"Literature is of the people," wrote Deleuze and Guattari, meaning that literature is read by the multitude and is not, like classical music and plastic arts, delimited to a small, specific, and elitist audience (Deleuze and

Guattari 1986). The way an author is looked upon by his readers, and his elevated status as "a spokesman of the nation," is nothing like the status of an eminent artist or musician, and this is still true in Israel. Consider, on the one hand, the status of the "canon"-defining Israeli authors Amos Oz, David Grossman, and A. B. Yehoshua. Their books are, unsurprisingly, rarely on the list of the best-sellers. The public buys and consumes a lot of books, just like other popular media, such as movies and light music. Unlike literature and its elitist ethos, however, photography is more simply "of the people." No doubt the number of people taking, distributing, and tagging photos through Facebook and Instagram is larger than those who read books, or for that matter, magazines, newspapers, and any printed material. The "visual turn" is evident in our experience: thinking through pictures, or visual thinking, is simultaneously more primal and more sophisticated, and it results in a totally different kind of culture.

Thus, on the one hand, it is obvious that our thought processes as children are molded by the first pictures etched in our brain. Acquisition of speech and language come after visual perception. The first words form in our cognition after the young brain has stored billions of life-scenes and given them meaning. On the other hand, visual thinking is very intricate and supplies us with a lot of information within a fraction of a second. Later on, by being exposed to a photo with multiple details and intricate symbolism, we manage to accrue very quickly and simultaneously a lot of information, pertaining to many different areas, and to instantly understand (at least some of) its meaning (Pedaya 2004). However, the meanings of an image are also determined within the public discourse, where opposing forces try to appropriate and define the relations between a photograph and the basic elements of the reality it captured.

This intricacy of photo-literacy, which underscores the negotiation of meanings between individuals and (hegemonic) public discourse—and between intuitive and reflective perceptions of images' implications—makes photo (a potentially) effective vehicle of democratization. Since the moment of its birth, photography was potentially available to the masses (Azoulay 2015), and it seems that now, with the advent of the digital technology and the abundant social networks, this option has become much more widespread. We are witnessing exhibitions of Instagram photos, a bustling traffic of smartphone pictures, and very impressive visual icons, privately created by the "populace." Many Israelis, for instance, maintain their own archive of photographs they took during participation in the 2023 mass protest against the government. These photos were taken from their point of view, reflecting their experiences, and emphasizing what is important to them. The democratic act, in this case, was "democratically" documented to preserve the "people's" outlook.

In his groundbreaking reflections on photography, Vilem Flusser argued that photographs "program" the ways we can view and understand the reality they display. The political discourse, therefore, owns the photographs (Flusser 2014, 80). This assertion reminds us that photos also comprise an antidemocratic element, which might help to control our gaze, our interpretations, and our actions when we encounter photographic images. Yet I believe that Flusser's argument becomes less relevant to contemporary profusion of photographs and the ability (and tendency) of almost all individuals to take pictures to narrate their experiences from their particular point of view. The number of photos the public produces might gradually erode the supremacy of the power-that-be to dictate the viewpoint and reduce the dictatorship of the racial structuring.

Toward a Conceptualization of the Oriental Modus in Photography

"It's a very regrettable fact," Flusser notes, "that a standard photography critic most of the time does not know how to discover, from the photo itself, the dramatic merging of the photographer's intention and the channel's program" (Flusser 2014, 80). "From channel to channel the photo renews its meaning," and it seems that the most significant change occurs in the transfer from the gallery to the museum (78–80). Once a photograph is exhibited under the roof of a museum, especially an important museum, it is taken out of the flood of photos we are deluged with, and it gains an inimitable halo. The greater part of canonic photography in Israel is the study of "a dramatic merging of the photographer's intention and the channel's program," namely, what happens in the local museums. Visitors of Israeli museums encounter various modes of flattery. In the celebrated exhibitions they can see, for instance, magnificent representations of scenery (Abramson 2009), via narcissistic sanctification of bourgeois domestication, "advanced" experimental structures—which bestow on the observer an illusion of being in "the Western avant-garde"—and enigmatic pictures to be deciphered only on the basis of knowledge previously shared by the photographer and the observer.

The move of photography from galleries to museum, combined with the aforementioned modes of flattery, which equate "quality" exhibitions with Western aesthetic traditions, has had a devastating impact on Mizrahi photographers and their depiction of Mizrahi life. While they may sometimes successfully get through the "gallery stage," the hegemonic "museum stage" remains an impassable moat. The Mizrahi modus in Israeli photography is nowadays characterized by very many valuable projects that remain one-time events and are relegated to oblivion.

Thus, for example, two wonderful exhibitions, by two Mizrahi women photographers, Dafna Shalom (*Moshe Dayan 53*, Gallery Kav 16, 2001, Irit Segoli, curator) and Vered Nissim (*The Daffodil*, Gallery "My Sister," 2007, Shula Keshet, curator). Both Shalom and Nissim are art school graduates, who exhibit advanced and professional photography together with a heart-rending repertoire of poverty. They thus create a world of photography that is not external to the persons photographed. Both these two creative photographers were suppressed and eliminated from the public's eye. In the following I shall offer a preliminary critique of Dafna Shalom's work, which has hardly been discussed elsewhere. This would allow me to focus on the modus of Mizrahi self-representation that Shalom proposes.

Shalom opted to closely record her neighbor family, living in 53 Moshe Dayan Street,·in Yad Eliahu quarter of Tel Aviv. The main body of Shalom's work represents a penetrating, unyielding visual research, which is a still ongoing photo project. Shalom resides in Tel Aviv and New York City, exhibited her work *Moshe Dayan 53* at Kav 16 gallery, located at the community center of Neve Eliezer, in 2001, while some other photos were displayed in the exhibition *Mother Tongue* in Ein-Harod Museum.

One of Shalom's photos depicts the interior of an apartment in the building where she grew up, and where her mother still lives today. Natalie, the project's protagonist, and her family, being the neighbors in the building, may be the reason for the lack of uneasiness that usually accompanies watching photos taken by a patronizing photographer. There is neither looking down here nor haughtiness. There is no staging, no strenuous effort to achieve some special composition, no meticulous frame. Indeed, it almost seems as if there's no camera, as the pictures do not conform to the well-known and accepted pattern of representing everyday figures and creating an artificial composition.

The camera and the photographer "conceal" themselves, and we feel as if a curtain is lifted, and we are invisible spectators in a family drama. Shalom stays focused on an essential question, what is the capability of a little girl to find privacy and to establish a private frame. For example, in the following picture there are three mattresses in a single room: sleeping together, getting up together.

The act of photography, it seems, allows Shalom a comeback to childhood, where she can now find and frame a private space for herself.

Figure 9.3. Dafna Shalom, item from the exhibition *Moshe Dayan 53*, Kav 16 Galeria, 2001. Irit Segoli, curator. *Source:* Courtesy of Dafna Shalom.

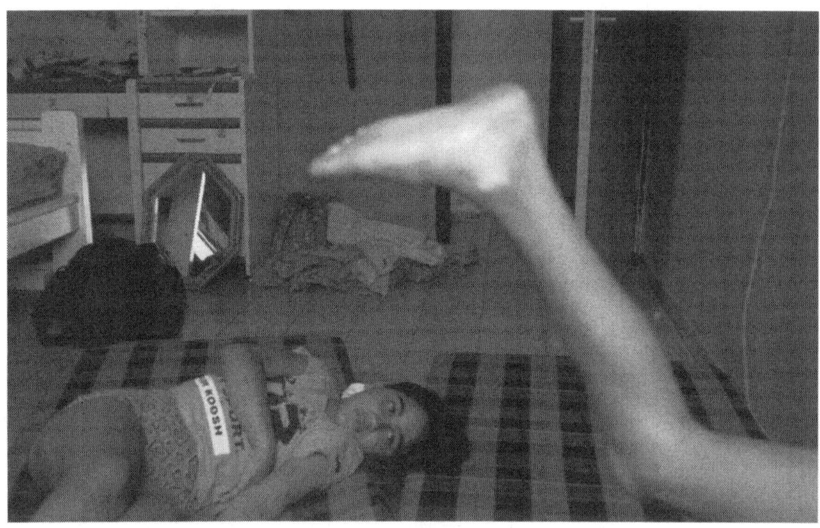

Figure 9.4. Dafna Shalom, item from the exhibition *Moshe Dayan 53*, Kav 16 Galeria, 2001. Irit Segoli, curator. *Source:* Courtesy of Dafna Shalom.

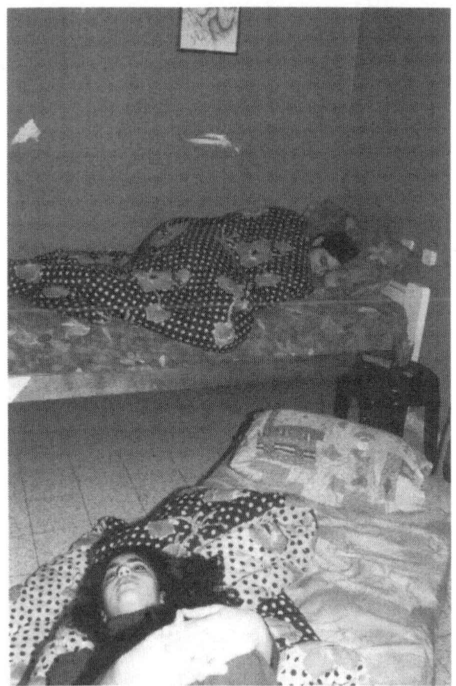

Maybe this is the place where some less conscious acts originate, such as the decision to "conceal the photographer," making it possible to know how "I had really been" and obtain an authentic representation of myself in the past, before "the imaginary I" took hold of me, as Shalom recounts:

> While growing up in Israel, a feeling of an "imaginary I" homed-in on me, a feeling which shaped my worldview. This made me adopt opinions, tastes and philosophy which led me to loath my parents' opinions, tastes, and spiritual world. This "imaginary I" took me on a broad process aimed at erasing my Mizrahi and adopting the Western way of life. My opinions, thoughts and tastes were shaped by that self-same "State of Israel." Its Education System did not allow an equal synthesis of Eastern and Western cultures. "The East" was never studied or formally taught and did not get adequate public exposure, where only Mizrahi cuisine represented the totality of Mizrahi culture. There was no History of Mizrahi history, not even a superficial attempt at researching it. I adopted this "point-of-view," actually this "blindness" relating to the Mizrahi society, and flattened my mother's persona accordingly. I looked upon her the same way society around her saw her. I spread a cover over her existence. I came to New York City on a quest. One of the reasons I stayed in this city is the basic, instinctive, urge to survive, the feeling that here I shall be able to grow and progress. It is reasonable to assume that I could have made a lot of progress in Israel too, but in New York I did not feel branded by any ethnic group or economic status. Today I am much more comfortable with these brands by race or social status referring to my place of origin. Before that, I preferred to be just Dafna. Is it avoidance? You might call it an escape, but very soon I found out that one cannot escape. And in New York I became much closer to the entity that I am: a woman, a Mizrahi woman, a woman of the working class. (Mendes Flor 2000, 9)

It seems these are the most significant social contexts in the photos: the progressive transformation of being a woman, a Mizrahi woman, and a woman of the working class. In the series of Shalom's photos, these three realms merge, each one of them leading to a different mode of interpretation.

A most acute problem of Mizrahi artists is the dread that using biographic material in their art will entail labeling them "nonsophisticated." According to the taste-setters, using popular material in art must carry an added meaning—be it irony, aloofness, metaphor that refers to an implicit observation or self-consciousness. Popularity by itself, it seems to be the commonly held wisdom, cannot be a legitimate alternative to aesthetics. As a result, Mizrahi photographers' subject matters are often regarded as "exotic." But exotic is merely a way to label them as marginal and irrelevant to everyday life. This is, in a way, ironic, since the people Shalom depicts are much more "normal," mainstream to Israeli society than, for instance, the lifestyle of the rich. Unlike the photographed Mizrahi Jews, wealthy celebrities and their life are represented in newspapers and in telenovelas as the "right" way to live—as models to be envied—not as subjects of anthropological study.

The exoticism of Mizrahi photographs is devastating also because it represents a profound misunderstanding of the artists' intentions. An artist takes photographs of his life, home, and roots. Instead of considering it as an inner search, a meaningful, deep process and introspection, critics present this as portrayals of the "other" or of an alien way of life, that is, as exotic imagery. What does this "Othering" do to the artist's identity? How does it affect his artistic choices? It seems that the triple "Otherness"—being a Mizrahi, a female, and of a lower socioeconomic status—is not worthy of being exposed, explored, and exhibited.

We look at a picture, any picture, while bearing a cultural baggage. Roland Barthes writes, "I reject all knowledge, any culture; I refuse to obtain anything through an eye which is not mine" (Barthes 1980). Is this possible? Is there a correlation between the cultural baggage of the observer-curator-critic and the photograph? What is the "right" treatment of a picture? Shalom has no "anthropological perspective," a point of view so prevalent in the application of the exotic attitude, where, in the words of Sigal Eshed, "the weak becomes attractive" (Eshed 2000, 10).

Yet this position also liberates. Shalom has no close-ups, no pleading or imploring looks, no pretense to tell the whole story in a single frame. She is free of the panache to be "exhibited." She creates a photographic string whose links are inseparable, where each photo tells a part of a story that is outside the frame, there is a continuation of life, a lot of activity. She introduces Israel's working-class heroes in 2001, who are so much different from the working-class heroes of Ashkenazi Zionists—the pioneer, the farmer, the contented factory worker—who until recently stood at the center of the Zionist ethos and its rhetoric.

Shalom recounted the Israeli reactions to the photos she received from friends in New York. On the one hand, there were such remarks as "this is a typical Israeli home," downplaying the photo, and completely ignoring the powerful social aspect the picture highlighted. On the other hand, some reacted with statements such as "who's interested in such a miserable and disgusting aesthetic; why on earth did you take these shots."

But this was precisely the point of this project—to remind viewers of normal Israeli life conditions, while urging them to consider why they find this disturbing. Another emphasis is on the Mizrahi female subject. Dafna Shalom took pictures of Natalie when she was eleven to thirteen years old. She tracks her sexual coming of age. In one of the pictures, we see the girl gazing at someone hidden from our eyes. There's only a bare leg, impudently flailing in the middle of the frame, as if "giving the finger" in a rude Oriental gesture.

Corporeality and its attributes are very much evident in figure 9.7: the colorful garments, the green, short, transparent blouse, the hygienic pads on the table, the folded clothes on the dining table, the white pail with its floor rag, situated in the corner, witness to the cleaning work done; the bare feet of Natalie on the wet floor and the rich, variegated setting of the

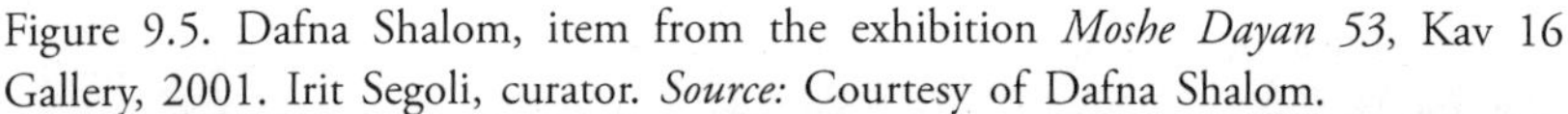

Figure 9.5. Dafna Shalom, item from the exhibition *Moshe Dayan 53*, Kav 16 Gallery, 2001. Irit Segoli, curator. *Source:* Courtesy of Dafna Shalom.

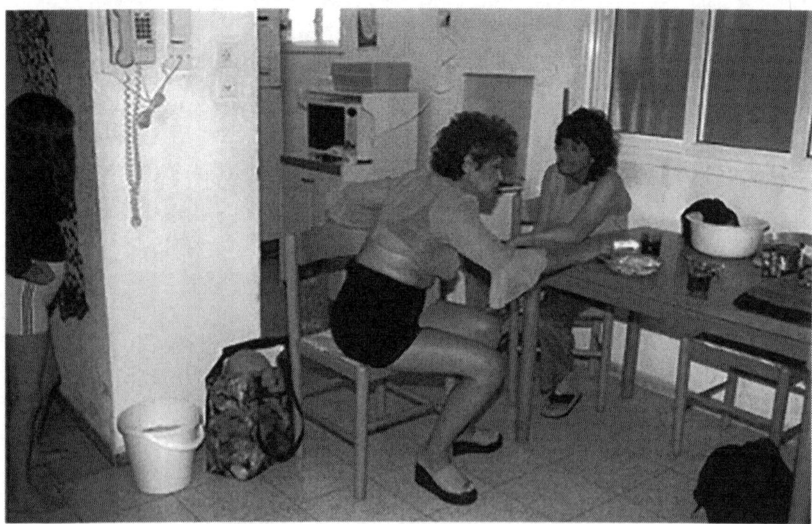

kitchen—all characteristic of the whole series. "While growing-up in such a family," Shalom noted, "your senses are continuously bombarded from all sides. The struggle for developing and maintaining one's ego happens in every household, but in circumstances such as these I think it's more difficult. This is a strangled individuality, wishing to erupt" (Alon 2002).

Shalom's works are currently not exhibited at any gallery in Israel or elsewhere. Notably, her exclusion from the professional milieu stands in a marked contrast to the extensive consumption of photographs depicting the poverty of the *Ma'abarot* in the 1950s. The reception of Shalom's photography is also far from the enthusiastic acceptance of the Israeli photographers who replaced reality with staged aestheticism (e.g., Adi Ness's staged photos presenting "Destitution," "Begging," or "Homelessness"; these staged and directed photographs present a procedure whose mechanism is fiction posing as documentary). The works of Shalom and Nissim grant us no escape hatch: we must cope with the visible, stark cruelty of the scene.

In 2010, Beit Ha-Omanim in Jerusalem exhibited the noteworthy series of portraits by Micah Simchon, *Makaam*, presenting the Jewish musicians from the Arab countries in Israel, who were relegated to an orchestra especially assembled for them—the Israel Broadcasting Service Orchestra, headed by Zuzu Musa. The bleak story of these musicians, who came to Eurocentric Israel, carrying the "wrong" cultural capital, is told in Eyal Halfon's movie *Chalery Baghdad*. The hypnotizing scenes successfully depict the uprooted, forlorn elderly musicians, who conceived themselves as "Europeans" in their Moslem countries, while here they were treated as "Mizrahi" in Israel. Just like Dafna Shalom's works, Simchon's project of portraits is still ongoing (similar to the exoticism of Mizrahi photography, highbrow Mizrahi music in Israel is not considered "Israeli" music, but rather as "ethnic," or "world" music).

Simchon's series was exhibited in 2013, in a marginal gallery. It did not get much media attention or critical acclaim, and of course no funds from the establishment. Simchon, who is personally acquainted with each and every one in the photos, was born and lived for many years in the poverty-ridden Musrara neighborhood in Jerusalem, where Mizrahi Jews were settled in houses that belonged to Palestinian-Arabs before the war in 1948. The profiles in the exhibition reflect the personal, intimate relationship with his subjects, and the uniform staging that he chose highlights the tension between the official stance and a comfortable family photo. Raz's words that "the representation of the Mizrahi male as primitive and violent created fictional ideologies about the sexual 'nature' of Mizrahi masculinity" come to mind (Sela 2001, 17), and it seems this caste-driven imagery, which is still a driving force in the public arena of Israel, blocks any possibility of a genuine representation of Mizrahi males in the artistic sphere. Simchon's portraits of these men demonstrate a clear path toward a different, fairer, and more realistic depiction of Mizrahi men as artists and as art in and of itself

Ever since the nineteenth century, photography had the potential to become the representative face of democracy—the populace could now have a true-to-the-original copy of their persona, whereas before only the nobility had the privilege of possessing official formal portraits of themselves (in the form of very expensive oil paintings). It is not surprising that many Mizrahi photographers sought to establish their place through portraits, seeking for the genuine visibility of Mizrahi Jews and wishing to draw attention to their subject matter (Alon 2014; Tzoreff 2014). This was their way of breaking with the Zionist traditions of photography and Zionist perception of Mizrahi Jews, as briefly described above.

Several fascinating yet overlooked Mizrahi artists still deserve a deeper study. I would like to mention here a few of them. The projects of Tamir Tzadok, whose photographs playfully and sophistically challenge the popular stereotypes that were distributed by the "Bourekas films" of the 1970s (where Mizrahi men were depicted as uneducated, sometimes violent, deceitful, but funny and often endearing). Joseph Dadon, Itzik Badash, and David Adika explore the Mizrahi body as well as Mizrahi homoeroticism. Hannah Sahar and Tal Shohat depict Mizrahi women in ways that, on the one hand are in dialog with the rich traditional representation of the Mizrahi woman in the history of art; and, on the other, rely on the prominent, nonthreatening sexual stereotypes (in contrast to the Mizrahi male), thus making it easier to "consume" the imagery. Yaakov Israel's project on "the mapping of Israel" presents a novel perspective that does not accept the codes dictated by the customary Israeli photography, and seeks to offer a novel horizon of representability. Many more are still waiting to be explored by unbiased scholars and critics.

This bounty of projects did not get to be routed toward the central bodies of the Israeli art sphere in the leading galleries and museums. Dispersion and dilution are characteristic of Mizrahi visual representation. Ella Shohat's studies, which marked the path for a critical analysis of the representation of Mizrahi Jews in Israeli culture, are available mainly in English. A quick look at the museum catalogs reveals the fortified and conservative character of the Israeli art establishment (cf. Alon and Keshet 2013; Ben Tzvi and Lerer 2001; Dekel 2013; Azoulay 2006). The peoples of dark color, the weakened, the Arabic, the Mizrahi—cannot enter through the gates of Israeli museums. They might sneak in, individually, woven within a hegemonic Ashkenazi, whitish lattice. As a strong, distinct mass, with aesthetic characteristics—this body of artists has no official place (Alon 2015). The Mizrahi modus in Israeli photography awaits a thorough and deep conceptualization.

Works Cited

Abramson, Larry, ed. 2009. *Holy Landscape*. Riesling.

Abutbool, Guy, Lev Greenberg, and Pnina Muzafi-Heller, eds. 2005. *Oriental Voices: Toward a New Mizrahi Dialog about the Israeli Society and Culture*. Masada.

Alon, Ktzia. 2002. "Restoring the Stolen Language" [in Hebrew]. *Panim* 22.

———. 2005. "On Jew, Christians, and Others." *Theory and Criticism* 26:175–99.

———. 2014. "Barefoot: A Reflection about Mizrahi Feminine Art." In *Bezalel: Reflections about Shoes*. Riesling.

———. 2015. "The Alternative Aesthetics." In *A Splash of Color and an Imprint*, edited by Shula Keshet. Achoty.

Alon, Ktzia, and Shula Keshet, eds. 2013. *Those Who Shatter the Walls*. Achoty.

Azoulay, Ariella, ed. 2006. "The Museum That Didn't Take Place" [in Hebrew]. Special issue of *Studio Art Magazine* 74.

———. 2012. "An Unbounded (Photography) Studio." In *Reality, Trauma and Internal Logic of Photography*, edited by Haim Lusaki. Spielmann Institute of Photography and Avi Ganor.

———. 2015. *Civil Imagination: A Political Ontology of Photography*. Verso.

Baraam, Michah. 2011. *An Inner Look*. Alexandra Noka.

Barthes, Roland. 1980. *Camera Lucida: Reflections on Photography*. Hill and Wang.

Bhabha, Homi. 1994. "The Question of the Other: Difference, Discrimination and Post-colonial Discourse." *Theory and Criticism* 5:79–105.

Ben Tzvi, Tal, and Yael Lerer. 2001. *Self-Portrait: Palestinian Women's Art*. Andalus.

Bourdieu, Pierre. 2004. *Issues in Sociology*. Resling.

Chinski, Sara. 2015. *The Social Grammar of Israeli Art*. Ha'Kibbutz Ha'Meuchad.

Dekel, Tal. 2013. *Women and Migration: Art and Gender in a Transnational Era*. Riesling.

Deleuze, Gilles, and Felix Guattari. 1986. *Kafka: Towards a Minor Literature*. University of Minnesota Press.

Eshed, Sigal. 2000. "Taking-On Form and Shedding Form, Extracts from the Exhibited Artists' Panel Discussion." In *Catalog of the Exhibition My Sister—Mizrahi Women Artists in Israel*, edited by Rita Mendes Flor. Beit Haomanim.

Flusser, Vilem. 2014. *Gestures*. University of Minnesota Press.

Gueta, Yehudit, and Ichilov Orit, eds. 2008. *Limbus—Place—Photography*. Hakibutz Hameuhad.

Hazan, Noa. 2009. "Learning to Discern Races in Hebrew." *The Bezalel Protocols: Photography and the Political Arena* 11.

———. 2013. "Looking Back from the East" [in Hebrew]. In *Those Who Shatter the Walls*, edited by Ktzia Alon and Shula Keshet. Achoty.

Hirsch, Dafna. 2007. "Zionist Physicians and Mixed Marriages." In *Racism in Israel*, edited by Yosi Yonah and Yehudah Shenhav. Van Lear Institute and Kibbutz Meuhad.

———. 2014. *"We Have Come to Bring You the West": Endowing Hygiene and Culture in the Jewish Society in the British Mandate Period.* Ben Gurion Institute for the Studies of Zionism, the University of Ben Gurion in the Negev.

Meltzer, Gilad. 2012. "A Yemenite Portrait: The House Models of Zionism." *Haaretz Literary Supplement*, March 28.

Mendes Flor, Rita, ed. 2000. *Catalog of the Exhibition My Sister—Mizrahi Women Artists in Israel, February 2000.* Beit Haomanim.

Nizri, Ygal, ed. 2000. *Mizrahi Semblance.* Babel.

Pedaya, Haviva. 2004. "The Exiled Voice." *Haaretz*, September 26.

Raz, Guy. 2012. *A Yemenite Portrait: Photography and Memory, 1881–1948.* Eretz Israel Museum.

Sela, Rona. 2000. *Photography in Palestine in 1930s and 1940s* [in Hebrew]. Hakibutz Hameuchad Publishing House; Herzliya Museum.

———. 2001. "One Hundred Years of Solitude." *Studio Art Magazine*, no. 124, 82–86.

Shenhav, Yehouda, Hanan Hever, and Pnina Motzafi-Haller, eds. 2002. *Mizrahi in Israel: A Critical Observation into Israel's Ethnicity* [in Hebrew]. Van Leer Institute Press; Hakibbutz Hameuchad.

Shohat, Ella. 1986. *Israeli Cinema: East-West and the Politics of Representation.* Palgrave-Macmillan.

Shovali, Rafi. 2012. "Each Yemenite Has a Name." *HaOketz*, August 3. https://www.haokets.org/2012/08/03.

Tzadok, Yosef. 1956. *Be'se'arot Teiman* [In Yemenite Storms]. Am Oved.

Tzoreff, Ronni. 2014. "Internalizing the Face: On the Visibility and the Invisibility of the Face of the Other." In *Broken Beads: Contemporary Artists on Their Moroccan Identity*, edited by Haim Maor. Ben Gurion University of the Negev.

Part IV

Jewish Photography as a Commentary on Crisis and Violence

Chapter 10

Photography as Agency

Self-assurance through Urban Documentation in the Works of Roman Vishniac and Abraham Pisarek

Joachim Schlör

Introductory Thoughts: Photography—Space—Agency

The main intention of this chapter is to offer a new reading of the work and the life trajectories of two photographers, Roman Vishniac (1897–1990) and Abraham Pisarek (1901–1983). I am particularly interested in the ways both personalities used photography as a means of self-understanding and self-expression: to capture the spaces and times that they lived in, and their own very specific place in that complex relationship. Both artists are well known for their documentary work on Jewish life before the Holocaust, Pisarek for his intimate and emphatic insight into Jewish life in Berlin under increasing Nazi rule, Vishniac for his travels to Eastern Europe and the documentation of what has become known as "a vanishing world." Consequently, both have been widely regarded as "Jewish photographers" because of their own background and because of the subject matter of their work (Vishniac 1983; Bourel 2010; Schlör 2012a). But in both cases, the body of work is larger and more varied, as are the life circumstances and the cultural and aesthetic influences. I would argue that, rather than their "Jewish sensibility" or heritage, it was the atmosphere of the big city, particularly Berlin in the 1920s, that helped them to create and to develop their own distinct approach to the visual world around them. I will map out this relationship between the artists and the city in spatial terms and use the concept of agency in order to emphasize the development of individuality vis-à-vis the urban environment.

In his contribution to the edited volume *Space and Spatiality in Modern German-Jewish History*, Michael Berkowitz has defined photography itself as a Jewish space: "Before the Nazi onslaught, photography was largely a Jewish space as a field of endeavor in Central Europe and beyond" (Berkowitz 2017, 246). Inspired by the spatial turn in the humanities and following up on a number of earlier publications by Charlotte Fonrobert and Vered Shemtov (2005), Julia Brauch, Anna Lipphardt. and Alexandra Nocke (2008), and Barbara Mann (2011), *Space and Spatiality* (2017) offers an overview of space-related approaches to Jewish history and culture and aims to show how a discussion of "Jewish space" can be made fruitful for different areas of study, including photography. Berkowitz uses the term in a very practical way: "What might be termed the Jewish space of photography was thus expansive and diverse, comprising working space, living space, commercial premises where Jews interacted with non-Jews, outdoor and indoor public spaces where photographers conducted their work, and spaces of material culture such as billboards, newspapers, and magazines" (Berkowitz 2017, 246). In the context of the Potsdam-based postgraduate program "Makom: Space and Place in Jewish Culture and History" (2001–2007), Julia Brauch, Anna Lipphardt, and Alexandra Nocke developed and discussed the category of *enacted space* in order to show how such spaces of Jewish involvement with the surrounding world have been constructed by human agency (Brauch, Lipphardt, and Nocke 2008, 1–25). This is a continuation of, but in some ways also a response to Henri Lefebvre's claim that space is fundamentally political and a social construct. These results of the Makom project add what has often been missing in Lefebvre's theory of social relations that create space: a human face. This is particularly important for our understanding of Jewish life in the late years of the Weimar Republic: "What kind of agency was possible for German Jews in times of crisis?" (Jünger 2020). Agency is not the same as free will, but it does contain the idea that humans make decisions and try to enact them in a given context. A very basic but useful definition has been brought forward by Eran Zelnik's assertion that agency is a deeply humanistic concept, "the conviction that the past should be told as a narrative in which people are the main protagonists and the 'agents' of change" (Zelnik 2015). In sociology, "agency" refers to the capacity of individuals to act independently and to make their own choices, based on their will, as opposed to given "structures" that limit or influence the opportunities that individuals have. Ideas drawn from the biographical research of Gerald Lamprecht (2001), Andreas Gestrich (1988). and Gabriele Rosenthal (1994), amongst others, demand a perspective "which views individuals in a permanent relationship with their environment" (Lamprecht 2001, 21). Individuals are neither heteronomous puppets nor completely free and autonomous; they are actors in what Bourdieu calls a "social space" constructed through relationships between individual actors, between those actors and the surrounding space, and in a constant state of flux (Bourdieu 1985, 5).

All life stories are individual and in their own ways extraordinary. Keeping this in mind, this chapter discusses the idea of agency in the—partly very similar, partly quite different—cultural situations that we come across in the works of Roman Vishniac and Abraham Pisarek: their move from towns in Russia and Eastern Europe to the city of Berlin; their discovery of the urban street and scenery as an area of self-expression; their perception of Jewish life under the threat of antisemitism and persecution in Germany and Eastern Europe; the necessity to survive in hiding or in emigration; and, most importantly, in the photographic strategies they both used. Taking photographs helped them, I would argue, to make a city their own and to present Jewish life and culture, with Jews as actors, as humans with will and initiative—not as victims and not, as was and is so often the case, seen through the eyes of the perpetrators.

Two Arrivals in Berlin

Roman Vishniac was born August 19, 1897, in his grandparents' *dacha* outside Saint Petersburg, in the town of Pavlovsk. He grew up in Moscow. His father was a manufacturer of umbrellas, his mother the daughter of diamond dealers—it was their wealth that allowed them to live in Moscow, outside of the Pale of Settlement. Fascinated by biology and photography, the young Roman filled his room with "plants, insects, fish and small animals." He received a microscope for his seventh birthday, connected it to a camera and photographed, as he remembers, "the muscles in a cockroach's leg at 150 times magnification" (Eisen 2019). He was schooled at home until the age of ten, attended a private school until seventeen, and then spent six years at the Shanyavsky Institute (now Russian State University for the Humanities) in Moscow, studying zoology and biology, and, later, taking a three-year course in medicine.

In 1918, antisemitism in Russia and the political situation after the revolution prompted the family to move to Berlin. Roman followed his parents and married Luta, or Leah, Bagg from Latvia, their children Mara and Wolf were born in Berlin. Studying Far Eastern art in his free time, researching endocrinology and optics, Roman developed his photographic skills on the streets of Berlin. The couple settled in the Wilmersdorf district, "home to a large community of affluent Russian Jewish expatriates, and began to engage with Berlin, "the epitome of a modern city: cosmopolitan, loud, vibrant, diverse, and full of recent immigrants," as curator Maya Benton wrote (Benton n.d.). While Benton makes a short reference to what Berkowitz has termed "the Jewish space of photography"—"many Russian Jews owned photography shops and studios, and Vishniac's family encouraged his pursuits" (Benton n.d.)—her main focus is on the new urban and modern space that he discovered and helped to create in the urban setting:

> In Berlin, his perspective as an outsider contributed to his inventive and dynamic images of life in the city and marked his transformation from amateur hobbyist to accomplished street photographer. This prodigious body of early work became increasingly influenced by European modernism as he captured the buzzing day-to-day life of the city: streetcar drivers, municipal workers and day laborers, marching students and children at play, bucolic park scenes and the intellectual café life of the bustling metropolis that was, in Vishniac's words, "the world's center of music, books, and science." (Benton n.d.)

This observation is in line with David Shneer's entry on "photography" in the *YIVO Encyclopedia*. Shneer places Vishniac in a spatial and temporal context with other "urban acculturated Jews [who] became important photographers throughout Eastern Europe" such as the Jewish graphic artist El Lissitzky (1890–1941), who "picked up a camera to create a fresh vision of socialist society," as well as André Kertész (1894–1985) and László Moholy-Nagy (1895–1946), who "built the field of photography in Hungary with their early street photography." Robert Capa (1913–1954), who left his native Budapest in 1931, at age 18, for Berlin is yet another example. Shneer calls these artists "acculturated East European photographers, who happened to be Jewish," and contrasts them to "Jewish photographers of the first half of the twentieth century who placed Jews at the center of their photographs." He names particularly Alter-Sholem Kacyzne (1885–1941), who "became one of the leading photographers of East European Jewish life in the interwar period" and worked for several different Yiddish publications as a photo correspondent in Poland—and Roman Vishniac (1897–1990), whom he dubs "perhaps the most famous Jewish photographer of the interwar period, used the camera more explicitly to capture traditional Jewish life that was, in his view, passing away before the camera's eye" (Shneer 2021).

I am not sure if this contrast really makes sense. In Vishniac's case, it seems safer to say that he started out in a similar way as Kertész and Capa, as an itinerant observer of the urban world, and that he *became* a "Jewish photographer" under the political circumstances that changed these cities so profoundly. In her project description "Spazieren in Charlottenburg," Maya Shabbat calls Berlin "the frontier of Western culture, an alternative city defying both East and West"—an "edge city" with an extraterritorial character. And she describes how some of the arrivals were interested in the "Scheunenviertel behind Alexanderplatz," whereas others "drifted to the suburbs of Berlin" and discovered Charlottenburg, the city of the "new west" (Shabbat 2020). Somewhere in between these two areas we also find the traces of our second protagonist, Abraham Pisarek.

Abraham Pisarek was born the son of the Jewish merchant Berek Pisarek and his wife Sura in Przedborz (in Russian Poland) in 1901. He attended *heder* (religious school) and a technical college in Lodz. Pisarek arrived in Germany in 1919, working in a variety of occupations, including in a factory in Herne. Like so many of his contemporaries, he traveled to Berlin from there, although the city was originally supposed to be nothing more than a stopover. In 1924, inspired by the Zionist movement, he left Germany for Palestine, then under the British Mandate, with the aim to become a *Chaluz*, a pioneer for the building of a Jewish homeland. Information about this period is scarce, but we know that he worked as a stonemason. After having contracted malaria, he returned via France to Germany and settled in Berlin-Reinickendorf. While this choice of settlement may not sound very urban—"die weiße Stadt" (the White City)—in Reinickendorf was indeed one of the emblematic projects of modern building and housing (Haspel and Jaegg 2007).

In 1928, Abraham Pisarek married his non-Jewish girlfriend, Berta Isigkeit. He attended evening classes in photography at the arts and trades college, became a member of the Reich Association of the German Press (*Reichsverband der Deutschen Presse*) in 1929, working for agencies such as Mauritius, for the *Arbeiter-Illustrierte-Zeitung* (Workers' Illustrated Newspaper; AIZ), and for Erwin Piscator's theater productions: a Berlin life, and above all a life within Berlin's incipient modernism. He documented the life of his family (their son Georg was born in 1929, and their daughter Ruth in 1931) in photographs that show cheerful children walking as they hold hands with a man who looks quite elegant with his glasses and hat, playing in front of the house or waving out of the window. Pisarek became known for his portrait photography involving famous contemporaries such as painter Max Liebermann, the president of Berlin's Academy of Arts and possibly the living symbol of Jewish achievement and success in a democratic Berlin.

In the years following the end of World War I, the German capital of Berlin—capital not of a "Reich" anymore, but of an insecure democratic republic—became one of the main centers for political, cultural, artistic, and scientific experiments (Peters 2015; Gay 1978, 170). At the same time, Berlin developed into the main arena for all contemporary Jewish fantasies, from assimilation to Zionism. The established Jewish community, settled there since 1671, an offspring of the Enlightenment, regarded itself as an integral part of German society and, in its large majority, believed that antisemitism and prejudice could be overcome in an age of rational thought, moving toward tolerance and diversity. For later arrivals from poverty-ridden and pogrom-infested Eastern Europe, Berlin symbolized the hope for a better life in the future (Saß 2012). All these hopes ended with the Nazi political victory in January 1933 and the outbreak of World War II in September 1939, but if we want to recreate the atmosphere of Roman Vishniac's and Abraham Pisarek's Berlin, it is necessary to regard the city from an "as-if-not" perspective. "As if" and "as-if-not" are mental constructions posed to help understand reality differently—namely, including all possible and even impossible outcomes—as presented and applied by German Jewish author Sammy Gronemann (1875–1952) in his 1920 novel *Tohuwabohu* and his 1927 story collection *Schalet oder Beiträge zur Philosophie des wenn-schon* (Kühne 2019, forthcoming). As a soldier in the Great War, Gronemann was deployed to Wilna, Kaunas, and Bialystok, and felt that the traditional lives and cultures of Jews in Eastern Europe he saw there were "authentic," whereas Jewish life in Germany had been corrupted by assimilation. In his literary work, Gronemann characterizes nearly all possibilities open to a young Eastern European Jew searching for an identity (and regards them all with irony and affection).

Roman Vishniac was such a young man, immigrating to Berlin in 1920 to join his parents. Scientific interests were his passion from a young age, but I want to find him on the streets of Berlin. "In Berlin," Gronemann wrote in his memoirs, "East and West are less geographical and more temporal terms" (Gronemann 2002, 273). While Berlin in this period became in certain ways a *Jewish space*, in the sense of Jewish cultural activity beyond the confines of the synagogue, there has never been an isolated Jewish quarter. The Scheunenviertel in Mitte, a center of Berlin Jewish life, received an influx of immigrants from Eastern Europe after 1880, including a large number of Hasidic Jews—easily recognizable through their dress and customs. The publicized snapshots of peddlers and beggars contributed to the othering and targeting of those immigrants. New living quarters in the western part of the city, from Schöneberg and Charlottenburg to Grunewald reflected a new geography of Jewish acculturation and integration. Roman Vishniac, whose family settled in one of the assimilated Jewish neighborhoods of west Berlin, turned to the streets of modern Berlin for his early photography. Whoever wanted to find his or her own place in the metropolis, needed to discuss and to negotiate their personal identity in relation to the whole city: to learn its language, to walk its streets attentively and with an eye for detail: streets, houses, shops, advertising, passersby.

Figure 10.1. Roman Vishniac, women walking with a baby carriage, Berlin, Germany, 1939. *Source:* Gift of Mara Vishniac Kohn, courtesy the Magnes Collection of Jewish Art and Life, University of California, Berkeley. Used with permission.

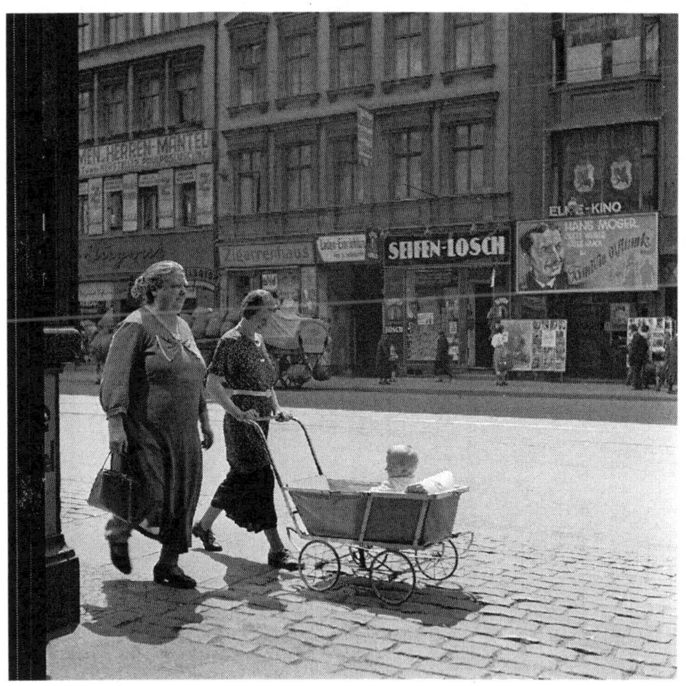

Influenced by Georg Simmel's observation of the ever-changing sensual and visual stimuli, intellectuals, scholars, and artists debated the roles played by the city street in shaping modern dangers and opportunities (Simmel 1950, 410). Some photographers have captured it as the theater for violent demonstrations and the rise of crime (Loberg 2018). To show the street in a peaceful and almost pastoral way, as Vishniac does here, depicting shops, a cinema, and a leisurely family stroll in the sunshine, could be taken as a sign of his arrival. He has developed, in short, what Berlin's main statistician Hermann Schwabe as early as 1870 had termed "ein Ich der Stadt," a personality that tries to make the city part of his or her own life, and vice versa: to become a full part of the city (Schwabe 1870, 150). It is the unplanned and unpretentious character of these photographs that we can relate to immediately: children playing on the street, traffic on city squares, a beer wagon driver, advertising columns, bus conductors taking a break, street repair workers, ships on the canal, the zoo—classical Berlin images that still show a very individual and emphatic angle. These images that were "rather unintentionally creating a random record of conventional daily life" (Fraser, Kohn, and Pomerance 2005, 11) belong to the "as-if-not" Berlin, the city of hopes. Mara Vishniac Kohn remembers: "Many decades later I asked my father, 'why did you chose Berlin?' He was surprised by the question. 'The world's center of music, books and science!' he explained. 'Of course, Berlin!'" (Vishniac Kohn 2005, 17–18). He made the attempt to make this city his, not just his home, but his own, and himself a part of it, with the help of his camera.

While the idea and practice of "walking in Berlin" has been studied through the image of the lonesome (and usually male) flaneur (Hessel 2016; for female walkers, see Elkin 2017), Vishniac offers a more down-to-earth view of the city as a living space for families amid the symbols of mobility and modernity. Following Sabina Becker, we should give the Weimar Republic the opportunity to "be seen as an era of its own, without losing sight of its failure. But the Weimar Republic and its culture really should not just be interpreted with an eye on 1933 and the inevitable transfer of power to Adolf Hitler and the Nazi party" (Kürten 2018). With the "humanistic concept" of agency in mind, we could argue that both artists tried their best to contribute to an alternative path of Berlin's history.

Becoming Jewish Photographers

Abraham Pisarek was excluded from the Reich Press Chamber (*Reichspressekammer*) and banned from working as a photographer. Neighbors complained

Figure 10.2. Roman Vishniac, German family walking between taxicabs in front of the Ufa-Palast movie theater, Berlin, late 1920s–early 1930s. *Source:* Gift of Mara Vishniac Kohn, courtesy the Magnes Collection of Jewish Art and Life, University of California, Berkeley. Used with permission.

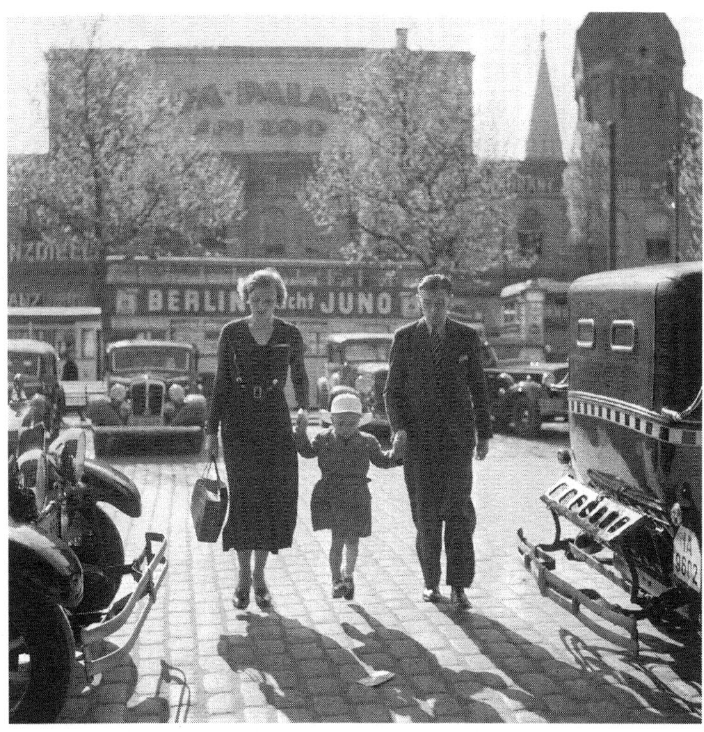

about the presence of "the Jew," and the housing society in Reinickendorf expelled the family in 1936, after having suggested to the "Aryan" mother that she should simply separate from "the Jew" if she wanted to stay (Rosenstrauch 1988, 42). As early as December 15, 1933, the consulate general of the United States of America wrote that "it is not at present possible to grant you an immigration visa. . . . It has been established that you are not eligible to emigrate to the United States. . . . It is not possible to say when your case could be reconsidered" (the letter is in the possession of Dr. Ruth Gross, Berlin. When the visa finally arrived, the USA was at war, and its consulate was closed). Pisarek was granted a work permit for the still-existent Jewish media (Diehl 1997) and for taking photographs related to the activities of the Jewish Cultural Association (*Jüdischer Kulturbund*), established in 1934.

Figure 10.3. Abraham Pisarek, life of Jewish couple. Walter (general secretary of Union of Jewish Cultural Unions) and Ruth Abelsdorf (secretary at Jewish Cultural Union) on the balcony of their flat on Olivaer Platz in Berlin-Charlottenburg 1936. *Source:* Courtesy akg images. Used with permission.

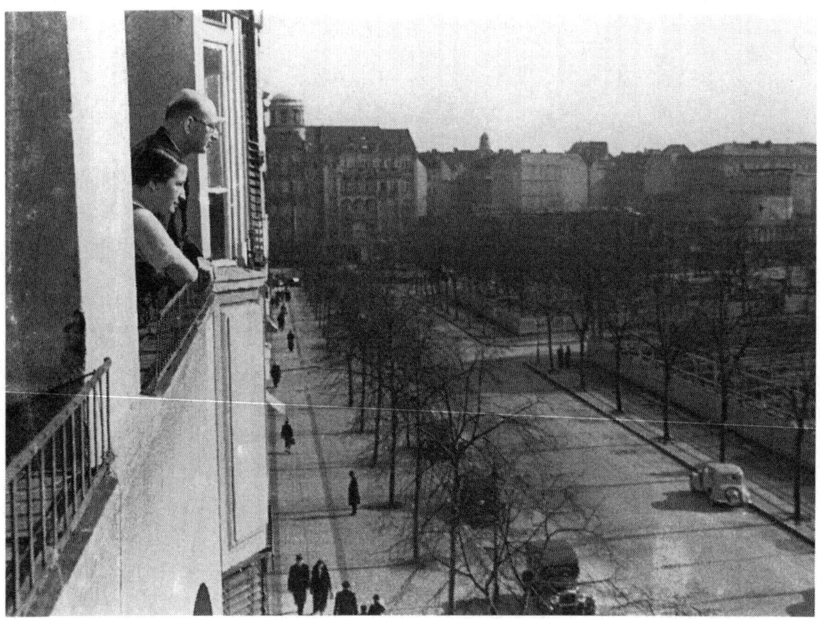

Jacob Boas, born in the concentration camp of Bergen-Belsen, described "the shrinking world of German Jewry" in an important text written in 1985: the increasingly limited, small world after 1933, when Nazi laws progressively restricted the access of Jews to public spaces (Boas 1986, 241). The city, whose process of opening up into a cosmopolitan metropolis had given its Jewish population room for development, closed itself off. The paths that had led Berlin's Jews through the entire city were blocked off, one by one. This observation is evidenced and illustrated by the photographs taken by Abraham Pisarek from this point onward. The place Berlin, which had become a *makom*—an arena for the German-Jewish, Jewish/non-Jewish negotiation of ideas and practical forms of living—was no longer accessible. This is captured in a photograph taken by Abraham Pisarek in 1936. Walter and Ruth Abelsdorf, both active members of the *Kulturbund*, are shown on the balcony of their flat in Charlottenburg, being forced to watch the busy city street from afar.

The story of the Jewish Cultural Association has been described and made the subject of critical discussion elsewhere (Geisel and Broder 1992). Some argue that actors, singers, and musicians (defined as Jews by Nazi law) who were no longer allowed to perform on the general stage and instead put on productions and concerts for Jewish audiences in this "tolerated" space supplied by the regime contributed to the development of a "new ghetto." Rabbi Joachim Prinz discussed this phenomenon in his sermon of April 17, 1935 (Prinz 1935, 3). Yet the activities of the Cultural Association can also be viewed as the continuation of the "Jewish Renaissance" (Bertz 1999) that began slowly to unfold before World War I. Steadily gaining momentum in the 1920s, young Jews in particular looked to this for an alternative to the excessively assimilated German position of the Central Association of German Citizens of Jewish Faith (*Central-Verein deutscher Staatsbürger jüdischen Glaubens*) on the one hand, and the Zionist striving for a Jewish state on the other. And was it not necessary for survival to create one's own intellectual and cultural space, to catch one's breath, to forget for a moment the external world of the now-inaccessible factual space, with its SA posts and denouncing neighbors, by staging productions of plays like Lessing's *Nathan the Wise* and performing compositions by Felix Mendelssohn-Bartholdy? Might this not have been essential to survival for those who could not get away?

Max Liebermann, whose portrait Pisarek had taken several times, was one of those who could no longer leave. Meir Dizengoff (the mayor of the young Hebrew city of Tel Aviv) and the poet Chaim Nachman Bialik had invited him to Palestine, but Liebermann's often quoted reply reflects the fatigue of an old man who had by then resigned himself (he had immediately stepped down from his post as president of the Academy of Arts in 1933) after such a successful life in Berlin. It also expresses the disappointment of the hope he had placed in Germany, in Berlin: the hope of belonging. "The repeal of equal rights weighs down on all of us like a terrible nightmare, and in particular on those who, like I, had devoted themselves to the dream of assimilation. . . . As difficult as it is, I have awoken from the dream that I dreamt all my life" (Brenner 2000, 231).

Max Liebermann died on February 8, 1935. His funeral at the cemetery on Schönhauser Allee was observed by Gestapo officers, and yet, Abraham Pisarek dared to take a few photographs. They look shadowy, almost unreal. The cold hand of the persecutors, who do not want evidence of their destruction to reach the public, reaches even into the most intimate of places, the place of death, the place that Jewish communities all over the

Figure 10.4. Abraham Pisarek, Max Liebermann's funeral at the Jewish Cemetery Schönhauser Allee, 1935. Funeral procession with Martha Liebermann, Heinrich Stahl (right), community leader, Dr. Alfred Klee (third from left) and others. *Source: Courtesy Bildarchiv Abraham Pisarek/akg images. Used with permission.*

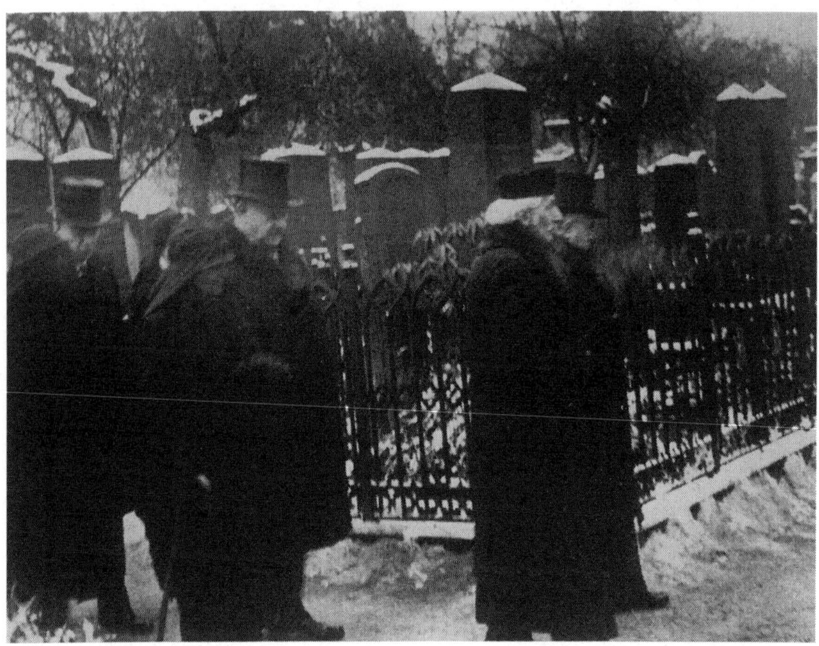

world always establish before all else: the cemetery. Pisarek's photographs therefore constitute an expression of agency and part of the still underresearched field of Jewish spiritual resistance.

In September 1933, a number of religious associations joined to form the Reich Association of German Jews (*Reichsvereinigung der Deutschen Juden*) and had to change its name in 1935 to Reich Association of Jews in Germany (*Reichsvereinigung der Juden in Deutschland*). Pisarek's photographs portray these organizations before they had been banned in an encouraging way, which highlighted continuity in their activities. These photographs were occasionally printed in the Jewish publications that had not been forced to cease publicaton yet, such as the *Israelitisches Familienblatt* and the *CV-Zeitung*. Pisarek documented Jewish life in Berlin until 1941, when his camera was taken away from him and he was obliged to carry out forced labor at Zeiss-Ikon and other factories.

Pisarek's photographs show the tension between life in an increasingly narrow world in Berlin, and the all-too narrow windows for escape constructed by Nazi law and the immigration regulations of possible countries of destination (Schlör 2012b, 13). They show families looking at maps and atlases at their living-room tables, assessing foreign countries' qualifications as new home countries. A mother is reading the letters written by her already-emigrated children (Maierhof, Schütz, and Simon 2004), and a teacher shakes the hand of her pupil who is about to leave. Pisarek uses his actor friends Behrend to stage and to illustrate the process of emigration—choosing a destination, collecting information at the emigration office, and, finally, taking their luggage to the Anhalter Bahnhof railway station. Jewish boys and girls take part in "preliminary apprenticeships" and preparatory courses for manual and agricultural work, in order to gain qualifications for life *elsewhere*. In many cases, their greatest hope lay in Palestine, Eretz Israel, and so Pisarek's attention was drawn to the activities of the Zionist movement. He documented the *Hachshara* (preparation) of youths in preparatory courses both in town (Niederschönhausen) and in the

Figure 10.5. Abraham Pisarek, Mr. and Mrs. Behrend at the emigration counselling session at the Hilfsverein, Oranienburger Straße 31. *Source:* Courtesy Bildarchiv Abraham Pisarek/bpk Bildagentur. Used with permission.

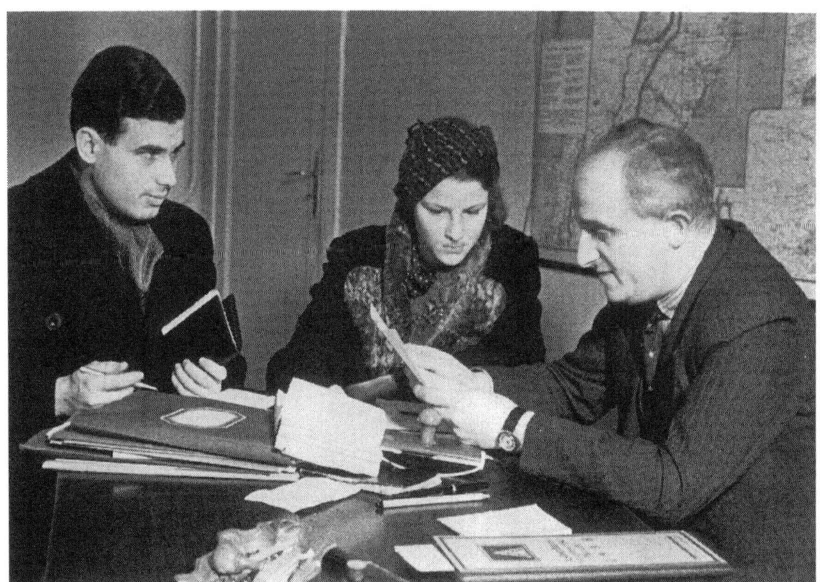

environs of Brandenburg (Gut Winkel, Ahrensdorf, Alt-Karbe). Studying all these activities, and their documentation in photography, helps to shift our perspective from the persecution *of Jews* to Jews as acting personalities.

Reluctantly and under the pressure of the circumstances after 1933, Abraham Pisarek became a witness and documenter of Jewish life in Berlin during the Nazi era. His pictures show the city in which this period of history—whose consequences continue to be felt, and which remains incomprehensible to this day—unfolded, its roads and buildings, and its people: the Berliners, Jews and their non-Jewish neighbors. In fact, the question as to who or what (people, buildings, streets) should be classified as "Jewish," and who had the power to make these decisions, leads us to the question of agency in Abraham Pisarek's work as a photographer under the Nazi regime. In stark contrast to the images "of Jews" produced by National Socialist propaganda, he uses his skills and his knowledge of the city to document life in Berlin from a Jewish perspective. As a Jew, as defined by the National Socialist laws, married to a non-Jew and the father of two children, robbed of his occupational security, Abraham Pisarek wandered the streets of a city that until then had seemed so familiar. Full of attentiveness and compassion, he walked through the neighborhood behind Alexanderplatz in which Jewish immigrants from Eastern Europe lived, and through the centers of Jewish religious life in Oranienburger Strasse. He took photographs of synagogues, schools, old people's homes and hospitals, and documented the donation of clothing and food by the Jewish Winter Aid (*Jüdische Winterhilfe*). He also captured the destruction wrought on Jewish institutions during the 1938 November Pogrom, also known as *Reichskristallnacht*. After he had been compelled to hand over his camera, Pisarek was pressed into forced labor and experienced liberation in 1945 (Unikower 1978).

Roman Vishniac's experience after 1933, when the Nazi regime "made it almost impossible for Jewish photographers to find work and it was dangerous for them to be seen taking professional photos in public," was similar at first, but his life and work then took a different direction. While Vishniac's gaze on people and street scenes in the capital city of Weimar Germany are marked by benevolence and sympathy, the later images give evidence of a pronounced distance, while, at the same time, they come across as more haunting and forceful.

One particular photographic strategy was pretending to take "tourist snaps" while secretly capturing the new reality behind them: Some look banal—blurry shots of people walking down a sunny city street—until you see the swastika flags fluttering from a shop in the corner of the frame,"

Figure 10.6. Roman Vishniac, Mara Vishniac posing in front of an election poster for Hindenburg and Hitler that reads, "The Marshal and the Corporal: Fight with Us for Peace and Equal Rights," Wilmersdorf, Berlin, 1933. *Source:* Gift of Mara Vishniac Kohn, courtesy the Magnes Collection of Jewish Art and Life, University of California, Berkeley. Used with permission.

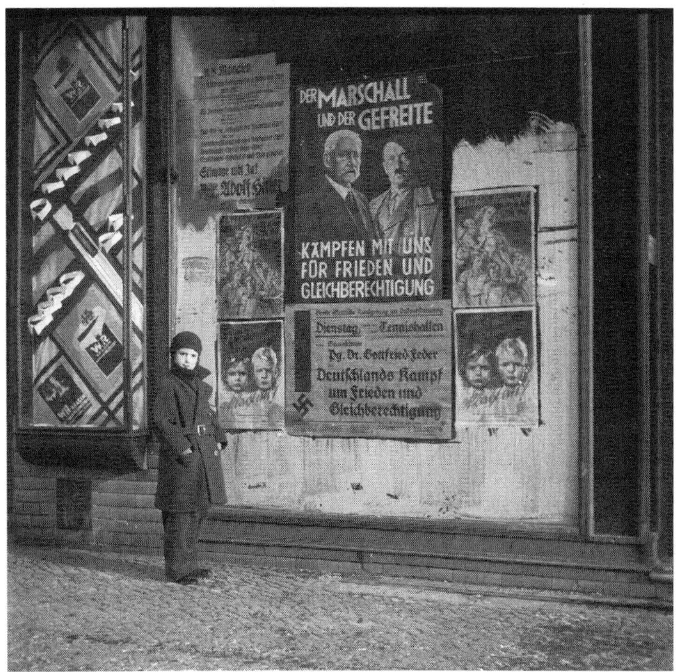

as Daniel Trilling comments. In other cases, Vishniac used his daughter Mara "as camouflage" and documented the emergence of Nazi imagery and language on the streets of Berlin (Trilling 2019).

In 1935, Roman Vishniac was commissioned by the Jewish Joint Distribution Committee (JDC) to take photographs of Jewish life in Eastern Europe—particularly of those people and forms of life that were under the most immediate threat: poor Jews; religious Jews; families and children; street markets in small towns and street scenes in Warsaw's crowded Jewish quarters; shops and carriages; bad housing conditions; people working and people without work. Vishniac traveled from Berlin to the Jewish quarters of Eastern European cities, from 1935 to 1938, posing as a traveling salesman, arrested from time to time by the police, and brought back several thousand photographs. "Through his photographs," Herbert Mitgang (1983) writes in an often-quoted report, "he sought to alert the rest of the world to the horrors [of the Nazi persecution]" (47). But this quotation is already part of the remarkable afterlife of this unique photographic collection. It is certainly true that this collection, published in 1983, decades after the destruction of Jewish life in Eastern Europe under German occupation, came to symbolize what had been lost: a vanished world—the world that Sammy Gronemann and so many others had regarded as the authentic, real world of Jewish culture. Some critics have observed a "lack of diversity" in this collection and suggested that he should have "photographed wealthier Jews, in addition to the poor Jews in ghettos" (Thornton 1971). Others cited "errors of focus and accidents of design" (Newhouse 2010). But we need to put both the celebration and the criticism of Vishniac's work in context and perspective: these photographic projects were commissions, with a specific purpose and goal that would not be met by photographing assimilated, affluent Jews.

Conclusion

Roman Vishniac's photographs of "a vanished world" have been the focus of many discussions—not just about photography, but about ethics and the art of memory in general. Writer Katja Petrovskaja framed the unease with which later generations look at the book with the following words: "He explains his intention through the catastrophe that has not yet occurred. He justifies his photography with a hidden camera by the urge to 'preserve' this world before it disappears, he opposes Hitler's racial madness, which ends with annihilation that was not foreseen at the time—not even in the worst nightmares. The photos have become documents of the disappearance, but they were not intended as such" (Petrowskaja 2020). The alleged "sentimentalization" is balanced, in my view, by the serious attempt to grasp, in photography, what Abraham Heschel in 1945 claimed as the essence of Eastern European Jewish life: its soul, that what we wish might not have been destroyed. Looking at, indeed studying these images might not provide us with a complete picture of Jewish life in Eastern Europe. But they do give us an insight into the Jewish spaces between Berlin and Warsaw, Riga and Odessa, and the many small towns in between, and an opportunity to think about the "as-ifs" and the "as-if-nots" of the twentieth century, through the eyes of an empathetic observer.

It is the camera that offers this insight, and it is the photographer who initiates it. Over time, however, the photographs themselves take on a kind of agency. Elizabeth Harvey and Maiken Umbach (2015) write that a case can be made for photographs "as objects that possess a degree of agency." Assemblages of people and objects—in our case, the life-worlds of Central and Eastern European Jewry before destruction, on the one hand, but also the earlier photographs that show the streets of Berlin as a space of Jewish/non-Jewish encounters and as a space of Jewish agency—constitute a social sphere that goes beyond "binary distinctions between the material and the semiotic, the active and the passive, the human and the nonhuman" (Harvey and Umbach 2015, 289). In that sense, Vishniac's and Pisarek's photographs contain—if this is the right word—the emotional responses that we need to learn to decipher.

In 1939, Vishniac's wife and children moved to Sweden to stay with Luta's parents, while Roman met with his parents in Nice, from where he traveled to Paris in late summer 1940. He was arrested and interned at Camp du Ruchard as a stateless person. With the help of his wife and the Joint Distribution Committee, he obtained a visa that allowed him to escape via Lisbon to the US with his family. He arrived in New York on New Year's Eve 1940. Without command of the English language, it was hard for him to find work. Still, some of his best portraits, including one of Albert Einstein in 1942, originated in this period. After his divorce from Luta and a new marriage to Edith Ernst, he gave up portraiture and turned to a new field, photomicroscopy. In 1957, he was appointed research associate at the Albert Einstein College of Medicine and later became a Professor of Creativity at the Pratt Institute, where he taught philosophy of photography.

Roman Vishniac died on January 22, 1990. In 2018, Vishniac's daughter Mara (Vishniac) Kohn donated the Vishniac archive of an estimated 30,000 items, including photo negatives, prints, documents, and other memorabilia to the Magnes Collection of Jewish Art and Life, a unit of the University of California at Berkeley's library system. There are few books on the history of Jewish Berlin that do not contain at least one photograph by Pisarek; his daughter Dr. Ruth Gross diligently preserves the heritage and has donated the original photographs to two different photographic agencies. In a 1977 film directed by Erwin Leiser, Roman Vishniac remembers his life trajectory as a series of arrivals and forced departures: "And then the thought jumps to the next stage. It's Berlin. And then the next stage again, chased away, first by Lenin, and then by Hitler, and then came Paris, and to Paris, to

France, to Free France . . . and then chased from France again, and on, on" (Leiser 1978). The spaces believed to provide a framework for agency and self-assurance proved to be instable, unreliable, and even dangerous. Today, the images both photographers left, and the stories connected to them, remain as symbols of an impressive effort to preserve the memory of Jewish presence—space and agency—in Berlin, Germany, and Europe.

Works Cited

Benton, Maya. n.d. "Berlin Street Photography, 1920s–30s." Accessed June 9, 2021. https://vishniac.icp.org/exhibition/berlin-street-photography-1920s-30s.

Berkowitz, Michael. 2017. "Photography as Jewish Space." In *Space and Spatiality in Modern German-Jewish History*, edited by Simone Lässig and Miriam Rürup. Berghahn.

Bertz, Inka. 1999. "Jewish Renaissance—Jewish Modernism." In *Berlin Metropolis: Jews and the New Culture, 1890–1918*, edited by Emily D. Bilski. Jewish Museum.

Boas, Jacob. 1986. "The Shrinking World of German Jewry, 1933–1938." *Leo Baeck Institute Yearbook* 31 (1): 241–66.

Bourdieu, Pierre. 1985. *Sozialer Raum und "Klassen": Zwei Vorlesungen*. Suhrkamp Verlag.

Bourel, Dominique, ed. 2010. *Les juifs à Berlin photographiés par Abraham Pisarek, 1933–1941*. Biro Éditeur.

Brauch, Julia, Anna Lipphardt, and Alexandra Nocke, eds. 2008. *Jewish Topographies: Visions of Space, Traditions of Place*. Ashgate.

Brenner, Michael. 2000. *Jüdische Kultur in der Weimarer Republik*. C. H. Beck.

Diehl, Katrin. 1997. *Die jüdische Presse im Dritten Reich: Zwischen Selbstbehauptung und Fremdbestimmung*. Conditio Judaica, 17. Niemeyer.

Eisen, Erica X. 2019. "Nothing Living Is Simple: On *Roman Vishniac Rediscovered*." *Threepenny Review*, no. 158. https://www.threepennyreview.com/samples/eisen_su19.html.

Elkin, Lauren. 2017. *Flaneuse: Women Walk the City in Paris, New York, Tokyo, Venice and London*. Chatto and Windus.

Fonrobert, Charlotte Elisheva, and Vered Shemtov. 2005. "Introduction: Jewish Conceptions and Practices of Space." *Jewish Social Studies*, n.s., 11 (3): 1–8.

Fraser, James Howard, Mara Vishniac Kohn, and Aubrey Pomerance. 2005. *Roman Vishniac's Berlin*. Nicolai Verlag.

Gay, Peter. 1978. "The Berlin-Jewish Spirit: A Dogma in Search of Some Doubt." In *Freud, Jews, and other Germans: Masters and Victims in Modernist Culture*. Oxford University Press.

Geisel, Eike, and Henryk M. Broder, eds. 1992. *Premiere und Pogrom: Der Jüdische Kulturbund, 1933–1942*. Siedler Verlag.

Gestrich, Andreas. 1988. "Einleitung: Sozialhistorische Biographieforschung." In *Biographie—sozialgeschichtlich*, edited by Andreas Gestrich, Peter Knoch, and Helga Merkel. Vandenhoeck & Ruprecht.

Gronemann, Sammy. 2002. *Erinnerungen an meine Jahre in Berlin*. Edited by Joachim Schlör. Philo.

Harvey, Elizabeth, and Maiken Umbach. 2015. "Introduction: Photography and Twentieth-Century German History." *Central European History* 48 (3): 287–99.

Haspel, Jörg, and Annemarie Jaegg. 2007. *Siedlungen der Berliner Moderne: UNESCO-Welterbe*. Deutscher Kunstverlag.

Hessel, Franz. 2016. *Walking in Berlin: A Flaneur in the Capital*. Scribe.

Jünger, David. 2020. "German-Jewish Agency in Times of Crisis, 1914–1938." Call for Papers. Accessed January 19, 2021. https://www.hsozkult.de/event/id/event-91891.

Kühne, Jan, ed. 2019. *Sammy Gronemann, Kritische Gesamtausgabe*. Vol. 2, *Tohuwabohu*. De Gruyter Oldenbourg.

———. Forthcoming. *Sammy Gronemann, Kritische Gesamtausgabe*. Vol. 4, *Schalet*. De Gruyter Oldenbourg.

Kürten, Jochen. 2018. "The Weimar Republic, a Pivotal Era." Interview with Sabine Becker. *DW*, December 14. https://www.dw.com/en/the-weimar-republic-a-pivotal-era-thats-more-than-the-berlin-babylon-clich%C3%A9s/a-46739003.

Lässig, Simone, and Miriam Rürup, eds. 2017. *Space and Spatiality in Modern German-Jewish History*. Berghahn.

Lamprecht, Gerald. 2001. *Feldpost und Kriegserlebnis: Briefe als historisch-biographische Quelle*. Studien Verlag.

Leiser, Erwin. 1978. *Die versunkenen Welten des Roman Vishniac*. Documentary. Erwin Leiser Filmproduktion

Loberg, Molly. 2018. *The Struggle for the Streets of Berlin: Politics, Consumption, and Urban Space, 1914–1945*. Cambridge University Press.

Maierhof, Gudrun, Chana Schütz, and Hermann Simon, eds. 2004, *Aus Kindern wurden Briefe: Die Rettung jüdischer Kinder aus Nazi-Deutschland*. Stiftung Neue Synagoge—Centrum Judaicum; Edition Berlin im Metropol Verlag.

Mann, Barbara. 2011. *Space and Place in Jewish Studies: Key Words in Jewish Studies*. Rutgers University Press.

Mitgang, Herbert. 1983. "Testament to a Lost People." *New York Times Magazine*, October 2.

Newhouse, Alana. 2010. "A Closer Reading of Roman Vishniac." *New York Times Magazine*, March 29.

Peters, Olaf, ed. 2015. *Berlin Metropolis: 1918–1933*. Prestel.

Petrowskaja, Katja. 2020. "Im Licht des Schattens." *Frankfurter Allgemeine Zeitung*, February 7.

Prinz, Joachim.1935. "Das Leben ohne Nachbarn: Versuch einer ersten Analyse." *Jüdische Rundschau*, April 17.

Rosenthal, Gabriele. 1994. "Zur Konstitution von Generationen in familienbiographischen Prozessen: Krieg, Nationalsozialismus und Genozid in Familiengeschichte und Biographie." *Österreichische Zeitschrift für Geschichtswissenschaften* 5 (4): 489–516.

Rosenstrauch, Hazel, ed. 1988. *Aus Nachbarn wurden Juden: Ausgrenzung und Selbstbehauptung, 1933–1942.* Transit Verlag.

Saß, Anne-Christin. 2012. *Berliner Luftmenschen: Osteuropäisch-jüdische Migranten in der Weimarer Republik.* Wallstein.

Schlör, Joachim, ed. 2012a. *Jüdisches Leben/Jewish Life in Berlin, 1933–1941.* Edition Braus.

———. 2012b. "Ausgrenzung, Heimatverlust, Neubeginn: Jüdische Auswanderung und die NS-'Volksgemeinschaft.'" In *Nationalsozialistisches Migrationsregime und Volksgemeinschaft,* edited by Jochen Oltmer. Verlag Ferdinand Schöningh.

Schwabe, Hermann. 1870. "Betrachtungen über die Volksseele von Berlin." In *Berlin und seine Entwickelung: Städtisches Jahrbuch für Volkswirthschaft und Statistik.* J. Guttentag.

Shabbat, Maya. 2020. "Spazieren in Charlottenburg." Staatsbibliothek zu Berlin, Preußischer Kulturbesitz. Blog-Netzwerk zu Forschung und Kultur, November 26. https://blog.sbb.berlin/spazieren-in-charlottenburg/.

Shneer, David. 2021. "Photography." *The YIVO Encyclopedia of Jews in Eastern Europe.* Accessed January 24, 2021. https://yivoencyclopedia.org/article.aspx/ Photography.

Simmel, Georg. 1950. "Metropolis and Mental Life." In *The Sociology of Georg Simmel,* translated by Kurt Wolff. Free Press.

Thornton, Gene. 1971. "The Two Roman Vishniacs." *New York Times,* October 31.

Trilling, Daniel. 2019. "At the Jewish Museum and the Photographers' Gallery." *London Review of Books,* February 22. https://www.lrb.co.uk/blog/2019/ february/at-the-jewish-museum-and-the-photographers-gallery.

Unikower, Inge. 1978. *Suche nach dem gelobten Land: Die fragwürdigen Abenteuer des kleinen Gerschon.* Verlag der Nation.

Vishniac, Roman. 1983. *A Vanished World.* Foreword by Elie Wiesel. Farrar, Straus and Giroux.

Vishniac Kohn, Mara. 2005. "Of course, Berlin! Remembering Roman Vishniac." In *Roman Vishniac's Berlin,* edited by James H. Fraser, Mara Vishniac Kohn, and Aubrey Pomerance for the Jewish Museum Berlin. Nicolai Verlag.

Zelnik, Eran. 2015. "Agency, Part I." U.S. Intellectual History Blog. Accessed March 28, 2021. https://s-usih.org/2015/10/agency-part-1/.

Chapter 11

Capturing Blind Spots

The Photographed and the
Not-to-Be-Photographed in Nazi Germany

Christoph Kreutzmüller and Theresia Ziehe

Upon entering the segment "Catastrophe (Reactions of Jews to the Persecution in Nazi Germany)" in the new core exhibition of the Jewish Museum in Berlin that opened in 2020, visitors are confronted with a panel of fifty photographs. All of them were taken in 1935, in the midst of a wave of brutal violence that both heralded and prepared the proclamation of the Nuremberg Laws. And all of them were taken by Jews. Prima vista they present a Jewish perspective. Still, many visitors are taken aback by the stark contrast the prints seem to show. Whereas one half of the pictures focus on anti-Jewish signposts as visible proof of discrimination and persecution, the other half shows sport, theater, and care—the "idyllic" side of Jewish life in Germany (Werner Fritz Fürstenberg Collection; Sonnenfeld Collection; Bildarchiv Abraham Pisarek). Taking this contrast and the photographic collection of the Jewish Museum in Berlin as a starting point, this chapter sets out to analyze both the pictured and the blind spots of photography of Jews in Nazi Germany. Who made photos, for whom, and for what purpose? Where were the limits of what should and could be photographed? And, assuming photographs are the foundation of shared memory, how do we think of or maybe even include the blind spots, that is, pictures that were never taken or were later destroyed because of persecution?

We start by sketching both what could and what would be photographed. In so doing, the chapter discusses the distribution of cameras in Germany in the 1930s, as well as the popular sujets and the themes considered dangerous to capture. As the boundaries became more fluid, we will discuss amateur as well as professional photography. In analyzing historical photography, particularly in the context of the Nazi regime—as in any dictatorship—it should be noted that not everything cameras caught was developed, printed, placed in albums, and ended up in the collection of museums such as the Jewish Museum in Berlin. Cameras, films, photos, and albums of Jews in Germany were not only destroyed during the war just like everybody else's, but also in the course of persecution itself. Moreover, owing to the persecution of their Jewish producers, some relevant photographs that have survived in museum collections are misplaced, mislabeled, or hidden in other collections or albums. This is why we, among others, did not only check the extensive photo collection of the Jewish Museum and photos that are shown in the permanent exhibition, but also various Jewish newspapers such as the *Jüdische Rundschau* (*JR*), *CV-Zeitung* (*CV-Z*), *Jüdisches Nachrichtenblatt* (*JN*), *Gemeindeblatt der Israelitischen Religionsgemeinde zu Leipzig*, and *Gemeinde-Zeitung für die israelitischen Gemeinden Württembergs* for traces of both, the to-be and the not-to-be photographed and will include certain aspects of non-Jewish photography in our discussion.

Jewish Photography in Nazi Germany: A Scattered Tradition

Photography became a mass phenomenon in the 1920s. Technical development—above all the introduction of small frame cameras—made photography easier and cheaper. In his preface to the second edition of his bestselling handbook *Der Photoamateur*, Hans Windisch rightly diagnosed in 1936 that the "photo amateur of today works differently . . . than ten years ago" (Windisch 1936, 5). Germany was not only one of the leading countries of camera and photo material production, but also home of millions of photographers (Milton 1999, 303–12). In the decade that preceded the outbreak of World War II, the number of German camera owners increased exponentially, from 3 percent of the population in 1927 (about two million camera owners) to 10 percent of all Germans in 1939 (Starl 1985, 98). The distribution was by no means even. By and large, younger middle-class residents in urban centers were much more likely to have a photographic device than old villagers. Of course, not everybody could afford a Leica. Many used the simpler and cheaper box cameras (Götz 2002). While many amateurs were happy with snapshots of family parties and outings, some were influenced and sought to replicate contemporaneous aesthetic trends—such as the modernism of the *Neues Sehen* (New Vision)—with their creative use of depth of field and their sensitivity to shadows and vectors. As indicated, the boundaries between amateur and professional photography became somewhat fluid. Many of the well-known photographers of the time were self-taught, such as Ilse Bing, Erwin Blumenfeld, André Kertész, Herbert Sonnenfeld, or Fred Stein (Ziehe 2018, 72–85).

Professional Jewish photographers were ostracized and banned from working as early as 1933 (Steinweis 1993). Many emigrated but were unable to recreate their former levels of success in exile, such as Erich Salomon or Lotte Jacobi (Weinke 2003, 29; Beckers and Moortgat 1997). Some only turned to photography in exile: "Dresden cast me out, that's how I became a photographer," Fred Stein once quipped (Ziehe 2020, 115). Others remained in Germany and found a niche existence as photojournalists for Jewish newspapers such as the *Jüdische Rundschau* or the *CV-Zeitung* until these newspapers were forced to cease publication after the 1938 November Pogrom (Ziehe 2016, 154–59). Working under Gestapo surveillance and censored by the Ministry of Propaganda, Abraham Pisarek, Arno Kikoker, and Herbert Sonnenfeld were forced to focus on what was allowed to be pictured: the positive aspects of Jewish life, religious and cultural events of the Jewish community as well as sports competitions. Others like Else Ernestine Neuländer-Simon, who had made a name of herself as Yva, tried to keep up their business in advertisement and fashion photography, but lost their customers. Yva had to close her once famous studio in 1938. Forced to work as a slave laborer, she was deported and murdered in Sobibor in 1942 (Stange 2010, 68–71). Even those who fled Germany could still be caught by the deluge of murder. Erich Salomon, for example, was arrested in the Netherlands in 1943 and murdered a year later in Auschwitz-Birkenau (Frecot 2004, 70).

With professional photographers either forced to emigrate or working under close scrutiny, scholars are increasingly paying more attention to amateur photography in Nazi Germany. It is unknown how many Jews in Germany had a camera. However, taking the average distribution in Germany as a starting point, we can assume that 10 percent of the Jews by the end of the 1930s had a photo device. This would mean that at least 20,000 families could document their lives in photographs. Accordingly reports on and advertisements for photography were widespread in Jewish newspapers and newsletters. Nearly all newspapers featured photo competitions by working groups of Jewish amateur photographers (*CV-Z* 1934, no. 13, 225; *JR* 1937, no. 11, 8; *JR* 1937, no. 81, 9; *CV-Z* 1937, no. 16, 124; *Gemeindeblatt Frankfurt am Main* 1934, no. 13, 118; *Gemeindeblatt Dresden* 1937, no. 13, 81). As a 1934 community newsletter in Frankfurt/ Main explained, these groups were founded to "cultivate and promote the art of photography among Jewish amateurs through mutual stimulation, lectures and work evenings, photo excursions, competitions, etc., and in particular to record Jewish cultural monuments from the past and present in photographs" (*Gemeindeblatt Frankfurt am Main* 1934, no. 12, 331). The advertisement sections of these Jewish papers became portable marketplaces, in which photography was strongly featured, including advertisements by photographers, photo studios, photo stores, photo suppliers, photo labs, drugstores, and advertisements for photo cameras, some appealing directly to photo amateurs (Kreutzmüller 2018; *Gemeinde-Zeitung für die israelitischen Gemeinden Württembergs* 1933, no. 9, 283). Some emphasized that they were the "only Jewish business in this branch" or the "only Jewish specialty store in Western Germany"; one photo studio offered cameras as bar mitzvah gifts (*Gemeindeblatt Leipzig* 1933/1934; *JR* 1937, no. 102, 6; *Gemeindeblatt Frankfurt am Main* 1933, no. 12, 133).

A close reading of the ads also reveals the importance of photography for future careers and emigration (*JR* 1938, no. 49, 12; *JR* 1937, no. 91, 11; *JR* 1937, no. 2, 10; *JR* 1938, no. 6, 8). Some ads explicitly highlight the advantages of photographic skills for emigration, while others advertised the leasing of photo booths for an "existence abroad," or stated that "emigrants can make a good living as photographers by buying inexpensive easy-to-use multiple cameras" (*JR* 1933, no. 75–76, 575; *JR* 1935, no. 103–4, 22; *CV-Z* 1938, no. 17, 438). The community newsletter in Leipzig listed "photographer" among the available Hachschara positions, while the one in Frankfurt/ Main offered photographer training under the headline "attention emigrants" (*Gemeindeblatt Leipzig* 1934, no. 10, 85; *Gemeindeblatt Frankfurt am Main* 1938, no. 16, 25). In 1937, the *CV-Zeitung* even made the point of listing "photographer" as the career opportunity for young women (*CV-Z* 1937, no. 16, 215). Sometimes photography permeated into personal ads when "photographers" were looking for marriage partners (*JR* 1933, no. 81–82, 644; *JR* 1937, no. 86, 8; *CV-Z* 1936, no. 15, 240). Many ads, including by professionals such as Herbert Sonnenfeld, promised to teach state of the art photography to amateurs who sought employment opportunity in

Germany and after emigration (*JR* 1933, no. 59, 371; *Gemeinde-Zeitung für die israelitischen Gemeinden Württembergs* 1934, no. 11, 19; *JR* 1938, no. 17, 20; *JR* 1937, no. 30, 8).

The November Pogrom brought an end to all Jewish newspapers, except the newly founded *Jüdisches Nachrichtenblatt*, that Rivka Elkin has analyzed recently (Elkin 2015). By late 1941, the *Nachrichtenblatt* had become a dire accumulation of official regulations that had to be published in due time (Krüger 1990, 11). Still, even in the first year of its publication, there are entries such as advertisements for photography courses or for photographers (*JN* 1939, no. 85, 3; *JN* 1939, no. 97, 3; *JN* 1939, no. 99, 3; *JN* 1940, no. 21, 3; *JN* 1940, no. 37, 4; *JN* 1941, no. 6, 3).

Prior to November 1938, Jewish newspapers had also provided an arena for the promotion of specific photo groups. The *Jüdische Rundschau*, for instance, mentioned frequently the activities of "Tmunah," a photo group of the Berlin Zionist association. The group offered free training courses to make "good and interesting Jewish pictures" and organized lectures, among others with Roman Vishniac and Fritz Eschen (*JR* 1934, no. 22, 10; *JR* 1935, no. 71, 13; *JR* 1936, no. 4, 14; *JR* 1936, no. 54, 12; *JR* 1936, no. 68, 12; *JR* 1936, no. 82, 14; *JR* 1937, no. 21, 14; *JR* 1938, no. 40, 14). The group also organized exhibitions that addressed both professional and amateur photographers (*JR* 1937, no. 69, 9; *JR* 1937, no. 99, 9; *JR* 1937, no. 101, 11; *JR* 1938, no. 40, 14). A newspaper article in 1938 describes an exhibition that resulted from the activities of the Tmunah photographic group, emphasizing "for the first time it has been possible to bring about a photographic exhibition showing only pictures of Jewish content" (*JR* 1938, no. 2, 14). Unfortunately, neither pictures of the exhibition nor a catalogue have survived. In November 1941, when systematic deportations had started, Jews were officially banned from owning cameras (Walk 2013, 355). Still, as the collection of the Jewish Museum in Berlin shows, some Jews did not follow the orders, kept their cameras, and continued taking photos.

Throughout the 1930s, Jews resorted to photography, even though this was still rather expensive, for a variety of reasons. Many were simply attracted by the new, modern technique and the novel ways of documenting their daily life. Yet, Jewish newspapers in Germany also underscored the particular significance of taking photos, *as Jews*, in the face of persecution. Rhetorically asking "Should Our Youth Take Pictures?" the *Jüdische Rundschau*, for instance, stressed in 1938 that "particularly for a scattered people, photography has a special meaning, because it connects separate parts to a whole, since it makes the distant visually imaginable" (*JR* 1938, no. 88, 5).

The article, which is devoid of any illustrations, describes technical details of photography and emphasizes the positive influence of the field of employment for youth. As more and more family members and friends emigrated to different parts of the world, photos became a way to communicate and keep a visual connection. Pictures showed how children grew up or what a family event someone had missed looked like. Of course, everybody who managed to emigrate would try to take all of these photos with them. After all, the family album was a prized possession—and a visual proof of the life they had left behind. Photographs were also a part of the process of emigration—and at times even of persecution. As emigration became an even more pressing issue, more and more photo studios offered passport photos in Jewish newspapers (*JR* 1938, no. 87, 7; *JR* 1938, no. 89, 9).

Many of the photos Jews had taken were never developed. Even more were destroyed in the war or stolen during or after the deportation. Many took their photo albums onto deportations trains, into the ghettos or the killing sites. Lili Jacob, who found and saved the famous album that staged the murder of the Hungarian Jews in Auschwitz-Birkenau from the SS's point of view recalled in 1959 that her family photo album was taken by her mother to the deportation, and disappeared when the family had to leave the luggage behind on the newly built *Rampe* (Bruttmann, Hördler, and Kreutzmüller 2019, 54–56). In Auschwitz-Birkenau the photos of the numerous albums were burned alongside individual prints the *Kanadakommando* found in the clothes of the murdered (report from a woman from Budapest n.d.). The efforts to hold on to photos also during escape attempts testify further to their significance. Alfred Benjamin took a few pictures of his wife with him when he escaped from an internment camp in France in 1942 and attempted to escape to Switzerland. Trying to illegally cross the border, he had a fatal accident in the mountains. The faded photographs were found on his body and were sent to his wife after the war.

Only a few deported Jews could rescue the image of their beloved in the midst of murder. Here, as in the case of photographs of individual persons, the contextual information is particularly important. Some of the inscriptions place rather ordinary portraits in a context of persecution and murder. Moreover, this additional information often emphasizes the meaning of the portraits themselves for the families and surviving relatives and the close ties to those depicted. The back of a portrait of Karl Düring, for example, displays the words, "the last passport photo, 1940, Daddy." Karl Düring had emigrated with his family to Belgium after the November Pogrom and was arrested and deported there after emigration plans failed.

Figure 11.1. Portait of Dora Davidsohn, France, c. 1941–1942. *Source:* Courtesy Jewish Museum Berlin, gift from Peter Schaul. Used with permission.

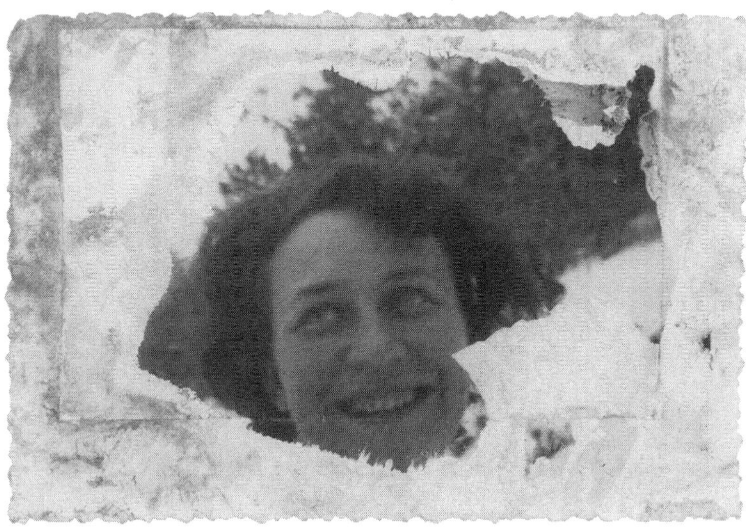

Figure 11.2. Helga Steinhardt with her son Denny, Berlin, 1941. *Source:* Courtesy Jewish Museum Berlin, gift from Rosa Oettinger. Used with permission.

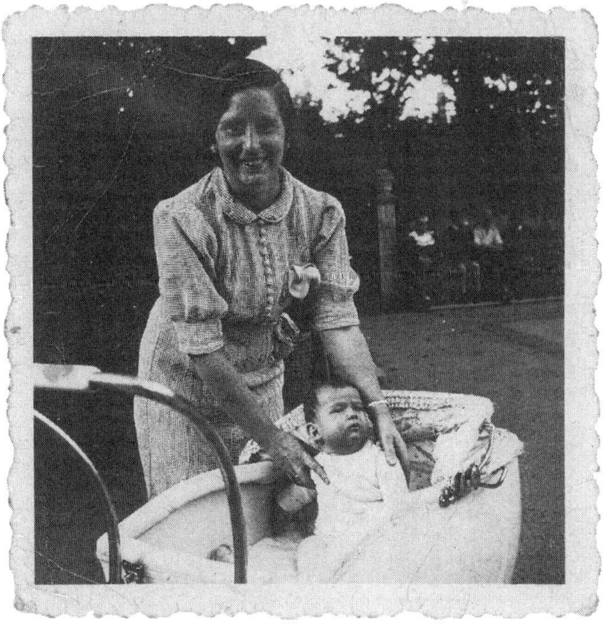

Unlike their father, the two daughters survived the persecution and later donated the photo to the Jewish Museum in Berlin. Even though it is not clear exactly when the inscription was made, it can be assumed that it was added later by one of the daughters and, thus, offers the perspective of the donor. Other photographs clearly identify the fate of the victims. "Cousin Helga with baby, 1941 Berlin, deported 1942," the inscription reads on a back of a photo showing a woman in elegant clothes walking with her son in a pram. The lady smiles into the camera, her hands resting on the baby. In the background there are more people sitting and trees that could belong to a park. Everything points to a relaxed situation in a public space. Here, too, the caption has been added later and contextualizes a seemingly carefree moment with the later fate of persecution in mind.

Jewish Photography in Nazi Germany: A Courageous Act

Photography in National Socialist Germany was perceived and restricted by ideological definitions and political affiliations. The criteria for who could photograph what were determined by racist principles, relying on proximity to the Nazi Party, local notoriety, and, of course, the chosen motifs. Officially, only fortifications and aerial views were subject to a ban on images in Germany in the 1930s (Windisch 1936, 193; Boll 2002, 80). Still, the documentation of violence needed the consent of the offenders or the support of the police. During the pogrom-like riots in Berlin in the summer of 1935, a Danish journalist was attacked by the crowd. Charged with investigating the case, the city's police chief Wolf-Heinrich Graf von Helldorff claimed that he had been attacked "because of his Jewish appearance" and because "he tried to photograph the crowd while standing in his car. By this behavior he was bound to incur the displeasure of the crowd, which was itself agitated" (Helldorf 1935). Needless to say, the film was destroyed. To this day only two fairly nondescript pictures of the riots have been found (Kreutzmüller and Weigel 2013, 26–27). On November 10, 1938, the *Manchester Guardian* reported: "Photographers who tried to take pictures of the wrecking operations were stopped by the police and one American photographer was arrested but later released." Despite the threat, some press agencies did take pictures. Even though these agencies' (non-Jewish) photographers enjoyed some kind of protection, none of them dared to show the perpetrators. Rather, the pictures document the calm after the storm, the completed destruction or the clean-up operations (Kreutzmüller and Weigel 2013). Yet, press agencies worked in the cities, especially in Berlin. In smaller communities hundreds of photos and films of the burning or smoldering synagogues were taken by local Nazis or onlookers doubling as voyeuristic witnesses (Hesse 2006, 149–68). Between 1940 and 1942 the deportation of Jews was photographed in about three dozen places, mainly in small towns. Out of the five cities with the largest Jewish communities in Germany (Berlin, Breslau, Frankfurt, Hamburg, and Cologne), only a few pictures from Breslau survived (Kreutzmüller 2022).

Looking at Jewish photography, the picture is even more fragmentary. In a larger collection of photos by Roman Vishniac, there are two photos that show his daughter Mara posing first in front of an election poster for Hindenburg and Hitler and then in front of a shop window with portraits of Hitler in Berlin in 1933 (Fraser, Vishniac Kohn, and Pomerance 2005). In these shots, Vishniac combines the omnipresence of the Nazi party with a portrait of his own daughter. The photographs can thus be read as a sign of the times, but also as a personal statement of the photographer. However, it became more and more difficult and dangerous for the persecuted to take pictures of persecution. Although the SA was supposed to be "disciplined" in the blockade of shops, doctors' surgeries, and lawyers' offices deemed to be Jewish, even non-Jewish photographers were attacked on April 1, 1933. Accordingly, only very few photos of those affected by the events have survived. In the archive of the Jewish Museum in Berlin, there is a letter with two photographs Elisheva Lernau took of the "boycott" of her father's office in Zweibrücken. The pictures show an SA man and an SS man standing alone on the pavement on an empty street. Leaning their sign with the inscription "Don't go to Jewish lawyers" against the wall of a house, they were probably waiting for passers-by. Above the two posts hangs a long flag—which seems to be the old flag of the Kaiserreich, which had been reintroduced by the Hitler-led government in mid-March 1933. It cannot be ruled out that the lawyer wanted to express his protest against the action and show that he was, as it was called at the time, "nationally minded." The nineteen-year-old Lernau took the photos at a considerable distance from her parents' flat, which was located opposite the law firm. In case of discovery, she was afraid of being sent "at least to a concentration camp" (Lernau 2003). Whether the young woman would really have been deported to a camp is uncertain. She certainly felt threatened, and this feeling was, no doubt, based on a concrete threat (Wünschmann 2015). When Adolf Vogel was seen taking two photos of the smeared shop windows of his father's business in Sandersleben, Anhalt, in 1934, the police searched his flat. However, Vogel had already sent the film to a brother living some distance away as a precaution. Still, the brother's flat was then also searched and the film confiscated (Vogel 1934; Wildt 2007, 138–42).

Beyond the difficulty of documenting violence in photographs, it was dangerous for Jews also to preserve such images. Perhaps that is why the photographs were sometimes documented in albums in inconspicuous family contexts. A photo album of Walter Roos, for example, shows different photographs of the owner, who was born in 1917 in the Palatine village of Brücken and managed to emigrate to the USA in 1936. The album contains typical photographs of family life: school, picknicks and outings, and the family business. One page in between seems inconspicuous at first glance. Yet a closer look reveals that it shows five images of a cemetery desecration in either 1934 or 1935 in Steinbach am Glan, including two damaged family graves (Roos n.d.). Due to the successful emigration, the photographs display the devastation of the cemetery at that time (Akermann 2020). Since the album also contains images from his life in the United States, it can be assumed that it was compiled after emigration.

The photo album of Rudi Barta offers a different example of "risky" Jewish photography (Barta n.d.). Barta, born in 1914, grew up in Berlin and was very active in the Jewish youth movement. In 1938, he managed to emigrate to Palestine with his newlywed wife. The album was given to him in 1937 for his birthday by two children he had cared for. It contains many photographs of the Jewish youth movement and Hachschara, mostly portraits of groups outdoors, including one shot of a group marching. Unfortunately, the picture is not well preserved, but Rudi Barta's memories, nevertheless, allow the image to be deciphered: At least four youths in shorts can be seen on a path in front of a forest, some of them marching behind each other. Rudi Barta is shown stretching his right arm forward in an allusion to a Hitler salute, making fun of the Hitler Youth. The picture was probably taken in 1935. Even though the group was certainly among themselves, photographing this scene was not without danger and even possessing and keeping such a photograph required courage.

In the summer of 1935, signs were put up in many communities forbidding Jews to enter. On a car trip from Berlin to Amsterdam, the businessman Werner Fritz Fürstenberg secretly photographed these signs and submitted them to the Central Jewish Information Office (the forerunner of the Wiener Library) in Amsterdam for documentation (Kreutzmüller and Ziehe 2019, 73–89). His pictures are currently presented at the beginning of the Jewish Museum of Berlin's exhibition segment "Catastrophe" along with photos taken by Pisarek and Sonnenfeld. The signs came part and parcel with a new wave of violence. In 1935, there were attacks on Jews in more than 350 places. One of the few known photos of these attacks was taken by Martin Marx in Groß-Gerau in Hesse. In this community, the synagogue had already been desecrated in 1934 (Schleindl 1990, 123). A year later, the house of the family's grain and feed store was repeatedly smeared with paint. It was against this background that Martin Marx decided to emigrate to the USA. Before he finally did so, he bought a camera and photographed his father inside the yard of the house, standing solidly with hands in his pocket right by the paint-smeared gate of the family's house (Historische Fotogalerie Familie Emil Marx n.d.). The photo reveals clear signs of other inscriptions that had already been washed away. Quite apparently, the house had been under attack for more than one day.

Figure 11.3. Martin Marx, Emil Marx at the door to the yard in front of his house, Groß-Gerau, 1935. *Source:* Courtesy Jewish Museum Berlin, gift from Ben Erwing. Used with permission.

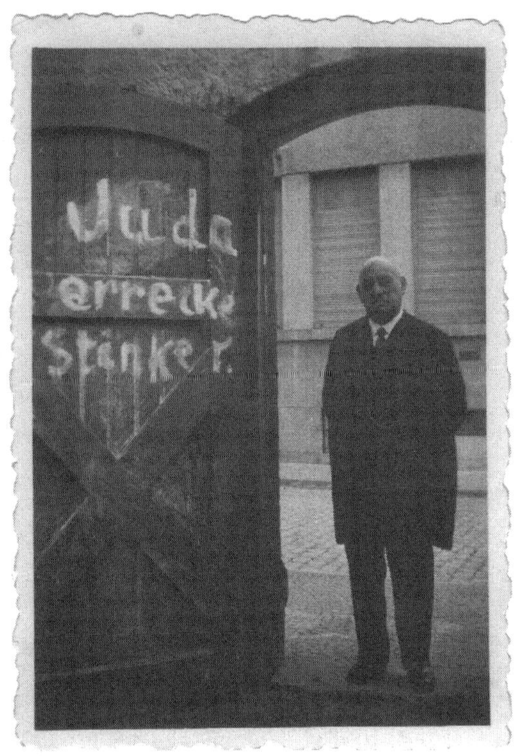

When Benjamin Cukiermann photographed his shop in Berlin-Friedrichshain in June 1938, which had been covered with paint by Nazis, a neighbor notified two policemen who arrested the merchant on the spot and handed him over to the Gestapo. As taking pictures on the street was too dangerous, one's own flat promised a certain degree of privacy. Indoor photography, however, was technically demanding. So far, only three series of photos are known to have been taken of Jews' homes ransacked and plundered by their neighbors in the pogrom in November 1938 (Schmidt 2014, 285–314). Hans Sachs took a series of nine photos in the family's flat in Nuremberg and attached them to files when he applied for compensation against the Federal Republic of Germany after the war. In a photo depicting the overturned kitchen buffet with fallen dishes and glassware, a lamp that Sachs used to illuminate the scene can clearly be seen.

Henry (Heinz) Bauer's photos were taken under very similar circumstances (Bauer 1938). Bauer recalled many years later that he came home from work on the evening of November 10 and "could not believe what he heard and saw there" (Bauer n.d.). His father had been deported to Dachau and his mother and little brother had remained behind in the flat, which had been devastated by the SA. Full of anger, he wanted to

Figure 11.4. Hans Sachs, destroyed apartment of the Sachs family, Nuremberg, 1938. *Source:* Courtesy Bayerisches Hauptstaatsarchiv. Used with permission.

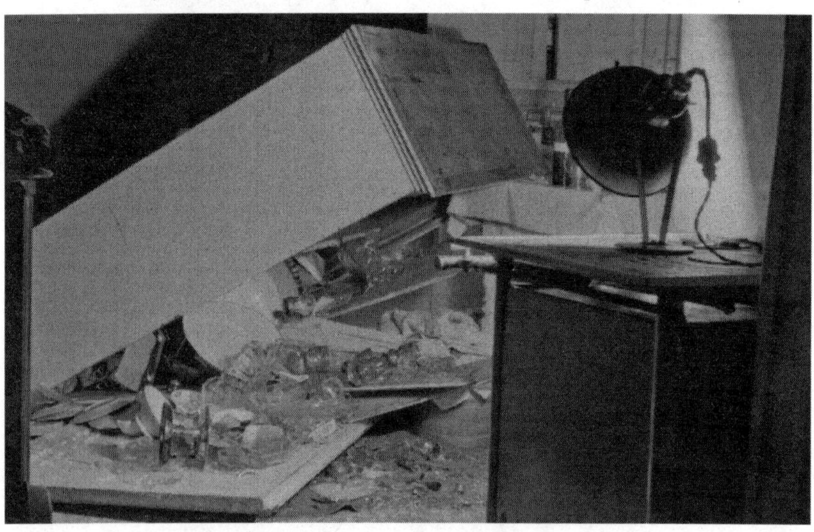

document what had happened to the family, so he took eight photos of the devastated flat. He was able to smuggle these photos (or the film) with him when he emigrated to the USA in 1939 and then also present them in his compensation proceedings. From his flat, the teacher Aron Höxter managed to take a photo on the morning of November 10 that is unique: it shows the removal of the Star of David from the roof of the still smoking ruin of the Dresden synagogue by the fire brigade (Ristau n.d.). Shortly before his emigration to Denmark in 1939, Georg Simon took a picture of the ruins of the synagogue in his hometown of Chemnitz, where his father had worked as a synagogue servant. In order not to attract attention, Simon shot the picture while riding past on his bicycle. He had to hide the camera under his coat (Nitsche and Röcher 2002, 155).

After that, taking photos became even more dangerous. Still, on December 4, 1941, two weeks after Jews were forbidden to have cameras, a picture was taken of Margot and Ernst Wachsner at their wedding (Wachsner and Wachsner 1941). They did not have much time to enjoy married life. One year and four months later, on March 1, 1943, the young couple was deported to Auschwitz-Birkenau and murdered.

Figure 11.5. Wedding of Helmut Gerson and Hildelotte Cohn, Berlin, December 12, 1941. *Source:* Courtesy Jewish Museum Berlin. Used with permission.

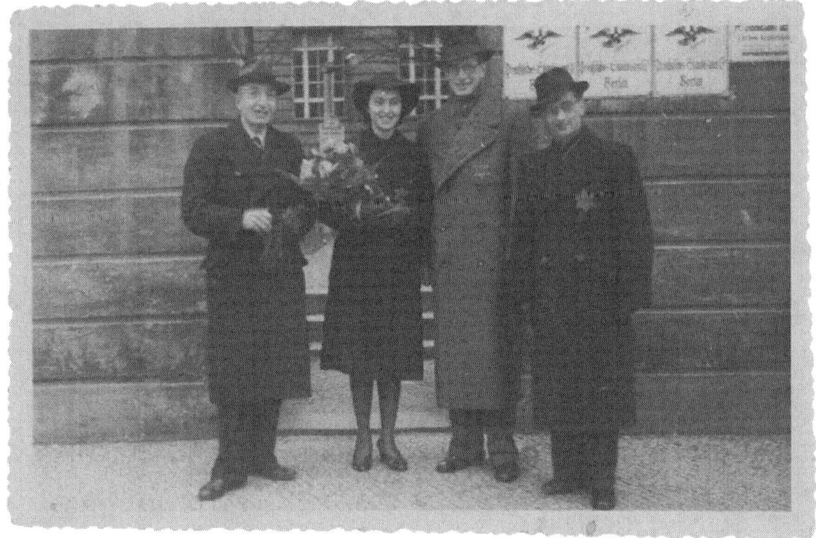

Before their deportation, the two had entrusted their photos to a close Christian friend who sent everything to Ernst's sister, whose daughter gave the material to Berlin's Jewish Museum. Eight days after Wachsner's wedding, and by chance, on the day Hitler discussed the final solution with the regional Nazi Party leaders in Munich, Hildelotte and Helmut Gerson married. Their wedding photo shows them standing in front of a Berlin registry office, with the two men serving as witnesses. All of them can be seen wearing the yellow star!

A real trove is the collection of Leonie and Walter Frankenstein. A year after their marriage in 1942, the couple decided to go underground. While being in hiding, their two sons were born. Still, the whole family survived. During Leonie's second pregnancy, she registered under a false identity at a center for people displaced by bombings. A few photos show Leonie and her son on the farm they were sent to and where they spent the spring and summer of 1944 (Walter and Leonie Frankenstein Collection; Rosemann 2017–2018). Another small collection shows students at the Jewish middle school in Berlin gathered in the courtyard of the Lindenstrasse synagogue, where the classes were held. The photos were taken in summer 1942 a few weeks before the Nazis closed down all Jewish schools. Some of the students carry visible yellow stars on their clothing. Only a few of the young people survived the Nazi period, among them the donor of the photo. And even after the closure of all Jewish religious institutions in the summer of 1942, community life went on. One of the photos of the museum collection even shows a Shavuot celebration in 1943 Berlin. It depicts seven people standing and sitting in a semicircle around a small, decorated table in a room that looks like a normal living room. The group of about twenty young people had evaded deportation. Calling themselves *Chug Chaluzi* (a Pioneering Circle), they were determined to contribute to the building of a Jewish homeland. In the middle of the Nazi capital Berlin, they often met to learn Hebrew and Zionist history and to celebrate holidays (Pomerance 2003, 86–91).

With the exception of Bremen, no pictures taken by Jews are known that capture the waves of deportations that began in the fall of 1941 (Kreutzmüller 2022, 144–45). Nonetheless, in the collection of the Jewish Museum Berlin, there is a photo showing Margarete Kuttner and her daughter Annemarie in their flat in Berlin's Uhlandstrasse. Between a desk and a large floor lamp, mother and daughter are depicted at a round table. To the right, in front, the end of a bed can probably be seen. While the mother's gaze rests on the daughter, the daughter looks forward into the void. According to her son's recollection, his sister took this photo with a

Figure 11.6. Margarete Kuttner, shortly before her deportation, with her daughter Annemarie, Berlin, 1943. *Source:* Courtesy Jewish Museum Berlin, gift from Paul Kuttner. Used with permission.

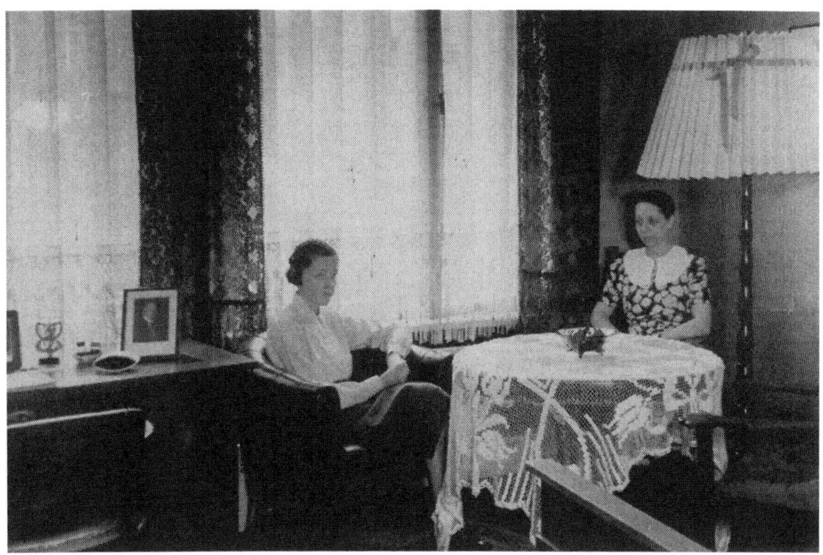

self-timer before she went into hiding. Margarete Kuttner could not decide to take this step. After she had filled out the declaration of assets on February 23, 1943, she was deported to Auschwitz-Birkenau three days later and was murdered there. Annemarie Kuttner survived—and was able to develop and preserve the photo of their last meeting before her mother's deportation.

Jewish Photography in Nazi Germany: The Transmission of Photographs until Today

Jewish photography in Nazi Germany is characterized by blind spots and the not-to-be photographed. The traces—the visual tradition as such—are especially scattered and frail and the remaining photographs have assumed the role of iconic artifacts of the Shoah. Photographing persecution was dangerous, but even when it was possible for Jews to take pictures, they were often not developed, destroyed during the war, or stolen during or after the deportations. Expecting her imminent emigration, Yva had sent her photo archive in a lift that got trapped. After the photographer had been deported and murdered, the contents of the lift were partly auctioned off and partly destroyed in a bomb raid (Stange 2010, 71). The almost complete destruction of Yva's work determines our perception of the photographer to this day. Even if her artist's name reappears occasionally in the press in the manner of a legend—often with a reference to her former famous apprentice Helmut Newton—Yva's life and work have remained largely unknown.

Even for Jewish photographers who survived, the experience of emigration and persecution continues to shape how their works are viewed and classified. In the case of Fred Stein, an entire group of works documenting events and demonstrations of the Front Populaire in Paris was destroyed, with a few exceptions. His wife sent the pictures to the Netherlands as the German troops approached Paris, as she considered it too dangerous to keep politically explosive material. There they were irretrievably destroyed by fire. Fred Stein's work might have been given a very different emphasis had these political motifs been preserved (Ziehe 2020, 115–22). The same probably holds true for the Central Jewish Information Office in Amsterdam. Much of the collection that had not been shipped to London was hastily destroyed in May 1940, when the German army invaded the Netherlands. This added to the losses by exclusion, persecution, eviction, and murder of many Jewish photographers—be they professional or amateur—which continues to affect the value accorded to these authors in the general history of photography today. Many are lost to memory or were only discovered years later, if at all. This results in permanent voids (Ziehe 2016, 154–59). Most of the photographs of the period, which are now in the collection of the Jewish Museum Berlin, for example, still exist today because they were taken into emigration. In the families, these are kept as important artefacts, often together with a lot of information and stories about the person depicted, often also linked to memories of people of whom there are no longer any photos.

There are different levels of information in the materials that have been handed down, which often fade more and more as they are passed on to next generations. This makes it all the more important for museum collections to document and preserve this information about the photographs: Who photographed what, when, and for whom? With whom do captions on the photographs originate, and when were they added? In the case of photo albums, further complex questions arise; here, individual photographs are usually combined into a new structure at a later date by persons other than the ones who had taken the images and are often additionally labeled again.

The already mentioned photographs of Werner Fritz Fürstenberg were given to the Jewish Museum in an album. In it, in addition to the twenty-six photos of anti-Jewish signposts from 1935, there are another eighteen photographs showing the destroyed Berlin in 1949. It is certainly no coincidence that both groups of photographs are related to each other in this manner: the exclusion of the Jews and the immense war damage. Without the photos it would have been impossible to prove that the five copies of an album that was used at the time to lecture on the "German Refugee Problem," and that the Wiener Library in London and the Leo Baeck Institute in New York hold, were not made by a Dutch motorcyclist, but by a German-Jewish businessman. Yet, it did not need an outsider. Against all odds (and showing great courage) a German Jew had made this pictorial documentation of the fate the Jews in Nazi Germany in 1935.

Regarding the photographs of Walter and Leonie Frankenstein, also mentioned above, Walter buried them during the time he and his family lived in illegality. After the war, he created various albums and of course the photos remain of great importance to him until today.

It is a great vote of confidence when such photographs are donated to the museum collection, and at the same time it is an obligation to document, contextualize, and preserve them. These photos help us understand what could have been and what was photographed by Jews in Nazi Germany. It, finally, enables us to grasp what was not depicted and the multitude of meanings that these acts bear.

Abbreviation

JMB   Jewish Museum Berlin

Works Cited

Akermann, Sabrina. 2020. "Das Fotoalbum der Familie Roos." www.jmberlin.de/node/7425.

Barta, Rudi. n.d. Photo album. *JMB*, Fremdbestand/1257/0.

Bauer, Henry. 1938. Photos. Museum of Jewish Heritage, New York. 1901.90.

———. n.d. Leo Baeck Institute Archives, New York. Manuscript Collection. AR 6347.

Beckers, Marion, and Elisabeth Moortgat. 1997. *Atelier Lotte Jacobi Berlin, New York*. Nicolai.

Bildarchiv Abraham Pisarek. Bpk Bildagentur, Berlin.

Boll, Bernd. 2002. "Das Adlerauge des Soldaten. Zur Fotopraxis deutscher Amateure im Zweiten Weltkrieg." *Fotogeschichte* 22 (85/86): 75–88.

Bruttmann, Tal, Stefan Hördler, and Christoph Kreutzmüller. 2019. *Die fotografische Inszenierung des Verbrechens: Ein Album aus Auschwitz*. WBG Academic.

Elkin, Rivka. 2015. *The Jüdisches Nachrichtenblatt: Standard-Bearer of Jewish Emigration from Germany during the Years 1938–1941* [in Hebrew]. Yad Vashem Publications.

Fraser, James Howard, Mara Vishniac Kohn, and Aubrey Pomerance, eds. 2005. *Roman Vishniacs Berlin*. Nicolai.

Frecot, Janos. 2004. *Erich Salomon, "Mit Frack und Linse durch Politik und Gesellschaft": Photographien, 1928–1938*. Schirmer-Mosel.

Götz, Hans-Dieter. 2002. *Box Cameras Made in Germany: Wie die Deutschen fotografieren lernten*. VfV Verlag.

Helldorf, Wolf-Heinrich Graf von, to Ministry of the Interior. 1935. Political Archive of the Foreign Office, Berlin. R 100269.

Hesse, Klaus. 2006. "Bilder lokaler Judendeportationen: Fotografien als Zugänge zur Alltagsgeschichte des NS-Terrors." In *Visual History: Ein Studienbuch*, edited by Gerhard Paul. Vandenhoeck & Ruprecht.

"Historische Fotogalerie Familie Emil Marx, Am Sandböhl 8." n.d. Accessed November 25, 2022. http://www.erinnerung.org/gg/haeuser/sb8_hist_marx.html.

Kreutzmüller, Christoph. 2018. *Printed under Pressure: Newspaper Advertisements of Jewish-Owned Businesses in Germany, 1933–1942*. Yad Vashem.

———. 2022. "A Deceptive Panorama: Photos of Deportations of Jews from Germany." In *Deportations in the Nazi Era. Sources and Research*, edited by Henning Borggräfe and Akim Jah. De Gruyter.

Kreutzmüller, Christoph, and Bjoern Weigel. 2013. *Kristallnacht? Bilder der Novemberpogrome 1938 in Berlin*. Kulturprojekte.

Kreutzmüller, Christoph, and Theresia Ziehe. 2019. "Crossing Borders in 1935: Fritz Fürstenberg's Photographs of Persecution in Nazi Germany." *Leo Baeck Yearbook* 64 (1): 73–89.

Krüger, Maren. 1990. "Herbert Sonnenfeld: Ein jüdischer Fotograf in Berlin, 1933–1938." Nicolai.

Lernau, Elisheva. 2003. Letter. *JMB*. 2004/127/29.

Manchester Guardian. 1938. "Photographer Arrested." November 10.

Milton, Sybil. 1999. "Photography as Evidence of the Holocaust." *History of Photography* 23 (4): 303–12.

Nitsche, Jürgen, and Ruth Röcher, eds. 2002. *Juden in Chemnitz: Die Geschichte der Gemeinde und ihrer Mitglieder*. Sandstein.

Pomerance, Aubrey. 2003. *Jüdische Zwangsarbeiter bei Ehrich & Graetz, Berlin-Treptow*. DuMont.

Report from a woman from Budapest, born 1915. n.d. Accessed November 25, 2022. http://www.degob.org/index.php?showjk=701.

Ristau, Daniel. n.d. "Ein Foto und seine Geschichte (3): Die Abnahme eines Davidsterns von der Dresdner Synagogenruine als Bildikone." Accessed November 25, 2022. http://bruchstuecke1938.de.

Roos, Walter. n.d. Photo album. *JMB.* 2020/72/0.

Rosemann, Anna. 2017–2018. "Erinnerungen aus dem Leben Walter Frankensteins." www.jmberlin.de/node/6137.

Schleindl, Angelika. 1990. *Verschwundene Nachbarn: Jüdische Gemeinden und Synagogen im Kreis Groß-Gerau.* Kreisausschuß.

Schmidt, Alexander. 2014. "Scheinbare Normalität: Drei Skizzen zur Geschichte der Nürnberger Juden 1918 bis 1938." In *Geschichte und Kultur der Juden in Nürnberg,* edited by Andrea Kluxen and Julia Krieger. Ergon.

Sonnenfeld Collection. *JMB.* FOT 88/500/0.

Stange, Heike. 2010. "Yva: Photographic Studio." In *Final Sale: The End of Jewish Owned Businesses in Nazi-Berlin,* edited by Christoph Kreutzmüller and Kasper Nürnberg. Aktives Museum.

Starl, Timm. 1985. *Die Bildgeschichte der privaten Fotografie in Deutschland und Österreich 1880 bis 1980.* Koehler & Amelang.

Steinweis, Alan. 1993. *Art, Ideology, and Economics in Nazi Germany: The Reich Chambers of Music, Theater, and the Visual Arts.* University of North Carolina Press.

Vogel, Adolf. 1934. Letter to Central-Verein deutscher Staatsbürger jüdischen Glaubens. July 9. Wiener Library, London. MF 55 (721/1/2397).

Wachsner, Margot, and Ernst Wachsner. 1941. Wedding picture. December 4. *JMB.* 2014/194/545.

Walk, Joseph, ed. 2013. *Das Sonderrecht für Juden im NS-Staat: Eine Sammlung der gesetzlichen Maßnahmen und Richtlinien—Inhalt und Bedeutung.* C. F. Müller.

Walter and Leonie Frankenstein Collection. *JMB.* 2010/164/2001-2005; 2011/73/41003 and 41004.

Weinke, Wilfried. 2003. *Verdrängt, vertrieben, aber nicht vergessen: Die Fotografen Emil Bieber, Max Halberstadt, Erich Kastan, Kurt Schallenberg.* Kunstverlag Weingarten.

Werner Fritz Fürstenberg Collection. *JMB.* L-2005/30/6.

Wildt, Michael. 2007. *Volksgemeinschaft als Selbstermächtigung: Gewalt gegen Juden in der deutschen Provinz 1919 bis 1939.* Hamburger Edition.

Windisch, Hans. 1936. *Der Photoamateur: Ein Lehr- u. Nachschlagebuch.* Photo-Schaja.

Wünschmann, Kim. 2015. *Before Auschwitz: Jewish Prisoners in the Prewar Concentration Camps.* Cambridge University Press.

Ziehe, Theresia. 2016. "Zur Situation jüdischer Fotografen und Fotografinnen in Berlin während des Nationalsozialismus." In *Karl Schenker: The Master of Beauty,* edited by Miriam Halwani. Walther König.

———. 2018. "Fred Steins Werk im Spiegel von Emigrationserfahrung und politischer Überzeugung." In *Fred Stein: Dresden Paris New York*, edited by Erika Eschebach. Sandstein.

———. 2020. "Der Fotograf Fred Stein." In *Beziehungsweise transatlantisch: Zum Verhältnis USA—Europa*, edited by Franziska Martinsen. Velbrueck.

Chapter 12

The Afterlife of the Barefoot Rabbi and the Making of an Iconic Holocaust Photograph*

YECHIEL WEIZMAN

There are certain images we know too well, such as the frightened boy from the Warsaw Ghetto, the old woman holding the hands of some unknown children on the way to the gas chambers in Auschwitz-Birkenau, and the man pointing a rifle at a mother trying to protect her child. While these iconic images do not represent the viewpoint of the Jewish victims—indeed, most of them were taken by the perpetrators of anti-Jewish atrocities—they have become by now metonymic representations of the Jewish fate that determine the aesthetic vocabulary of a global Holocaust memory. As such, they are constantly being reproduced and often abstracted out of their original context to become "visual shorthand for the Holocaust" (Wollaston 2010, 439).

One of these iconic Holocaust photographs features a religious Jewish man wearing a *tallit* (prayer shawl) and *tefillin* (phylacteries), which appear to have been damaged and torn apart. He is standing in the middle of a square, barefoot, his head bowed down, and his hands folded across his chest. At his feet, we notice several men, lying down facing the ground,

---

*I would like to thank Yohai Cohen for providing me a copy of the captioned photograph analyzed in the chapter as it was displayed in Yad Vashem's museum and Shlomo Strauss for sharing the source on architect Yeshayahu Ilan and his buildings with me. I would also like to thank Krzysztof Kocjan for his useful comments.

their hands behind their backs. Behind the man, there are around eight Germans in uniforms, some staring directly at the camera, others clearly amused by the scene. This single photograph was, and still is, the subject of various historical (mis)interpretations regarding the nature of the depicted events, the location of the scene, the fate of the photographed people and the circumstances behind its creation and discovery. These conflicting versions gave birth to numerous analyses, including theological readings, and turned the photograph into a decontextualized and recontextualized emblem of both Jewish suffering and spiritual defiance.

This chapter deconstructs the myths surrounding the photograph and traces its concrete and symbolic trajectories in museums, memorial sites, family narratives, and academic and popular publications across the world (Lower 2021; Porat 2010; Shneer 2020). Analyzing the multiple lenses through which the photograph, as a historical document *and* an image, is

Figure 12.1. Moshe Hagerman standing in the market square in Olkusz, as part of the events of "Bloody Wednesday," July 31, 1940. *Source:* Courtesy of the Emanuel Ringelblum Jewish Historical Institute in Warsaw, Poland. Used with permission.

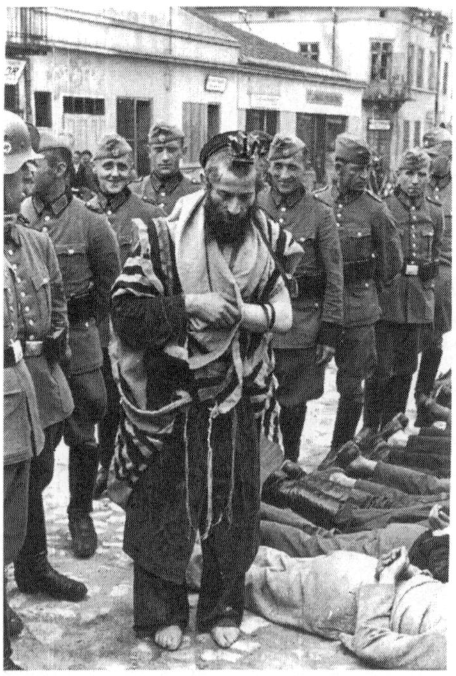

being framed, understood, and reproduced, this case study shows how certain iconic Holocaust images are prone to become malleable objects, susceptible to Rashomonic accounts invoked by different actors to support competing ideological, political, and historiographical narratives.

This case study also demonstrates the extent to which our historical knowledge and cultural memory of the Holocaust and other atrocities is intrinsically dependent on perpetrators' photography. What happens when we try to understand, or remember, the Holocaust through German photographic documentation? What are the ethical implications of visualizing and contemplating Jewish history through photographs of Jews as persecuted objects? Highlighting the problems (and temptations) of seeing Jewish history through the victimizers' lens, I wish to critically analyze the various framings and uses (or abuses) of iconic Holocaust photographs, but also try and see them as part of a creative-hermeneutical attempt to reclaim and subvert the oppressive German gaze.

But let us first focus our gaze on the man in the center. Moshe Yoel Hagerman, the son of Yitzhak and Malka, was born in 1898 in Olkusz, a midsized town in southern Poland between Kraków and Katowice. On the eve of World War II around one quarter of the 10,000 local inhabitants were Jewish. In many of the written and oral postwar accounts attached to the photo, Hagerman is presented as the town's rabbi or the local *dayan* (religious judge). Yet he was neither. Hagerman worked as a *melamed*, teaching Torah to young children, directly employed by the Jewish community (Starostwo Powiatowe Olkuski n.d.). He was married to Fruma (born 1903), and they had four kids: Yitzhak Paltiel (born 1923), Avraham Leyb (born 1925), Malka Fayga (born 1929), and Shaul Nathan (born 1930).

The chain of events that condemned Hagerman to stand barefoot in the square and to become an endlessly reproduced symbol of Jewish humiliation unfolded on July 15, 1940. By then, Olkusz was annexed to the Third Reich, bordering the General Government from the east. The Jews were still living in their houses at that time, but they were already ordered to wear a white armband with a Star of David and were subjected to economic restrictions, forced labor, and arbitrary violence. On this mid-July day, a German policeman who served in the local civil administration was shot dead during the night in his house, which had been confiscated from a local Polish physician. The identity of the assailants was unclear. According to local rumors, the murder was committed by Polish underground fighters, but later it turned out that he was probably killed by armed robbers who broke into the house. As a reprisal, the next day, the Germans gathered twenty Poles (non-Jews) from the region and executed them outside of town (Kocjan 2017, 37).

The second stage of the collective punishment took place two weeks later. This time, Jews were also targeted. Early in the morning on Wednesday, July 31, members of the German Police and *Sicherheitsdienst* (SD), the Security Service of the SS, started moving from house to house and violently forced all adult men (between fifteen and fifty-five according to several versions), Jews and non-Jews, to report to several concentration points around town, where they were beaten and abused for several hours. The largest group was brought to the market square where they had to lie down, facing the ground, under the blazing sun until the afternoon (Dressen, Riess, and Klee 1988, 7–15). Although most Jewish recollections of this day describe it as an attack singling out solely Jews, the German policemen did not differentiate between Jews and non-Jews, who were lying side by side on the square. The men were hit with clubs and whips; some suffered kicks to their heads. Others were selected randomly and forced to run back and forth while carrying rocks or underwent various forms of physical torture. According to several accounts, two men, one of them an Olkusz-born American Jew, died from their wounds. A few days later, as some versions recall, a local priest who was badly injured passed away in the hospital. Polish and Jewish witnesses recall that for several days the square was tainted in red from the blood of the victims (Blumenfeld 1996; Dror-Blady 1998; Forman 1996; Mentle-wicz, Szczygieł, and Zubowa 1984; Sypień 2020; Rotner 1998; Vaytsman 1997; Yashiv 1972). Many of the persecuted men could hardly walk back to their homes and needed several days to recover from what later came to be known as "Bloody Wednesday"—*Der Blutiker Mitvokh* in Yiddish or *Krwawa Środa* in Polish, reflecting the two distinct memory cultures that determined the conflicting perception of the events.

The local Polish commemorative events and historical publications surrounding *Krwawa Środa* in the postwar decades portrayed the events in the framework of the Polish-national martyrdom and tended to ignore the fate of the Jews, exhibiting mostly photographs that do not show the particular abuse of the Jews. Though both Jews and Christians were indeed targeted that day, traditional-looking Jews received a special treatment, as both Jewish and Polish accounts recall, and as is evident from the available rich photographic documentation (Levin and Uziel 1998, 14–15). As in other parts of Nazi-occupied Poland, the abuse and humiliation of Jews was not ordered from above but was rather a spontaneous practice performed by the German occupation forces, many of them coming into contact for the first time with those "Jews from the east," who figured prominently in Nazi propaganda (Uziel 2001). As occurred in Olkusz on this day, several Jews had their beards cut off and were forced to pose for the camera in derogatory positions. It is not clear what exactly led to the encounter between the Germans and the man who would become, unwillingly, the Jewish emblem of "Bloody Wednesday." Testimonies of Olkusz survivors claim that Moshe Hagerman was met by a group of policemen who barged into his house and found him in the middle of the morning prayer, wearing *Tefillin* and *Tallit* (Yashiv 1972, 128). After being led to the square, some two minutes' walk from his house, at a certain point he appeared to have caught the attention of the unknown photographer whose camera followed him throughout his day of torments. Hagerman figures in several other photos, in which he was told to pose for the camera in various degrading positions, alone or together with other Jews. In some of the photographs his *Tefillin* are still intact while in others he is bareheaded. In one of the photographs (fig. 12.2), we see him accompanied by a young man, who was identified as his nephew Lejbush, as he is being forced by a German policeman to dive in the nearby river, fully clothed.

Figure 12.2. Moshe Hagerman being forced to dive in the river. Olkusz, July 31, 1940. *Source:* Courtesy of the Emanuel Ringelblum Jewish Historical Institute in Warsaw, Poland. Used with permission.

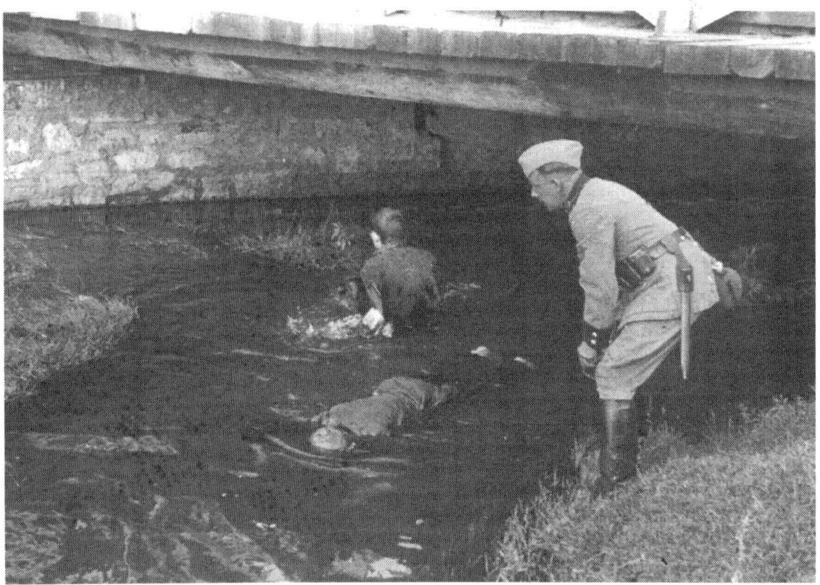

Figure 12.3. Moshe Hagerman (encircled) stands with a group of Jews in the market square. Olkusz, July 31, 1940. *Source:* Courtesy Photo Archives of Yad Vashem. Used with permission.

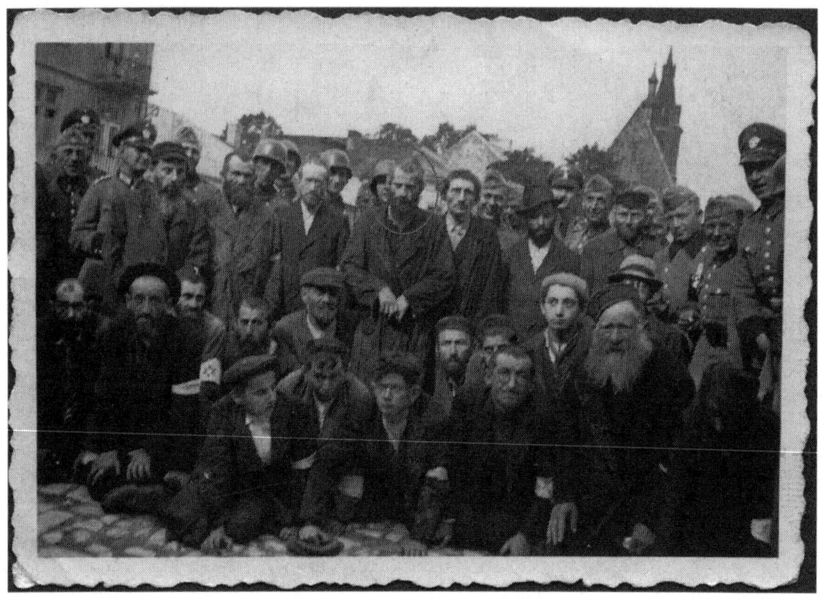

In a video testimony recorded by Yad Vashem, David Dror-Blady (1998) provided details on the minutes leading to the moment captured in the most iconic frame. Dror was among those who were forced to lie down in the square, and he recalls that he was positioned very close to where Hagerman was standing, to the extent that he could see how the Germans split apart the black parcel of the *tefillin* and ordered him to place it again on his head. According to his version, right before the destruction of the phylacteries, one of the Germans asked Hagerman to explain the nature of those items he is wearing. After Hagerman explained that these are ritual objects used for prayer, the German said: "But God is no longer with you, the Jews, he is with us," pointing on his belt's buckle which was inscribed with the writing "Gott Mit Uns" (God with us). At the end of this long Wednesday, Hagerman—like the rest of the town's men—returned to his house injured and abused. Not long after, Hagerman, together with the entire Jewish community, was incarcerated in the local ghetto. From there, in June 1942, Hagerman and his family, along with the vast majority of the Jewish community, were deported by trains to Auschwitz where they were probably murdered in the gas chambers immediately upon their arrival (Kocjan 2017, 102–45).

Like other iconic "heroes" of the Holocaust, Moshe Hagerman owes his sad fame to the perpetrators' visual documentation. From the early days of the invasion of Poland, the camera became a "metonymic extension of the Nazi weaponry" (Prager 2008, 22). Whether made by professionals from the propaganda units attached to the advancing troops or by amateur photographers—German soldiers, policemen, and civilians who brought their cameras with them to their posting—the perpetrators' photographic documentation is the major source for visual historical evidence of the crimes against the Jews and other groups (Levin and Uziel 1998; Loewy 1997; Struk 2004). Whereas photographs capturing the actual killings are very scarce, there is an abundance of photos from the ghettos as well as from earlier stages of the war in the east. Scenes depicting the poverty and hunger in the ghettos' streets were published in propaganda publications, entrenching and corroborating the perception of the Jews as a deadly and dangerous threat and thus justifying their persecution as a crucial act of self-preservation. At the same time, sights of humiliated and defeated Jews (and other, mainly Slavic populations) were used to convey a victorious message from the front (Knoch 2001).

While representatives from the propaganda units often had clear objectives when taking pictures—very often carefully designing the mise-en-scène and giving direct stage instructions to the Jews—personal photos taken by nonprofessionals were far less orchestrated and seemed to have multiple purposes and different motives. Soldiers and policemen in transit would often capture images from the ghettos out of stereotypically fueled curiosity or exotic fascination, while others appear to have been motivated by a sense of historical awareness and a wish to document the events—whether out of a feeling of ideological superiority or, to a lesser extent, some moral sensibilities and a desire to document the atrocities of war (Gutterman and Springer-Aharoni 2013). Very often those who carried their personal camera were not merely taking pictures, but rather documenting their own abuse and humiliation of Jews, particularly those who appeared to them as bearing "typical" characteristics. Many of these items were reproduced and found their way home to Germany as postcards sent from the front to the families. Similar to official photographs, they also appeared in the press and newsreels. Such images also circulated among the occupation forces, who would collect and purchase them as souvenirs and trophies. Negatives, prints, and even entire albums were found at the end of the war by the liberating forces and the survivors, in deserted German posts or on the bodies of fallen soldiers (Gutman and Gutterman 2002). We do not know who stood behind the camera on that particular Wednesday in Olkusz's market square, but most probably it was not the work of any propaganda unit, but rather a spontaneous documentation of a policeman who wished to capture the abuse of the town's population, particularly the Jews, turning the camera into a participating observer in the scene and taking an active part in the humiliation.

The Circulation of the Photograph

There exist several dozen photographs documenting the events of "Bloody Wednesday" in Olkusz, and stories of the circumstances behind their development and discovery are varied. According to a popular version in Olkusz, repeated in slightly different nuances in local publications and memoirs, after the violent events several armed Germans brought the negatives to the studio of the local photographer Włodzimierz Dębiec, forcing him to develop them. As the story goes, Dębiec risked his life and secretly kept some prints of the photographs for future generations (Dziechciarz 2018). The Polish photographer placed these copies in a box and buried it in the garden until the end of the war. He later brought it to the postwar Polish authorities. Interestingly enough, however, according to this local story the secret prints were not those showing persecuted Hagerman. Instead, they depicted the general terrorization of the town's men.

Jewish accounts of the negatives' recovery tell a similar story, but frame it precisely around the single photograph showing Hagerman surrounded by the laughing Germans. These accounts emphasize the Jews' part in disseminating the memory of "Bloody Wednesday" and further narrate it as a particular anti-Jewish event. In later testimonies, Olkusz survivors also mentioned a Polish photographer as the one who made the secret prints, but claimed it was a woman. After the war, when the first Jews returned to town, this version goes, she approached them and deposited the negatives in the hands of the few survivors—who later brought the materials to Jewish institutions (Dror-Blady 1998; Ziegler 1995). Other sources give an entirely different version of the photograph's discovery. According to the caption accompanying Hagerman's photo published in a 1983 Polish edition of

Adam Czerniaków's diary from the Warsaw ghetto, the photograph, which shows "bodies of Jews and smiling Germans," was found on the body of a dead German soldier (Fuks 1983, 240).

The rapid and extensive circulation and reproduction of the photograph after the war make it hard to unequivocally trace its provenance, but it appears that, as early as the 1950s, many Holocaust documentation and commemoration centers around the world received copies of the photo, directly or indirectly, through one source—the Jewish Historical Institute in Warsaw (ŻIH). Established in 1947 as the successor of the Central Jewish Historical Commission, one of the institute's main tasks was to collect testimonial sources of the destruction of Polish Jewry, among them photographs. The ŻIH soon became a leading arbiter in preserving and interpreting the visual documentation of the Holocaust in Poland.

According to the ŻIH, the original print, from which probably all other copies were reproduced, arrived in their possession shortly after the war, through one of the different branches of the Jewish Historical Commission that operated in Poland in the immediate postwar period, collecting testimonies and evidence of the genocide. On the back of this particular print, we can notice a stamp of "Photo-Winkler" from Görlitz, a city located on the German-Polish post-1945 border. Such a photo studio did exist in Görlitz under the management of Adolf Winkler and probably was still active in the first postwar years. While the negatives were never found, the stamp on the back of the photo, the fact that it arrived at a very early stage at the ŻIH, and the latter's experts who examined the photo, allow us to conclude with high probability that this single photo stored in Warsaw is most probably an original one, that is—developed directly from the negative in the German studio. When and how the negative arrived in Görlitz and how the original print ended up back in Poland remain unknown. Among the many photographs from "Bloody Wednesday," only one other carries the stamp of "Photo-Winkler"—the photo of Moshe Hagerman and his nephew forced to dive into the river (fig. 12.2).

The first identification of the photograph occurred in 1948 by workers of the Jewish Historical Institute in Warsaw. According to the hand-written text on the back of the original photo, it depicts "a Jew in liturgical vestments among victims of terror surrounded by Nazi soldiers." Another text identifies the scene as taking place in the formerly Polish city Lwów (after 1945 Lviv in Ukraine), and the man at the center as a *melamed* named Löffler, from Tokarzewskiego St. 26. The source for these details is mentioned

Figure 12.4. The back of Moshe Hagerman's original photograph. *Source:* Courtesy of the Emanuel Ringelblum Jewish Historical Institute in Warsaw, Poland. Used with permission.

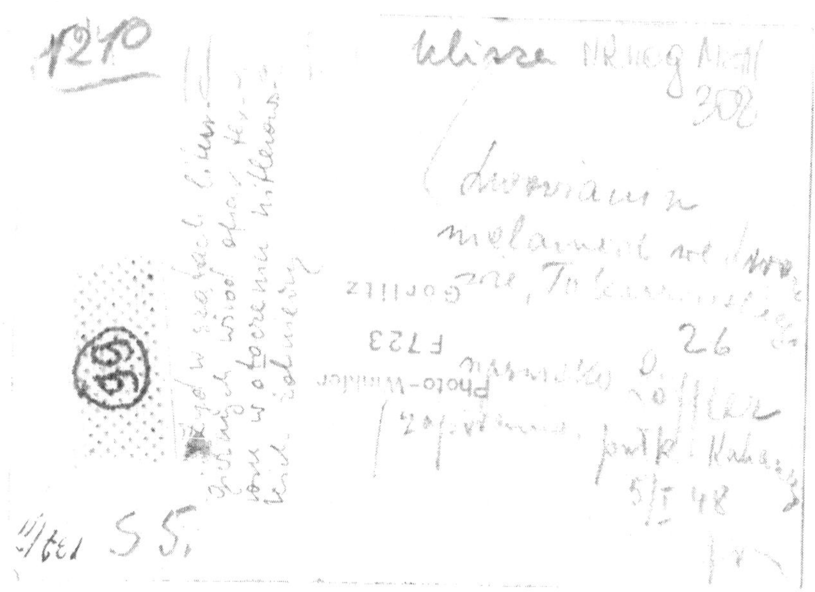

as Colonel David Kahane, the Chief Rabbi of the Polish Army, who gave his testimony in 1948. This version remained the official identification of the ŻIH archive until the early 2000s. Archives and research centers around the world that received copies of the photos have also presented them as originating from Lwów.

While this early attempt of identification, albeit wrong, represented a perception of the photograph as a historical source depicting specific incidents and people, in its later trajectories this historical-forensic approach was abandoned, as the photograph entered the symbolic-visual vocabulary of the emerging Jewish and universal memory of the Nazi atrocities. Already during the 1950s, it started appearing in exhibitions and publications and became an often-reproduced image (Schoenberner 1960, 36). In most instances, the photograph appeared either without any specific or localized context, or merely illustrating the humiliation, abuse, or murder of the Jews. When concrete details did appear, they were always false and tended to portray the events in generalized, archetypical terms. An article titled "*Kiddush Hashem* [martyrdom] in the Ghettos," published in the New-York based, Yiddish newspaper *Forverts* on the Holocaust Memorial Day in 1959, was accompanied by a half-sized photo of Hagerman. The caption went as follows: "A scene from Warsaw ghetto. A barefoot rabbi is reciting Kaddish over the murdered Jews in Warsaw ghetto, wearing *tallit* and *tefillin* as the Nazi murderers are laughing" (Menes 1959).

The paradigmatic status of the Warsaw ghetto in the Jewish memory in the first postwar decades, as a metonym of the Holocaust, might account for the choice to place the scene in the Warsaw ghetto—a location that is both specific and an abstract realm of memory—but various locations were also mentioned. On an undated old postcard, which can still be found in online public auctions, the photo bears the inscription "Tormenting Jews in Minsk [Belarus]," in English and Russian. In a publication from the 1990s,

Figure 12.5. Moshe Hagerman in the market square in Olkusz, July 31, 1940 (inscribed as "Kiddush Hashem [martyrdom] in the Ghettos"). *Source: Forverts,* April 19, 1959.

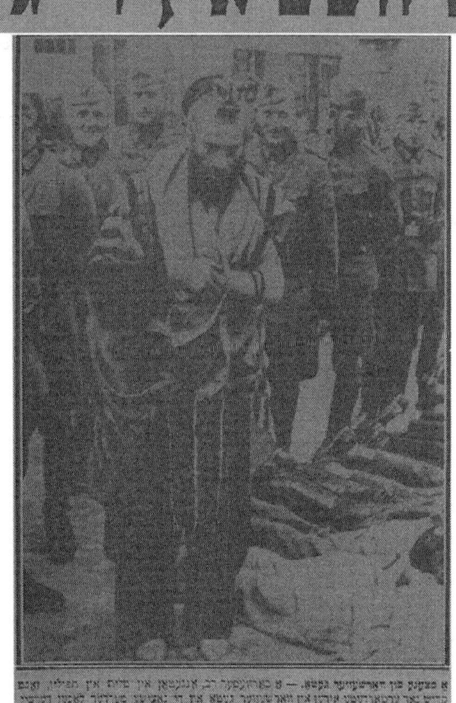

the photo is claimed to capture a massacre in Żarki, a small town not far from Olkusz, wherein "a Jew wearing his prayer shawl and phylacteries recites Kaddish over bodies of Jews murdered by the Germans" (Arad 1990, 81).

The Kaddish version became one of the most popular explanations attached to the photograph, framing it as a graphic visualization of traditional patterns of Jewish memorialization and further turning the anonymous man into an emblematic Jewish martyr. Insisting to put the words of the ancient Jewish prayer in Hagerman's mouth, might have also reflected the wish to endow the Jewish victims with a certain agency, thus perhaps inverting the original essence of the photograph as an act of humiliation, created by and for the victimizers.

In the 1960s, several survivors from Olkusz stumbled upon the photograph and immediately recognized the events and identified Hagerman.

Figure 12.6. Moshe Hagerman in the market square in Olkusz, July 31, 1940 (inscribed as "Tormenting Jews in Minsk," undated postcard). *Source:* Public domain.

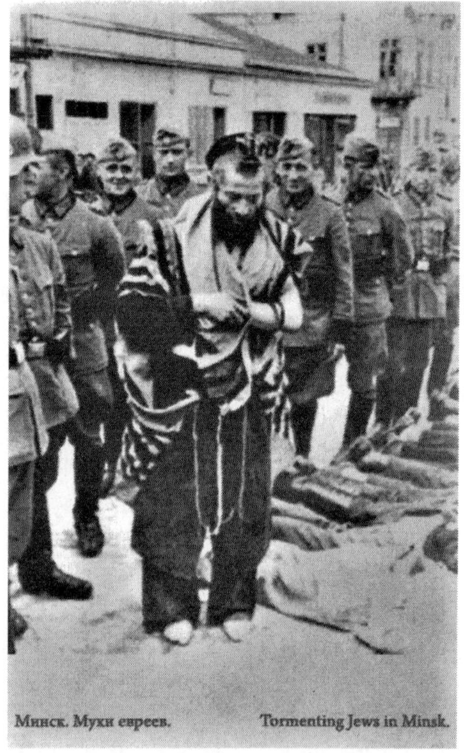

In 1972, with the publication of Olkusz's Yizkor-book, it appeared together with an elaborated historical context, but this did not affect the creative interpretations from further circulating and evolving. With the opening of the old historical museum of Yad Vashem in the 1970s, the enlarged photograph accompanied, uncaptioned and unidentified, the part of the exhibition on "Persecution and Atrocities." From conversations with senior Yad Vashem employees, I learned that over the years visitors used to hear various interpretations from the museum guides, which usually provided false details, arguing that the people lying down are dead and that Hagerman would soon join them.

In a 1990 letter to Yad Vashem, Mosheh Vaytsman, an Israeli survivor from Olkusz who was among the men persecuted in 1940 in the square, requested that the institution tell the real story behind the photo. Leaving it uncaptioned and unexplained, he argued, falsifies history and disrespects the victims. In response, Yitzhak Arad politely thanked him, but wrote: "The information you provided us in your letter is indeed important and we strictly preserve it. However, we usually don't mention the name of photographed people or personal details, but rather the event in its historical context" (Arad 1990). This short correspondence is telling, as it reflects two competing understandings regarding the meaning and use of Holocaust photographs and of their mnemonic significance. Arad's response expressed a perception—common in Holocaust institutions until the 1990s—which tended to treat photographs as a vessel of collective memory and a means to convey some general historical message. Conversely, the survivor's personal appeal scoffs at the idea of obscuring the individuality of the depicted victims in favor of deriving some generalized, historical impression, and insists that treating the photograph as a concrete historical document is the only adequate memorialization. In 1993, after the renovation of Yad Vashem's museum, a caption was eventually attached to the photo that indeed ascribed it to Olkusz. Yet again, it provided the usual story: "A Jew in a prayer shawl and desecrated phylacteries jeered by German soldiers as he is forced to recite the prayer for the dead over the bodies of murdered Jews, Olkusz, Poland 1940."

Mosheh Vaytsman, the author's grandfather, stood at the center of another episode connected to the photograph when in 1998, the weekly leaflet *Sichat Hashavua* (Talk of the Week) distributed in synagogues in Israel by Chabad (Hasidic dynasty, a.k.a. Lubavitch), shared with its readers a "recent revelation" on the origins of the photograph and the identity of Hagerman, following the alleged discovery of an old Swiss-Yiddish newspaper clip that brought the story behind the photo. The report again told the version according to which Hagerman was allowed to say Kaddish over his dead brethren before joining them, bringing a direct quote from a "wartime diary" of Mosheh Vaytsman, who, according to the leaflet, died in the Holocaust and left a testimony on what had happened in Olkusz on this day (Brod 1998).

The saga of misidentification and misinterpretation of this single photograph unfolded also outside the boundaries of Israel. In 1995, it was exhibited in Germany as part of the controversial "Wehrmacht Exhibition," which revealed the involvement of the German army in war crimes and civilians' murder during WWII, thus dispelling the long-standing myth according to which the Wehrmacht's soldiers were not involved in the Holocaust. Apart from the nationalist and defensive backlash against the exhibition, critics have also argued that several of the photographs presented in the exhibition as evidence of the Wehrmacht's crimes are false, since the perpetrators are not soldiers of the army, but rather the SS, SD, or even Soviet forces. One of the contested photographs was that of Moshe Hagerman, which was shown in the original exhibition with the caption: "A selection in a Polish city. An amateur photo from a series." The accompanying historical catalog argued that doctors and commanders of the Wehrmacht carried out the selection, and further narrated the scene. "The rabbi, the main motif of the photograph, stands calm, resigned to his fate and at the same time aloof," explained the text, and suggested that he was either selected to death as an old man who is unable to work or was held accountable for the entire community as a member of the Jewish Council (*Judenrat*) (Heer and Naumann 1995, 488–89). In the revised version of the exhibition six years later, the photograph from Olkusz was no longer included after it turned out that soldiers of the army were not involved in the events and that the story of this particular selection never happened (Struk 2004, 232n30).

Horizons of Expectation

False interpretations and competing identifications of Holocaust photographs are not a new phenomenon (Porat 2010; Struk 2004, 200–206). The versatile and creative accounts that were often attached to the photographs were encouraged by the lack of historical details on many of the depicted events and by a general archival policy that usually did not treat photographs as historical evidence, but rather as symbolic images of certain aspects of the Holocaust. This phenomenon is also a result of the need to "identify" oneself in the historical image, and of the symbolic and iconic status of the photo that legitimizes its decontextualization and flaccidity (Kielbach 2009). The extent to which a certain photograph acquires this Rashomon-like status is therefore a result of our own expectations and interpretive patterns, and the evocative power of the photograph, its composition, and its symbolic potential. When we look at such images, writes Brad Prager, "our understanding of them is predicated on the projection of knowledge and desire—or, one could say, horizons of expectation—onto those we see depicted" (Prager 2008, 34).

In the case of the famous photograph from Olkusz, these "horizons of expectation" coincided with its specific content and form, which appear to possess all of the visual traits to become such malleable, symbolic representation. Almost everything in the photograph begs for a figurative interpretation and seems to converge around a clear and scripted symbolic nexus. The uniqueness of the photo is located both in the presence of charged symbolic objects and gestures and in the relations between its elements. The traditional appearance of Hagerman, his deformed religious articles and shabby clothes, and his lowered, submissive gaze stand in contrast to the confident and nonchalant posture of the Germans, their amused and curious expression and direct stare, and the neatness and order of their physical appearance. It almost seems as if someone directed this scene to conform to a known and expected narrative. Every button in the Germans' uniforms is in place, the hunters and the hunted fulfill their role in this eternal struggle between the evil perpetrators and helpless victims. The juxtaposition of the lying, faceless Jews and the upright expressive Germans creates a symmetrical contrast, as if to set the stage for Moshe Hagerman, whose central and special role is also emphasized by his bare feet, as opposed to the high German boots and the lying men's shoes.

The composition of the photograph works to distinguish Hagerman from the surroundings and creates the impression that he is placed in an internal sphere of his own, at the same time vulnerable and inviolable, almost protected from the terror around him. This somewhat unbreakable persona is all the more emphasized by the position of his hands, folded as a shield, protecting some inner untouchable self. The circumstance that Hagerman is barefoot also supports this reading, as it is both as a symbol of humiliation and a semiotic marker of the proximity to the divine presence. The symbolic power and iconic potential of the photo, thus enable us to understand how and why so many viewers allowed themselves to arrive at the almost foregone conclusion after this visual build-up—condemning Moshe Hagerman to be "shot after he is shot," to paraphrase Marianne Hirsch, as an omnipresent martyr, abused and sublime at once (Hirsch 2001, 24).

It is precisely this combination of horror and sublimity that constitutes the lure of iconic Holocaust photographs and accounts for their ahistorical and abstract status (Brink 2000). Several scholars have critically emphasized the extent to which iconic Holocaust photographs delimit our opportunity for historical understanding and prevent us from inquiring into the use and origins of the photographs (Brink 2000; Crane 2008; Hirsch 2001). But while the prevailing perception of such images tends to decontextualize the historical reality, at the same time they are often being recontextualized into a sophisticated narrative that seeks to transcend and redeem the past, in a way that "exemplifies sacrifice and redemption" at the same time (Brink 2000, 143).

Cornelia Brink terms such photographs "secular icons," but the reception of Moshe Hagerman's image is everything but secular. Fitting into the familiar pattern of Jewish martyrdom and religious resilience, the humiliated man, who seems to possess an unbreakable inner essence, surrounded by his tormentors and wearing his desecrated crown, barefoot and looking down the earth, also evokes the most iconic Christian imagery. Encountering this photo for the first time, the suffering Hagerman reminded Olgerd Dziechciarz, a Polish poet and journalist from Olkusz, of the famous painting *Christ Carrying the Cross* by Hieronymus Bosch. "I cannot help thinking that the painting and this photograph have something in common. They are so mystically charged that I can see God's hand in both of them. Moshe Hagerman, just like the other Jew from almost two thousand years ago, has a face full of inner peace. It is as if he does not care that there are people around him who want to degrade him" (Dziechciarz 2002).

The association to the Nazarene was also made by the Polish-born, Israeli author Ka-Tsetnik (Yehiel De-Nur), when contemplating the same photograph. He too, reads Jesus into his vision of Hagerman's image, but invertedly "re-Judaizes" him through his creative interpretation of the photograph, in which he sees a revelatory moment of transcendence in the face of pure evil. In his last, and most enigmatic, book, *Shivitti: A Vision* (originally published in 1987 in Hebrew), Hagerman figures as a leitmotif and a divine revenant who accompanies the author's hallucinatory impressions recorded under the influence of LSD, with which he was treated in the Netherlands in an attempt to cure his acute post-traumatic syndrome. In the forward to this psychedelic and mystical reenactment of his Auschwitz experience, he mentions the photograph of "the Jew on the wall," which is hung over his desk.

> For the first time I took note that the normally square case of the head tefillin was spread into three peaks, like the three strokes in the Hebrew [letter] *Shin* (ש), and was perched like a crown on the head of the Jew. . . . Any moment now a bullet would dispatch him to join the row of corpses lined at the feet of the rollicking German fraternity of warriors. But it was not the moment of shooting that was of significance here. Anyone could see this, once in touch with the hidden light radiating from the face of the Jew. . . . Just look at the serenity on his face! And at those eyes, the way he looks down at the spot where he will fall in another moment! His hands are folded, defying description, as does the light beaming from his bare feet . . . before he falls among the dead lined up on the ground, the horizons suddenly flare blue into other-worldly incandescence such as I've never seen. (Ka-Tsetnik 1998, xvii–xix, 5)

De-Nur might have been disappointed to learn the true story behind the photograph. His mystical analysis, however, provides an articulated rationale to the common narrative that elevated the confrontation between the victims and the victimizers to a dramatic, symbolic level and inevitably places the captured events as a deterministic prelude for the ultimate *Kiddush Hashem*—which is also portrayed as a moment of epiphany. His reading of Hagerman's image reflects the extent to which photographs became both a mnemonic medium and a prism through which we understand the meaning of Jewish history after the Holocaust. The Jew is transformed from a humiliated victim into a triumphant martyr, who defies the German attempt to crush his spirit, turning the photo into an iconic one, in the original religious sense of the word.

Seen in this light, it is understandable why attempting to provide a concrete and detailed historically contextualized explanation of the photograph threatens to interfere with the irresistible temptation of transcending the photograph to theological dimensions. Knowing that Hagerman, as well the rest of the Jews in the photo, returned to their houses at the end of that day, it might be hard to treat the photo as a "photographic image of transcendence," as posited by David Patterson (2018, 209). Moshe Hagerman is thus being deprived of his individuality and becomes a vessel for divine presence, and the concurrent Nazi attempt to destroy it. "It is . . . a photograph of the Nazi assault on transcendence itself," writes Patterson (211). But this attempt, he argues, is doomed to fail, and only reinforces what it wishes to destroy. "Rabbi Hagerman is surrounded not by the wings of the Angel of Death but by those who would obliterate the Angel of Death, the Angel of a Thousand Eyes, who is also an emanation of the glory of the Infinite" (211).

This attempt to extract some redemptive meaning in the image of the suffering and humiliated Hagerman has also received a surprising permanent manifestation in spatial terms. The Architect Yeshayahu Ilan, who designed several monumental synagogues and *yeshivoth* in Israel, was inspired by the famous photograph from Olkusz while conceiving his unique buildings, whose roofs are shaped in the form of spread wings. The desecrated *tefillin* on Hagerman's head appeared to him "as some kind of a winged '*Shin*' [the

Figure 12.7. Pachad Yitzhak Yeshiva, Har-Nof, Jerusalem, early 2020s. Photo by Yechiel Weizman. *Source:* Courtesy of the photographer.

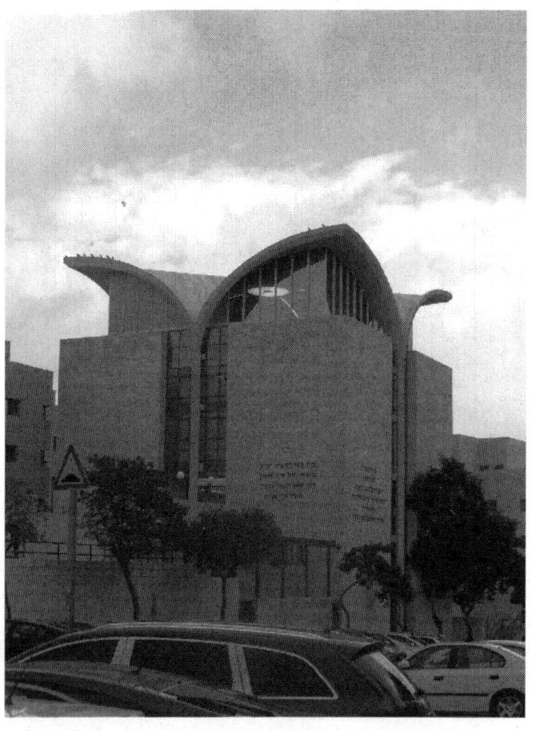

Hebrew letter *v*]" (Ilan 1992, 52). The image of the obliterated-winged *tefillin* reminded him of the Talmudic story of Elisha the man-of-the-wings (*Elisha ba'al kenafayim*), who disobeyed the Romans' prohibition to wear *tefillin* and managed to escape execution thanks to a miraculous intervention that turned his *tefillin* into wings of a dove. Combining these two sources, Ilan integrated the image of the degraded religious object into his architectural signature, expressing the sublime inversion of the Jewish persecution. As can be seen in the photograph below, the three wings–shaped roof of the building of the Jerusalemite *Yeshiva* he designed, is supposed to resemble both the Hebrew letter *Shin* (*v*), which is printed on the *tefillin*, as well as the torn item on Hagerman's head—which appears to be split into three parts.

Since the early 2000s, Holocaust institutions around the world have been putting an emphasis on meticulous research of visual materials and attempts have been made to identify the protagonists and the historical reality captured in photographs. With the opening of the new museum in Yad Vashem in 2005, the iconic image from Olkusz appeared in the new exhibition, this time with an elaborated and correct depiction of the events, and with Hagerman's name. But this did not stop the photograph from being circulated, cropped, misinterpreted, and used in various theological and ideological contexts—now aided by the rapid development of digital reproduction methods and social media. Once in a while, Hagerman is used in Facebook discussions as a polemical tool, in order to protest, for example, against the alleged mocking of the *tefillin* in the famous Israeli satire show *Eretz Nehederet*, or to attack those who oppose attempts to persuade high school students in Tel-Aviv to wear *tefillin*. In all of these heated posts, the logic was patent; "How dare you mock or oppose the *mitzvah* of *tefillin*, while the victims of the Holocaust gave their life to wear it" (Hagag 2018).

The digital afterlife of Moshe Hagerman demonstrates the innumerable circulation of Holocaust images and their unlimited flaccidity and applicability, but in a sense, these examples are merely a new manifestation of the *mesirut-nefesh* (self-sacrifice) trope in Jewish tradition—which acquires its authoritative visual ratification through the iconic status of certain photographs in the age of technological reproduction. The fusing of such photographic evidence with rooted ideological patterns and mnemonic practices constitutes a traditional-modern Jewish way of seeing Jewish suffering and devotion, which functions as a powerful and persuasive interpretative mechanism of Jewish history. Ironically, this emotional line of reasoning makes use of the Nazi humiliating gaze in order to propagate a narrative of proud Jewish identity. In a New York internet bulletin of *Chabad* New York, Hagerman was again invoked by an author who reported on his encounter on a plane with "a group of young Israeli youth who belonged to a certain anti-religious movement." After failing to convince them to put on *tefillin* and being laughed at, he was approached by a woman who asked his permission to talk to the boys, assuring him that she will be able to persuade them "in two minutes." After telling the group about her parents who survived the Holocaust and "built a true Jewish home founded on *Torah* and *Mitzvos*," she told them about the photograph and asked them, "which man in the picture do you identify with, the Jew or the Nazi?" In an instant, writes the reporter, all members of the group rolled up their sleeves and asked to put on the *tefillin* (Elisha 2017).

While Hagerman's image continues to be reevoked, reproduced, and remolded as an argumentative token in the public sphere, recently it returned "home," to the concrete space of present-day Olkusz. Only after Hagerman became a worldwide poster boy for the Jewish humiliation and sublimity, he was adopted also as a local symbol, a representation for the fate of Olkusz's murdered and absent Jews. When visiting the town today, one can see him accompanying memorial plaques and public billboards, cropped and abstracted from the larger photograph, as some sort of saint in his own monadic transcendence universe. But his transformation into the town's Jewish logo transpired as part of a bitter and dissonant local struggle on the commemoration of the Holocaust and World War II in the public space. After decades of collective forgetfulness of the town's Jewish fate and focus on the Polish suffering, Hagerman's image was summoned by local non-Jewish activists to reconquer and redesign the town's mnemonic land-scape, forcing the current inhabitants to come to terms with the unsettling Jewish past but also generating a defensive and nationalist backlash against the "Judaization" of the wartime narrative. Since the 2000s, local politi-cians and activists from Olkusz, for example, have repeatedly complained that Holocaust museums and publications around the world are portraying the events of "Bloody Wednesday" as solely anti-Jewish, while completely ignoring the persecution of the Christian-Polish population (Dańko 2006).

The omnipresence of Holocaust photographs has created a new system of visual representations and eidetic language through which we understand, imagine, and remember the Jewish fate. This post-Holocaust "way of seeing," however, is based mainly on a photographic endeavor that was an integral part of the dehumanization and humiliation of the victims. "When we confront perpetrator images," Marianne Hirsch reminds us, "we cannot look independently of the look of the perpetrator" (Hirsch 2001, 26).

Figure 12.8. The cropped image of Moshe Hagerman printed on memorial tablets in the Jewish cemetery, the place of the former synagogue, and the market square in Olkusz. Photo by Yechiel Weizman. *Source:* Courtesy of the photographer.

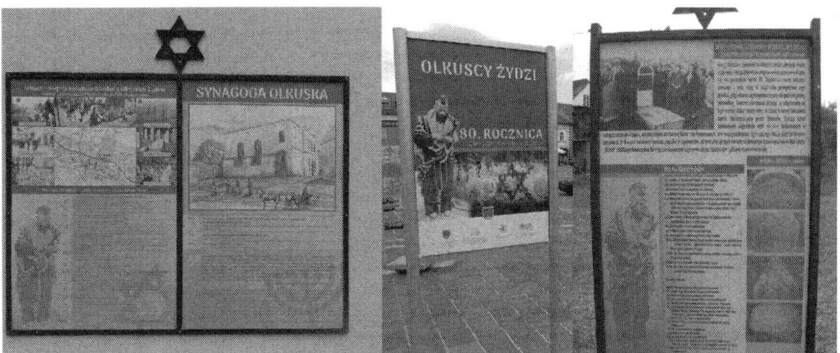

Some scholars have suggested that the adequate ethical course of action to deal with such materials is "choosing not to look" or adopting a "ban" on images created by and for the victimizers (Crane 2008, 22). But as Ulrich Baer argues, "To insist that the meaning of Nazi-photographed images is established exclusively by their creators' intentions and uses, implies that the Nazis have subdued the force of critical analysis with their murderous assault on the means of respectful commemoration" (Baer 2002, 174). The many afterlives of the photograph from Olkusz, while often depriving its protagonist of his individuality and falsify history, in many ways demonstrate how Nazi visual documentation is being "reclaimed" in order to emphasize Jewish resilience in the face of horror. There is a certain insistence to extract a deeper, higher meaning from the Jewish helplessness, thus inverting the original meaning invested in the photograph by the perpetrators. The problematic act of decontextualizing and exploiting the image of the barefoot Hagerman is perhaps some kind of a hermeneutical act of reappropriating the gaze, which turns Nazi visual documentation *of Jews* into *Jewish photography* and transforms the Jewish victims from the camera's passive objects to its agent subjects.

As for Moshe Hagerman, he will probably continue to stand in the square, forever barefoot, forever cropped, forever copy-pasted, caught in the intersection of opposing gazes and trapped between the wish to salvage him from the reach of the Nazi lens and the refusal to release him from his many roles he has come to fulfill so well.

Works Cited

Arad, Yitzhak, ed. 1990. *The Pictorial History of the Holocaust*. Macmillan.

———. 1990. To Mosheh Vaytsman. Private archive of the author.

Baer, Ulrich. 2002. *Spectral Evidence: The Photography of Trauma*. MIT Press.

Blumenfeld, Sam. 1996. Interview 18894. Interview by Lillian Gewirtzman. Visual History Archive, USC Shoah Foundation. August 22. https://vha.usc.edu/testimony/18894.

Brink, Cornelia. 2000. "Secular Icons: Looking at Photographs from Nazi Concentration Camps." *History and Memory* 12 (1): 135–50.

Brod, Menchem. 1998. "Every Photograph Has a Name" [in Hebrew]. *Sichat Hashavua*, no. 625 (December 25).

Crane, Susan A. 2008. "Choosing Not to Look: Representation, Repatriation, and Holocaust Atrocity Photography." *History and Theory* 47 (3): 309–30.

Dańko, Ireneusz. 2006. "Władze Olkusza prostują przekłamania Yad Vashem." *Gazeta Wyborcza Kraków*, July 14. https://krakow.wyborcza.pl/krakow/7,44425,3485687.html.

Dressen, Willi, Volker Riess, and Ernst Klee. 1988. *Schöne Zeiten: Judenmord aus der Sicht der Täter und Gaffer*. Fischer Verlag.

Dror-Blady, David. 1998. Interview 0.3, 11107. Yad Vashem Archives. October 10.

Dziechciarz, Olgerd. 2002. "Książka o Zagładzie." *Gazeta Krakowska*, December 12.

———. 2018. "'Krwawa środa' w oczach Henryka Osucha." *Olkuski Przegląd*, August 19. https://przeglad.olkuski.pl/krwawa-środa-w-oczach-henryka-osucha/.

Elisha, Bentzion. 2017. "Story: 'Which Man Do You Identify With?'" *CrownHeights.info*, July 11. https://crownheights.info/something-jewish/583804/story-man-identify/.

Forman, Tzila. 1996. Interview 0.3, 3747379. Yad Vashem Archives. April 4.

Fuks, Marian, ed. 1983. *Adama Czerniakowa dziennik getta warszawskiego*. Państwowe Wydawnictwo Naukowe.

Gutman, Israel, and Bella Gutterman, eds. 2002. *The Auschwitz Album: The Story of a Transport*. Yad Vashem Publications.

Gutterman, Bella, and Nina Springer-Aharoni, eds. 2013. *The End! Radom and Szydlowiec through the Eyes of a German Photographer*. Yad Vashem Publications.

Hagag, Tsahi. 2018. "In Eretz Nehederet They Are Using Tefillin as a Setting for a Joke . . ." [in Hebrew]. Facebook, May 18. https://www.facebook.com/TsHagag/posts/420953698316262/.

Heer, Hannes, and Klaus Naumann, eds. 1995. *Vernichtungskrieg: Verbrechen der Wehrmacht 1941–1944*. Hamburger Institut für Sozialforschung.

Hirsch, Marianne. 2001. "Surviving Images: Holocaust Photographs and the Work of Postmemory." *Yale Journal of Criticism* 14 (1): 5–37.

Ilan, Yeshayahu. 1992. "Places" [in Hebrew]. In *The Synagogue's Structure in Israel, 1948–1992*. Bezalel Academy of Arts and Design and the Ministry of Education and Culture. Exhibition catalog.

Ka-Tsetnik. 1998. *Shivitti: A Vision*. Gateway.

Kielbach, Judith. 2009. "Photographs, Symbolic Images, and the Holocaust: On the (Im)Possibility of Depicting Historical Truth." *History and Theory* 48 (2): 54–76.

Knoch, Habbo. 2001. *Die Tat als Bild: Fotografien des Holocaust in der Deutschen Erinnerungskultur*. Hamburger Edition.

Kocjan, Krzysztof. 2017. *Zagłada olkuskich Żydów*. Fundacja Kultury AFRONT.

Levin, Judith, and Daniel Uziel. 1998. "Ordinary Men, Extraordinary Photos." *Yad Vashem Studies* 26:280–93.

Loewy, Hanno. 1997. "'. . . Without Masks': Jews through the Lens of 'German Photography,' 1933–1945." In *German Photography 1870–1970: The Power of a Medium*, edited by Klaus Honnef, Rolf Sachsse, and Karin Thomas. Dumont.

Lower, Lower. 2021. *The Ravine: A Family, a Photograph, a Holocaust Massacre Revealed*. Head of Zeus.

Menes, A. 1959. "Kiddush Hashem in the Ghettos" [in Yiddish]. *Forverts*, April 19.

Mentlewicz, Lesław, Bogdan Szczygieł, and Gabriela Zubowa, eds. 1984. *Krwawa środa 1940: Z dawnych dni ziemi olkuskiej*. Wydział Kultury, Kultury Fizycznej i Sportu Urzędu Miasta Gminy Olkusz.

Patterson, David. 2018. *The Holocaust and the Nonrepresentable: Literary and Photographic Transcendence*. State University of New York Press.

Porat, Dan. 2010. *The Boy: A Holocaust Story*. Melbourne University Press.

Prager, Brad. 2008. "On the Liberation of Perpetrator Photographs in Holocaust Narratives." In *Visualizing the Holocaust: Documents, Aesthetics, Memory*, edited by David Bathrick, Brad Prager, and Michael D. Richardson. Camden House.

Rotner, Bella. 1998. Interview 48316. Interview by Anita White. Visual History Archive, USC Shoah Foundation. October 26. https://vha.usc.edu/testimony/48316.

Schoenberner, Gerhard. 1960. *Der gelbe Stern: Die Judenverfolgung in Europa 1933 bis 1945*. Bertelsmann Sachbuchverlag.

Shneer, David. 2020. *Grief: The Biography of a Holocaust Photograph*. Oxford University Press.

Starostwo Powiatowe Olkuski. n.d. File 240. Archiwum Państwowe w Katowicach [State Archive in Katowice].

Struk, Janina. 2004. *Photographing the Holocaust: Interpretations of the Evidence*. Routledge.

Sypień, Jacek. 2020. *Krwawa Środa 1940 w Olkuszu: wybór źródeł*. Instytut Pamięci Narodowej—Komisja Ścigania Zbrodni przeciwko Narodowi Polskiemu & Urząd Miasta i Gminy Olkusz.

Uziel, Daniel. 2001. "Wehrmacht Propaganda Troops and the Jews." *Yad Vashem Studies* 29:27–65.

Vaytsman, Moshe. 1997. Interview 31636. Interview by Miriam Thau. Visual History Archive, USC Shoah Foundation. May 18. https://vha.usc.edu/testimony/31636.

Wollaston, Isabel. 2010. "The Absent, the Partial and the Iconic in Archival Photographs of the Holocaust." *Jewish Culture and History* 12 (3): 439–62.

Yashiv, Zvi, ed. 1972. *The Olkusz Yizkor Book* [in Hebrew and Yiddish]. Organization of Former Residents of Olkusz in Israel.

Ziegler, Walter. 1995. Interview 4410. Interview by Neil Smith. Visual History Archive, USC Shoah Foundation. August 8. https://vha.usc.edu/testimony/4410.

Part V

The Jewish Gaze on the Other "Others"

Migration, Colonialism, Minorities

Chapter 13

Moving Views

Global Routes of Jewish Refuge as
Spaces of Early Humanitarian Seeing

Rebekka Grossmann

A baby is lying on a frayed mat, sleeping. Its long black hair has been shaved on the sides according to Chinese custom. The child is covered with a white cloth; a smaller piece of cotton serves as a pillow. The scene looks peaceful, but two elements undermine the alleged harmony. The first is the angle of our gaze. The camera has captured the baby from above and behind its head. Its forehead reflects the dim light; the rest of the room seems darker. The impression of distance and darkness is strengthened by the silhouette in the front right, probably a piece of furniture preventing the visitor from further approaching the make-shift crib.

The German-Jewish photographer Lotte Errell took this photograph during her trip to China in the years 1931 and 1932. The respective collection, however, is not merely a compilation of views. Errell also provided lengthy captions to explain the scene to interested viewers. In this case, the caption states, "Silk spinning mill in Shanghai. While the mothers work, the babies lie underneath the spinning chairs."

Errell's caption locates the baby on the floor under a loom of its working mother. It discloses that this baby is only one of many "living" under their mothers' chairs. With the knowledge of the distress of poverty

Figure 13.1. Lotte Errel, a baby underneath a silk spinning mill in Shanghai, 1931–1932. *Source:* Courtesy Fotografische Sammlung, Museum Folkwang.

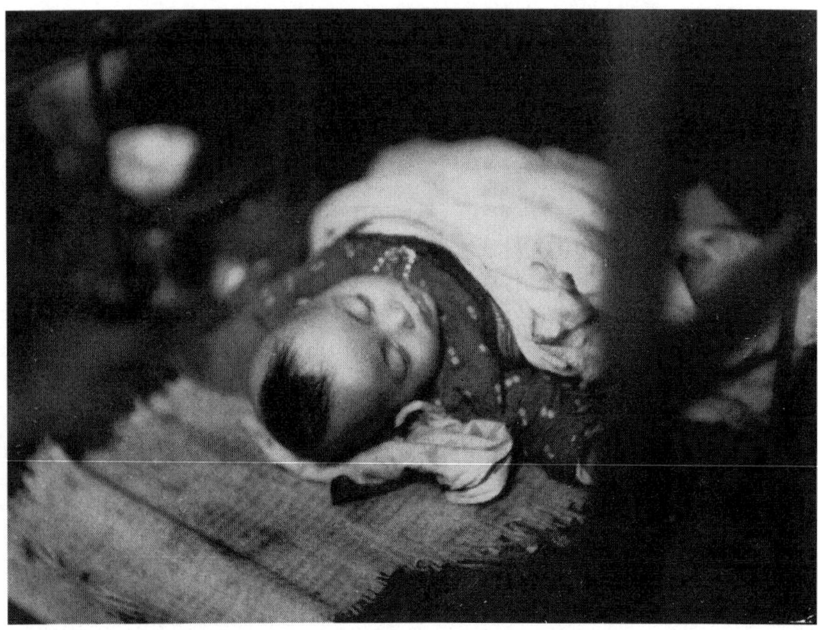

Figure 13.2. Lotte Errell, the back of the silk spinning mill photograph, 1931–1932. *Source:* Courtesy Fotografische Sammlung, Museum Folkwang.

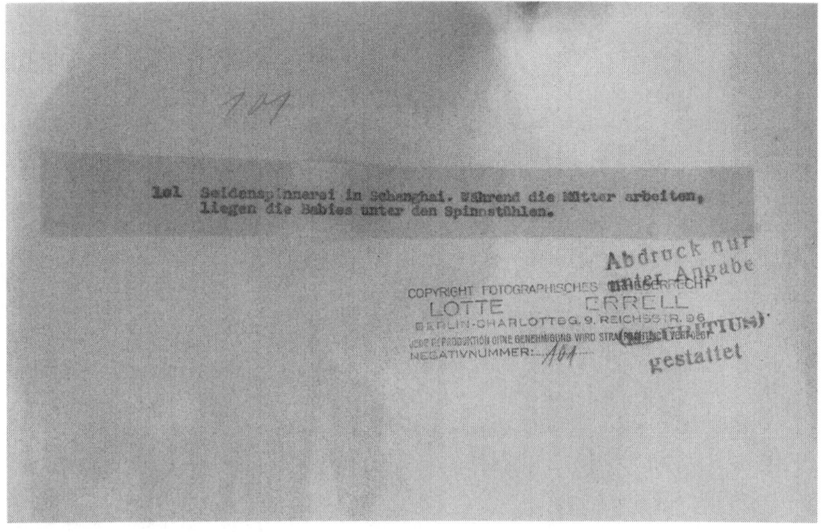

and hard labor the cloth covering the baby appears dirtier, the mat looks yet more meager. The high angle corroborates the cultural superiority of the observing camera. But without this camera, the baby's fate would remain unknown. A different detail on the back of the photograph shows that it was conceived as a piece of news. Errell was sent to China by the Ullstein publishing house to send back regular reports (Errell n.d.[c]). But the image circulated further. This print was purchased by the German Mauritius agency. Another print of the same motif was sold to the Associated Press. In a respective report titled "Child Labor," Errell further described the conditions of Chinese women and children working in silk production. While mothers "stored" their babies under their desks, older children were forced to help prepare the silk for spinning. Their "little arms," Errell writes, work as fast and as exact as a machine, but their heads seem to live a "soulless life" (Errell n.d.[d], 5–6). A few lines later, the observer adds that she does not report on this kind of Chinese poverty to evoke criticism or condescension. Instead, she hoped to alert viewers to the suffering of others: the material conditions of the family simply did not allow for surviving without the help of children and mothers.

This chapter is set at the intersection of Jewish travel—voluntary at first, later turning into migratory transit—and journalistic investigation during the twilight years of the Weimar Republic and the early years of National Socialism. It follows photographers like Errell who, being Jewish, discovered travel as a refuge from political radicalism, and a way that facilitated their continuing communication with the audiences of their native Germany. Their major "accomplices" were news editors and global news outlets, who turned the images they provided and the views and sensitivities they carried into news. Employing channels of photographic transfer and the globalization of the media, which emerged at around the same time, these travelers' photographs crossed the globe as pieces of information that only they as nomads in transit could transmit (Myers 2009; Schlör 2014; Presner 2007).

The globalization of news media gained momentum during the interwar years. Respective scholarship offers a methodological space to explore ideas transported and visibilities communicated along global routes (Lawrence and Tavernor 2019, 2–3; Fehrenbach and Rodogno 2015; Hight and Sampson 2002; Grandin 2004). In particular, it allows for investigating travel and migration as a laboratory of the kind of humanitarian visibility that enhanced an awareness of political causes in colonial contexts and mediated distances between home and abroad. At the same time, scholarship of media globalism highlights the ways travel and journalism were—and continue to be—dominated by Western ideologies, beliefs, and communicative structures, which influenced the flow and content of information (Curran and Park 2000, 5–6; Barnett 2010, 12). The interwar encounters of traveling Jews with the colonial landscape, however, extend beyond the study of global journalism. The photographers I discuss below were not merely visitors from a wealthy world who came to explore the periphery of modernity. "Exploration" is complemented by the negatively connoted "rootlessness" (Clifford 1997, 31); photographic encounters are strained by the additional experience of closures, restrictions, and separation. Photographers like Errell traveled as the objects of actual or implicated violence at home. This position of refugee-Westerners complicates the "asymmetry of vulnerability" normally embedded in similar photographic practices (Rothberg 2019, 28). It demands a reading of the respective photographs as a combination of the colonial and the displaced gaze.

This chapter approaches such photographic encounters from the vantage point of Jewish refugees on global roads. It argues that the simultaneous identification with the Western perspective and the excluded Jewish point of view forged a particular kind of photographic encounter. Recent scholarship indicates the importance of frontline photographers (and agencies, such as Magnum) in the formation of postcolonial imagery and its place in the public discussion of colonialism in the West (Bair 2020; Bear 2010). My analysis highlights the contribution of displaced photographers in transit to this discourse: photographers whose views preceded and laid the ground for the humanitarian camera of the 1940s, 1950s, and 1960s. In what follows, I consider Lotte Errell's works and those of some of her colleagues as a case study for the overlooked contribution of (traveling) Jewish refugees to this way of humanitarian seeing. The images they produced, I argue, indicate a particular awareness of subaltern stories of suppression, presumably instigated by the photographers' own exclusion. This sensitivity is evident in the use (and development) of a documentary style that presents an unfiltered image of subaltern experiences. The images also shed light on the ways these photographers sought to market their views for large audiences of newspaper readers through extended journalistic connections made, at least partially, on the same routes of travel and displacement.

Early Travel Photography between Curiosity and Solidarity

Errell's trip to China was not her first expedition. In 1928, the twenty-five-year-old photographer had accompanied the German ethnographer

Gulla Pfeffer on a trip to the Gold Coast (present-day Ghana) and Togo (Schilling 2010, 145). Another companion on the trip was the filmmaker Friedrich Dalsheim. Dalsheim's presence and Errell's training as a photographic autodidact and assistant to her husband Richard Errell (who made up a new, less Jewish sounding name for himself from his initials, R. L., formerly being Richard Levy) must have created an atmosphere of artistic and journalistic exchange and fueled aspirations (Wiethoff 1997, 6). Errell's photographs speak of a rather visible desire to counter the tradition of the ethnographic gaze. This position was in opposition to her companion Pfeffer, who by then had made a name for herself as a collector of artifacts for the Berlin ethnological museum (Schilling 2010, 145). Upon her return, Errell succeeded placing her images in different illustrated magazines and she also published her travel account in a book, *Kleine Reise zu Schwarzen Menschen* (Little Journey to Black People; 1931). The written accounts that are paired with the photographs are not free of racist stereotypes and generalizations. The captions are ambiguous and partially differ from the captions given to the same photographs in an article in the illustrated magazine *Atlantis*, suggesting that the photographed people were able to play a variety of "African roles" in the Western readers' imagination (Anonymous 1930). The photographs, however, speak a language that seems to enter a process of disavowal of the objectification and instrumentalization of the ethnographic camera. By contrast to conventional ethnographic imagery, Errell's low angles, close ups, and dynamic portraits of individual "protagonists" convey the aspiration to avoid ethnic-based generalizations and to pay attention to individual fragments and details (Schilling 2010, 145; Wiethoff 1997, 9–10). This impression is strengthened by the fact that the text of the book never immediately refers to the images (Wiethoff 1997, 10). In moving women into the center of attention and providing detailed information about their lives and work, Errell discloses her interest in connecting between women's experiences across the globe. In Africa, she began to develop a visual language of female solidarity that she would expand during further travels, weaving women's stories into her written and visual accounts. Her works are among the earliest examples of an export of the kind of objectivity she picked up at home and that would direct her gaze at the fates of the marginalized of China and central Asia.

Some of Errell's photographs continued to perpetuate Western ethnographic approaches. This is evident, for instance, in her highlighting of the (semi-)nudity of her subjects, or when she includes images of local crafts and fashions as a generic means to characterize and categorize actions and appearances (Ryan 1997, 149–53; Hight and Sampson 2002, 2–5). At the

Figure 13.3. Lotte Errell, *A Woman from Monrovia*. 1931. *Source:* Lotte Errell. *Kleine Reise zu Schwarzen Menschen*. Brehm Verlag, 1931.

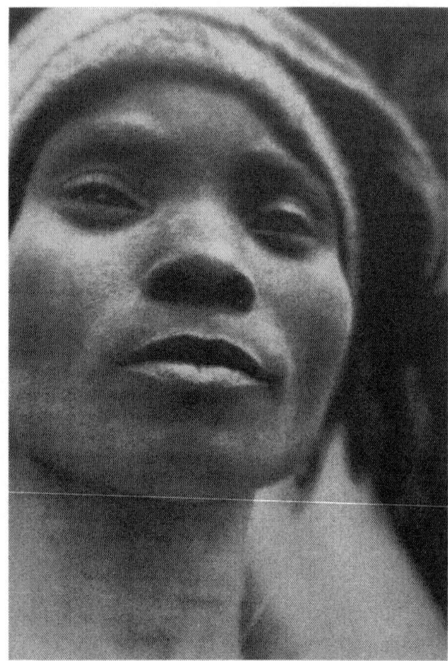

same time, the text and images betray a certain awareness of the challenge of the photographic depiction without intrusion. A photographic series of a little boy, for example, grants him space to display different reactions to the presence of the camera. Some parts of Errell's writings, moreover, question the effects of European colonial advances; she judges the double standards of British colonial rule with sarcasm (Errell 1931, 11).

Errell was not alone in pointing at the exploitative essence of colonial rule by extending the reformatory and inclusive gaze of the documentary camera to her African subjects. Toward the late 1920s, travel photography increasingly gained the interest of central and western European photojournalists, who sought to meet audiences' desires for a new kind of reportage that featured semi-ethnographic insights into foreign cultures (Wiethoff 1997, 7). Illustrated news outlets promptly began to send their photographers abroad, equipped with new cameras that were easier to handle and did not require long exposure times (Gidal 1972, 20–27). One of the first journalists to bring vistas of foreign countries home to the feuilletons of Viennese papers was the Jewish-Austrian writer Alice Schalek (Klaus 2014;

Manojlovic 2012). Other Jewish and non-Jewish pioneers of travel photography were Martin Munkacsi and Walter Bosshard, who had a particular interest in illuminating readers and viewers at home on the political struggles or transformations in colonial contexts such as India. Younger photographers such as the German-Jewish photographer Tim Gidal would later state that the travel and reports of people like Bosshard of the late 1920s and early 1930s inspired their own journeys and works (Gidal 1972, 26). Esteemed journalists and travel writers like Richard A. Bermann, who wrote under the nom de plume Arnold Höllriegel, or the French Albert Londres, recognized the value of traveling with photographers. When traveling through West Africa in 1930, Bermann was accompanied by the German-Jewish photographer Hans Casparius, who helped him supply illustrated reports for the *Berliner Tageblatt*. In one of his reports, Bermann hints at the value of the camera of his photographing fellow, which made him see clearer the face of a people whose character had been "distorted by imperial Europe's coins, its pennies." "The photographer," Bermann continues, "mercilessly" educates the writer "to see every single person" (Müller and Eckert 1995, 249). The new images and texts struck a chord with an audience that had seen a decade of rising international treaties. As traditional reports on life in imperial contexts made way for active discussions of international concerns, the world began to grasp the potential of traveling journalists who sought to expand political and social debates beyond one's own borders. Humanitarian photography had provided imagery of global social questions as early as the nineteenth century (Fehrenbach and Rodogno 2015, 4). But only the regular presence of global concerns in local papers was able to grant a sustained awareness of political and humanitarian themes beyond the usual circles of reformers and philanthropists (Fehrenbach and Rodogno 2015, 9, 11). While traditional ethnographic reports continued to appear, journalism became one of the main channels of communicating new, global social questions, and Jewish photographers in transit would continue forging visual codes that shifted from a civilizing rhetoric to an actor-centered perspective (Rodogno and David 2015, 235). Casparius, for example, not unlike Errell, took close-ups of the people he met, allowing them to fill the scene instead of populating it for more complete views of exotic spaces.

The successful publication of their photographs from Africa gained photographers like Casparius and Errell further appointments. Bermann would continue to take Casparius on his travels and Errell was asked by Ullstein to take a trip to China and send reports for the publisher's various news outlets and magazines.

China between *Alltag* and Crisis

Taken at a time of increasing racial discrimination in Weimar Germany, Errell's sights of China can be perceived as a performance of an active agenda of global solidarity with minorities and marginalized groups. Her photographic and written accounts of China attest to intensive encounters with both the local population and international colleagues who would further shape her routes. Some of her reports are influenced by the demands of the press market at the time; her stories featured in Ullstein's important outlets such as *Uhu, Berliner Illustrierte Zeitung,* and *Koralle.* For Ullstein's *Die Dame,* for example, she provided images and reports like "The Everyday Life of the Chinese Woman." The article offered further space for Errel's manifold observations of the intricacies of women's lives in different global contexts.

Figure 13.4. Lotte Errell, portrait of a Chinese woman. *Source:* Lotte Errell. "Der Alltag der Chinesischen Frau: Als Gast in Chinesischen Familien," *Uhu* 9 (1933): 87.

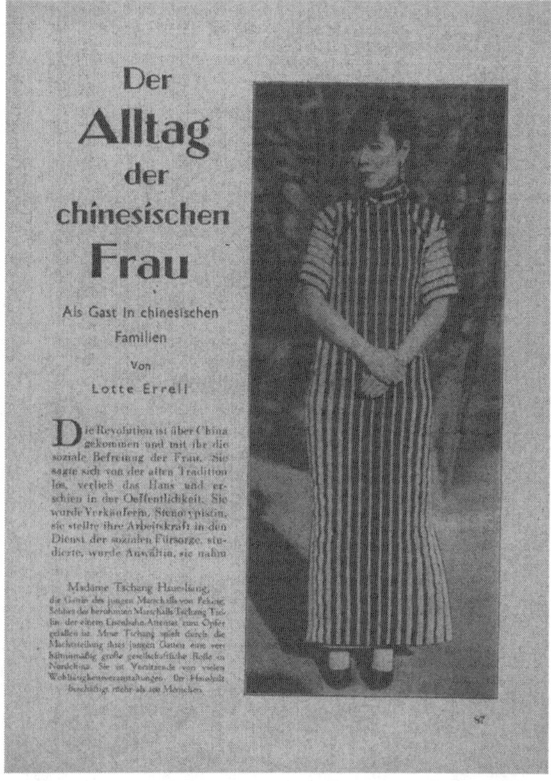

Her portrayal of everyday life in China appears to counter the exoticization of Chinese women. It suggests, on the one hand, that their habits and styles can be compared to those of European women. On the other hand, Errell portrays them as women with individual preferences and intricacies, from the female soldier over the wives of bankers or politicians to a Buddhist nun or Chinese students. The focus of the camera is on their different appearances and postures that the photographer observes from varying angles.

While some of the women Errell encountered spoke several languages and were interested in and informed about European politics and culture, Errell acknowledges a certain reluctance in most women to reveal much about their lives. Her report aimed at bringing both Chinese everyday life and its social questions closer to German audiences. It also emphasized, however, the impression of a persistent distance between the women in China and those

Figure 13.5. Lotte Errell, two portraits of Chinese women. 1933. *Source:* Lotte Errell. "Der Alltag der Chinesischen Frau: Als Gast in Chinesischen Familien," *Uhu* 9 (1933): 88.

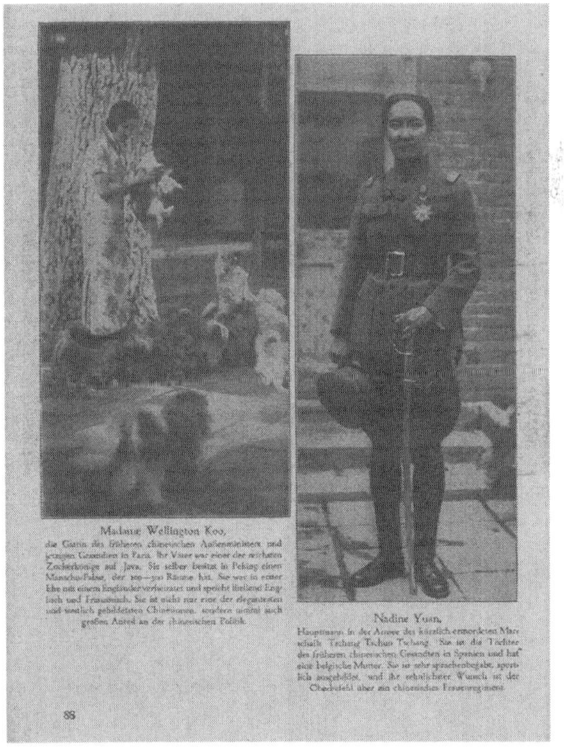

of Europe. Except for the soldier Nadine Yuan, the women do not meet the photographer's gaze. In most cases, this refusal of eye contact seems to be a sign of agency, denying the gaze the proximity of the encounter. In contrast to nineteenth-century Chinese portraits (Hung 2016, 34–35), Errell's protagonists are active participants in the photographic event. By granting her subjects distance, she corrects the scrutinizing gaze of the Oriental camera, focused almost solely on the eroticized body. This does not mean that Errell is denied close contacts. Indeed, the deliberate interplay of proximity and distance allows her to add nuances to the visual characterization of her subjects. The close-up portrait of the nun, emphasizing the simplicity she has chosen for her life, differs from the relative distance to Madame Wellington Koo, who is surrounded by her loyal dogs at what seems to be the wealthy family's estate. In encouraging the interplay of different photographic ranges Errell merits Chinese cultural independence from the West. The women Errell's camera captures do not change their behavior, or divert their attention, at the presence of the Western photographer. They maintain their individual interests and appearances, which makes it more difficult to read their portraits as projection screens to the desires and expectations of the Orientalist observer.

Figure 13.6. Lotte Errell, Chinese students and a Bhuddist nun. 1933. *Source:* Lotte Errell. "Der Alltag der Chinesischen Frau: Als Gast in Chinesischen Familien," *Uhu* 9 (1933): 90–91.

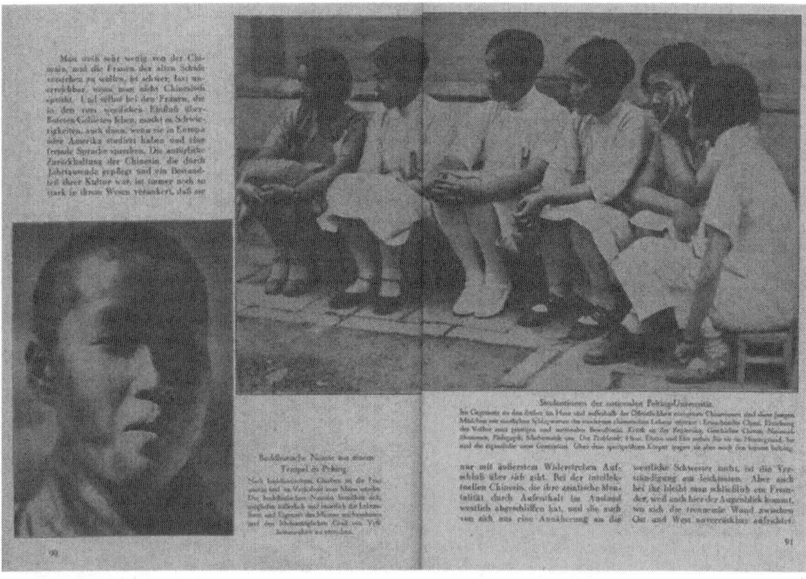

Errell stayed in China for more than a year, which enabled her to study the country and build ties with fellow travelers and local journalists. Respective networks gained her private meetings such as with China's foremost opium magnate Du Yusheng, and granted her permission to document controversial aspects of Chinese realities such as the ongoing practice of the mutilation of women's feet as a relic of Chinese traditional beauty ideals. Labor or the lack of it likewise takes center stage in many of her photographic works. Some of Errell's images are radically direct, pointing the gaze of her audiences to China's social questions including the fate of Shanghai's unemployed. One image of photographs depicting Chinese poverty shows three men sitting on the sidewalk in front of shop windows.

The first carries an apathetic look, staring into the distance beyond the frame. Two other men sit next to him at a distance, each one securing their space, both burying their faces in their hands and laps. Together they embody an evolution of poverty and misery with each one tilting forward a bit more until no face is visible. The man in the middle does not wear a shirt, a large dark spot on his shoulder suggests an injury or dirt. Similar stains on the ground in front of him direct the attention back to the mark

Figure 13.7. Lotte Errell, "Unemployed in Shanghai." 1931–1932. *Source:* Courtesy Fotografische Sammlung, Museum Folkwang.

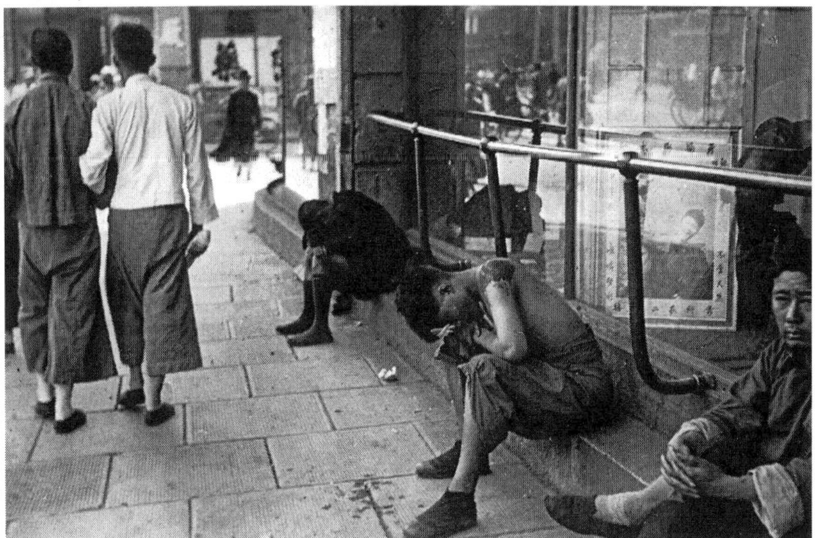

on his arm, connecting him visually with the beaten pavement. The third person is entirely dark, almost invisible. His deeper, crouching pose makes him appear yet smaller, suggesting the final stage in an evolution of poverty and distress. As if to underscore his fate, his silhouette mirrors in the glass window behind him, "doubling" his presence in the photograph. Two men walk past the desolate scene, the photographer catches them and thereby snaps a moment of indifference and potentially even disdain for those sitting by the wayside. The steps of the passersby are synchronous, their trousers near-identical, in their similarity they become replaceable alluding to the many others passing by hour by hour and inviting the spectator to adopt their position. Behind the window, a framed portrait of a joyful person—potentially a Chinese royal dignitary—creates the contrapuntal equivalent to the scene, broadcasting the ease and joy of Chinese life toward passersby and adding to the insensitivity the men are met with. Bicycles mirroring in the shop window allude to the dynamic lives of fellow Chinese men and women with work and income.

The slightly tilted angle—probably owing to the fact that the photograph is a snapshot—underscores the impression of instability that governs these men's lives. Taken from the side, by a photographer who appears to be timid of intruding, the image creates an immediacy that denies the ethnographic staging of Errell's Chinese subjects. Moreover, by explicitly pointing the camera at social differences, Errell counteracts the "curatorial imperative" of earlier travel photography that was eager to preserve "authentic" views for future generations. Choosing to show the difficult fate of the unemployed endows her photographs with a demanding, even accusing tone. The metamorphosis of poverty they represent doesn't leave much more than pity for the decomposed lives of the three men. This tendency recalls the works of earlier traveling photographers in China, such as the British John Thompson (1837–1921), who used photographs of the opium trade, the mutilations of women's feet, or unemployment to establish the narrative of China as uncivilized and in need of Western support (Ryan 1997, 165–66). In fact, British homeless and unemployed at home were sometimes compared with Oriental "types" not to emphasize the connections between the countries but to further degrade the former in an act of distinction and exclusion (Ryan 1997 176–78, 180). Earlier traditions drew connections between the physical appearance, social standing, and character of the photographed. However, in the meantime, a major economic crisis had hit the Western world that rendered the problem of unemployment one of mass concern. Errell seemed to choose to connect the stories of the Chinese workers with the topic of mass unemployment at home inspired by a kind of reformatory camera that pointed to the urgency of social change. This inspiration to point to the global dimension of social problems must be assumed to have originated in her ongoing travels, which at this point presented a way to avoid working in the increasingly polarized climate of Weimar Germany. By the time the photograph of the unemployed was taken, Errell and many of her Jewish colleagues were faced with the menace of National Socialism. For many of them, the threat at home necessitated a life of constant traveling, of transit.

Errell's photographs of the French journalist and travel writer Albert Londres, and the obituary she wrote for him after his tragic death in 1932, also demonstrate the extent to which other traveling journalists she met on her journeys inspired her investigative gaze. In her text about him, she acknowledges her fascination with the journalism he championed, which connected social challenges and suffering of different parts of the globe (Errell, n.d.[b]). This inspiration was not only one-sided. Their correspondence suggests that the two travelers were not only engaged in a passionate affair, but that they also shared similar views on minority rights and on their representations. The non-Jewish writer Londres, who in 1930 had written a favorable account of Zionism in Palestine, shared with the Jewish photographer a commitment for advocating global solidarity and propagating the self-determination of minorities (Londres [1930] 1997).

But Errell did not only import visual codes of the kind she had picked up at home. Her photographs also divert from the Weimar documentary style and its modes of observation and show that her travels shaped her photographic approaches additionally. Her hybrid camera speaks directly to the early strategies of the humanitarian gaze, which combined the recognition of similarities between distant cultures with a reminder of the (European) spectator's ability to help (Lawrence and Tavernor 2019, 3). The message that the fate of unemployment, for example, was shared by countless other men and women across the globe would play into an international language of humanitarian responsibility that was shared a by a growing "international community" (Barnett 2010, 102). Errell, like various other Jewish colleagues, would take this humanitarian tone with them and further develop it once the road became their home. It must be considered a form of knowledge and expertise acquired on a journey that, for some, would last years (Lässig and Steinberg, 2017).

Travel as Refuge

After January 1933, many of the journalists working for the liberal press were immediately at risk of being removed from their jobs; Jewish journalists were among the first to be actively excluded if not arrested (Vowinckel 2013, 473). A common reaction was to use assignments abroad to stay away from Germany. Richard Bermann, who lost his job at the *Berliner Tageblatt* in early 1933, and his photographing colleague Hans Casparius were quick to leave the country for a trip to Libya a few weeks later (Müller and Eckert 1995, 264, 275, 293). In a diary entry from this trip, Bermann admitted: ". . . the unknown I turn to is clearer than the amorphous I leave behind." (Müller and Eckert 1995, 278). He considered the option of staying in the Middle East for good and indeed spent long periods traveling outside of Germany before he finally emigrated to the United States in 1938 (278, 299). Moreover, he convinced Casparius to settle in Vienna instead of going back to Berlin after their return from North Africa. From Vienna, Casparius traveled to Palestine and thereafter settled in London (Feld 1993, 56). Other Jewish photographers and photojournalists, such as Tim Gidal, Fritz Henle, and Ferenc Berkó likewise turned to travel overseas, while continuing to supply some of their former German contacts with images (Gidal 1984, 116–20; Honnef and Weyers 1997, 63, 227, 292). Robert Capa who had gained essential skills as a photojournalist in Berlin left for Paris and, later, Spain, followed by a trip to China where he covered the Japanese invasion. Some regarded transit as exile from the place they called home, whereas others embraced the ongoing travel as a new kind of stability, free of the haphazardly emerging policies of exclusion. The contacts they had built with international agents and local colonial authorities before 1933 would offer some extent of financial stability; at times, they even saved lives.

Lotte Errell changed her travel plans on her way back to Germany from China more than once and tried to find ways to extend her stay (Errell, n.d.[a], 1, 4–6). While her images found much appreciation at home after her return—she was even able to exhibit them at the prestigious Galerie Nierendorf in 1933, sponsored by I.G. Farben—she was eager to leave Germany (Errell n.d.[c]). In early 1934, the Associated Press sent her to England and Ireland and, subsequently, to Iran to portrait the Shah and the Swedish crown prince Gustav Adolf during an official state visit to the country (Errell n.d.[c]). Her images illustrated articles in the *Münchner Illustrierte Presse* and the *Berliner Illustrierte Zeitung* (Wiethoff 1997, 17). A few weeks later, in December 1934, she was informed that she could no longer work as a photojournalist for German newspapers or agencies

(Reichsverband der deutschen Presse 1934). Others continued to supply German papers and agencies for some more months. The German-Jewish photojournalist Alfred Eisenstaedt, for instance, was able to sell his images of Ethiopia to the Berlin office of the Associated Press in the months preceding the 1935 Italian invasion (Honnef and Weyers 1997, 138; Eisenstaedt 1966, 163). Eisenstaedt, who had developed an awareness of current events in international politics by covering international conferences, such as the League of Nations gatherings, portrayed the country as confident, actively confronting the injustice of colonial rule (Eisenstaedt 1966, 8). His photographs helped to support Ethiopian criticism of a European lack of intervention grounded in a prevailing paternalism toward a "less-developed" Africa (Barnett 2010, 92–93). At the same time, Eisenstaedt, like others, saw the country through a European lens, profiting from and waiting for a kind of progress instigated by Western exports. Images of the kind he took sold well among papers across Europe, even in Germany, which supported Mussolini's colonial endeavors.

Figure 13.8. Lotte Errell, "Iran in the past. A glimpse in the mirror before this young nurse is going out." c. 1934. *Source:* Courtesy Fotografische Sammlung, Museum Folkwang.

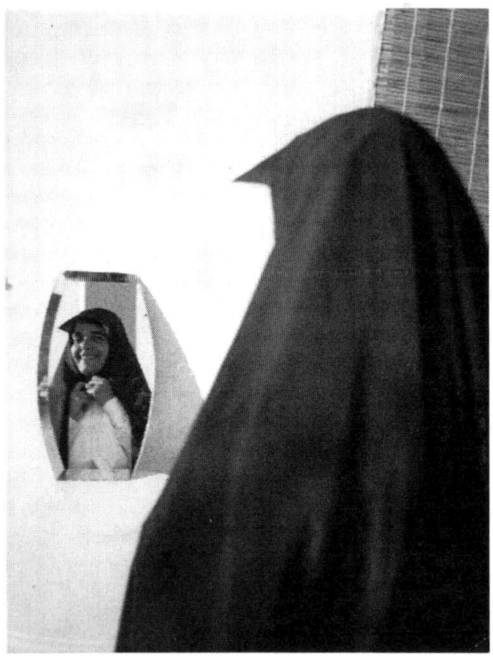

Lotte Errell's photographs of these years are subject to a similar ambivalence. In her images of Iran, Iraq, and Kurdistan, taken during the mid-1930s, she returned to covering the everyday lives of the people she met and observed, especially those of women. A photograph of a nurse in Iran offers an example of Errell's attempts to pierce the tighter norms and traditions of Muslim societies. She has captured the nurse from behind, a long black veil covers her back. The window on the side is closed with a blind. And yet her face is visible through a mirror hanging on the opposite wall.

Together the mirror and the camera's lens provide for a double mediation of the woman's smiling face. While her head is turned away, the mirror makes it visible; the camera extends this visibility and turns it into a mobile image, carrying it out of the room. The mediation, however, comes with visual "edits"—while disclosing her smile the mirror reduces the size of the woman's face, the large veil continues to dominate the room. The same mediation, moreover, turns the woman into a picture hanging on the wall, "freezing" the moment and replicating the capture of the photographic act. The camera, thus, locates the woman at a liminal threshold between the presentness of the mirror and the pastness of a photograph. On the one hand, the image is an unmitigated encounter with an individual similar to the viewers in the west. On the other hand, the framing of the face by the mirror on the wall endows it with an aura of the unknown, maybe exotic. It grants the nurse her own story, in a curious interplay of proximity and distance, revelation and closure, but it also captures her in a moment directed by the photographer. The stark contrasts between agency and powerlessness, past and present are replicated visually by that of the black veil and the white wall.

The caption of the picture does away with some of the temporal liminality, situating it firmly in one point in time, the "past." This active positioning risks returning to a more ethnographic pattern, but at the same time it radiates the "double consciousness" of a female Jewish migrant in transit as the owner of the camera on the one hand and a refugee on the other (Messner 2023, 31). Is Errell's "dating" the image an act of judging the woman's appearance or her social and cultural background? Or did she choose this caption only years after the image was taken? Moreover, much of the documentary gaze she developed in China seems absent. Instead, the photograph follows a more formalist style, similar to the photographs taken in Africa. This shift could be explained with Errell's isolation at this point, no longer able to actively communicate by means of journalistic accounts, taking the images for herself and according to her own artistic aspirations.

Unlike some of her traveling contemporaries, who would go on to portray the political transformations around the globe in the early 1940s, such as Tim Gidal traveling India, Errell's images of Central Asia remain focused on traditional appearances, and they rarely offer glimpses of change. Nevertheless, photographs like that of the nurse add individual faces to an archive she created of realities still largely unknown in the West.

Her photographs of Iran, Iraq, and Kurdistan belong to the last images professionally produced and circulated by Errell. In 1938, she traveled to the United States for a few months where she got in touch with her contacts of the Associated Press and met colleagues, including Alfred Eisenstaedt, who by then had gone on to pursue a career in New York (Errell 1942b; Wiethoff 1997, 15). Her stay gained her additional assignments in the Middle East—even with *Life* magazine—which, however, she would not be able to accomplish due to bureaucratic hurdles (Errell 1942a). And yet, her colleagues would prove crucial on a different front, when in the summer of 1942 Errell was arrested in Baghdad on charges of being an enemy alien, potentially a German spy, even as she had lost her German citizenship in November 1941. This suspicion sent her on an odyssey throughout the British Empire, to Palestine and from there to Kenya and Uganda. She stayed in Africa more than two years until her case was resolved. Repeated letters from former contacts at different news outlets and agencies eventually had the British authorities abandon their charges. In the meantime, her elderly mother and father who had remained in her native Münster were killed in Theresienstadt and Auschwitz respectively.

By the end of the war, the documentary camera that had been carried into a region that would later be dubbed the Global South was there to stay. It would become the handmaid of a humanitarian gaze that "went global" (Barnett 2010, 2). Cornell Capa, Robert Capa's brother, would term this way of seeing that of the "concerned photographer" (Capa 1968). Alfred Eisenstaedt traveled back to different African countries in the mid-1950s, where he documented their way to independence. In his memoirs, he describes the changes Ethiopia had undergone in the years since he had seen it last (Eisenstaedt 1966, 163–64). The lens of the former German Jewish traveler—both privileged and excluded—had not lost the certain tone of the superior eye, which provides informed comment on the development of the "younger" society. At the same time, Eisenstaedt's first visit in the region during the turbulent 1930s seemed to have made him, just like his fellow excluded photographers, susceptible to the needs and desires of a country preparing for self-determination. Other former stateless travelers, too, would return to the contexts and themes they had first met in transit. Tim Gidal would use the images he took in India during the early 1940s for the inaugural issue of a book series for children that, in the spirit of Edward Steichen's 1955 *Family of Man* exhibition, would spread Western liberal values and a "utopian globalism" through messages of unity (Turner 2012, 83). Photographic insights of this kind were considered suitable agents to suggest bonds between the audiences and the photographed subjects, supposed to evoke the existence of one, shared global time zone and the absence of ethnic and cultural differences (Barnett 2010, 56). Hans Casparius lost his travel companion Richard Bermann to illness in 1939 when the latter died in a sanatorium just after he had emigrated to the United States. Casparius stayed in London. Finally, Lotte Errell returned to Europe in the late 1940s. She would not resume her profession as a photojournalist. But her articles and images that had brought China, Africa, and Central Asia closer to Europe were to inspire a new generation of photographers following them in expanding the documentary lens to gain humanitarian traits.

Conclusion

The photographic perspectives observed here were the hybrid results of racial exclusion and the privileges of Western travelers. As Jews, the photographers embarked on paths of escape and rescue. As photographers, they acted as communicators of the social questions of their time. The works of German-Jewish photographers like Errell, Gidal, Casparius, or Eisenstaedt and the journalistic discourses they were influenced by not only provided for close encounters. Their gaze and stories also presented objects of exchange, offering a way to grant their interlocutors visibility in international news coverage. As such their accounts reflect the transition of views from the ethnographic to the humanitarian camera, encouraging awareness and even coalitions (Rothberg 2019, 203). Their photography, created to be turned into a global commodity, endowed them with the knowledge of observers of a reality that was still largely unknown to audiences in the West. These perspectives granted them the agency of experts that shaped their role and standing as international commentators. Moreover, their stories attest to the creation of a global cohort of journalists inspiring one another. Despite their times of transit, which often extended across long periods, photographers and editors kept in touch continuing to communicate and share views and viewpoints. The wartime odyssey of Errell saved out of British confinement by former photo agents and journalists is only one example of the network of émigré photographers that reached across the globe.

None of the photographers and journalists would have been able to travel the countries they saw without employing the privilege of their European background that gained them the necessary trust by the imperialist authorities of these regions. For this reason, they were also prone to perpetuate, to a certain extent, views that these empires had forged, contributing to a "salvage paradigm" that would become a tenacious feature of humanitarian photography shaped by the "paradox of emancipation and domination" (Pinney 1998, 45–56; Barnett 2010, 11). Visibility and care, thus, also meant aid and support of the kind that risked prolonging hierarchies of knowledge and power (Barnett 2010, 12, 14).

Yet the encounters were more than mere acts of "cosmopolitan solidarity" (Rothberg 2019, 31); instead, they were colored by the journalists' projections of their own exclusion as Jews onto the objects of imperial rule. Their journeys were results of haphazardly realized departures, shaped by deeply ingrained structures of racial distinction at home, which instigated a new implication of photographic seeing, driven by the desire to create new, lasting collaborative bonds the nature of which is subject to ongoing research. Not all photographic encounters were of a similar reflectivity, but those photographers who hoped to participate in the journalistic discourses of their time and forge new paths of global communication oriented themselves on the kind of reformatory perspective elaborated in the photojournalistic circles that had shaped them. The blend of skepticism of national sovereignty, empathy for anti-colonial resistance and the remnants of ethnographic fascination paired with internationalist narratives that are reflected in the works of these travelers shaped the history of photojournalism and the genealogy of humanitarian seeing. It would turn their photographs of wartime travel into a documentary language influencing postwar cultural discourses of photographic globalism.

Works Cited

Anonymous. 1930. "Die Ewe, ein Negerstamm der Goldküste: 8 Aufnahmen von Lotte Levy-Errell." *Atlantis: Länder, Völker, Reisen*, no. 6 (June).

Bair, Nadya. 2020. *The Decisive Network: Magnum Photos and the Postwar Image Market*. University of California Press.

Barnett, Michael. 2010. *Empire of Humanity: A History of Humanitarianism*. Cornell University Press.

Bear, Jordan. 2010. "Magnum Orbis: Photographs from the End(s) of the Earth." *Visual Studies* 25 (2): 111–23.

Capa, Cornell. 1968. *The Concerned Photographer: In Memory of Werner Bishof, Robert Capa and David Seymour.* Grossman.

Clifford, James. 1997. *Routes: Travel and Translation in the Late Twentieth Century.* Harvard University Press.

Curran, James, and Myung-Jin Park. 2000. "Beyond Globalization Theory." In *De-westernizing Media Studies*, edited by James Curran and Myung-Jin Park. Routledge.

Eisenstaedt, Alfred. 1966. *Witness to Our Time.* Viking.

Errell, Lotte. 1931. *Kleine Reise zu schwarzen Menschen.* Brehm Verlag.

———. 1942a. "Lotte Sostmann (nom de plume: Lotte Errell), born Rosenberg." Fotografische Sammlung, Museum Folkwang.

———. 1942b. To Leon Daniel. Fotografische Sammlung, Museum Folkwang.

———. n.d.(a). "China." Manuscript. Fotografische Sammlung, Museum Folkwang.

———. n.d.(b). "Chinesisches Allerseelen." Manuscript. Fotografische Sammlung, Museum Folkwang.

———. n.d.(c). Curriculum vitae. Fotografische Sammlung, Museum Folkwang.

———. n.d.(d). "Kinderarbeit in China." Unpublished manuscript. Fotografische Sammlung, Museum Folkwang.

Fehrenbach, Heide, and Davide Rodogno. 2015. *Humanitarian Photography: A History.* Cambridge University Press.

Feld, Hans. 1993. "Portrait of an Eccentric: Hans Casparius: Photographer and Film-Maker." *Film Exil: Stiftung Deutsche Kinemathek* 3:43–62.

Gidal, Tim. 1972. *Deutschland: Beginn des modernen Photojournalismus.* Bucher.

———. 1984. "A Photo Reporter in Israel." *Ariel* 57:106–22.

Grandin, Greg. 2004. "Can the Subaltern Be Seen? Photography and the Affects of Nationalism." *HAHR: Hispanic American Historical Review* 84 (1): 83–111.

Hight, Eleanor M., and Gary D. Sampson. 2002. *Colonialist Photography: Imag(in)ing Race and Place.* Routledge.

Honnef, Klaus, and Frank Weyers. 1997. *Und Sie haben Deutschland verlassen müssen . . . Fotografen und ihre Bilder 1928–1997.* PROAG.

Hung, Wu. 2016. *Zooming In: Histories of Photography in China.* Reaktion.

Klaus, Elisabeth. 2014. "'Alles ist klingend, romantisch, ästhetisch': Die Kriegsberichterstatterin und Fotografin Alice Schalek." *Fotogeschichte: Beiträge zur Geschichte und Ästhetik der Fotografie* 34 (134): 19–26.

Lässig, Simone, and Swen Steinberg. 2017. "Knowledge on the Move: New Approaches toward a History of Migrant Knowledge." *Geschichte und Gesellschaft* 43 (3): 313–46.

Lawrence, Michael, and Rachel Tavernor. 2019. Introduction to *Global Humanitarianism and Media Culture*, edited by Michael Lawrence and Rachel Tavernor. Manchester University Press.

Londres, Albert. (1930) 1997. *Le Juif errant est arrivé*. Arléa.

Manojlovic, Katharina. 2012. "Strolling through India: The Austrian Photographer and Journalist Alice Schalek." *Austrian Studies* 20:193–205.

Messner, Anna Sophia. 2023. *Palästina/Israel im Blick: Bildgeographien deutsch-jüdischer Fotografinnen nach 1933*. Wallstein.

Müller, Hans-Harald, and Britta Eckert. 1995. *Richard A. Bermann alias Arnold Höllriegel: Österreicher-Demokrat-Weltbürger*. K. G. Saur Verlag.

Myers, David. 2009. "Editor's Introduction: The Condition of Travel." *Jewish Quarterly Review* 99 (4): 437–38.

Pinney, Christopher. 1998. *Camera Indica: The Social Life of Indian Photographs*. University of Chicago Press.

Presner, Todd Samuel. 2007. *Mobile Modernity: Germans, Jews, Trains*. Columbia University Press.

Reichsverband der deutschen Presse. 1934. To Lotte Errell. Fotografische Sammlung, Museum Folkwang.

Rodogno, Davide, and Thomas David. 2015. "All the World Loves a Picture: The World Health Organization's Visual Politics, 1948–1973." In Fehrenbach and Rodogno (2015).

Rothberg, Michael. 2019. *The Implicated Subject: Beyond Victims and Perpetrators*. Stanford University Press.

Ryan, James R. 1997. *Picturing Empire: Photography and the Visualization of the British Empire*. University of Chicago Press.

Schilling, Britta. 2010. "Crossing Boundaries: German Women in Africa, 1919–33." In *German Colonialism and National Identity*, edited by Michael Perraudin and Jürgen Zimmerer. Routledge.

Schlör, Joachim. 2014. " 'Solange wir auf dem Schiff waren, hatten wir ein Zuhause': Reisen als kulturelle Praxis im Migrationsprozess jüdischer Auswanderer." *Voyage: Jahrbuch für Reise- und Tourismusforschung* 10:226–46.

Turner, Fred. 2012. "The Family of Man and the Politics of Attention in Cold War America." *Public Culture* 24 (1 [66]): 55–84.

Vowinckel, Annette. 2013. "German (Jewish) Photojournalists in Exile: A Story of Networks and Success." *German History* 31 (4): 473–96.

Wiethoff, Dorothee. 1997. "Fahrten zu fremden Welten: Ein Beruf entsteht." In *Lotte Errell: Reporterin der 30er Jahre*, edited by Ute Eskildsen. Museum Folkwang.

Chapter 14

Politics and Pictures

Jewish American Photographers
and Black Americans, 1938–1964

Deborah Dash Moore

In an article for *Commentary* magazine in 2003, William Meyers, himself both a photographer and critic, describes a meeting he organized back in the 1990s about Jews and photography. He sought then to understand the extraordinary presence of Jews in twentieth-century photography. Why so many Jews became photographers intrigued him, but he also wondered why they chose to make the kinds of pictures they did. At one point in the discussion he had queried, "Why was it that of all the ethnic groups in New York City in the 1930s and 1940s, it was the Jews who took it into their heads to go to Harlem and photograph the blacks there?" Naomi Rosenblum, a teacher, wife of the left-wing photographer Walter Rosenblum, and author of *A World History of Photography*, promptly replied, "We weren't Jews; we were leftists" (Meyers 2003, 47).

The American studies scholar Alan Trachtenberg offers a middle ground between Meyers and Rosenblum. "A way of being-in-the-world, a shared culture, Yiddishkeit probably does come into play in the work of many photographers connected with that culture," he acknowledges, "especially its secular humanism, its liberal and socialist proclivities." The latter connected Jewishness or Yiddishkeit with politics, specifically left-wing politics. In reference to the New York Photo League (1936–1951), Trachtenberg elaborates: "Jewish socialist humanism," he writes, "seems a more plausible consensus among the generation of the Photo-League at least, the 1930s group of socially conscious documentary photographers based in New York" (Trachtenberg 2003, 24). A "socially minded artists' collective that was born in the New Deal and expired during the Cold War," as the critic J. Hoberman described it, the League mostly attracted New York Jews interested in photography (Hoberman 2012). At the Photo League, aspiring photographers argued over the very issues that engaged Meyers, namely, what kinds of pictures were worth taking. And while Meyers focused on one of their collective projects, Harlem Document, League photographers also produced other collaborative neighborhood studies. Chelsea Document, photographed during the late 1930s, overlapping with Harlem Document, explored a poor Irish American neighborhood on Manhattan's West Side.

Meyers' reflections touch briefly on the complicated relationship of politics and pictures. They also implicitly adumbrate a kind of New York Jewishness informing that relationship. Most of the photographers associated with the Photo League were the children of working-class Jewish immigrants. They grew up in the city, attended its public schools, and learned to walk its streets aware of the gendered codes of behavior governing those streets. When they discovered cameras—often in high school, at a time when high schools were starting to add camera clubs as an extracurricular activity—they gradually recognized how they could use photographs to come to understand their city and themselves. The pictures that they took—straight, often unposed photographs, outdoors, with natural light—expressed not only their aesthetic but their personal point of view, a perspective influenced by their politics.

The photographer Sy Kattelson never thought of the Photo League as Jewish. It was a "New York thing," he recalled. There were a lot of Jewish people there. But they were left-wing photographers. "That's what brought us together" (Sy Kattelson, personal communication, August 2, 2008). Kattelson's elision of a "New York thing" with "a lot of Jewish people" articulates common contemporary assumptions. At the New York Photo League, Jews could easily ignore their Jewishness because they set the tone of the debates, they filled the classes, they shared the darkroom. The Photo League was, in short, a typical second-generation New York Jewish organization: secular, politically engaged, vibrant, a place where Jews felt comfortable and set a pattern for the non-Jewish minority.

Naomi Rosenblum articulated a pervasive political self-consciousness among Jewish photographers. Like Kattelson, she dismissed the Jewish element, giving priority to politics and a self-chosen identity rather than an ascribed one. However, her statement only opens discussion because "leftism"—whether of the socialist or communist or Popular Front or anti-fascist or even New Deal democratic variety—does not, in fact, translate directly into ways of seeing. Neither, of course, does Jewishness. Both Rosenblum and Meyers connect New York Jews photographing Blacks with left-wing politics.

Trachtenberg adds: "To choose documentary or street or reportage photography as a vocation is to choose to study contemporary American society and culture as a vocation, as a way of focusing your attention, your creative and critical abilities on the here and now" (Trachtenberg 2003, 25). It is possible that Jewishness motivates that choice, or alienation and a desire to overcome it, or political hope, or even just voyeurism. Meyers thought that for Jewish photographers, photography "was a way out of a parochial Jewish environment into what seemed to be larger, more universal, worlds of art and politics" (Meyers 2003, 47).

This chapter does not posit among photographers an ideal Jew or Judaic standard. Nor does it suggest that any photo can be essentially Jewish regarding subject or subjectivity. Religious studies scholar Laura Levitt proposes that "what makes an image Jewish is literally how it is framed, who sees it and where" (Levitt 2002, 468). Photography seems to promise a simple window on reality, yet it is a contingent process of perceptual interactions. The critic Max Kozloff devotes the final chapter of his long catalog essay accompanying an exhibit at the Jewish Museum in 2002 on "New York: The Capital of Photography" to what he calls a "Jewish sensibility." Jewish photographers, he suggests, understood the city as "not so much a place to be described as a setting that poses a question: what is the relatedness of seer and seen, as influenced by the social orders represented by the city?" Kozloff suggests that efforts to answer this question produce a Jewish style of photography. Characteristically these photographs participate in an ongoing search for solidarity, understood not as a fact "to be taken for granted," but rather as "a created and always liquid condition, reversible as a tide" (Kozloff 2002, 70–75).

There is no kit of essential ethnic attributes, though Kozloff does point to Jewish engagements with modernity and, accordingly, to modes of diasporic consciousness. The concept of ethnicity can serve as an umbrella under which people who refer to one another as "Jew" can be usefully discussed together. An *ethnic* collectivity is known from within through *cultural* patterns of association, such as religious, linguistic, national, historical, and artistic. *Class* variables also shape these relationships.

Photo historian Ya'ara Gil-Glazer complicates this assessment. She contends that although League photographers "believed in the power of art to generate social change," two rather different subschools existed at the Photo League (Gil-Glazer 2019, 360). One group, organized around Aaron Siskind and the Harlem Document project, reflected Kozloff's Jewish sensitivity "tainted by an estranged ambivalence." The other group centered around Sid Grossman, an influential teacher at the Photo League, a member of the Communist Party who was engaged in the Chelsea Document project. Grossman's students tended to connect Jewish sensitivity with "socialist egalitarian idealism" and a "deep identification" with Blacks (366). Differences in their approaches appear in the political, ethical, and aesthetic dimensions of their photographs of Black Americans.

In the 1930s and 1940s Jewish American photographers involved with the New York Photo League regularly documented Black life in the city, whether as part of collective projects such as Harlem Document or as individuals interested in urban street culture. Radical politics, including commitments to communism and socialism, motivated many of these photographers. Yet they tended not to focus on explicitly political subject matter. Rather than using their cameras just to present heroic imagery of May Day parades, eviction protests, and political rallies, they chose to represent the human dimensions of poor and working-class New Yorkers, both Black and white, to foster a sense of urban community and an experience of shared common ground. Their choices set them apart from other photographers of New York, who gravitated to picturing the city's distinctive, monumental architecture and its expressions of wealth.

Often invisible to white photographers, Blacks when pictured tended to be portrayed according to contemporary stereotypes. Meyers proposed that "leftism provided these Jews with a way of seeing." He then elaborated: "They could photograph blacks, and migrants, and derelicts, and gangsters, the dispossessed and homeless because they had a social framework in which these subjects could be understood" (Meyers 2003, 47). In fact, League photographers rarely pictured migrants, derelicts, gangsters, the dispossessed, and homeless. These were popular ways of seeing Blacks, which they rejected. Instead, League photographers pictured Blacks as fellow New Yorkers.

The ascendancy of anti-communism in the postwar decade frightened many left-wing Jewish photographers (Desjardin 1993; Tucker 2011, 72–85). The New York Photo League, placed on the Attorney General's list as a subversive organization in 1947, closed its doors in 1951 (Tucker 2001, 9–20; Klein 2012, 10–29). Ironically, the shuttering of the Photo League occurred even as some of its most politically radical photographers turned toward expressive forms of picture-taking. Nervous about street photography, a number chose fashion photography as a politically safe venue (Sy Kattelson, personal communication, August 20, 2008).

These shifts among New York Jewish photographers in the 1950s occurred as the civil rights movement was gathering momentum in the South. Here Black Americans engaged in direct political action, the kind usually pictured by photojournalists. As the nation's gaze shifted southward, several Jewish American photographers gravitated to these scenes of struggle. Their photographs presented Black Americans as ordinary Americans, drawing upon some of the imagery from the 1930s and 1940s. As these photographs conveyed the dignity of the political struggle for equal rights and respect, they showed Americans a vision of integration as a moral stance. Their posture reflected the impact of World War II. Although few Jewish photographers explicitly discussed the war and the murder of millions of European Jews, many felt the war's horrors. Those who served in the armed forces returned with a changed perspective on the United States and a commitment to eliminate discrimination, against Jews and Blacks (Moore 2004, ch. 8).

One way to understand how Jewish politics intersects with photography in pictures of Black Americans is to start with the Photo League before moving to pictures taken in response to the civil rights movement.

Consider these two photographs of Black boys, one by Jerome Liebling and the other by his teacher, Walter Rosenblum, the husband of Naomi Rosenblum. Both Liebling and Rosenblum grew up in immigrant Jewish households. Like many Jews who became photographers, Liebling received his first camera as a gift from his father, a restaurant worker and strong unionist who loved America. Liebling promptly began taking pictures of poor people to convince his father of his false faith in the United States. After a three-year stint in the military during World War II, Liebling returned to attend Brooklyn College on the GI Bill. There he met Walter Rosenblum, a member of the Photo League (Jussim 1978, 3–11). Like Liebling, Rosenblum served in the Signal Corps during World War II; unlike Liebling, Rosenblum's father was Orthodox, not a union man. Both photographers embraced left-wing politics. Both joined the Photo League (Rosenblum 1983, 1019–21).

"It was a whole environmental experience that changed you because of the influences that you came in contact with," Rosenblum explained about the League. "Photography then became part of a total cultural superstructure which related to an economic and social climate of which it was a part." This Marxist interpretation of society affected self-perception. "And you began consciously or subconsciously," he continued, "to develop an understanding of who you were and what you were about." In joining the Photo League, Liebling recalled how he "was filled with ideas and ideals about documentary photography, the Bauhaus aesthetic, photojournalism, filmmaking, and how all of this related to politics." He discovered "many like-minded people" at the League who shared his politics and taught him how to think about photography. "Rosenblum led me through the streets," he recalled, "and helped me establish where my sympathies would lie" (Liebling 1995, 16). Those sympathies, shaped by his politics, lay with the poor, the working classes, and Black Americans.

A decade separates Liebling's photo taken on the Lower East Side from Rosenblum's rooftop photo taken as part of a League project on Pitt Street, in the same neighborhood. Yet both share common attributes picturing a

Figure 14.1. Walter Rosenblum, *Boy on Roof, Pitt Street, New York*, 1938. *Source:* © Photo by Walter Rosenblum. All Rights Reserved. Used by permission of the Walter Rosenblum Archive.

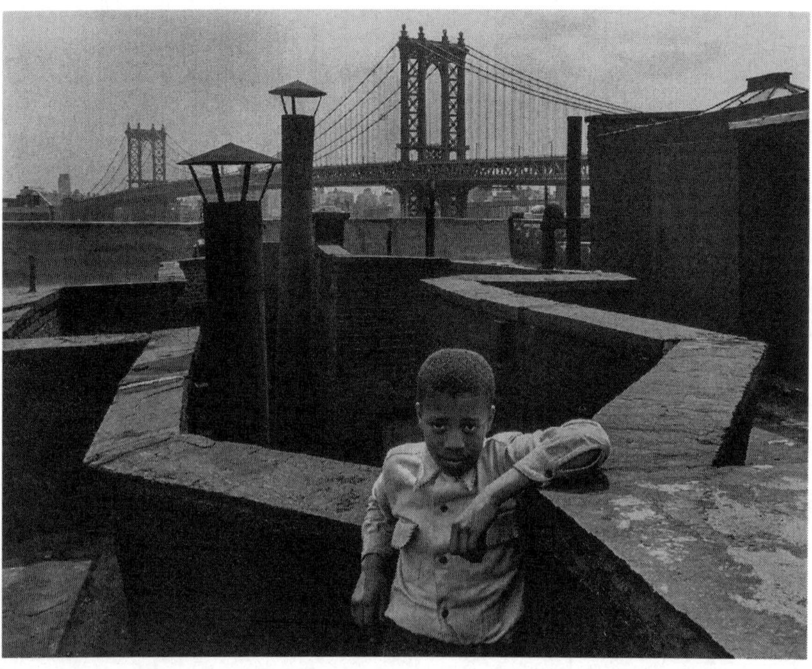

young boy looking up at the photographer with a serious demeanor. In Rosenblum's photo, the boy appears at the lower third of the image, centered. His willingness to pose for the photographer is reflected in his somewhat nervous expression. Behind him the abstract drama and aesthetics of rooftop ledges zig and zag in a modernist mode to accommodate tenement-housing laws requiring airshafts between buildings. In the distance, directly above his head, soars the Manhattan Bridge, adding a measure of architectural beauty to the attributes of poverty so visible on these tenement roofs.

In Liebling's photo, a similar sense of apprehension registers on the boy's face although he opens his lovely wool coat in a generous gesture to show off his shorts and white shirt. The boy occupies most of the frame, inviting attention to how well he is dressed in matching cap and coat in contrast to his poorly laced shoes. Although the sidewalk provides most of the portrait's backdrop, a fender of a car parked at the curb echoes the arc of the boy's head and hat.

Figure 14.2. Jerome Liebling, *Butterfly Boy, New York City*, 1949. *Source:* Courtesy Jerome Liebling Photography LLC. Used with permission.

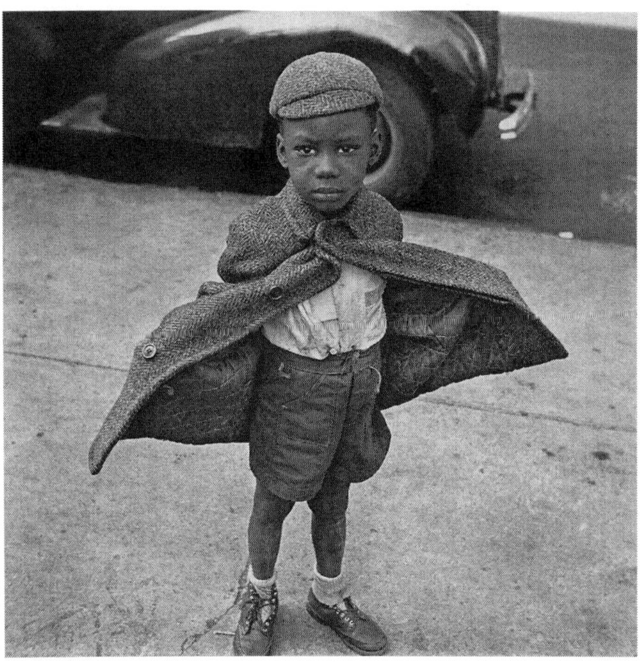

The politics in these pictures are largely implicit, as are their Jewish dimensions. The curator and critic Maurice Berger accuses Jews who photographed in Harlem of failing to grasp the burden of responsibility inherent in documenting Blacks. Jewish photographers' "status as white Americans and cultural intruders, however, made them more than just objective witnesses," he argues (Berger 2011, 30–46). "It also implicated them in the complex social dynamic they were documenting. Thus, in more subjective and introspective hands," Berger suggests, "Harlem might also have served as a place to study some of the essentials of white existence—especially the white racial attitudes and beliefs that infiltrated and conditioned the lives of virtually every one of its residents" (39). Yet both photographs taken on the Lower East Side endow their subjects with dignity and humanity as well as individuality. They invite identification and appreciation if not social critique or introspection. They suggest recognition by these Jewish photographers of the boys as individuals rather than as representations of a particular condition. Each boy posed for what he probably thought of only as a white male photographer. Despite their youth, both men had status and authority in the boys' eyes. The cameras they carried disguised Liebling's and Rosenblum's own socioeconomic marginality as working-class college students, their situation when they took the photographs.

What occurred behind the exchange of looks evident in each photo can only be surmised. Rosenblum made it a practice to ask people if he could take their picture. He regularly returned to the block to give individuals a print of their portrait. Given the location on the tenement roof, reached only by stairs, rather than on the sidewalk, Rosenblum likely gave the boy a photograph. A photograph of Rosenblum setting up to take the picture with a large format camera on a tripod also shows the boy sitting on the roof's ledge, relaxed, with one arm draped around his knee. Rosenblum is grinning at the boy, who appears engaged. When he took the photo in 1938, Rosenblum was taking a class with Grossman at the Photo League. Liebling's decision to ignore the Fifth Avenue Easter parade of well-to-do men and women for a Black alternative to the holiday in what was still considered a Jewish neighborhood probably reflected the intersection of his Jewishness and his politics. Liebling's title, *Butterfly Boy*, suggests that the boy's wide-armed gesture reminded him of a beautiful moment before flight. It is also possible that the title ironically invited attention to the boy's social situation, rather than merely the aesthetics of the pose.

Unlike Liebling and Rosenblum, the Jewish American photographer Helen Levitt regularly photographed in Harlem. She tended to keep her politics to herself. Growing up in Bensonhurst, Brooklyn, a mixed Italian and Jewish, mostly middle-class neighborhood, Levitt confessed that she found Black people "extremely exotic." She wanted to photograph the working class and their "conditions," understood as a political term that drew attention to exploitation and oppression. As she later admitted, "I was affected by the time," that is, the Great Depression of the 1930s and the flourishing of radical politics in New York (Gopnik 2001). She did not join the Photo League, although she exhibited there. Levitt fell in love with photography as a teenager and left high school to pursue her passion. In the late 1930s, she started taking photographs on the streets of New York City, mostly of women and children, and never stopped. According to literary and photography scholar Sara Blair, the communist Black writer Richard Wright saw "Levitt as an artist of the camera who uses her instrument as a poetic and subjective means of expression, creating images that have the capacity to evoke infinite wonder" (Blair 2007, 71).

Levitt's shot of children dancing outside a radio store conveys an understanding of street photography as subjective communication without

Figure 14.3. Helen Levitt, jitterbug dancers, New York, c. 1940. *Source:* © Film Documents LLC, courtesy Galerie Thomas Zander, Cologne. Used with permission.

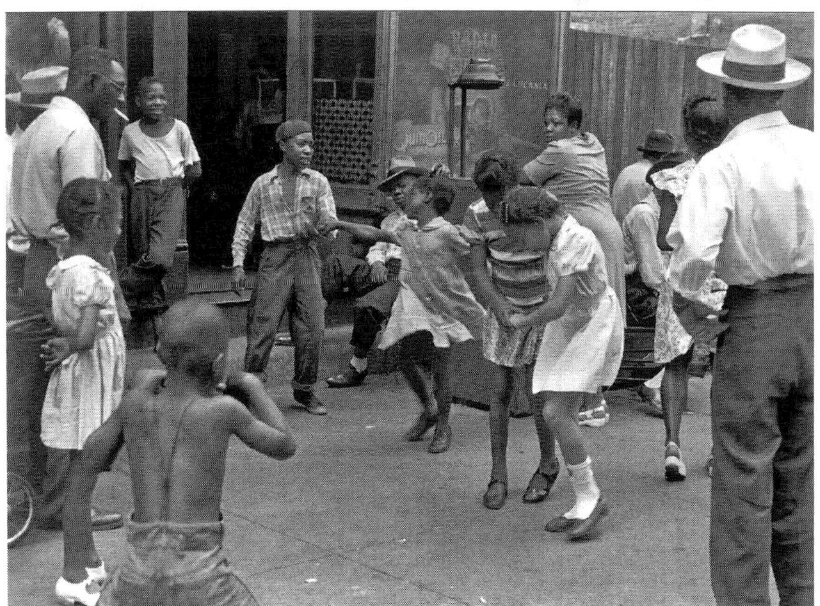

an explicit political agenda. Blair sees her Harlem work as insistently evading "doctrinaire readings of poverty and delinquency, framing the ghetto street as a site of dynamic social interaction, agency, and expressive power. In so doing," Blair argues, "it significantly altered the documentary contract between photographer and subjects, and consequently between the documentary image—uncontrived and subjective rather than instrumental and objective—and its viewer" (Blair 2007, 71). Is this what it looks like to photograph in Harlem not as an ideological leftist? Or did Levitt's blend of political inclinations and unselfconscious Jewishness spark her fascination with the dynamic social interaction and creative agency visible on city streets, especially in poor neighborhoods? In many ways, that combination of politics and Jewishness instantiated what it meant to grow up in New York City during the Great Depression as a child of immigrants.

In 1940 Jews were the largest single ethnic group in the city, accounting for approximately 30 percent of the population. Jewish residential concentration—in Brooklyn neighborhoods like Bensonhurst, where Levitt grew up—made Jewishness part of public life, not necessarily something private and personal. Jewish institutions lined the streets of such neighborhoods; local food stores catered to Jewish tastes, including the kosher practice of separating meat from dairy products. Yiddish signs adorned stores, emphasizing just how Jewish New York was. In such a milieu, New York Jews could easily ignore their Jewishness, as long as they were not looking for a job with the telephone company or seeking to live in certain neighborhoods in Queens (Moore 1981).

Trachtenberg comments that a street photographer commits "to confronting unstaged reality. It's a way of connecting and disconnecting at the same time, like any enterprise of study, like reflective thought itself" (Trachtenberg 2003, 25). A political perspective guides a street photographer's choices of what to photograph. Picturing Black life on the street can be seen as a quotidian project or it can be understood as an insistent reminder that Black Americans were part of the city's social fabric. For Levitt, Black children dancing the jitterbug on the streets on a hot summer day epitomized New York City as much, if not more, than its skyscrapers and fabulous views of lower Manhattan from the Brooklyn waterfront.

To these questions about how to interpret Levitt's photograph one must add an acknowledgment of Levitt's vulnerability as an unaccompanied young woman on New York's streets and her nerve in flouting gendered conventions (Brookfield 2020). Conventions of looking on city streets constrained women, although a woman with camera around her neck asserted her right to stare. Female street photographers often exposed their intentions as they observed others. Unlike many male photographers, they usually avoided direct exchanges with their subjects. Unavoidably, the frisson of gendered attention was not an uncommon aspect of photographic interactions. For Jewish women photographers, the personal was political (Moore 2010, 282–304).

Unlike Levitt, Vivian Cherry espoused political radicalism, adopting her Jewish mother's communist commitments rather than her immigrant father's liberalism. She grew up first in Yorkville and then in the Bronx, attending May Day celebrations with her mother. Cherry wanted to be a dancer and only discovered photography because she needed a job. Developing and printing photographs at Underwood and Underwood inspired her to try to take pictures herself. "All day long, I was looking at these photos, and I thought 'I can do that.'" In 1947, she joined the Photo League and studied with Sid Grossman. "But even more important was what happened after class," she recalled, "everybody going to Sid's loft, talking about photography, looking at each other's work" (Hartman 2008). Those conversations helped to build a shared understanding of photography and aesthetics, as well as their political valence.

Figure 14.4. Vivian Cherry, a woman and child paused on the thresholds of their tenements, New York, 1940s. *Source:* Courtesy Daniel Cooney Fine Art. Used with permission.

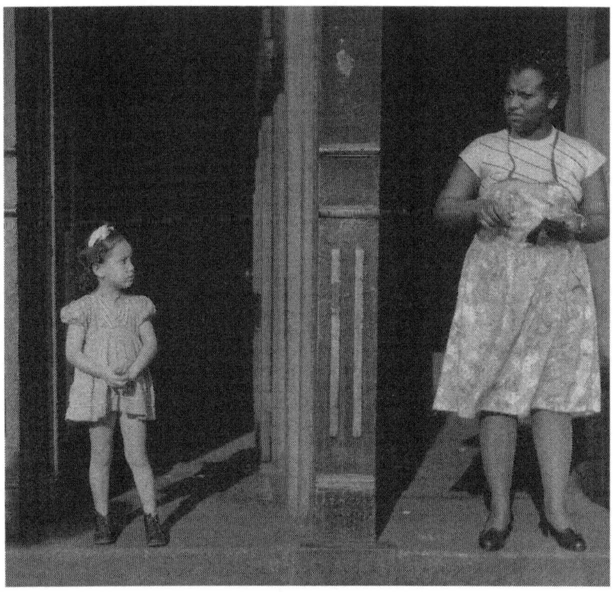

Cherry's photograph of a woman and child paused on the thresholds of their tenements conveys a powerful relationship. Both woman and girl would probably be called Black, though the former is dark, and the latter is not. The potential tension between the two conveyed in the image prompts questions about their unarticulated relationship: will this girl child with a pretty bow in her hair grow up to be the serious woman wearing glasses, an apron, and nylons? Does she recognize this adult from the neighboring tenement? Can this photo be construed as mirroring a mother and daughter relationship? Do the different shades of blackness undermine fixed racial categories? Or maybe, do they prompt a universalization of the experience, transforming the photograph into a comment on generational relations between two working-class females? As the photographer Keith McManus astutely observed: "I don't think still photography is very good at answering questions. More often it poses questions, and I think that's one of the most endearing qualities of still photography" (Francisco 2016). Like the Black boys photographed by Rosenblum and Liebling, the girl seems anxious. Perhaps she is not allowed outside alone. She stands still, gazing upward as if assessing her next move. Who, it seems to query, is in charge here?

Rosenblum, Liebling, Levitt, and Cherry all grew up in New York City, the children of Jewish immigrants. The city that felt half-Jewish in those years shaped the kinds of photographers they became as well as the politics they pursued. New York was a union town. Its left-wing politics sustained competition between socialists and communists, as well as a third party, the American Labor Party. This was not Weegee's experience.

Before he became Weegee, a famous photojournalist, he arrived on the Lower East Side as a Jewish child from Hungary named Usher Fellig (anglicized to Arthur). He barely finished grade school. His parents' poverty and his father's piety spurred him to seek employment as a young teenager and to disavow Jewish religious practice. He did, however, celebrate Jewish holidays, at least through their foods. Eventually he turned to photography. The art historian Samantha Baskind argues that his "voyeuristic eye" captured "overtly Jewish" subjects as well as those "less explicitly Jewish" but nonetheless "influenced by Jewish values" (Baskind 2010, 61). In the 1930s he made his reputation covering murders, fires, and the kind of mayhem associated with the urban underground. "A photojournalist chronicling crime and disaster in New York, Weegee specialized in capturing the aftermath of these tragedies, selling his photographs to newspapers and tabloids" (62–63). Yet when he went to Harlem to cover the riot in August 1943 that expressed wartime anger at segregation, discrimination, exploitation, and the absence of equality and civil rights, he presented far less sensationalized images than in his other work (Capeci 1977). Rather than picture the violence (five people were killed and 400 were injured), the looting of stores or the mass arrests of 500 people by police, Weegee photographed the aftermath.

Many of the stores looted in the riot were Jewish, a reflection of the area's past when Harlem was a Jewish neighborhood (Gurock 1979). Weegee's photos for the liberal anti-fascist New York newspaper *PM* sympathetically portrays Harlem's Black residents. On one photo, titled *Boy Caught in Boarded-up Harlem Store*, Weegee noted on the back of the print, "FEAR. This was an aftermath of the HARLEM riot . . . a drug store that had been looted and then closed by the owner . . . some kids then sneaked in to look for cigarettes . . . candy etc . . . someone in the house heard the noise and called the cops . . . this photo shows one of the boys coming out of the boarded up store . . . a detective is waiting for him . . . notice the fear on the boys [*sic*] face . . ." (Weegee 1963). Weegee's notes elaborate on freedom from fear, one of President Franklin Delano Roosevelt's four freedoms, an American war goal and one denied to Black Americans. His notes also endow the boy with a measure of innocence: he is looking for cigarettes or candy, not drugs. These notes mesh with *PM*'s pro–New Deal political position, one that Weegee also supported (Milkman 1997).

Weegee returned to the political theme of freedom from fear in an image from October 1943, this one associated with the violation of civil rights. On West 166th Street between Edgecombe and Amsterdam Avenues in Washington Heights, in northern Manhattan, two buildings had just started to accept Black tenants. The block was literally the color line. One block south was Black; one block north was white. Then on the night of October 16, vandals attacked a young family of four when the police patrols were off. Three photos appeared in *PM* to accompany an article headlined, "Police Called to Give Negroes Freedom from 'Fear.'" Weegee's photos portray evidence of white New Yorkers' hatred of Blacks. A group of men had attacked an apartment building where Blacks had been allowed to rent, vandalizing the radiators, and throwing bricks through the glass entry door. His two photographs of the Lythcott family transmit self-respect in the face of injustice (Bonanos 2018, 185).

Weegee later published the powerful image of Bernice Lythcott and her son, Leonard, uncropped, a "director's cut" as it were, in his 1945 book, *Naked City*. This updated version of a mother and child conveys more than a deep humanity in the face of injustice. It bespeaks a Jewish perspective on Black Americans, seeing them as an integral and equal part

Figure 14.5. Weegee, Berenice Lythcott and her son, Leonard, October 17, 1943. Printed in Weegee's *Naked City*, 1945. *Source:* Courtesy Weegee (Arthur Fellig)/ International Center of Photography, via Getty Images. Used with permission.

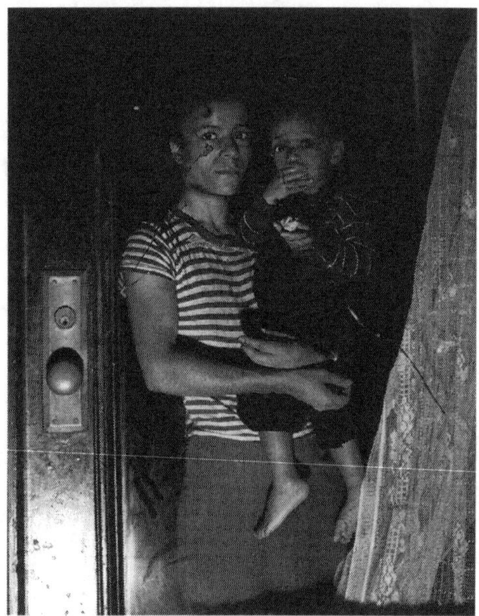

of American society. Christopher Bonanos, Weegee's biographer, writes: "Leonard has his eyes wide, and his hand to his mouth, as if stunned. It is a more traditional news picture than Weegee is known for making, and it's technically better than most of them, too, with relatively subtle highlights and careful framing that didn't require cropping. It's a great, penetrating image of a hard American moment, a portrait that holds its own." Bonanos argues it deserves the same attention as Dorothea Lange's *Migrant Mother* as an icon of American suffering (Bonanos 2018, 186). The photo evokes the Madonna's redemptive resilience. The flash lighting illuminates Bernice Lythcott's face, bounces off the door handle and highlights the jagged line of broken glass against the deep blacks of the hallway where she stands. Delicate white lace curtains on the side emphasize a dignified domesticity brutalized. Indeed, Lythcott's penetrating gaze and her child's munching on a snack contrast vividly with the doorway that frames their frustrated effort to acquire decent housing in Washington Heights, on the fringes of Harlem. Weegee's photo calls out in a Jewish idiom for justice, not pity; respect, not condescension (*PM Daily*, October 18, 1943).

In the text accompanying the photograph in *Naked City*, Weegee writes, "Discrimination . . . that's the one ugly word for it. . . . The solution I don't know, but here's one of the reasons for race riots . . . a poor white neighborhood." Weegee elaborates: "The occupants of the tenements are white bus drivers, streetcar conductors, elevator operators, shipping clerks, etc . . . poorly paid white people who get themselves pushed around all day by people they come in contact with in their work and by their straw bosses." He then concludes, "So the ones that get pushed around themselves, now started pushing others around by throwing rocks into the windows." Weegee references race, not ethnicity, but New Yorkers would have recognized his description of transit workers as referring to Irish Americans who predominated in that line of work. He also explicitly cites their economic exploitation as a source of the violence. His critique of capitalism is subtle, but present. The photograph of Lythcott and accompanying text open the section of the book called "Harlem" (Weegee 1975, 190).

Left-wing Jewish photographers continued to photograph during the 1950s, portraying Blacks with dignity and empathy. Later, they received the label of "concerned photographers" to reframe their putatively dangerous politics. "Images at the passionate and truthful best are as powerful as words can ever be," explained Cornell Capa, who came up with the new term. "If they alone cannot bring change, they can, at least, provide an undistorted mirror of man's actions, thereby sharpening human awareness and awakening conscience" (Capa 1972). Jewish photographers' visual inventory of alternative images challenged stereotypes of Blacks as criminals or poor, bedraggled, victims of violence regnant in the popular press. However, the rise of the civil rights movement drew some Jewish photographers into the orbit of specifically political photography. Working as photojournalists, Jewish photographers covered the freedom rides and sit-ins, as well as the marches to integrate southern cities. Their Jewish sympathies lay with the young Black men and women fighting for an equal society, one that would also benefit them as Jewish Americans.

Bruce Davidson entered this realm after completing a series on white Catholic teenagers who were part of a Brooklyn gang. In 1961 he volunteered to cover the freedom riders on assignment for the *New York Times*. "We were an interracial band of brothers and sisters, the first of its kind," recalled John Lewis, a young Black divinity school graduate at the time. "A circle of trust—six blacks and seven whites—traveling by bus through the heart of the Deep South to test the *Boynton v. Virginia* Supreme Court ruling that banned segregation on interstate buses and in public facilities."

Then he added: "Each of us was willing to put our bodies on the line and to die if necessary" (Lewis 2002).

The trip politicized Davidson. Unlike New York Jewish photographers who had absorbed politics growing up in the city as the children of immigrants, Davidson arrived in New York after college and military service. Years later he recalled walking into a meeting "late one evening in Montgomery"; it was the home of a local resident, John Lewis, "who wore a large bandage on his head covering a wound inflicted in a previous bus ride beating." Despite the bandage, Lewis "calmly presided over the group" that was going to ride. Accompanied by National Guard troops with "grim faces and fixed bayonets," the freedom riders arrived safely in Jackson, Mississippi. As they exited the bus, all were arrested. Davidson returned to New York, "but kept thinking about the courageous youths who were now in jail. They had risked their lives for freedom. For the first time I was exposed directly to segregation and its oppression." By 1962 Davidson had "the youth from the Freedom Rides and the South on my mind" (Davidson 2002). He carried his new political consciousness into photographs of Blacks in New York City that extended his awareness of the Black freedom struggle (Goldberg 2016, 63–86).

Figure 14.6. Bruce Davidson, *USA. New York City. 1962. Black Americans. Source:* Courtesy Magnum Photos. Used with permission.

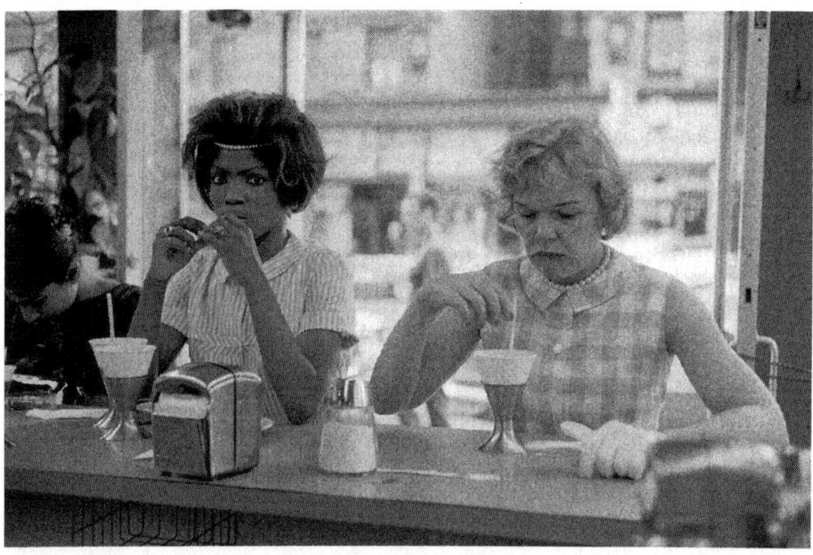

Although lunch counters were integrated in New York City, Davidson's photograph of two women, one black and one white, reflects his heightened consciousness of the politics of equal rights wracking the United States. Neither woman talks; they merely sit next to each other. But that politically resonant posture reverberates in 1962 because this simple opportunity was denied Black Americans throughout the South, and even in some northern cities. As historian of photography Deborah Willis observes, "The photo of two women seated at a restaurant counter—one white, the other black—could have [been] captured during demonstrations in the South or during a chance encounter at a New York City luncheonette" (Willis 2002).

The photograph makes its statement not only through its subjects but also through the equal lighting and attention given to both women. The Black woman notices Davidson and glances at him. The rhinestone ornament in her hair, straightened as was the style then, contrasts with the more conventional pearl necklace around the white woman's throat, not to mention her white gloved hand. "People were accustomed to seeing photographs from the civil rights movement that were filled with drama, menace, and violence, which the print media and television lapped up" (Goldberg 2016, 78). The photography and art historian Martin A. Berger contends that these popular photographs limited white sympathy for Blacks, since the former identified not with the Black victims but with the white victimizers (Berger 2011). Jewish photographers like Davidson, Leonard Freed, and especially Danny Lyon, took different photographs. "We all remember fire hoses and police dogs," averred Julian Bond, a Black leader of the Student Nonviolent Coordinating Committee (SNCC). "Danny Lyon makes us remember the people and the forgotten places, too" (Bond 1992, 7). Like Lyon, Davidson's photos also documented other aspects of Black American life, in the North as well as the South.

Davidson continued photographing in Mississippi, at the 1963 March for Jobs and Freedom on Washington, and then the 1965 Selma to Montgomery, Alabama, march. Many of his photographs were published in magazines. The civil rights leader John Lewis recalled that "we would take his photographs from newspapers and magazines, enlarge them, put them on bulletin boards, and ask people to meet. They became," he explained, "tools to mobilize, educate, and inspire. His photographs make this part of our history real" (Lewis 2002). Davidson subsequently assembled these photographs into a book under the rubric, *Time of Change*.

Davidson had started taking pictures as a boy. After his parents' divorce, he grew up in his mother's childhood home in the Chicago suburb of Oak

Park. His mother worked full time, and his religiously observant immigrant grandparents helped with childcare. Davidson received a camera, a gift from his uncle, for his bar mitzvah when he turned thirteen. When his mother remarried, the family moved up into the secure precincts of the middle class. Photography accompanied Davidson during his college years as well as his brief semester at Yale, and then into military service. He arrived in New York City too late to join the Photo League (Goldberg 2016, 11–30).

Older than Davidson, Leonard Freed also inclined to photographing outsiders. He earned a living as both a photojournalist and documentary photographer. The son of Jewish immigrant parents, Freed grew up in Brooklyn, and aspired to become a painter but turned to photography and film, "committed to documenting social injustice" (Kozloff 2002, 187). He photographed both Blacks and Jews. As a young man in the early 1950s conscious of the murder of six million Jews in the Holocaust, he photographed Hasidic Jews in New York before moving to Amsterdam. Over the course of several years, he pictured the evolving postwar scene there and in Germany. Aware of the political reverberations of his photographs, he published his first book on Jews from Amsterdam and several years later a book *Jews in Germany Today*, a politically provocative project. Then, in Berlin, he photographed a Black American soldier guarding the Berlin Wall separating East and West. "We, he and I, two Americans," he wrote. In Europe he was a Jew, conscious of that identity only a short time after the end of the war. Now he acknowledged another identity. "We meet silently and part silently. Between us, impregnable and as deadly as the wall behind him, is another wall. It is there on the trolley tracks, it crawls along the cobblestones, across frontiers and oceans, reaching back home, back into our lives and deep into our hearts: dividing us, whenever we meet. I am white and he is Black" (Freed 2020, 16). Moved by the encounter and wanting to photograph the burgeoning civil rights movement that promised a chance to overcome this segregation, Freed returned to the States in 1962 (Capa 1968).

Along with many other photographers, in August 1963, he traveled to Washington, DC, to photograph the March on Washington for Jobs and Freedom. Freed's photograph of a woman in the crowd, intently listening and applauding, with the Washington Monument rising in the middle of the photograph in the background, illustrates an attention to quotidian details that made his photographs so effective. He does not photograph Martin Luther King, Jr., or any of the other speakers. His photo shows crowds of people, immaculately dressed, mostly Black Americans with whites standing alongside them in solidarity, together with the landmark that identifies the

Figure 14.7. Leonard Freed, *USA. Washington, D.C. August 28, 1963. The March on Washington*. March on Washington. *Source:* Courtesy Magnum Photos. Used with permission.

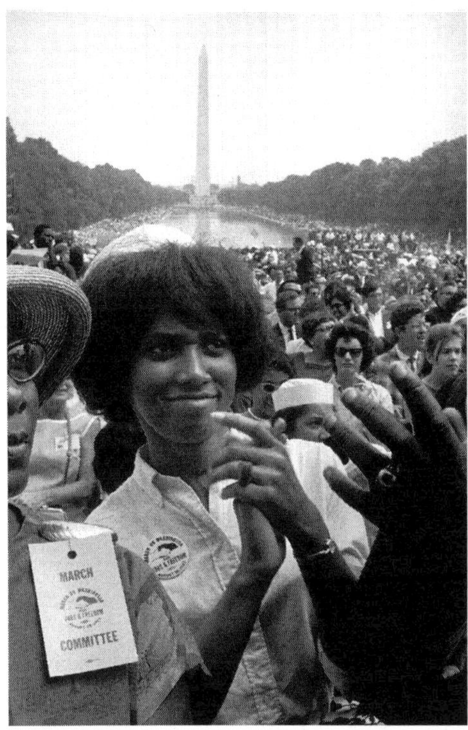

scene. Freed is down in the crowd. The woman ignores the photographer; she directs her gaze at the speakers' platform. Although photographs are silent witnesses, the visibility of hands clapping suggests an audible third dimension, much as the music animated the dancers in Levitt's photo.

Looking back on Freed's photographs of the March on Washington, Bond observed how "many are dressed as if for a Sunday gathering, a special event demanding respect from all in attendance. For the participants," he writes, "this was both a serious and a happy occasion, a chance to exercise their rights and to petition their government for a redress of ancient grievances. The marchers are at once sober, somber, and gleeful—proud to be present as they sense that history is being made" (Bond 2013, ix).

"What sort of man is the photographer?" Freed asked rhetorically. "The mounted police charge. The blood flows while I see it all as my private stage setting. We are dancing a public ballet. I look for the relationship of forms. This is my super–art appreciation course. All of this while a beaten woman screams. And I tell myself, I'm doing this for her, so none will forget this day" (Capa 1968). Freed's consciousness of the photographer's role as witness informed his photographs, whether of Jews or Blacks. They were political statements, indelibly linked to history and memory, the history he had lived as a teenager during World War II and the memory of Jewish suffering and death. In the book that he later published on the March on Washington, Paul Farber wrote appreciatively how "Freed sought images in which he could bring the marchers and the layers of their social landscape into a shared frame" (Farber 2013, 105).

Danny Lyon also went to Washington, albeit reluctantly, as a photographer for SNCC. Although John Lewis as head of SNCC was one of the speakers, SNCC activists were not happy with the rules governing the march. Lyon photographed SNCC members singing, not something participants were supposed to do. His iconic photo of the march, later made into a poster, pictures two men caught in the rapture of the moment. One bald-headed man looks down but raises his arm, his fingers snapping. The other closes his eyes and claps his hands. There are no identifying features here: no Washington Monument, no buttons proclaiming the cause of the day, no crush of the crowd. Without information from Lyon about where it was shot, the photo is mute regarding its place and time. Its power stems from its effective and dramatic simplicity; it conveys iconic struggle, prayer, exaltation. Here, a theatrical moment has been preserved as a monument framed dramatically against the sky. The arm reaching upwards toward heaven's judgment upstages both Washington Monument and Lincoln Memorial, on whose steps the speakers had gathered. In SNCC's poster, a large NOW is printed next to the man's raised hand.

Thirteen years younger than Freed, Lyon was also born in Brooklyn but grew up in a middle-class home in Queens. He started taking photographs as a teenager. As a freshman at the University of Chicago in 1959, one of his pictures won a prize at a university art festival. He took photographs for the student newspaper and covered some of the student protests. Starting in 1962, Lyon worked for SNCC as its official staff photographer. As Blair notes laconically, Lyon ran along with his camera as fellow activists prayed, sang, marched, and were arrested, but he "could not hold hands and sing" (Blair 2007, 203). He had to step out and take their picture.

Drawn to the radical milieu of early 1960s Chicago, Lyon dreamed of changing the world. A history major, he hitchhiked down to Mississippi in

Figure 14.8. Danny Lyon, *USA. Cairo, Illinois. 1962. SNCC demonstration at the Cairo pool. Source:* Courtesy Magnum Photos. Used with permission.

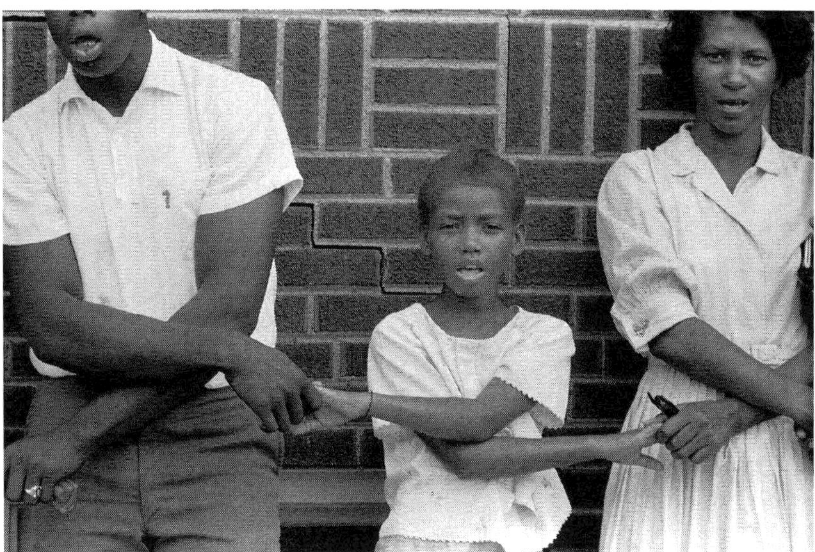

1962. But he took the pictures that would link him with SNCC in Cairo, Illinois. The town, located on the historical border between slavery and freedom, attracted Lyon. He discovered it by reading *Huckleberry Finn*. There he met John Lewis in a church. "I had seldom been in a church before and had never heard a black preacher," Lyon recalled. "The speech, delivered in a heavy, rural Alabama accent, seemed to come up out of him, out of centuries of abuse, and explode from this unassuming young man. His voice was high pitched and trembling with emotion. John's speech would have converted anyone, and it converted me." Perhaps even more astonishing, the speech led to action. Lyon had been used to college students debating and discussing, not acting. The small group of men, women, and children walked out of the church and over to the town's only public swimming pool, which was segregated. After being denied entrance, they stopped to pray. "Then they stood in the street singing, and when a blue pickup truck drove down the center of the street straight at them, a game of chicken ensued as the truck slowed and the demonstrators moved out of the way, except for one defiant thirteen-year-old girl, who stood her ground until the truck knocked her down" (Lyon 1992, 26).

Lyon photographed the men, women, and children praying as a protest against segregation. One photograph of John Lewis kneeling with others, including the brave young girl, became famous because SNCC used it as a poster. They printed 10,000 copies, selling them at a dollar apiece to raise money. But this photograph of the young girl singing captures the moral power of innocence. She holds crossed arms with a man and woman. Lyon focuses on her, placing her front and center in the photograph against the plain brick wall. His mission, he later admitted, was to "create photographs that would be stronger, more truthful, and more powerful than *Life* magazine." He "believed in the power of photography," which "could change the world" (Lyon 2009, 6–7). In part that power came from photography's reality, its ability to picture individual people, people Lyon came to believe in. Bond admitted that Lyon produced "a true picture—not just photographs—of the movement and its promise. That promise failed. Danny Lyon's work is pictures both of what was and of what might have been" (Bond 1992, 7).

These photographs by Freed and Lyon portray activist politics, a blend of instant history and portraiture. Had they been taken in the 1930s, they might have been considered political photographs. But to the extent that they are political, linking ethical principles with demands to overthrow an unjust regime of Jim Crow, their aesthetic follows no party line. In fact, despite both Freed's and Lyon's desire to use photography to expose injustice and further the cause of freedom and equality, neither adheres to an aesthetic of social realism. Instead, their vision appears more grounded in the humanity of the photographic encounter. Crucially, since this encounter involved Black Americans, they employed the photographic emulsion needed to register the diversity of skin color in the range of black and white film.

Looking back on Freed's photographs of the March on Washington, the Black critic Michael Eric Dyson credits him for picturing a "rainbow of blackness that floats above prescribed definitions of beauty and intelligence. Dark-skinned blacks who were usually only photographed in buffoonish extravagance," Dyson argues, "get from Freed a forgiving realism that rescues the blackest blacks from the wasteland of stereotype and restores them to majestic ordinariness." In the racial politics of the 1960s, not only legal rights but also the very humanity of Black Americans were at stake. Dyson characterizes the photos as possessing a "moral beauty" (Dyson 2013, 5–6). His observations indicate the expanded dimensions of political pictures by the 1960s as well as the impact of a several decades of documentary images by Jewish photographers portraying Blacks.

Scholars seem to be comfortable with the notion of "the radical camera"—the title of a show on the New York Photo League in 2012 at the Jewish Museum—but uncomfortable with a possible show titled "the Jewish camera." Naomi Rosenblum appears to have won the argument with William Meyers. Why? Why, per Naomi Rosenblum, does radicalism inflect photographic choices and perceptions and Jewishness does not? Is it because one is ideological and affirmed and the other is largely unacknowledged and ignored? Both, I would argue, are in the mix. Photography is a medium of exchanges: gifts, loans, trades, and thefts. Photographers learn how to see, and discover, as Liebling put it, where their sympathies lie. A photograph invites stares, but having captured an observant gaze for the duration, it structures a viewer's interactions with it. It may be true that when a photo of someone is "taken," as is said, their soul is at risk; but it's equally plausible to feel that a photograph also draws sustenance from those who look at it. As the philosopher John Dewey suggests, a "work of art" does not "work" except as it can use the desires and memories of its audience. "The work takes place when a human being cooperates with the product so that the outcome is an experience that is enjoyed because of its liberating and ordered properties" (Dewey 1958, 214).

The photographs by Rosenblum and Liebling, by Levitt and Weegee, as well as by other Jewish photographers whose work there has not been space to discuss, paved the way for Jewish American photographers to shoot political pictures in the 1960s according to a different calculus. It was not enough, then, to be leftists; not enough to be, as Jews, not quite white; not enough to be New Yorkers. To be able to see beyond stereotypes, to picture Blacks with compassion and dignity, to identify them as moral victims of injustice and seekers of the truth, one needed to bring all these elements together with a sense of the camera's liberating possibilities, its potential to transcend differences and even as art to, as Lyon put it, "change men and transform society" (Lyon 2009).

This Jewish embrace of the power of photography brings it into the history of American Jews. Photography offered Jews, who often lacked other means, a tool potentially to remake the world and to make history. In producing authentic documents of an era, Jewish photographers possessed the ability to shape future generations' understanding of the past. As Lyon later recognized, "My photographs—made because I had studied history, made because I loved to make them, made under direction from Forman and the office—were used to help create a public image for SNCC" (Lyon 1992,

30). They let people see the world through Jewish eyes: its humanity and its injustices and its hopes for political change. In reclaiming this history of Jewish photographers' pictures of Black Americans lies the possibility of broadening and complicating both American Jewish history and memory.

Works Cited

Baskind, Samantha. 2010. "Weegee's Jewishness." *History of Photography* 34 (1): 60–78.

Berger, Martin A. 2011. *Seeing through Race: A Reinterpretation of Civil Rights Photography*. University of California Press.

Berger, Maurice. 2011. "Man in the Mirror: Harlem Document, Race, and the Photo League." In *The Radical Camera: New York's Photo League, 1936–1951*, edited by Mason Klein and Catherine Evans. Yale University Press.

Blair, Sara. 2007. *Harlem Crossroads: Black Writers and the Photograph in the Twentieth Century*. Princeton University Press.

Bonanos, Christopher. 2018. *Flash: The Making of Weegee the Famous*. Holt.

Bond, Julian. 1992. Foreword to *Memories of the Southern Civil Rights Movement*, by Danny Lyon. University of North Carolina Press.

———. 2013. Foreword to *This Is the Day: The March on Washington*, by Leonard Freed. J. Paul Getty Museum.

Brookfield, Molly Miller. 2020. "Watching the Girls Go By: Sexual Harassment in the American Street, 1850–1980." PhD diss., University of Michigan.

Capa, Cornell, ed. 1968. *The Concerned Photographer: The Photographs of Werner Bischof, André Kertész, Robert Capa, Leonard Freed, David Seymour ("Chim") and Dan Weiner*. Grossman.

———. 1972. Introduction to *The Concerned Photographer 2: The Photographs of Marc Riboud, Roman Vishniac, Bruce Davidson, Gordon Parks, Ernst Haas, Hiroshi Hamaya, Donald McCullin, W. Eugene Smith*, edited by Cornell Capa. Grossman.

Capeci, Dominic J., Jr. 1977. *The Harlem Riot of 1943*. Temple University Press.

Davidson, Bruce. 2002. Afterword to *Time of Change: Civil Rights Photographs, 1961–1965*. St. Ann's.

Desjardin, Fiona. 1993. "The Photo League: Aesthetics, Politics, and the Cold War." PhD diss., University of Delaware.

Dewey, John. 1958. *Art as Experience*. Capricorn.

Dyson, Michael Eric. 2013. "August March." In *This Is the Day: The March on Washington*, by Leonard Freed. J. Paul Getty Museum.

Farber, Paul M. 2013. "Afterword: In Leonard Freed's Footsteps." In *This Is the Day: The March on Washington*, by Leonard Freed. J. Paul Getty Museum.

Francisco, Jason. 2016. "Esther Bubley." *#PhotosWeLove* (blog), May 8. https://medium.com/photos-we-love.

Freed, Leonard. 2020. *Black in White America 1963–1965*. Reel Art.

———. 2013. *This Is the Day: The March on Washington*. J. Paul Getty Museum.

Gil-Glazer, Ya'ara. 2019. " 'We Weren't Jewish (We Were Concerned Photographers)': The Photo League's Archive of Black Lives in New York." *Jewish Culture and History* 20 (4): 359–81.

Goldberg, Vicki. 2016. *Bruce Davidson: An Illustrated Biography*. Magnum Legacy. Magnum Foundation; Prestel.

Gopnik, Adam. 2001. "Improvised City: Helen Levitt's New York." *New Yorker*, November 11. https://www.newyorker.com/magazine/2001/11/19/improvised-city.

Gurock, Jeffrey S. 1979. *When Harlem Was Jewish, 1870–1930*. Columbia University Press.

Hartman, Susan. 2008. "A New York Street Photographer Keeps on Clicking." *Christian Science Monitor*, March 26. https://www.csmonitor.com/USA/Society/2008/0326/p20s01-ussc.html.

Hoberman, J. 2012. "The Radical Camera: New York's Photo League, 1936–1941." *Artforum*, April 19. https://www.artforum.com/print/reviews/201204/the-radical-camera-30580.

Jussim, Estelle. 1978. "The Photographs of Jerome Liebling, a Personal View." In *Jerome Liebling: Photographs, 1947–1977*. Friends of Photography.

Klein, Mason. 2011. "Of Politics and Poetry: The Dilemma of the Photo League." In *The Radical Camera: New York's Photo League, 1936–1951*, edited by Mason Klein and Catherine Evans. Yale University Press.

Kozloff, Max. 2002. *New York: Capital of Photography*. Jewish Museum; Yale University Press.

Levitt, Laura S. 2002. "New York: Capital of Photography." *American Jewish History* 90 (4): 466–68.

Lewis, John. 2002. Foreword to *Time of Change: Civil Rights Photographs, 1961–1965* by Bruce Davidson. St. Ann's.

Liebling, Jerome. 1995. *The People, Yes*. Aperture.

Lyon, Danny. 1992. *Memories of the Southern Civil Rights Movement*. Lyndhurst Series on the South Center for Documentary Studies. University of North Carolina Press.

———. 2009. Preface to *Memories of Myself: Essays by Danny Lyon*. Phaidon.

Meyers, William. 2003. "Jews and Photography." *Commentary* 112 (1): 45–48. https://www.commentary.org/articles/william-meyers/jews-and-photography/.

Milkman, Paul. 1997. *PM: A New Deal in Journalism, 1940–1948*. Rutgers University Press.

Moore, Deborah Dash. 1981. *At Home in America: Second Generation New York Jews, 1920–1940*. Columbia University Press.

———. 2004. *GI Jews: How World War II Changed a Generation*. Harvard University Press.

————. 2010. "Walkers in the City: Young Jewish Women with Cameras." In *Gender and Jewish History*, edited by Marion A. Kaplan and Deborah Dash Moore. Indiana University Press.

PM Daily. 1943. "Police Called to Give Negroes 'Freedom from Fear.'" October 18.

Rosenblum, Walter. 1983. Interview with Walter Rosenblum by Colin Osman. *Creative Camera*, no. 223–24, 1019–25.

Trachtenberg, Alan. 2003. "The Claim of a Jewish Eye?" *PaknTreger* 4 (4): 20–25.

Tucker, Anne Wilkes. 2001. "The Photo League: A Center for Documentary Photography." In *This Was the Photo League: Compassion and the Camera from the Depression to the Cold War*, edited by Anne Wilkes Tucker, Claire Cass, and Stephen Daiter. Stephen Daiter Gallery; John Cleary Gallery.

————. 2011. "A Rashomon Reading." In *The Radical Camera: New York's Photo League, 1936–1951*, edited by Mason Klein and Catherine Evans. Yale University Press.

Weegee. 1963. *Boys Caught in Boarded-Up Harlem Store*. Gelatin Silver, 34 x 27. International Center of Photography. https://www.icp.org/browse/archive/objects/boys-caught-in-boarded-up-harlem-store-1.

————. 1975. *Naked City*. DaCapo.

Willis, Deborah. 2002. Introduction to *Time of Change: Civil Rights Photographs, 1961–1965*, by Bruce Davidson. St. Ann's.

Chapter 15

Beyond Black and White

Jews, African Americans, and Africa in Photography, Film, and Television

Michael Berkowitz

For most of those interested in the historical confluence of African Americans and Jews in the United States (beyond the orbit of the current volume), photography may not seem an obvious point of contact (Blight 2018). Television and film, however, are among the more conspicuous realms where Jews and African Americans have long interacted, in addition to music. Marc Dollinger's highly acclaimed *Black Power, Jewish Politics: Reinventing the Alliance in the 1960s* employs no images—the absence of which is not regarded as problematic (Dollinger 2018; Donnella 2018). Likewise, Cheryl Lynn Greenberg, in *Troubling the Waters: Black-Jewish Relations in the American Century*, does not dive deeply into visual culture—despite the opening scene of Rabbi Abraham Joshua Heschel (1907–1972) and Rev. Martin Luther King, Jr. (1929–1968), marching "side by side from Selma to Birmingham in 1965," which "symbolized for many the powerful 'black-Jewish' alliance" (Greenberg 2006, 1). The creatively designed dust jacket of her book, however, features a much-reproduced photograph of King with Heschel that is divided in half.

Greg Robinson and Robert Chang's recent anthology on ethnic and racial minority relations, in which Jews and African Americans figure prominently, includes neither figures nor dedicated chapters involving realistic representations (Robinson and Chang 2017). Certainly, it is possible to

Figure 15.1. Book dust jacket image, Cheryl Lynn Greenberg, *Troubling the Waters: Black Jewish Relations in the American* Century (Princeton University Press, 2006). Pamela Lewis Schnittter, designer. Photo from Bettmann/CORBIS (no photographer attributed). *Source:* Courtesy of Princeton University Press, with assistance from Cheryl Lynn Greenberg. Used with permission.

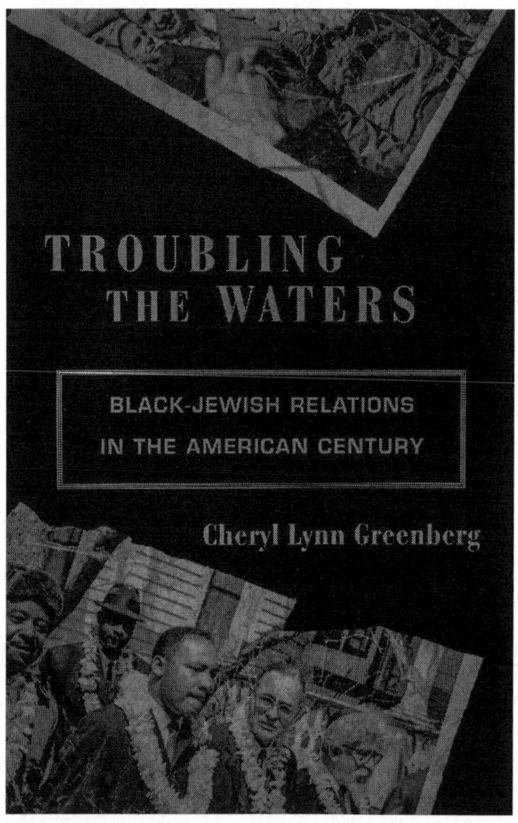

produce important scholarship without illustrations. But for a field such as ethnic and racial minority relations, in which imagery has played such an immense role, one may assume that the subject might merit engagement.

In contrast to the abovementioned studies, Susannah Heschel emphasized the significance of the fact that her father, Abraham Joshua Heschel, "appears beside Martin Luther King Jr. in several of the most iconic photographs of that time." Iconic, that is, especially for Jews, such as its use by Greenberg and numerous others. Heschel is careful to qualify, however, that "we've become so used to these images that it's easy to forget how unusual the friendship between Heschel and King was in its day" (Heschel 2018).

The photographer whose work features in Heschel's article (and apparently Greenberg's cover image) is John C. Goodwin (1941–2017). Goodwin stood out in his cohort as a Gentile, but more notably as a son of a white Baptist pastor who was outspoken on human rights, tolerance, and opposition to US involvement in Vietnam. Both father and son were sensitive to antisemitism and racism (Pekow n.d.). Such use of the pictures of Goodwin is not confined to scholarly work. A colorized image of Heschel and King also graces the cover of Richard Michelson and Raul Colon's *As Good as Anybody*, a successful children's book about the two men's "walk toward freedom" (Michelson and Colon 2008). From a theory-driven approach, literary-history scholar Sara Blair deftly interweaves photography, Jews, and African Americans into an analysis of "the other half" on New York's Lower East Side, which complements her earlier, interdisciplinary interpretation of the Harlem Renaissance. Blair's excellent work, however, is tightly focused on specific precincts of New York and privileges self-consciously creative expressions and artists (Blair 2018, 2007). There is little doubt, however, that issues surrounding the representation of minorities in film, television, and media have fueled ongoing controversies and myths not only between Black and White Americans, but specifically, African Americans and Jews.

This chapter peers into infrequently explored encounters between Jews, African Americans, and Africa, and their explicit intersections with photography, extending to film and television. It highlights selected, freighted meetings between Jewish professionals in photography and film, and shall focus on two men who rarely have been approached as Jewish historical subjects: Omar Oscar Marcus (1910–1980) and Eliot Elisofon (1911–1973) (Elisofon and Flukinger 2000; Kart 2014). The memorial exhibit for Elisofon in 1974, for example, was entitled *Tribute to Africa* and took place at the Museum of African Art in Washington, DC. Each man held sophisticated ideas on photography and thought deeply about how different types of people were represented. They believed and demonstrated that photographers were responsible for the mediation of her or his subjects. There is no basis, however, to assume that the photographic practices of these men were distinctly "Jewish," or that their Jewish background predisposed them to a particular style or approach to aesthetics.

Omar Oscar Marcus and Eliot Elisofon in Context

Although the individuals prominent in the following discussion, Marcus and Elisofon, are not among the most famous photographers, they provide instructive cases for examining relations between Jews and Blacks, in large part due to their connections to larger streams and personalities in popular culture. Elisofon by most measures was far more successful than Marcus, and had a widely recognized impact on the work of many contemporaries. Marcus, however, vicariously, set himself against the famed British "society" photographer, Cecil Beaton (1904–1980) when he undertook an opportunity to shoot Harlem's Black community (Vickers 2020). While Beaton was not the only photographer who aestheticized fashion and Western social life with a racist leaning, he is one of the few photographers who landed himself in the midst of an antisemitic scandal. Marcus went on to become a sympathetic photographer of modernizing Africa in the subsequent decades. Earlier he had been recognized for portraying Muslims and Islam, cutting across racial divides, with compassion. We do not know if Beaton took any notice of Marcus's challenge to him. Yet we can detect prescient discernment about racism in Marcus's critical reading of the words and images of Beaton, whose popular books have thus far escaped close scrutiny. Beaton was, however, famously embroiled in an antisemitic controversy in June 1938 that did not seriously impair his career or reputation (Berkowitz 2015, 18–19, 216–18).

Decades later Eliot Elisofon was accused, unjustly in my estimation, of being racially insensitive as a producer/director and cinematographer, in reactions to his presentation of African history and culture to television audiences (Polier 1972). Elisofon became the target of criticism as part of general apprehension about white people telling the stories of Africans and African Americans. One of Elisofon's greatest passions was African art, which comprised a major component of his film-work for television and a significant portion of his photographic practice.

Elisofon's advocacy for, and productions concerning African art may serve as a bridge to a brief reflection on the photographers Alfred Stieglitz (1864–1946), Helmut Gernsheim (1913–1995), and Peter Pollack (1909–1978). Stieglitz displayed "Negro Art"—not a derogatory term—as early as 1914, along with modern art and photography, in his New York galleries (Stieglitz 2008). Both Pollack and Gernsheim were collectors of and investors in African art. The activity and personal correspondence of all three reveal a deep ethical consciousness, in every respect, when dealing with these cultural products. Intensive research into the conception and cultivation of museum exhibitions and collections of African art, I suspect, may reveal a Jewish connection similar to what has been shown about the involvement of Jews in the reception and dissemination of modern, abstract art, as discussed recently by Charles Dellheim. Dellheim goes so far as to assert that it was "Jews who made the art world modern" (Dellheim 2021).

In the 1940s, Helmut Gernsheim pioneered a historical approach to photography collecting and scholarship. Simultaneously he began collecting African art and treating it as worthy of respect in the canon of fine arts. Peter Pollack, an American Jew, worked along parallel tracks, for a brief period allied with Gernsheim, in the United States (Berkowitz 2011). American-born photographer Eliot Elisofon took this impulse of openness to African art even further. He became a critical interlocutor between African culture and the West, and facilitated—to no small extent—the establishment of the African art history museum on the National Mall in Washington, DC. Elisofon also was central to the serious presentation of African history on television, which led to a painful clash between him and writer Maya Angelou. The lack of comment on this affair, however, reveals that these Jewish photographers have been, until recently, largely lost to history and memory. (A richly-deserved, substantial biography of Eliot Elisofon is being prepared by Elisofon's daughter, Elin, which promises to fill this lacuna.) The experience of Elisofon exposes both the potential and the pitfalls of Jews engaging Black culture, identity, and history though photography and film.

It is fitting, but not acknowledged for its importance, that the cover image of one of the first photography books produced by the National Museum of African American History and Culture (in 2014, before the opening of the museum itself), *Through the African American Lens*, was taken by a Jewish artist, Elisofon. Dated circa 1937, the image depicts African American photographer Zack Brown who is taking images of dapper men in Harlem (Smithsonian National Museum of African American History and Culture 2014, cover, 58–59).

The photograph is reproduced in fuller form in the volume, but there is no discussion of Elisofon or other Jewish photographers in this book, such as Leonard Freed (1929–2006), Alexander Alland (1902–1989), and Joe Schwartz (1913–2015). Elisofon professed that Black people themselves should be enabled and encouraged in their own image-making. Interestingly, Maurice Berger's *New York Times* review of the 2015 exhibition commented that Elisofon's photo challenged the then-dominant view of Black urban life, focusing on dignity instead of suffering, self-possession instead of defeat, happiness instead of sorrow. Mr. Elisofon's picture also reminds us of the powerful role of photography in African-American life, how the medium—and black photographers—helped reshape the image of a people (Berger 2015).

Figure 15.2. Eliot Elisofon, *Photographer Zack Brown Shooting Dapper Men in Harlem,* c. 1937. Book soft cover [exhibition catalogue], *Through the African American Lens* (Smithsonian National Museum of African American History and Culture, 2014). *Source:* Courtesy of the Smithsonian National Museum of African American History and Elin Elisofon. Used with permission.

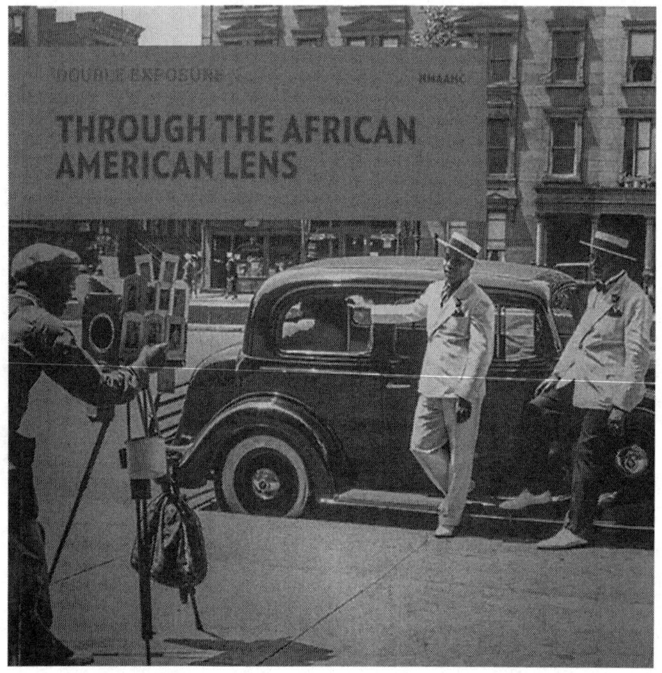

It is important to recall, in framing this chapter, that Jews were tremendously overrepresented as photographers, and in the photographic trades overall, in Europe, from the mid-nineteenth century to the Holocaust, and in the United States from the turn of the century until the 1970s (Berkowitz 2011). It is not surprising, therefore, that Jews, as photographers, photography editors, and writers, helped to shape Africa's presentation to the world in realistic media and influenced Africa's evolving relationship with the arts and culture in the West. A more comprehensive overview of this topic would integrate photographers who are well known, such as Ylla (Camilla Koffler), Paul Strand, Robert Capa, Alfred Eisenstaedt, and Arnold Newman—all of whom were earnestly devoted to Africa and Africans. Because Marcus and Elisofon articulated, in prose, their approach to

Africa and Africans, however, revisiting their lives and work, in this subject matter, is especially instructive.

There is no reason to expect the name Omar Oscar Marcus to mean anything to even the most avid scholars of European Jewish history and the history of photography. A potted biography of Marcus, by Hebrew University, which vanished from its English-language website of the Truman Institute, stated that he "was a press photographer," born in Berlin in 1910. He was a descendant of the noted eighteenth-century Rabbi Akiva Eger, and it was said that his family's history in Berlin could be traced back several generations (There are two famed rabbis named Akiva Eger, of 1722–1758 and 1761–1837) (Marcus n.d.). Yet Marcus has been honored by the Hebrew University of Jerusalem with a large-scale exhibition including selections of his writing and photographs, and, moreover, by the establishment of a prize to recognize attempts to foster understanding between Jews and Arabs. As a press photographer, Marcus was best known for being the first non-Muslim to photograph prayer at Mecca. Among Arabs in numerous settings, he was able to pass as a Muslim in part due to his facility in Arabic (which he denigrated as limited, but apparently was effective). Marcus did, in fact, have great respect for Arabs and their diverse cultures. Many of his observations of the *yishuv*, the Jewish settlement in Palestine, and Zionist-Arab relations, turned out to be more perceptive than those typically voiced by his Jewish peers. He believed that there was no possibility of a permanent solution to the Arab-Zionist, later the Arab-Israeli conflict if Jews did not make a determined effort to understand and appreciate their Arab counterparts, which meant learning their language and customs. He retained the name "Omar" for his entire life.

Despite the accolades by the Truman Institute of Hebrew University, Marcus's story is not one of consistent success and personal fulfillment. For much of his life Marcus struggled financially, his relations with friends and colleagues were tense and strained, and his family—whose support he may have taken for granted—apparently did not play a major role in his life. Part of the reason, I believe, for Marcus's lack of noted achievement in photography and cinematography is that he did not conform to many of the informal codes of the time.

Marcus can be appreciated, however, as a pioneer of international press photography. Part of his success in this area derives from the extent to which photojournalism was in large part a Jewish domain (Vowinckel 2016). Marcus's place within the milieu, though, was odd. Believing that the future was one of "color," he aspired to become a color cinematographer.

Marcus did some work in this area, but he remained frustrated. Marcus felt that he was underappreciated for his expertise. He was one of the first cameramen to capture the famed Indianapolis 500 (automobile race) in color for American television (Marcus 1951a).

The segment of his life that seemed to have left the most indelible imprint was the time he spent in Britain, especially Scotland, during the 1940s. Despite a rather tempestuous, brief stay, he identified himself primarily as a "Scot" from that time forward, and his politics were moderate to right-wing Tory (Marcus 1949, 1951a, 1951b, 1964, 1973a, 1973b, 1973c, 1952). He did, however, loathe the disgraced United States president, Richard Nixon (Marcus 1973a). This political hodge-podge, which was bizarre for most "cameramen" in the United States, where he hoped to ply his trade, meant he did not fit with the leftist-union politics that dominated the time. He eventually relocated to Mexico. In Mexico, he carried himself as a proud British expat, and he even earned part of his living from teaching English. After his death, though, the segment of his legacy that remained, most strongly, was as an interlocutor between Arabic speakers and the wider world. Although it is not surprising that Marcus has been rediscovered in this way, I wish to point out the dissonance between his later life and that which was featured in his memorialization. There is no reason to believe that he was unsympathetic to the Zionist movement and modern Israel, but it was not his utmost concern. Among the few references to Israel is a comment that he has "No news from my brother!" during a period of tension in the Middle East (Marcus 1973b). He does not seem to have made any effort to join his family in Israel, and his interest in Zionism, even the Arab world, seemed to wane when he struck out for the United States. In 1972, he coldly related to a friend that he had not seen his father for thirty-nine years (Marcus 1972).

The discussion that follows will comment on Marcus's early influences and career as a press photographer, his brief but consequential stay in Britain, his frustrating sojourn to the United States, and his relocation to Mexico. Our chief concern, though, is one specific assignment that was exceptionally meaningful to him for a "Negro" newspaper in Harlem.

Marcus became renowned "in the 1930s for his fascinating photos of North Africa and Arab countries, some of them taken at great personal risk. His pictures of the Middle East are full of gripping tales of kings and princes he met on his many travels on behalf of the Associated Press." Although it was fleeting, "world fame came to him in 1935 with the publication of his photos of worshippers at Mecca, which was closed to Westerners. When he became known as a photographer in the Arab world, he took the name 'Omar,' which sounds Arabic, and is made up of the first syllables of his first and last names, Omar Marcus" (press release n.d.).

This story of his name may not be the whole truth. He seems to have converted, sincerely, to Islam, and changed religious faiths at least one more time after that. Not quite understanding what it meant for photographers to undertake assignments, the Hebrew University publicity describes Marcus as "wandering around the world" and eventually settling in Mexico City, "where he taught the art of color movie photography at the university. He was killed in a road accident in Mexico in 1980 and buried in Jerusalem." The official biography concludes with his memorialization in 1984, when the "Omar Oscar Marcus Fund for Understanding and Peace between Arabs and Jews" was established at the Hebrew University's Truman Institute. It specified that "as a Jew, as a man involved with the culture of the Middle East, and as a citizen of the world, Omar Marcus saw great importance in working towards peace in general and between Jews and Arabs in particular" (press release n.d.). It is unclear when this prize ceased to be awarded.

There is nothing either incorrect or objectionable about the characterization of Marcus by the press office of Hebrew University. This depiction, however, reveals only a few facets of an extremely complicated individual and career. As much as the Hebrew University wished to praise him, some of the cutting-edge dimensions of Marcus's career went unnoticed. Overall, his profession, as a photographer, cinematographer, and television cameraman, was influenced—both helped and occasionally hindered—by his identity as a German Jew, eventually a German Jewish refugee, and later an English and Scottish expatriate. He obtained work through German-Jewish connections, yet he also was discriminated against as a foreigner. He was both an Anglophile and a Scotch patriot, becoming a British citizen in 1942. He was still working as a press photographer into the 1970s, supplying pictures for some of the same papers that had employed him forty years earlier, and, perhaps more remarkably, into the 1960s he was relying on his knowledge of local languages and customs in order to obtain the desired story and pictures (Marcus 1973a, 1973b, 1963). He was a fairly astute observer of the world around him—although he did not seem to possess much savvy in understanding what sense others made of him. His writings also are intriguing, because he was a Jew operating in what may be considered heavily Jewish fields—first, photography per se, and, later, cinematography and television. Yet, he was a loner. He was never "one of the boys" and he was no "ladies man." He might have been homosexual. This may be why so many names are blotted out in the archives. It is not surprising that the Hebrew University information service is reticent to relate that, from a religious perspective, Omar Oscar Marcus was more at home in the Church of Scotland than any synagogue. Although when he prayed as a Muslim, in order to be accepted in their midst, he was evading his background as a Jew, it seems that he did so with respect. He remained an outsider among outsiders, even though some aspects of his attitude and experience were quite typical of his larger cohort. Photography was his greatest passion, but he neither embraced nor understood the playful relationship with machismo and irreverence that was much so much a part of how most photographers of his time styled themselves. The conflicted Jewish identity of Marcus was not only manifested in his forays into the Near East—but through his engagement with African Americans in the United States and Africans in Africa, the latter as both traditional and modernizing people. Although it is difficult to define precisely, Marcus possibly had an affinity for those he thought were disparaged and misunderstood.

The brief biographical treatments present Marcus as more of a politically concerned photographer than is actually warranted. Marcus, like the vast majority of professional photographers, mainly took pictures of what he was paid to photograph. He traveled to several Mediterranean countries on behalf of the Associated Press. One of his many assignments was to cover the Italian colonial war in Abyssinia in 1937, alongside leading photojournalists such as Robert Capa and Alfred Eisenstaedt. Marcus lived in Egypt for several years and studied Arabic. "He achieved special recognition for his photographs of worshippers in Mecca[,] becoming the first non-Muslim to gain entry into the city (at the risk of his life). . . . When Marcus returned to London at the end of the 1930s, the English newspaper *The Star* referred to him as 'Marcus of Arabia'" (*Star* 1936). There is an overtly romantic, "Orientalizing," even death-defying twist to the story and its presentation—showing Omar in Arab dress—which no doubt was intended to draw on the publicity from earlier that year accorded to the infinitely more famous "Lawrence of Arabia." It was said that he had "a knack of picking up languages with extraordinary rapidity. He speaks and writes Arabic fluently and can speak a half dozen African languages with equal ease. At Jeddah during the pilgrimage, he, a European acted as interpreter for two Moslems who spoke a different tongue. He knew both."

His own account is less dramatic and more qualified. "I was on my way back from Abyssinia," he told a *Star* reporter, "and decided I would like to see Jeddah at the most interesting time of the year, the time of the pilgrimage to Mecca. All the pilgrims pass through Jeddah on their way to Mecca, an hour and a half's car journey away. No non-Muslim, of course, is allowed in Mecca. Even if he found his way he would be doomed unless he knew every movement and detail of the ritual. But I secured some pictures of the pilgrims near Jeddah." Here Marcus himself explains that his photographs of the pilgrims come not from Mecca, but Jeddah. However, there is a possibility that he did supply press photos from Mecca, but trying to avoid threats in the future, stated that he merely made it to Jeddah. Omar's second best-known public outing was his 1936 encounter with Emir Abdullah Ibn Hussein, then ruler of Transjordan. Around that time Omar had a number of brushes with celebrity, if not greatness. During World War II, "Marcus stayed in England where he was interned for a short time because of his German nationality. In 1940 he joined the British Army and was dismissed in 1942, obtaining British citizenship." There is no clue why he was "dismissed" in 1942 (Marcus n.d.).

Between his stint in the United States and his relocation to Mexico, in the late 1950s Marcus was assigned to photograph an expedition to Africa for the Twentieth Century Fund. His pictures appeared in *Tropical Africa* (1960), a two-volume work by the research director of the foundation, George H. T. Kimble (biographical note n.d.). The photos have been frequently reproduced. Thus, while today he is mostly recognized for his sympathetic photographs of the Arab world, Marcus was equally committed to presenting the lives of Africans and African Americans to broader audiences (Marcus 1952).

In 1950, during one of his periods of underemployment, Marcus was especially proud of himself for having completed a project he initiated, namely, a "photographic essay on the re-housing and re-habilitation of Harlem slum-dwellers." According to a letter Marcus wrote in 1952, the project

> met with the most unexpected success. The story, comprising 38 pictures, was shown the Publisher and owner of *Our World*, a monthly illustrated for the coloured people. He was fascinated by the pictures and the story treatment, asked for my fee, called in his treasurer and within 7 minutes from entering his office I was presented with a handsome cheque. "There's just one picture missing," the publisher said. "One of yourself in Harlem—I'm going to assign one of my photographers to make arrangements for this with you!" (Marcus 1952)

To Marcus this was a deeply satisfying response.

Figure 15.3. Omar Marcus, "A New World in the Old. The physical features of most colleges are first-class, and unsegregated (Dakar, School of Medicine and Pharmacy)." George H. T. Kimble, *Tropical Africa*, vol. 2, *Society and Polity* (Twentieth Century Fund, 1960). *Source:* Reproduced by permission of the Century Foundation.

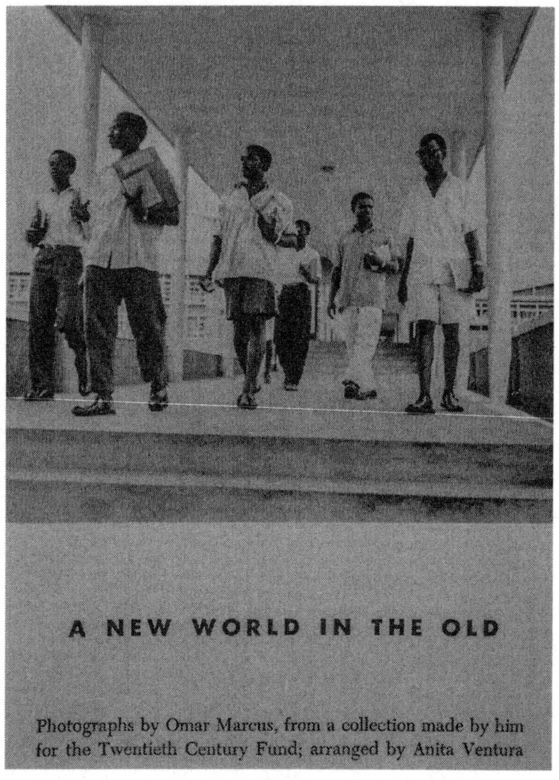

Later Marcus was contracted to produce a photo essay for *Our World* (1952), which was presented as, "A Scot Peeks at Harlem Society. Here is New York's Negro 400, as seen by a visitor accustomed to photograph society." This "400" was the term that referred to the elite cohort of Harlem. The lead photo featured Mrs. Betty Alston, wife of Dr. Garlan Alston of Brooklyn, who was, in Marcus's opinion, a "lady of grace and elegance, with corngold hair." She is pictured with her father, Grenier Turner. It is, indeed, a beautiful photo. In the essay Marcus explained:

When I started this . . . almost everybody I met told me there was no Negro society. . . . True, there is no lazy leisure class as we find among the whites. Most Negroes have got to go wherever

Figure 15.4. Omar Marcus, "Neither modern still nor ancient lore recognize differences of person or sex." George H. T. Kimble, *Tropical Africa*, vol. 2, *Society and Polity* (Twentieth Century Fund, 1960). *Source:* Reproduced by permission of the Century Foundation.

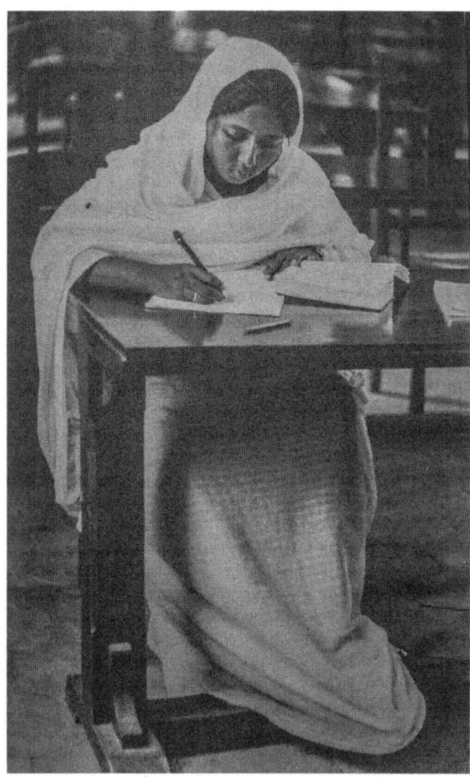

they are by hard work, ingenuity, and thrift. But many of the Negroes I met had culture, learning, intelligence, and charm equal to and sometimes, superior to many whites I have met. Negroes have been only 85 years out of slavery. In that short time, they have made tremendous progress. To a Britisher who thinks of society in terms of centuries, it is stupendous. *It is even more difficult to understand when one thinks of the racial obstacles Negroes still have to face.* (Marcus 1950; emphasis added)

In pursuing this endeavor, it was vital for Marcus that Beaton had preceded him as a photographer of Harlem—and that Beaton's treatment of Harlem was abhorrent. Part of his essay is sectioned off with the heading "Cecil Beaton's

Figure 15.5. Omar Marcus, "Any day in a medical laboratory (Institut pour la Recherche Scientifique en Afrique Centrale, Lwiro, B.C.)." George H. T. Kimble, *Tropical Africa*, vol. 2, *Society and Polity* (Twentieth Century Fund, 1960). *Source:* Reproduced by permission of the Century Foundation.

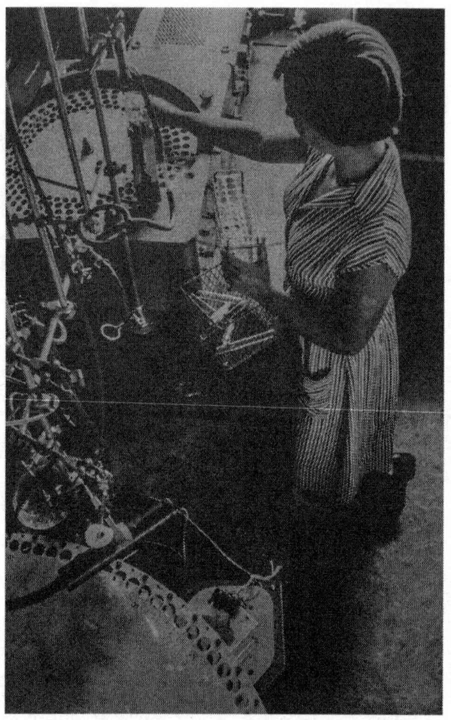

Story." "Some years ago," Marcus wrote, "Cecil Beaton, English society writer-photographer, came to New York and later published a book in which he mercilessly slandered Negroes" (Marcus 1950). Marcus was largely correct, but the story is more complicated. At the time of Marcus's article, Beaton had published two different editions of his book, *A Portrait of New York*, in 1938, and a revised edition in 1948. Marcus, though, had more than sufficient grounds for condemning Beaton. In the more subdued second edition, Beaton nevertheless sought to highlight the Black photographers of Harlem whose assignments would invariably reflect poorly on the community. Mainly, Beaton wrote, they shot corpses opportunistically, " 'Apotheosis' pictures," and "anything from a high-yellow fiancée to an intricate scalp operation." "High-yellow" to Beaton was derogatory for mixed-race, a category to which

Figure 15.6. Omar Marcus, "Soccer for the fun of it, at 10,000 feet above sea level (near Addis Ababa)." George H. T. Kimble, *Tropical Africa*, vol. 2, *Society and Polity* (Twentieth Century Fund, 1960). *Source:* Reproduced by permission of the Century Foundation.

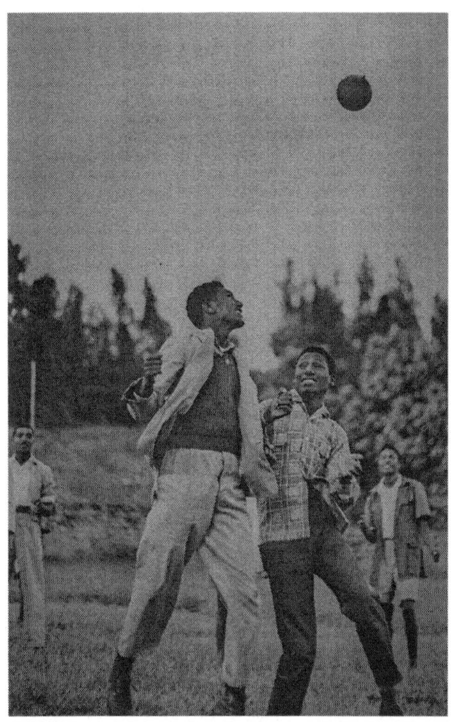

he often, scathingly revisited. Unsurprisingly, many of Beaton's comments are highly sexualized, such as his detailed discussion of Black female impersonators at the annual Mardi Gras Ball (Beaton 1948, 104, 179).

For Marcus, Beaton's gaze at Harlem's society was outrageous and needed correction. He asserted that Beaton had "painted a lurid picture of a Harlem penthouse apartment where 'imitation ivy climbs round the hot-pipes in the hall,' of 'enormous black-mammas' sitting in chairs and a 'hostess . . . tipping cigarette ash into a fancy biscuit-tin.' What utter nonsense! Beaton couldn't have seen much" (Marcus 1950). While Beaton's text did contain contradictory and occasionally complimentary nods to African Americans, his elitism and racism—also directed against the Irish and Jews—was vicious (Beaton 1938, 172–74, 179).

Marcus, by contrast, wished to put his spotlight on well-educated and politically active Harlem residents, such as the Wright family. He emphasized that "Dr. Louis T. Wright is an internationally famous surgeon, one of the first to work with aureomcin [sp., aureomycin]," a recently introduced antibiotic treatment for bacterial-, viral-, and rickets-related diseases, which also was used for typhus. A man with a great sense of humor and common sense, according to Marcus, Wright also was distinguished as "the Chairman of the Board of the National Association for the Advancement of Colored People [NAACP]." Marcus noted that Louis Wright's family also belong to this emerging social group. He described Wright's daughters, Jane and Barbara, as "doctors in their own right, both civil, charming cultured mothers." Moreover, "Mrs. Corrine Wright, herself, [is] a former teacher, a woman of depth and character." Marcus continued with thick descriptions of two other families with whom he had become acquainted and was profoundly impressed. "In time," he wrote, "with God's help, they might give the white people a lot to think about—like how to live and enjoy it" (Marcus 1950).

Alas, Marcus did not find much other work in New York. Continuing his peripatetic lifestyle, in 1957 Marcus travelled to Mexico, initially as a correspondent for the *Daily Express* of London. "He contributed to various film productions in Mexico" and was later hired to teach "cinematography at the [Ibero-American] University of Mexico City" (Typescript n.d.). He returned to the United States in 1968, settling in Chicago, and four years later went back to Mexico City. The official accounts record that Marcus "died on April 11, 1980, after a traffic accident. He was buried at the Har Hamenuchot cemetery in Jerusalem, next to his parents" (Marcus n.d.). But his end was more prolonged and painful. The accident was a hit-and-run trauma, from which he never totally recovered; Marcus described it as "depressing" and "soul-destroying" (Marcus 1978). There may, however, be some other Jewish threads that merit further investigation. Among Marcus's many projects were collaboration with the Spanish poet Manuel Altolaguirre (Marcus 1978; Leo Baeck Institute Finding Aid n.d.). Altolaguiree worked on a number of films, and apparently one of the most notable was *El cantar de los cantares* (Song of Songs; dir. Manuel Altolaguirre, 1959). Perhaps he found some solace, or nourishment for his urge to create compelling picture-stories in this work. Yet for much of his life he was an unhappy cosmopolitan. His time in Edinburgh might have been the brightest, with Harlem and Africa among the highlights.

Similar to Marcus, Eliot Elisofon also sought to integrate Islam and Africa into a universal cultural inheritance that deserved to be as respected as that of "the West" (Elisofon 1965b; Elisofon 1966; Elisofon 1965a). In his television work, Elisofon was especially esteemed by an informal fraternal order of directors who had great regard for the still photography that accompanied cinematography (Dimitri 1967). Born in New York in 1911, Elisofon's mother took him regularly to art museums and he spent hours drawing in them as a child. He later turned to watercolors. Quite early in life he realized that there was a complex and complementary relationship between art and photography, including the notion that a photograph of a work of art could be a work of art in itself (Elisofon n.d.). We might see this as something of an inversion of Walter Benjamin's well-worn assertion of "the work of art in the age of mechanical reproduction," which argued that the artwork loses its "aura," its specialness, through photography.

After graduating from Fordham, a Catholic university in the Bronx, he embarked on a career as a professional photographer. His work for *Life* magazine includes photos of Americans praying at St. George's Episcopal Church in Manhattan for the victims of the 1938 November Pogrom in Berlin. According to his *New York Times* obituary, prior to the American entry into World War II, he "covered the London blitz, and in 1942 accompanied United States troops to Africa as a photographer/correspondent for *Life*. After photographing the first landing at Casablanca, Morocco, in November 1942, he covered the Tunisian campaign. During the war he was also attached to the Pacific Fleet. On assignments from *Life* after the war he drove from Cape Town to Cairo, and did photographic studies of art and architecture temples of India and in Angkor Wat, Cambodia." Following extensive work in South America, in 1950 he "climbed with his cameras to 16,000 feet in the Mountains of the Moon in the Belgian Congo" (*New York Times* 1973). "Elisofon's photography has a place in New York's Museum of Modern Art and the Art Institute of Chicago, among other museums," and his books on Africa, such as *The Sculpture of Africa*, with text by William Fagg, and *The Nile*, were largely products of his original research.

"He was a research fellow in primitive art with Harvard's Peabody Museum and a member of the Royal Anthropological Society. He collected French impressionist paintings and primitive works from Africa, the South Seas and South and Central America, as well as American folk art" (*New York Times* 1973).

Elisofon's photographs from Africa have been sharply, publicly criticized. When his work was exhibited at the Museum of African Art in Washington, DC, in 2014, Raoul Granqvist, an Africanist at Umea University in Sweden, lambasted it as "old, updated, worse" (Granqvist 2014). He not only

Figure 15.7. Door. Senufo artist. Mid-20th century, Wood, iron. 134.9 × 73 × 7.9 cm. Bequest of Eliot Elisofon. Photograph by Brad Simpson. *Source:* National Museum of African Art, Smithsonian Institution. Used with permission.

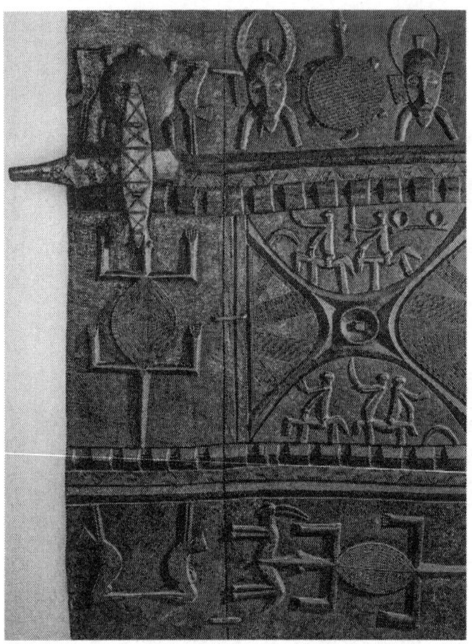

wished to cast aspersions on Elifson's efforts, but also how it was extolled by Susan Stamberg on National Public Radio. A decade earlier, the initial controversy from the show was stimulated by an article by Maya Angelou, which was a most unpleasant surprise to Elisofon. As a rejoinder to a review of the Westinghouse Broadcasting series *Black African Heritage* by Angelou (Angelou 1972a), Elisofon wrote to the *New York Times* TV Mailbag. It is worth reproducing his letter in full:

> I found Maya Angelou's article, which refers to my Westinghouse Broadcasting series, "Black African Heritage," both complimentary and disturbing. Since Miss Angelou is an outstanding and extremely articulate black American, her thoughts are particularly important.
>
> Miss Angelou states that the culture of Africa is not caught only in masks and dances, tribal Chiefs and musical instruments. This is surprising since she narrated the third program, "The Slave

Coast," in which we showed, among other subjects, weaving, pottery making, wood carving, bronze casting and architecture as well as song and dance.

No one program can do everything. But I believe that there are many unspoken references and effects which came through to the audience. For example, the sequence on the talking drums of the Yoruba not only demonstrated a sophisticated versatility in music and communication, but also the respect the people had for their tribal chief. Miss Angelou has forgotten the sequence on the coast of Ghana whence millions of slaves were shipped to the Americas. She also ignores our inclusion of the women warriors of Abomey, a feminine phenomenon in African history.

We made four films for as wide an audience as possible. We meant to entertain people and hoped to inspire them with a new appreciation of Africa in general. How many would watch a professional discussion of matrilineal inheritance, which Miss Angelou thinks is most important? I could make a documentary film for a foundation or a university, but not a film for a general television audience. This subject might be "much more relevant to today's needs than a perfect photograph of a much-photographed Benin mask," writes Miss Angelou. (Elisofon 1972)

Simply put, Angelou's criticism was a personal affront to Elisofon, and it stung. She belittled the photography that was at the heart of his vocation and mission as well as the television series. He retorted: "I doubt that one percent of the audience has ever seen the greatest of the Benin art before. Was it not important to show our audience that Africans were producing these works of art in the Middle Ages? We also showed Nok terra-cotta heads made 2,000 years ago, an extraordinary achievement." Elisofon also responded to her remark that the show had failed to exhibit African intellectualism:

Miss Angelou writes that "Timbuktu is mentioned but we are not informed that one of mankind's oldest universities was situated in that country." An exact quote from Ossie Davis's narration in the second program, "The Bend of the Niger," follows: "A salt caravan comes to Timbuktu past Sankore Mosque which dates from the early 14th century. Timbuktu was both a commercial and intellectual center. It was famous for its schools where theology, history, law and government were taught."

> Finally, I am very disturbed by Miss Angelou's statement about me, "and yet the photographer is not as committed to the subject as a black American must be."
>
> This is a bad blow and I am surprised that she sounds just as prejudiced against all whites as are too many of her contemporaries. I drove alone from Capetown to Cairo in 1947, published the most comprehensive book on African sculpture in 1958, produced a book tracing the Nile from it source to the sea in 1964, and was director of creative production of the four-hour ABC Africa TV special in 1967. I have made eight trips to Africa in all. Before the black revolution, most black Americans were either ashamed of Africa—and why not, since the Tarzan image was the only one they were familiar with—or they just did not care.
>
> Being white does not mean I love Africa less than a black American, or that I do not have the capacity to understand its vast, complex structure of traditions and culture. Do you have to be Jewish to understand the Old Testament? Or be Greek to understand Plato and appreciate the Acropolis? The concept of "black for blacks only" is my biggest quarrel with Maya Angelou, who I believe is one of the most gifted Americans of our time. (Elisofon 1972)

It seems that Maya Angelou was made a narrator in order to replace Bill Cosby, who did not appear in the production. The original letter of agreement listed her as a "singer." Angelou was featured in the publicity leading up to the show's airing, to which there is no indication of any objection on her part. Along with brief biographies of Julian Bond, Ossie Davis, and Gordon Parks, Angelou was described as serving as the Northern Coordinator for the Southern Christian Leadership Conference at the behest of Martin Luther King, Jr. (Angelou 1971).

Angelou's personal response to Elisofon's letter in the *New York Times* only seems to have passed between them. On May 25, 1972, she wrote Elisofon that

> I am distressed that you were distressed with the *New York Times* article. I am distressed that you misunderstood the point of the article. In effect, I was saying that, although in my youth I studied Judaism and have visited and taught in Tel Aviv, if I were to do an article on Israel I could never approach the task

with the same emotion as one whose relatives had suffered at Dachau and died in that madness. It is no intention of mine to underestimate your past, present and future contributions to all of us. Nor do I intend to risk what I hope will grow into a lifetime friendship, carrying out a feud in the newspapers which will entertain Sunday readers. Your art and perception make you one of my heroes and I thank you for that. Liberation and peace,

Maya (Angelou 1972b)

This exchange between Elisofon and Angelou is all the more distressing because they obviously admired each other tremendously. In months, Elisofon would be dead, shortly before his 62nd birthday. Elisofon had intended, through meticulous and creative photography, cinematography, and history, to draw Africa and Africans, including their labor and culture, into the purview of the West. For him, as well as photographers Stieglitz, Gernsheim, and Pollack, the monetization of African art, its placement in museums and galleries, and valuation by established auction houses had been a part of this process. Elisofon was smart enough to know that most people, White or Black, would never visit Africa and spend the time and effort as he did to comprehend and contextualize its culture. There was much more of a chance, though, that they might buy a book with exquisite photos of African people, their art, and their culture that was treated with integrity. It was even more likely, though, for them to tune into a TV show that they might find captivating.

Abbreviations

EEC   Eliot Elisofon Collection
HRC   Harry Ransom Center, University of Texas, Austin
LBIA   Leo Baeck Institute Archives, New York
OOMC Omar Oscar Marcus Collection

Works Cited

Angelou, Maya. 1971. Letter of agreement to Miss Maya Angelou, November 18. 51.4 Elisofon Series II. Film and Television projects "Black African Heritage" [The Slave Coast] III. G. C. [Guinea Coast], EEC, HRC.

———. 1972a. "For Years, We Hated Ourselves." *New York Times*, April 16.

———. 1972b. Maya Angelou to Eliot Elisofon, May 25, 1972. 51.9, Elisofon Series II Film and TV projects "Black African Heritage" Group W Publicity, 2 of 3, EEC, HRC.

Beaton, Cecil. 1938. *Cecil Beaton's New York*. Lippincott.

———. 1948. *A Portrait of New York*. P. T. Batsford.

Berger, Maurice. 2015. "African American Life, Double-Exposed." *New York Times*, April 17. https://archive.nytimes.com/lens.blogs.nytimes.com/2015/04/17/african-american-life-double-exposed/.

Berkowitz, Michael. 2011. "'Jews in Photography': Conceiving a Field in the Papers of Peter Pollack." *Photography and Culture* 4 (1): 7–28.

———. 2015. *Jews and Photography in Britain*. University of Texas Press.

Biographical note [about Omar Marcus]. n.d. OOMC, LBIA.

Blair, Sara. 2007. *Harlem Crossroads: Black Writers and the Photograph in the Twentieth Century*. Princeton University Press.

———. 2018. *How the Other Half Looks: The Lower East Side and the Afterlives of Images*. Princeton University Press.

Blight, David W. 2018. *Frederick Douglass: Prophet of Freedom*. Simon and Schuster.

Dellheim, Charles. 2021. *Belonging and Betrayal: How Jews Made the Art World Modern*. Brandeis University Press.

Dimitri [?]. 1967. To Eliot Elisofon [Time-Life], January 20, 1967. File 48.4, Elisofon series II. Film and TV projects "Man Builds Ancient Egypt" 1965, EEC, HRC.

Dollinger, Marc. 2018. *Black Power, Jewish Politics: Reinventing the Alliance in the 1960s*. Brandeis University Press.

Donnella, Leah. 2018. "Exploding Myths about 'Black Power, Jewish Politics.'" *Code Switch: Race in Your Face*, NPR (National Public Radio), June 4. https://www.npr.org/sections/codeswitch/2018/06/04/613683819/exploding-myths-about-black-power-jewish-politics.

Elisofon, Eliot. 1965a. Correspondence with Blaustein. 48.2 Elisofon series II. Film and Television projects. EEC, HRC.

———. 1965b. Correspondence with Arthur Odell. March 10. EEC, HRC.

———. 1966. Correspondence with Kohner. EEC, HRC.

———. 1972. "Being White, Do I Love Africa Less?" Letter to the editor, "TV Mailbag." *New York Times*, May 14, D 17.

———. n.d. Story fragment. Contained in correspondence [possibly to Leonard Lyons]. File 60,12, Series VII, correspondence, 1930s–1940s. EEC, HRC.

Elisofon, Eliot, and Roy Flukinger. 2000. *"To Help the World to See": An Eliot Elisofon Retrospective*. Harry Ransom Humanities Research Center, University of Texas at Austin.

Granqvist, Raoul J. 2014. "Eliot Elisofon's Africa: Old, Updated, Worse." February 13. https://africasacountry.com/2014/02/eliot-elisofons-africa-old-updated-worse.

Greenberg, Cheryl Lynn. 2006. *Troubling the Waters: Black-Jewish Relations in the American Century*. Princeton University Press.

Heschel, Susannah. 2018. "Two Friends, Two Prophets: Abraham Joshua Heschel and Martin Luther King Jr." *Plough Quarterly*, no. 16. https://www.plough.com/en/topics/community/leadership/two-friends-two-prophets.

Kart, Susanne. 2014. "Eliot Elisofon Archives at the National Museum of African Art, Smithsonian Institution." *Visual Resources: VR-Routledge* 30 (1): 106–9.

Leo Baeck Institute Finding Aid. n.d. Description of "Series III, Subseries 1: Printed Material. and Writings." OOMC, LBIA.

Marcus, Omar. 1949. Fragment of postcard from Marcus [no recipient given]. January 31. OOMC, LBIA.

———. 1950. "A Scot Peeks at Harlem Society: Here is New York's Negro 400, as Seen by a Visitor Accustomed to Photograph Society." *Our World*, August, 11. AR5650, OS [oversized documents]. OOMC, LBIA.

———. 1951a. Fragment of letter. August 11. OOMC, LBIA.

———. 1951b. Letter to "Gordon." November 17. OOMC, LBIA.

———. 1952. Letter to Col. Mackinnon. March 2. OOMC, LBIA.

———. 1963. Letter to Lee Davis (New Orleans) from Mexico City. January 23. OOMC, LBIA.

———. 1964. Letter to Taylor Mills (Motion Picture Association of America). January 2. OOMC, LBIA.

———. 1972. Letter to "Vera" sent from Chicago. October 7. OOMC, LBIA.

———. 1973a. Letter to "Ellen." April 5. OOMC, LBIA.

———. 1973b. Letter to unidentified correspondent. July 1. OOMC, LBIA.

———. 1973c. Letter to "Gwen and Eddy." November 5. OOMC, LBIA.

———. 1978. Letter to a blacked-out recipient. September 16. OOMC, LBIA.

———. n.d. Hebrew University internet entry [print-out.] OOMC, LBIA.

Michelson, Richard, and Raul Colon. 2008. *As Good as Anybody*. Knopf.

New York Times. 1973. "Eliot Elisofon, Photo-Journalist, Writer and Painter, Dies at 61." April 8, 81.

Pekow, Suzanne. n.d. "King's Last Year: Photographs by John C. Goodwin." *APM Reports*, Minnesota Public Radio. Accessed November 27, 2021. https://features.apmreports.org/arw/king/goodwin.html.

Polier, Rex. 1972. Review of Black African Heritage Film in the *Evening Bulletin*, Philadelphia, March 20. 51.8 Elisofon Series II. Film and Television Projects "Black Africa Heritage." Westinghouse publicity clippings, press release, correspondence, itineraries. HRC.

Press release [about Omar Oscar Marcus]. n.d. "Exhibition Material." OOMC, LBIA.

Robinson, Greg, and Robert S. Chang. 2017. *Minority Relations: Intergroup Conflict and Cooperation*. University Press of Mississippi.

Smithsonian National Museum of African American History and Culture. 2014. *Though the African American Lens*. Double Exposure. Smithsonian National

Museum of African American History and Culture, in association with D. Giles.

Star. 1936. "Marcus of Arabia Here Again/Young Man Who Has Cheated Death/ They call him Omar." June 10.

Stieglitz, Alfred. 2008. "Negro Art Exhibition." Half-tone reproduction, 10.6 × 14.1 cm. In *Camera Work* 48, 1916. And in *Camera Work: The Complete Photographs, 1903–1917.* Taschen.

Typescript [sheet describing foreign language documents concerning Omar Marcus]. n.d. Omar Oscar Marcus collection, box 1, file 1, LBIA.

Vickers, Hugo. 2020. *Cecil Beaton: The Authorised Biography.* Hodder.

Vowinckel, Annette. 2016. *Agenten der Bilder: Fotografisches Handeln im 20. Jahrhundert* Wallstein.

Contributing Authors

Ktzia Alon is an independent scholar of Mizrahi culture and literature. She is the author of fifteen books on Mizrahi poetry, arts, prose, and photography, including *Photo Opp: The Other Side of Israeli Photography* (2017; in Hebrew); *The Black Rebellion Rose* (2014; in Hebrew); and *Oriental Israeli Poetics* (2011; in Hebrew). She is the owner and the director of Gama Press.

Dora Apel is the W. Hawkins Ferry Endowed Chair Professor Emerita of Modern and Contemporary Art History at Wayne State University. As an art historian, cultural critic, and author, her work focuses on visual culture and politics; trauma and memory; gendered, racial, and ethnic oppression. Her books include *Memory Effects: The Holocaust and the Art of Secondary Witnessing* (2002) and *Imagery of Lynching: Black Men, White Women, and the Mob* (2004), among others that focus on imagery of war and urban ruination. Her most recent book, *Calling Memory into Place* (2020), in which she transitions from the scholarly to the personal, considers the dynamic nature of memory and memorials, the ways in which memory can be mobilized for social justice, and the ways in which memory is embodied, including her family's experience of the Holocaust and her own experience of breast cancer treatment.

Ofer Ashkenazi is professor of history and the director of the Koebner-Minerva Center for German History at the Hebrew University of Jerusalem. His publications include the monographs *Still Lives: Jewish Photography in Nazi Germany* (2025, coauthored with Rebekka Grossmann, Sarah Wobick-segev, and Shira Miron); *Anti-Heimat Cinema: The Jewish Invention of the German Landscape* (2020); *Weimar Film and Modern Jewish Identity* (2012); and *A Walk into the Night: Reason and Subjectivity in Weimar Film* (2010).

Michael Berkowitz is professor of modern Jewish history at University College London and author, most recently, of *Jews and Photography in Britain* (2015). His previous monographs include *The Crime of My Very Existence: Nazism and the Myth of Jewish Criminality* (2007); *The Jewish Self-Image* (2000); and *Zionist Culture and West European Jewry before the First World War* (1993).

Noam Gal is a scholar and curator of the arts in the camera-age as well as a senior lecturer at the Art History Department, the Hebrew University of Jerusalem. Between 2013 and 2021, he served as chief curator of photography at the Israel Museum Jerusalem. Gal's main exhibition projects featured the art of Richard Avedon, Berenice Abbott, Ron Amir, Ilit Azoulay, Tomoko Sawada, Roi Kuper, Micha Bar-Am, and Chen Cohen. Gal is the curator and author of *A Modern Love*, the first survey in Hebrew of modernism in photography. Gal's essays appeared internationally in *Critical Arts*, *African Identities*, *Art Journal*, and *Photographies* along with numerous local venues. His book project *The Movers: Israeli Art in the Third Millennium* is forthcoming in 2025.

Rebekka Grossmann is assistant professor of migration history at Leiden University. In her research she explores the connections of visual culture, migration, and politics with a special focus on Jewish history. Her first monograph, currently under review, investigates the role of the camera as agent, observer, and critic of Jewish nation-building. In a new project she traces the impact of Weimar German culture on Cold War discourses of global connectivity. Together with Ofer Ashkenazi, Sarah Wobick-Segev, and Shira Miron, she is the coauthor of *Still Lives: Jewish Photography in Nazi Germany*, which is forthcoming in 2024. She has also published her research in key journals such as *Jewish Social Studies*, the *Leo Baeck Institute Yearbook*, *Naharaim*, and *Israel Studies*.

Marianne Hirsch is a professor of comparative literature and gender studies emerita at Columbia University. She writes about the transmission of memories of violence across generations, combining feminist theory with memory studies in global perspective. Her books include *The Generation of Postmemory: Writing and Visual Culture after the Holocaust* (2012) and the coedited volume *Women Mobilizing Memory* (2019). She has also coauthored two books with Leo Spitzer: *Ghosts of Home: The Afterlife of Czernowitz in Jewish Memory* (2010) and *School Photos in Liquid Time: Reframing Difference* (2020).

Michele Klein is an independent scholar. She served as guest curator for three exhibitions of Jewish art and is the National Jewish Book Award winner for *A Time to be Born: Customs and Folklore of Jewish Birth* (1998). She now studies nineteenth-century Jewish portrait albums, focusing on the social and cultural history embedded within them.

Christoph Kreutzmüller is codirector of the #Last Seen-Project, analyzing photos of deportations of Jews out of Nazi Germany at the Selma Stern Center for Jewish Studies in Berlin. Among his publications are the acclaimed study on the Lili Jacob Album *Die Inszenierung des Verbrechens: Ein Fotoalbum aus Auschwitz* (with Tal Bruttmann and Stefan Hördler Darmstadt, 2019) and *Fixiert: Fotografische Quellen zur Verfolgung und Ermordung der Juden in Europa: Eine pädagogische Handreichung*, 2nd ed. (with Julia Werner, 2016).

Daniel H. Magilow is professor of German at the University of Tennessee, Knoxville, and coeditor-in-chief of *Holocaust and Genocide Studies*. His research centers on photography and film and their intersections with Holocaust studies, Weimar Germany, Nazi Germany, and postwar memory. He is the author, coauthor, editor, or translator of six books, including *The Photography of Crisis: The Photo Essays of Weimar Germany* (2012); *Holocaust Representations in History: An Introduction* (2015); *Nazisploitation! The Nazi Image in Low-Brow Cinema and Culture* (2011); *In Her Father's Eyes: A Childhood Extinguished by the Holocaust* (2008); and, most recently, *The Absolute Realist: Albert Renger-Patzsch's Collected Writings, 1923–1967* (2023).

Deborah Dash Moore is Jonathan Freedman Distinguished University Professor of History and professor of Judaic studies at the University of Michigan. A historian of American Jews, she specializes in twentieth-century urban history. Most recently, she has written a comprehensive history of New York Jews, *Jewish New York: The Remarkable Story of a People and a City* (2017). Her forthcoming book, *Walkers in the City: Jewish Street Photographers of Mid-Century New York* (2023) extends her interest in urban Jewish history to photography. Currently she serves as editor in chief of the Posen Library of Jewish Culture and Civilization, a ten-volume anthology of original sources translated into English from the biblical period to 2005, selected by leading scholars.

Amos Morris-Reich holds the Geza Roth Chair of Modern Jewish History, is the director of the Stephen Roth Institute for the Study of Contemporary Antisemitism and Racism, and is a professor in the Cohn Institute for the

History and Philosophy of Science and Ideas, at Tel Aviv University. He is the author of *The Quest for Jewish Assimilation in Modern Social Science* (2008); *Race and Photography: Racial Photography as Scientific Evidence, 1876–1980* (2016); and *Photography and Jewish History: Five Twentieth Century Cases* (2023).

Thomas Pegelow Kaplan is the Louis P. Singer Endowed Chair in Jewish History and a professor of history at the University of Colorado Boulder. He works in Holocaust and genocide studies, modern German and Jewish history, protest movements in the global 1960s, historical methodology and theory, and transnational history. His books and edited collections include *Taking the Transnational Turn: The German-Jewish Press and Journalism beyond Borders, 1933–1943* (2023; in Hebrew); *Police and Holocaust* (with Thomas Köhler, Jürgen Matthäus, and Peter Römer, 2023; in German); *Petitions Resisting Persecution: Negotiating Self-determination and Survival of European Jews* (with Wolf Gruner, 2020); and *The Language of Nazi Genocide: Linguistic Violence and the Struggle of Germans of Jewish Ancestry* (2009).

Johannes Schlör has been professor for modern Jewish/non-Jewish relations and a member of the Parkes Institute at the University of Southampton, UK, since 2006. His research interests include the cultural history and the ethnography of migration and mobility, of modern urban life, and the reflection of history in the individual experience. Recent publications: *Escaping Nazi Germany. One Woman's Emigration from Heilbronn to England* (2021) and *Im Herzen immer ein Berliner: Jüdische Emigranten im Dialog mit ihrer Heimatstadt* (2021). He is the editor of the journal *Jewish Culture and History* and coeditor of the online journal *Mobile Culture Studies*.

Lisa Silverman is professor of history and Jewish studies at the University of Wisconsin–Milwaukee. She is author of *Becoming Austrians: Jews and Culture between the World Wars* (2012) and coauthor with Daniel H. Magilow of *Holocaust Representations in History: An Introduction* (2015). Her next book, *The Postwar Antisemite: Culture and Complicity after the Holocaust*, is forthcoming.

Leo Spitzer is a professor of history emeritus at Dartmouth College. He writes about responses to colonialism and cultural "in-betweeness," Jewish refugee memory, and traumatic witnessing and its transmission. His books include *Lives in Between: Assimilation, Marginality, Exclusion in the Era of Emancipation* (1998) and *Hotel Bolivia: The Culture of Memory in a Refuge* *from Nazism* (1998). He has also coauthored two books with Marianne Hirsch: *Ghosts of Home: The Afterlife of Czernowitz in Jewish Memory* (2010) and *School Photos in Liquid Time: Reframing Difference* (2020).

Jonathan Stafford is a research fellow for the project "Archipelagic Imperatives: Shipwreck and Lifesaving in European Societies since 1800" at the Leibniz Zentrum für Literatur- und Kulturforschung, Berlin. His current research is concerned with the historical genealogies of the humanitarian imperative to save lives at sea, particularly engaging with the emergence of moral norms around the nexus of technological and aesthetic experience. His publications include *Imperial Steam: Modernity on the Sea Route to India, 1837–74* (2023) and the forthcoming edited volume *Moral Seascapes: Maritime Ethics and Aesthetics in the Modern Era* (2024).

Maiken Umbach works as professor of modern history at the University of Nottingham, and as chief academic advisor at the National Holocaust Museum. Her research focuses on the question of what photography can reveal, and obscure, for how we understand, commemorate, and teach about National Socialism and the Holocaust. Recent publications include the coauthored book *Photography, Migration, and Identity: A German-Jewish-American Story* (with Scott Sulzener, 2018), the edited volume *Private Life and Privacy in Nazi Germany* (with Elizabeth Harvey, Johannes Hürter, and Andreas Wirsching, 2019), and the article "Jewish Photos and Holocaust Testimony: A Complex Relationship" (with Alice Tofts, 2022).

Yechiel Weizman is a lecturer at the Israel and Golda Koschitzky Department of Jewish History and Contemporary Jewry at Bar-Ilan University, Israel. He completed his PhD at the University of Haifa and was a research fellow at the Leibniz Institute for Jewish History and Culture–Simon Dubnow, in Leipzig. He is the author of *Unsettled Heritage: Living Next to Poland's Material Jewish Traces after the Holocaust* (2022).

Theresia Ziehe is curator of photography at the Jewish Museum Berlin (JMB). Among others, she is a member of the team of curators for the museum's new permanent exhibit. At the JMB, she curated several temporary exhibits, including *Frédéric Brenner—Zerheilt* (2021); *Im Augenblick: Fotografien von Fred Stein* (2013); and *Russen Juden Deutsche: Fotografien von Michael Kerstgens seit 1992* (2012). She is the author of numerous articles on Jewish photographers and photography such as "Zur Situation jüdischer Fotografen und Fotografinnen in Berlin während des Nationalsozialismus" (2016); "Crossing Borders in the Summer of 1935: Fritz Fürstenberg's Photographs of Persecution in National Socialist Germany" (with Christoph Kreutzmüller, 2019); and "Jüdische Perspektiven in der Fotografie der NS-Zeit: Aus den Beständen des Jüdischen Museums Berlin" (2022).

Index

Page numbers followed by *f* refer to figures.